Lecture Notes in Computer Science

Commenced Publication in 1973
Founding and Former Series Editors:
Gerhard Goos, Juris Hartmanis, and Jan van Leeuwen

T0238627

Editorial Board

Anna Isabel Esparcia-Alcázar
Anikó Ekárt   Sara Silva   Stephen Dignum
A. Şima Uyar (Eds.)

Genetic Programming

13th European Conference, EuroGP 2010
Istanbul, Turkey, April 7-9, 2010
Proceedings

 Springer

Volume Editors

Anna Isabel Esparcia-Alcázar
Universidad Politécnica de Valencia, Instituto Tecnológico de Informática
Camino de Vera s/n, 46022 Valencia, Spain
E-mail: anna@iti.upv.es

Anikó Ekárt
Aston University, Computer Science
Aston Triangle, Birmingham, B4 7ET, UK
E-mail: a.ekart@aston.ac.uk

Sara Silva
INESC-ID Lisboa
Rua Alves Redol 9, 1000-029 Lisboa, Portugal
E-mail: sara@kdbio.inesc-id.pt

Stephen Dignum
University of Essex, School of Computer Science and Electronic Engineering
Wivenhoe Park, Colchester, CO4 3SQ, UK
E-mail: sandig@essex.ac.uk

A. Şima Uyar
Istanbul Technical University, Computer Engineering Department
Room Nr. 3302, Maslak, 34469 Istanbul, Turkey
E-mail: etaner@itu.edu.tr

Cover illustration:
"Pelegrina Galathea" by Stayko Chalakov (2009) Aston University, UK

Library of Congress Control Number: 2010922339

CR Subject Classification (1998): I.2, F.1, J.3, F.2, I.5, D.1

LNCS Sublibrary: SL 1 – Theoretical Computer Science and General Issues

ISSN	0302-9743
ISBN-10	3-642-12147-0 Springer Berlin Heidelberg New York
ISBN-13	978-3-642-12147-0 Springer Berlin Heidelberg New York

springer.com

© Springer-Verlag Berlin Heidelberg 2010
Printed in Germany

Typesetting: Camera-ready by author, data conversion by Scientific Publishing Services, Chennai, India
Printed on acid-free paper   06/3180

Preface

In its lucky 12+1 edition, during April 7–9, 2010, the European Conference on Genetic Programming (EuroGP) travelled to its most easterly location so far, the European City of Culture 2010, Istanbul, Turkey. EuroGP is the only conference worldwide exclusively devoted to genetic programming and the evolutionary generation of computer programs.

For over a decade, genetic programming (GP) has been considered the new form of evolutionary computation. With nearly 7,000 articles in the online GP bibliography maintained by William B. Langdon, we can say that it is now a mature field. EuroGP has contributed to the success of the field substantially, by being a unique forum for expressing new ideas, meeting, and starting up collaborations.

The wide range of topics in this volume reflect the current state of research in the field, including representations, theory, operators and analysis, novel models, performance enhancements, extensions of genetic programming, and various applications. The volume contains contributions in the following areas:

- **Understanding GP behavior** and **GP analysis** include articles on crossover operators and a new way of analyzing results.
- **GP performance** presents work on performance enhancements through phenotypic diversity, simplification, fitness and parallelism.
- **Novel models and their application** present innovative approaches with artificial biochemical networks, genetic regulatory networks and geometric differential evolution.
- **Grammatical evolution** introduces advances in crossover, mutation and phenotype–genotype maps in this relatively new area.
- **Machine learning** and **data mining** include articles that present data mining or machine learning solutions using GP and also combine data mining and machine learning with GP.
- **Applications** range from solving differential equations, routing problems to file type detection, object-oriented testing, agents.

This year we received 48 submissions, of which 47 were sent to the reviewers. The papers underwent a rigorous double-blind peer review process, each being reviewed by at least three members of the International Program Committee from 20 different countries. The selection process resulted in this volume, with 21 papers accepted for oral presentation (43.75% acceptance rate) and seven for poster presentation (58.33% global acceptance rate for talks and posters). Papers were submitted, reviewed, and selected using the MyReview conference management software. We are sincerely grateful to Marc Schoenauer of INRIA, France, for his great assistance in providing, hosting, and managing the software.

EuroGP 2010 was part of the Evo* 2010 event, which included three additional conferences: EvoCOP 2010, EvoBIO 2010 and EvoApplications 2010 (formerly known as EvoWorkshops). Many people helped to make this event a success. Firstly we would like to thank the great community of researchers and practitioners who contributed to the conference by both submitting their work and reviewing others' as part of the Program Committee. The hard work of both sides resulted in a high-quality conference. The local team (Gülşen Eryiğit, Şule Gündüz Öğüdücü, Sanem Sarıel Talay, Ayşegül Yayımlı) led by A. Şima Uyar must also be thanked: the smooth development of the conference has been their feat. Also thanks to Cecilia Di Chio for helping maintain the official EvoStar website, and to H. Turgut Uyar, who was in charge of the local information website.

We also thank the following institutions for their financial support: Istanbul Technical University, Microsoft Turkey, and the Scientific and Technological Research Council of Turkey.

We would also like to express our sincerest gratitude to our invited speakers, who gave the inspiring keynote talks: Kevin Warwick, of the University of Reading, UK, and Luigi Cavalli-Sforza of the Stanford School of Medicine, USA.

We especially want to express a heartfelt thanks to Jennifer Willies and the Centre for Emergent Computing at Edinburgh Napier University. Ever since its inaugural meeting in 1998 this event has relied on her dedicated work and continued involvement and we do not exaggerate when we state that without her, Evo* could not have achieved its current status.

April 2010

Anna I Esparcia-Alcázar
Anikó Ekárt
Sara Silva
Stephen Dignum
A. Şima Uyar

Organization

Administrative details were handled by Jennifer Willies, Edinburgh Napier University, Centre for Emergent Computing, Scotland, UK.

Organizing Committee

Program Co-chairs: Anna Isabel Esparcia-Alcázar (Universidad
    Politécnica de Valencia, Spain)
    Anikó Ekárt (Aston University, UK)
Publication Chair: Sara Silva (INESC-ID Lisboa, Portugal)
Publicity Chair: Stephen Dignum (University of Essex, UK)
Local Chair: A. Şima Uyar (Istanbul Technical University,
    Turkey)

Program Committee

Hussein Abbass	UNSW@ADFA, Australia
Lee Altenberg	University of Hawaii at Manoa, USA
Lourdes Araujo	UNED, Spain
R. Muhammad Atif Azad	University of Limerick, Ireland
Wolfgang Banzhaf	Memorial University of Newfoundland, Canada
Xavier Blasco	Universidad Politécnica de Valencia, Spain
Anthony Brabazon	University College Dublin, Ireland
Nicolas Bredeche	Université Paris-Sud, INRIA Futurs, CNRS, France
Stefano Cagnoni	University of Parma, Italy
Philippe Collard	Laboratoire I3S (UNSA-CNRS), France
Pierre Collet	LSIIT-FDBT, France
Ernesto Costa	Universidade de Coimbra, Portugal
Michael Platel Defoin	University of Auckland, New Zealand
Antonio Cioppa Della	University of Salerno, Italy
Ian Dempsey	NCRA and Pipeline Financial Group, Inc., USA
Federico Divina	Pablo de Olavide University, Spain
Marc Ebner	Universität Tübingen, Germany
Francisco Fernández de Vega	University of Extremadura, Spain
Gianluigi Folino	ICAR-CNR, Italy
Christian Gagné	Université Laval, Canada
Steven Gustafson	GE Global Research, USA
Jin-Kao Hao	LERIA, University of Angers, France
Simon Harding	Memorial University of Newfoundland, Canada

Table of Contents

Oral Presentations

Genetic Programming for Classification with Unbalanced Data......... 1
Urvesh Bhowan, Mengjie Zhang, and Mark Johnston

An Analysis of the Behaviour of Mutation in Grammatical Evolution ... 14
*Jonathan Byrne, Michael O'Neill, James McDermott, and
Anthony Brabazon*

Positional Effect of Crossover and Mutation in Grammatical
Evolution 26
Tom Castle and Colin G. Johnson

Sub-tree Swapping Crossover and Arity Histogram Distributions 38
Stephen Dignum and Riccardo Poli

Novelty-Based Fitness: An Evaluation under the Santa Fe Trail 50
John Doucette and Malcolm I. Heywood

An Analysis of Genotype-Phenotype Maps in Grammatical Evolution... 62
*David Fagan, Michael O'Neill, Edgar Galván-López,
Anthony Brabazon, and Sean McGarraghy*

Handling Different Categories of Concept Drifts in Data Streams Using
Distributed GP 74
Gianluigi Folino and Giuseppe Papuzzo

An Indirect Approach to the Three-Dimensional Multi-pipe Routing
Problem 86
Marcus Furuholmen, Kyrre Glette, Mats Hovin, and Jim Torresen

Phenotypic Diversity in Initial Genetic Programming Populations 98
David Jackson

A Relaxed Approach to Simplification in Genetic Programming 110
Mark Johnston, Thomas Liddle, and Mengjie Zhang

Unsupervised Problem Decomposition Using Genetic Programming..... 122
Ahmed Kattan, Alexandros Agapitos, and Riccardo Poli

GP-Fileprints: File Types Detection Using Genetic Programming 134
*Ahmed Kattan, Edgar Galván-López, Riccardo Poli, and
Michael O'Neill*

A Many Threaded CUDA Interpreter for Genetic Programming 146
    W.B. Langdon

Controlling Complex Dynamics with Artificial Biochemical Networks ... 159
    Michael A. Lones, Andy M. Tyrrell, Susan Stepney, and Leo S. Caves

Geometric Differential Evolution on the Space of Genetic Programs 171
    Alberto Moraglio and Sara Silva

Improving the Generalisation Ability of Genetic Programming with
Semantic Similarity based Crossover 184
    *Nguyen Quang Uy, Nguyen Thi Hien, Nguyen Xuan Hoai, and
    Michael O'Neill*

Evolving Genes to Balance a Pole 196
    Miguel Nicolau, Marc Schoenauer, and Wolfgang Banzhaf

Solution-Locked Averages and Solution-Time Binning in Genetic
Programming.. 208
    Riccardo Poli

Enabling Object Reuse on Genetic Programming-Based Approaches to
Object-Oriented Evolutionary Testing 220
    *José Carlos Bregieiro Ribeiro, Mário Alberto Zenha-Rela, and
    Francisco Fernández de Vega*

Analytic Solutions to Differential Equations under Graph-Based
Genetic Programming 232
    Tom Seaton, Gavin Brown, and Julian F. Miller

Learning a Lot from Only a Little: Genetic Programming for Panel
Segmentation on Sparse Sensory Evaluation Data 244
    *Katya Vladislavleva, Kalyan Veeramachaneni, Una-May O'Reilly,
    Matt Burland, and Jason Parcon*

Posters

Genetic Programming for Auction Based Scheduling.................. 256
    Mohamed Bader-El-Den and Shaheen Fatima

Bandit-Based Genetic Programming................................ 268
    Jean-Baptiste Hoock and Olivier Teytaud

Using Imaginary Ensembles to Select GP Classifiers 278
    Ulf Johansson, Rikard König, Tuve Löfström, and Lars Niklasson

Analysis of Building Blocks with Numerical Simplification in Genetic
Programming.. 289
    David Kinzett, Mengjie Zhang, and Mark Johnston

Fast Evaluation of GP Trees on GPGPU by Optimizing Hardware
Scheduling 301
    Ogier Maitre, Nicolas Lachiche, and Pierre Collet

Ensemble Image Classification Method Based on Genetic Image
Network 313
    Shiro Nakayama, Shinichi Shirakawa, Noriko Yata, and
    Tomoharu Nagao

Fine-Grained Timing Using Genetic Programming 325
    David R. White, Juan M.E. Tapiador,
    Julio Cesar Hernandez-Castro, and John A. Clark

Author Index... 337

Genetic Programming for Classification with Unbalanced Data

Urvesh Bhowan, Mengjie Zhang, and Mark Johnston

Evolutionary Computation Research Group,
Victoria University of Wellington, New Zealand
{urvesh.bhowan,mengjie.zhang}@ecs.vuw.ac.nz,
mark.johnston@msor.vuw.ac.nz

Abstract. Learning algorithms can suffer a performance bias when data sets only have a small number of training examples for one or more classes. In this scenario learning methods can produce the deceptive appearance of "good looking" results even when classification performance on the important minority class can be poor. This paper compares two Genetic Programming (GP) approaches for classification with unbalanced data. The first focuses on adapting the fitness function to evolve classifiers with good classification ability across both minority and majority classes. The second uses a multi-objective approach to simultaneously evolve a Pareto front (or set) of classifiers along the minority and majority class trade-off surface. Our results show that solutions with good classification ability were evolved across a range of binary classification tasks with unbalanced data.

1 Introduction

Classification is a systematic way of predicting class membership for a set of examples using properties of the examples [1]. This is a non-trivial task; many real-world data sets involve a large number of examples, high dimensionality, and complicated relationships between classification rules and example properties. Genetic Programming (GP) is an evolutionary technique which has been successful in building reliable and accurate classifiers to solve a range of classification problems [2][3][4].

However, working with unbalanced data sets is still a major obstacle in classifier learning [5][6]. Data sets are unbalanced when they have an uneven distribution of class examples, that is, when at least one class is represented by only a small number of examples (*minority class*) while the other class(es) make up the rest (*majority class*). Unbalanced data sets are common; fraud detection [7], medical diagnostics [8], financial risk modelling [9], and image recognition [10][11] are just a few examples.

Recent research has shown that using an uneven distribution of class examples in the learning (or training) process can leave the learning algorithm with a performance bias: poor accuracy on the minority class(es) but high accuracy on the majority class(es) [5][12]. This is because traditional training criteria such as overall success or error rate can be influenced by the larger number of examples from the majority class [12]. However, as the minority class often represents the main (or *positive*) class in many class imbalance classification problems, accurately classifying examples from this class

A.I. Esparcia-Alcazar et al. (Eds.): EuroGP 2010, LNCS 6021, pp. 1–13, 2010.

can be *at least* as important, and in some scenarios more important, than accurately classifying examples from the majority class [7][13].

Addressing this learning bias to find classifiers that are accurate on both classes is an important area of research [5][12]. In GP, much work has focused on directly adapting the fitness function in class imbalance problems; this includes using fixed misclassification costs for minority class examples to boost classification rates [8][14], or training metrics that are insensitive to the learning bias such as the Area under the ROC Curve (AUC) [15] or the average accuracy of each class [4][16]. While these techniques have improved performance, results often focus on gains in minority class accuracy with little analysis on the effects of the overall *classification ability* of evolved solutions [4][14][16]. These objectives are usually in conflict, that is, increasing the performance of one class can result in a trade-off in performance for the other [16][17].

This paper aims to address these issues by developing two different GP approaches to the class imbalance problem. The first uses a traditional single-objective GP system and focuses on adapting the fitness function to evolve classifiers with good overall classification ability across both the minority and majority classes. We present four improved fitness functions for classification with unbalanced data, and compare the overall classification ability of evolved solutions using the AUC, as well as a detailed analysis of the individual class performances using these fitness functions. The second approach uses a multi-objective GP (MOGP) system to simultaneously evolve a *Pareto front* (or set) of classifiers along the optimal minority and majority class trade-off surface. Based on the popular NSGA-II algorithm [18], the MOGP approach uses the notion of Pareto ranking in fitness to treat these two objectives separately in the learning process. This offers the advantages of discovering insights into the performance trade-off inherent in a particular classification task, and the ability to readily choose a preferred solution along the evolved Pareto front after the search process [19].

The rest of this paper is organised as follows. Section 2 outlines the GP framework. Section 3 describes the improved GP system using the new fitness functions. Section 4 briefly outlines the multi-objective GP approach. Section 5 presents the unbalanced data sets, and full experiment results and analysis. Section 6 concludes this paper and gives directions for future work.

2   GP Framework for Classification

This section outlines the program representation, classification strategy, fitness function and evolutionary parameters used in our basic GP framework.

2.1   Program Representation and Classification Strategy

A tree-based structure was used to represent genetic programs [2]. We used feature terminals (example features) and constant terminals (randomly generated floating point numbers) in the terminal set. We used a function set including the four standard arithmetic operators, $+$, $-$, $\%$, and $\times$, and a conditional operator, if. The $+$,$-$ and $\times$ operators have their usual meanings (addition, subtraction and multiplication) while $\%$ means *protected* division, that is, usual division except that a divide by zero gives a result of zero. Each of these four operators take two arguments and return one. The conditional if function takes three arguments. If the first is negative, the second argument is returned; otherwise it returns the third argument. The if function allows a program to contain a different expression in different regions of feature space, and allows discontinuous programs rather than insisting on smooth functions.

For the classification strategy we translated the output of a genetic program (floating point number) into two class labels using the division between positive and non-positive numbers. If the genetic program output is positive or zero, the example is predicted as belonging to the minority class, otherwise the example is predicted as the majority class.

2.2 Standard Fitness Function for Classification

A typical fitness measure in classification is the success or error rate of a solution on the training examples [3][14][16]. Using the four outcomes for binary classification shown Table 1, the overall classification accuracy can be defined by equation (1).

$$f_{overall} = \frac{TP+TN}{TP+TN+FP+FN} \tag{1}$$

Table 1. Outcomes of a two-class classification problem

	Predicted Object	Predicted non-object
Actual Object	True Positive (TP)	False Negative (FN)
Actual non-object	False Positive (FP)	True Negative (TN)

2.3 Evolutionary Parameters

The ramped half-and-half method was used for generating programs in the initial population and for the mutation operator [2] . The population size was 500. Crossover, mutation and elitism rates were 60%, 30%, and 10% respectively, and the maximum program depth was 8 to restrict very large programs in the population. The evolution ran for 50 generations or until an optimal solution was found. Half of each data set was randomly chosen as the training set and the other half as the test set, both preserving the original class imbalance ratio.

3   Improving GP with New Fitness Functions

Recent research has shown that the standard GP fitness function for classification, $f_{overall}$ (eq. 1), can be unsuitable for some class imbalance problems as it can favour solutions with a performance bias. Adapting the fitness function to consider the accuracy of *each class* as equally important has lead to improvements in minority class accuracy [4][16][20]. However, these developments offer little analysis on the effects on the overall *classification ability* of evolved classifiers [16][17]. To address this we present four improved fitness functions for classification with unbalanced data with the goal of evolving classifiers with a good AUC. It must be mentioned that the AUC itself is difficult to use directly in the fitness function as it significantly increases training times. This is due to the computational overhead required to calculate the AUC (i.e., a ROC curve must be constructed) for every solution in the population during fitness evaluation. Note, the term "class observation" is used below to describe aspects of these improved fitness functions; this term corresponds to the output of a genetic program when evaluated on an example from either the majority or minority class.

3.1   New Fitness Functions for Classification with Unbalanced Data

New Fitness Function 1. In many classification problems, correctly classifying examples from the minority class (true positives) can be more important than correctly classifying examples from the majority class (true negatives). In equation (2), $f_{weighted}$ uses a weighted average of the true positive (TP) and true negative (TN) rates. We evaluated five different weighting factors, 0.5, 0.55, 0.6, 065, 0.7 and 0.75, for each classification task. When $W=0.5$ in $f_{weighted}$, the classification accuracy of both classes is treated as equally important. When $W>0.5$, minority class accuracy will contribute more to program fitness than majority class accuracy by factor W.

This fitness function is designed to investigate two aspects. The first is how to effectively balance between TP and TN rates as demanded by a particular classification task. The second aspect is whether classifiers evolved with stronger accuracy on the minority class (i.e., W in favour of the TP rate), will have better *classification ability* compared to classifiers evolved when the fitness function treats the accuracy of both classes as equally important.

$$f_{weighted} = W \times \left(\frac{TP}{TP + FN} \right) + (1 - W) \times \left(\frac{TN}{TN + FP} \right) \qquad (2)$$

New Fitness Function 2. The function $f_{correlation}$ (eq. 3) is based on the well-known statistical measure, the correlation ratio, which measures the relationship between linear statistical dispersions within sets of class observations [21]. The correlation ratio can be adapted for classification to measure how well two sets of genetic program class observations are *separated* with respect to each other. The higher the correlation ratio for a program classifier, the better the separation of class observations. The goals of this new fitness function are to explore the effectiveness of new separability-based evaluation metrics in program fitness, and investigate whether this particular metric will evolve solutions with good classification ability compared to typical accuracy-based metrics in fitness.

To estimate the correlation ratio r in equation (3), let class observation P_{ci} represent the output of a genetic program classifier P when evaluated on the ith example belonging to class c, where N is the number of total examples, N_c is the number of examples in class c, and M is the number of classes (note that $N=\sum_{c=1}^{M} N_c$).

$$r = \sqrt{ \frac{\sum_{c=1}^{M} N_c(\bar{\mu}_c - \bar{\mu})^2}{\sum_{c=1}^{M} \sum_{i=1}^{N_c} (P_{ci} - \bar{\mu})^2} }$$

Here $\bar{\mu}_c$ represents the mean of class observations for class c only, and $\bar{\mu}$ represents the overall mean of both minority and majority class observations:

$$\bar{\mu}_c = \frac{\sum_{i=1}^{N_c} P_{ci}}{N_c} \text{ and } \bar{\mu} = \frac{\sum_{c=1}^{M} N_c \bar{\mu}_c}{\sum_{c=1}^{M} N_c}$$

The correlation ratio r will return values ranging between 0 and 1, where values close to 1 represent a better separation of class observations and values close to 0 represent a poor separation [21]. However, for classification it is preferable that the class observations are not simply well separated, but separated according to the classification strategy, that is, minority class observations should be positive numbers and majority class observations negative. This ordering preference is incorporated into the fitness function in equation (3) using an indicator function $I(.)$, which takes the means of all minority and majority class observations as inputs and returns 1 if the mean of the minority and majority class observations are positive and negative, respectively, or 0 otherwise. Fitness values from this fitness function range between 0 and 2, where values close to 2 represent optimal fitness and values close to 0 poor fitness.

$$f_{correlation} = r + I(\bar{\mu}_{min}, \bar{\mu}_{maj}) \tag{3}$$

3.2 Recently Improved Fitness Functions for Class Imbalance

Two recently improved fitness functions for class imbalance are presented below. These were shown to improve minority class accuracy in evolved solutions using unbalanced training data [16]. However, a detailed analysis of the classification ability of evolved solutions using these improved fitness functions was not previously explored.

Improved Fitness Function 1. The function f_{errors} (eq. 4) uses new performance objectives in combination with the (equally-weighted) accuracy of each class in program fitness. These new objectives measure the "level of error" for each class, and are designed to add a finer-grain to the fitness landscape – this can guide greedy hill-climbing search better [3]. The "level of error" aims to differentiate between solutions which score the same classification accuracy on each class but with different internal classification models. Solutions with smaller levels of error for each class are *closer* to correctly labelling any incorrectly predicted examples; these solutions will have better classification models and are favoured over solutions with a larger levels of error.

The level of error, Err_c, for class c in Equation (4) is estimated using the largest and smallest incorrect genetic program class observation (i.e., program output value) for a particular class, P_c^{mx} and P_c^{mn}, respectively. As the genetic program class observations can be positive or negative numbers, the absolute value is taken. These values are scaled to between 1 and 0 where 1 indicates the highest level of error and 0 the lowest. Optimal fitness for this fitness functions is obtained by scoring 1 on all four objectives.

$$f_{errors} = \frac{TP}{TP + FN} + \frac{TN}{TN + FP} + (1 - Err_{min}) + (1 - Err_{maj}) \tag{4}$$

where

$$Err_c = (|P_c^{mx}| + |P_c^{mn}|)/2$$

Improved Fitness Function 2. The function f_{wmw} (eq. 5) uses the Wilcoxon-Mann-Whitney (WMW) statistic, a well-known approximation for the Area under a ROC Curve (AUC) without having to construct the ROC curve itself [15]. This fitness function also explores the use of a separability-based metric directly in program fitness. However, the WMW statistic can be computationally expensive to calculate [4] [22].

In Equation (5), P_i and P_j represent minority and majority class observations, respectively; and N_{min} and N_{maj} correspond to the number of examples in the minority and majority class, respectively. Equation (5) conducts a series of pairwise comparisons (i.e, example-by-example) between minority class and majority class observations, collecting "rewards" (1 point) when indicator function $I(.)$ enforces two constraints. The first constraint ($P_i > 0$) requires that minority class observations are positive (i.e., correctly labelled). The second constraint ($P_i > P_j$) requires that minority class observations are *greater* than majority class observations; this constraint establishes an ordering of class observations.

The pairwise ordering of class observations in f_{wmw} can be useful in program fitness as solutions are rated not only on their classification accuracy per class, but also by how *separable* these class observations are. For example, if two solutions S_1 and S_2 have the same individual class accuracy, this fitness function will rank the solution with a better ordering of class observations as fitter.

$$f_{wmw} = \frac{\sum_{i=1}^{N_{min}} \sum_{j=1}^{N_{maj}} I(P_i, P_j)}{N_{min} \times N_{maj}} \tag{5}$$

where

$$I(P_i, P_j) = 1 \text{ if } P_i > 0 \text{ and } P_i > P_j, \text{ and } 0 \text{ otherwise.}$$

4   Improving GP with Multi-objective Search

In traditional evolutionary multi-objective optimisation (EMO), the evolutionary search is focused on improving the set of *non-dominated* solutions until they are optimal [23]. This requires two major adaptations to canonical (single-objective) GP: modifying the evolutionary search algorithm to evolve of a Pareto front (of solutions), and using Pareto Dominance in fitness. The multi-objective GP (MOGP) approach used minority and majority class accuracy as the two learning objectives.

4.1   Evolutionary Search Algorithm

MOGP is based on the well known EMO algorithm NSGA-II [18]. We used NSGA-II because it is a fast and simple algorithm, and performs well compared to other EMO algorithms across a range of problem domains [23][18]. In NSGA-II the parent and offspring populations are merged together at every generation. The fittest individuals of this combined parent-child population are then copied into a new population (archive population). The archive population serves as the parent population in the next generation (the archive population size is also 500). The offspring population at every generation is generated using traditional crossover and mutation operators; the archive population is used to preserve elitism in the population over generations. The classification strategy, function and terminal sets, and evolutionary parameters remain the same as the single-objective GP approach. The basic idea of MOGP can be seen in [19].

4.2 MOGP Fitness

Fitness in NSGA-II comprises of two hierarchical aspects: non-dominance rank and a "crowding" distance measure [18]. The non-dominance rank serves as the primary fitness attribute – "crowding" is only used to resolve selection when the non-dominance rank is equal between two or more solutions. Non-dominance rank measures how well a solution performs on all objectives with respect to every other member in the population. In Pareto dominance, a single solution *dominates* another solution if it is at least as good as the other solution on all the objectives and *better* on at least one objective [23]. The non-dominance rank for a solution is the number of other solutions in the population that dominate the given solution. The optimal non-dominance rank is 0. "Crowding" is an estimate of solution diversity based on Euclidean distance between solutions in *objective-space*. Solutions in densely populated areas of objective-space (similarly performing solutions) are penalised to a greater extent over solutions in sparsely populated regions to promote solution diversity in the population.

5 Experiment Results

5.1 Unbalanced Data sets

Four benchmark binary classification problems were used in the experiments based on their uneven distribution of class examples. The first two, Spect and Yeast, are from the *UCI Repository of Machine Learning Databases* [24]. The second two, Face and Pedestrian, are well-known image classification problems. Face is a collection of face and non-face image cut-outs from the Center for Biological and Computational Learning at MIT [10], and Pedestrian is a collection of pedestrian and non-pedestrian image cut-outs from the Intelligent Systems Lab at the University of Amsterdam [11].

Figure 1 shows example pedestrian and non-pedestrian (1.a), and face and non-face (1.b) images. Low-level pixel statistical features corresponding to the mean and variance of pixel values around certain local regions within each image were used as image features. These features represent overall pixel brightness/intensity and the contrast of a given region. Details can be seen in [25].

SPECT Heart data. This data set contains 267 records derived from cardiac Single Proton Emmision Computed Tomography (SPECT) images. There are 55 instances of the "abnormal" class (20.6%) and 212 instances of the "normal" class (79.4%), a class imbalance ratio of approximately 1:4. Each SPECT image was processed to extract 44 continuous features, these were further pre-processed to form 22 binary features (F_1–F_{22}) that make up the attributes for each instance [24]. There are no missing attributes.

Yeast data. This data set contains 1482 instances of protein localisation sites in yeast cells. There are eight numeric features calculated from properties of amino acid sequences (F_1–F_8) [24]. This is a multi-class classification problem; there are nine distinct classes each with a different degree of class imbalance. For our purposes, we decomposed this data set into *many* binary classification problems with only one "main" (minority) class and *everything else* as the majority class. We use a "main" class containing 244 minority class examples (16%), an imbalance ratio of 1:5.

Pedestrian image data. This data set contains 24,800 PGM-format cut-outs split into 4,800 pedestrian (19.4%) and 20,000 (80.6%) non-pedestrian (background) images, an imbalance ratio of approximately 1:4. These images are 19×36 pixels in size, and 22 pixel statistics were extracted as features F_1–F_{22} [25].

Face image data. This image data contains 30,821 PGM-format cut-outs split into 2,901 face (9.5%) and 28,121 (90.5%) non-face (background) images, an imbalance ratio of approximately 1:9. These images are 19×19 pixels in size, and 14 pixel statistics were extracted as features F_1–F_{14} [25].

(a)   (b)

Fig. 1. (a) Example pedestrian and non-pedestrian, and (b) face and non-face, images

5.2   AUC Results: GP Fitness Functions

Table 2 presents the classification results of the GP system using the standard fitness function for classification (eq. 1), and the improved fitness functions for class imbalance (eq. 2–5). All the experiments were repeated 50 times with a different random seed used for every run. Table 2 reports the average (and standard deviation) AUC on the test set and average training time using each fitness function on the classification tasks. The average training times are presented in seconds (s), minutes (m) or hours (h). For each task the fitness function with the best AUC performance is underlined, and for function $f_{weighted}$ the weight factor W with the best AUC performance is highlighted in italics. If the best AUC is the same for two or more functions, we prefer the result with lower standard deviation.

The AUC was chosen as the primary evaluation measure because it is known to be a good estimate of classification ability in class imbalance learning [6][15]. The AUC is insensitive to the class imbalance learning bias and considers the classification performance across varying classification thresholds. Standard evaluation metrics such as overall accuracy or error rate can lead to the deceptive appearance of "good looking" results when classifier performance suffers the learning bias [16][17]. The AUC was estimated using the trapezoidal technique, that is, as the sum of the areas of individual trapezoids fitted under the points of a given ROC Curve [15]. Note that the MOGP is not included in Table 2 as this requires the AUC of the *set* of evolved Pareto-front solutions to be considered – we leave this comparison as future work.

Table 2. AUC results and training times using GP fitness functions on the classification tasks

Fitness Function		Spect		Yeast		Pedestrian		Face	
		AUC	Time	AUC	Time	AUC	Time	AUC	Time
Overall	(eq. 1)	0.71 ± 0.15	1.8s	0.72 ± 0.09	8.0s	0.80 ± 0.13	1.4m	0.63 ± 0.11	1.5m
Weighted$_{50}$		0.71 ± 0.05	2.5s	0.75 ± 0.05	12.7s	0.91 ± 0.03	3.2m	0.79 ± 0.04	4.1m
Weighted$_{55}$		0.70 ± 0.07	3.3s	0.72 ± 0.06	14.7	0.92 ± 0.05	4.3m	0.78 ± 0.05	6.4m
Weighted$_{60}$	(eq. 2)	0.71 ± 0.05	3.2s	0.75 ± 0.05	14.7	0.92 ± 0.02	4.2m	0.78 ± 0.05	6.6m
Weighted$_{65}$		0.74 ± 0.04	3.2s	0.74 ± 0.05	14.7	0.90 ± 0.05	4.3m	0.77 ± 0.06	6.4m
Weighted$_{70}$		0.69 ± 0.04	3.3s	0.75 ± 0.02	14.6	0.90 ± 0.04	4.3m	0.76 ± 0.06	6.4m
Weighted$_{75}$		0.71 ± 0.05	3.3s	0.73 ± 0.07	14.7	0.89 ± 0.05	4.1m	0.76 ± 0.05	6.5m
Correlation	(eq. 3)	0.74 ± 0.05	1.5s	0.79 ± 0.02	7.4s	0.91 ± 0.02	4.2m	0.83 ± 0.01	4.3m
Errors	(eq. 4)	0.72 ± 0.05	3.1s	0.78 ± 0.03	17.0s	0.91 ± 0.03	5.3m	0.80 ± 0.04	6.0m
WMW	(eq. 5)	0.73 ± 0.05	5.1s	0.79 ± 0.03	69.3s	0.93 ± 0.01	4.5h	0.82 ± 0.02	5.8h

5.3 Individual Class Performances: GP Fitness Functions *vs.* MOGP

Table 2 provides a "single-figure" value of classification performance for a particular task. However, it is also important to consider the individual minority and majority class accuracies when evaluating classifier performance. Figure 2 shows the average minority and majority class performance using the GP fitness functions, along with the results of the MOGP approach on the classification tasks. This allows for a visual-based interpretation of the performance trade-off exhibited by a particular GP fitness function, as well as a direct comparison between the performance of solutions found using the (single-objective) GP and MOGP approach.

For fitness function $f_{weighted}$ only two weight factors are included in Figure 2. These are using $W=0.5$ and the W value with the highest corresponding AUC from Table 2 for a particular task (unless the optimal W was 0.5). This allows for a comparison when the accuracy of each class is equally weighted in the fitness function ($W=0.5$), and when minority accuracy is weighed higher (by some optimal amount). The optimal weighting for the Spect, Yeast, Pedestrian and Face tasks were 0.65, 0.7, 0.6 and 0.5, respectively.

All MOGP experiments were also repeated 50 times with a different random seed for every experiment. Summary attainment surfaces were used to approximate a *average-performing* and the *best-performing* evolved Pareto front of solutions with respect to all experiments; both these fronts are presented in Figure 2. Attainment surfaces summarise multiple evolved Pareto fronts of solutions (i.e., multiple MOGP experiments) into a single approximated set of solutions. The "average" set are those solutions with a 50% probability of attainment (median surface) and the "best" set those solutions with the lowest probability of attainment (first surface), with respect to all experiments [26].

Analysis of Learning Bias

According to Table 2, function $f_{overall}$ (eq. 1) produced relatively low AUC results compared to the other fitness functions. Figure 2 shows that these solutions were biased toward the majority class in all tasks, that is, majority class accuracy was high ($\geq 90\%$) but minority class accuracy low ($< 50\%$). As the level of class imbalance increases

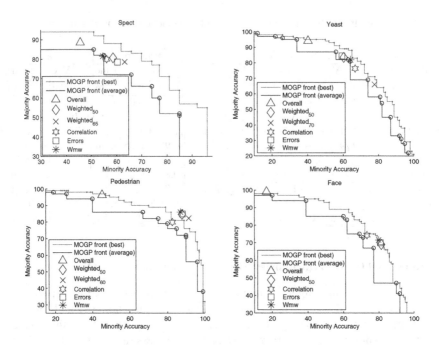

Fig. 2. Average class performance of solutions using GP with six fitness functions (blue markers), and the "best" and "average" MOGP Pareto-approximated fronts (red and blue lines) on the classification tasks. The horizontal axis represent minority class accuracy and vertical axis majority class accuracy. Note that the axis ranges are different in each plot.

for a particular task, more examples were classified as belonging the majority class. These results show that this fitness function is ill-suited for these class imbalance tasks as evolved solutions had comparatively low classification ability and did not learn to classify the minority class examples very well.

Analysis of New Fitness Functions

Table 2 shows that the four improved fitness functions succeeded in improving classification ability (compared to $f_{overall}$) by evolving solutions with higher AUC performances. This suggests that these improvements to the fitness function had a beneficial effect on the classification tasks. However, Figure 2 illustrates the variation in class performance when different GP fitness functions are used. In each case, a different minority and majority class trade-off is exhibited. Some trends across the tasks include:

1. The fitness functions that consistently achieved the best AUC results were the separability-based functions $f_{correlation}$ (eq. 3) and f_{wmw} (eq. 5). This suggests that these new separability measures were effective training criteria for these classification tasks. However, the training times using f_{wmw} were significantly higher on the large data sets (hours instead of minutes), due to the overhead in calculating the WMW statistic during fitness evaluation. The training times using $f_{correlation}$

were comparably low – suggesting that this fitness function was the most effective in quickly evolving solutions with high AUC on these classification tasks.

2. The new "level of error" measure in program fitness (eq. 4) produced better AUC performances in three classification tasks (exception was Pedestrian) with only a relatively small increase in training time, compared to without ($f_{weighted}$ where W is 0.5). This suggest that this new program measure was effective in improving classification performance in some of the tasks, and provides a useful new direction for further improvements to the fitness function for class imbalance.

3. In $f_{weighted}$ (eq. 2), the best AUC results when W was weighted in favour of minority class accuracy ($W>0.5$) was marginally better in most tasks compared to an equal weighting ($W=0.5$); the exception was Face where the best AUC was achieved using an equal weighting. However, this fitness function produced the highest minority class accuracies in all tasks indicating that for some problems (Spect and Pedestrian), the improvement in minority accuracy did not negatively impact on majority class accuracy as the AUC was also improved. For other tasks (Yeast and Face) this improvement in minority accuracy came at the expense of majority accuracy. This suggests that weighting the minority class accuracy higher (by some optimal amount) *can* improve classification ability (compared to an equal weighting) but that this is problem specific.

Analysis of MOGP Pareto Fronts

Figure 2 shows that the MOGP approach evolved a diverse set of solutions along the minority and majority class trade-off surface for the classification tasks. MOGP found *multiple* good solutions around the important middle region of the trade-off surface where the two objectives are at their highest together. This is an important advantage of MOGP over traditional (single-objective) GP. In the latter, only one solution is found along the objective trade-off surface, whereas in MOGP the decision-maker can *a posteriori* choose a preferred classifier from the evolved Pareto front with the desired objective trade-off.

6 Conclusions

The goals of this paper were to develop and compare two genetic programming techniques to class imbalance learning by evolving classifiers with good classification ability on both the minority and majority classes, and investigate the performance trade-off inherent in optimising these two conflicting objectives. These goals were achieved by examining the classification performance of evolved solutions using both our new GP fitness functions and our Pareto-based multi-objective GP.

The improved fitness functions for class imbalance found solutions with better AUC results than the standard GP fitness function for classification, which produced solutions with poor minority class accuracy on the classification tasks. The new separability-based program metrics in fitness generally achieved the best AUC on the classification tasks with the function using the correlation ratio being the most effective in quickly evolving solutions with a high AUC. The new "level of error" measure improved solution performance compared to without. Weighting the true-positive rate higher than the true-negative rate in the fitness function only improved classification ability for *some* tasks when compared with an equal weighting.

Using the multi-objective GP, a single experiment evolved multiple solutions with good individual class accuracies allowing users to choose between these solutions depending on their requirements. This can be advantageous compared to canonical (single-objective) GP where only a single solution is evolved in a single experiment.

In terms of future work we plan to evaluate these improved fitness functions, and develop new fitness functions, using more class imbalance problems. We also plan to investigate the AUC of the evolved MOGP solutions along the Pareto front.

References

1. Breiman, L., Friedman, J., Olshen, R., Stone, C.: Classification and Regression Trees. Wadsworth and Brooks (1984)
2. Koza, J.R.: Genetic Programming: On the Programming of Computers by Means of Natural Selection. MIT Press, Cambridge (1992)
3. Winkler, S., Affenzeller, M., Wagner, S.: Advanced genetic programming based machine learning. Journal of Mathematical Modelling and Algorithms 6(3), 455–480 (2007)
4. Doucette, J., Heywood, M.I.: GP classification under imbalanced data sets: Active sub-sampling and AUC approximation. In: O'Neill, M., Vanneschi, L., Gustafson, S., Esparcia Alcázar, A.I., De Falco, I., Della Cioppa, A., Tarantino, E. (eds.) EuroGP 2008. LNCS, vol. 4971, pp. 266–277. Springer, Heidelberg (2008)
5. Chawla, N.V., Japkowicz, N., Kolcz, A.: Editorial: Special issue on learning from imbalanced data sets. ACM SIGKDD Explorations Newsletter 6, 1–6 (2004)
6. Weiss, G.M., Provost, F.: Learning when training data are costly: The effect of class distribution on tree induction. Journal of Artificial Intelligence Research 19, 315–354 (2003)
7. Fawcett, T., Provost, F.: Adaptive fraud detection. Data Mining and Knowledge Discovery 1, 291–316 (1997)
8. Holmes, J.H.: Differential negative reinforcement improves classifier system learning rate in two-class problems with unequal base rates. In: Koza, J.R., Banzhaf, W., Chellapilla, K., et al. (eds.) Proceedings of the Third Annual Conference Genetic Programming 1998, pp. 635–644. Morgan Kaufmann, San Francisco (1998)
9. Pednault, E., Rosen, B., Apte, C.: Handling imbalanced data sets in insurance risk modeling. Tech. Rep., IBM Tech Research Report RC-21731 (2000)
10. Sung, K.-K.: Learning and Example Selection for Object and Pattern Recognition. PhD thesis, AI Laboratory and Center for Biological and Computational Learning. MIT (1996)
11. Munder, S., Gavrila, D.: An experimental study on pedestrain classification. IEEE Transactions on Pattern Analysis and Machine Intelligence 28(11), 1863–1868 (2006)
12. Monard, M.C., Batista, G.E.A.P.A.: Learning with skewed class distributions. In: Advances in Logic, Artificial Intelligence and Robotics, pp. 173–180 (2002)
13. Song, D., Heywood, M., Zincir-Heywood, A.: Training genetic programming on half a million patterns: an example from anomaly detection. IEEE Transactions on Evolutionary Computation 9, 225–239 (2005)
14. Eggermont, J., Eiben, A., van Hemert, J.: Adapting the fitness function in GP for data mining. In: Langdon, W.B., Fogarty, T.C., Nordin, P., Poli, R. (eds.) EuroGP 1999. LNCS, vol. 1598, pp. 193–202. Springer, Heidelberg (1999)
15. Bradley, A.P.: The use of the area under the ROC curve in the evaluation of machine learning algorithms. Pattern Recognition 30, 1145–1159 (1997)

16. Bhowan, U., Johnston, M., Zhang, M.: Differentiating between individual class performance in genetic programming fitness for classification with unbalanced data. In: Proceedings of the 2009 IEEE Congress on Evolutionary Computation, CEC 2009 (2009)

17. Patterson, G., Zhang, M.: Fitness functions in genetic programming for classification with unbalanced data. In: Orgun, M.A., Thornton, J. (eds.) AI 2007. LNCS (LNAI), vol. 4830, pp. 769–775. Springer, Heidelberg (2007)

18. Deb, K., Pratap, A., Agarwal, S., Meyarivan, T.: A fast elitist multi-objective genetic algorithm: NSGA-II. IEEE Transactions on Evolutionary Computation 6, 182–197 (2000)

19. Bhowan, U., Johnston, M., Zhang, M.: Multi-objective genetic programming for classification with unbalanced data. In: Li, X. (ed.) AI 2009. LNCS (LNAI), vol. 5866, pp. 370–380. Springer, Heidelberg (2009)

20. Parrot, D., Li, X., Ciesielski, V.: Multi-objective techniques in genetic programming for evolving classifiers. In: Proceedings of the 2005 Congress on Evolutionary Computation (CEC 2005), September 2005, pp. 1141–1148 (2005)

21. Fisher, R.A.: Statistical methods for research workers, 14th edn. Oliver and Boyd (1970)

22. Yan, L., Dodier, R., Mozer, M.C., Wolniewicz, R.: Optimizing classifier performance via the Wilcoxon-Mann-Whitney statistic. In: Proceedings of The Twentieth International Conference on Machine Learning (ICML 2003), pp. 848–855 (2003)

23. Coello, C., Lamont, G., Veldhuizen, D.: Evolutionary Algorithms for Solving Multi-Objective Problems, 2nd edn. Genetic & Evolutionary Computation Series. Springer, US (2007)

24. Asuncion, A., Newman, D.: UCI Machine Learning Repository, University of California, Irvine, School of Information and Computer Sciences (2007),
http://www.ics.uci.edu/~mlearn/MLRepository.html

25. Bhowan, U., Johnston, M., Zhang, M.: Genetic programming for image classification with unbalanced data. In: Proceedings of 24th International Conference on Image and Vision Computing, Wellington, New Zealand, pp. 316–321. IEEE Press, Los Alamitos (2009)

26. Knowles, J., Thiele, L., Zitzler, E.: A tutorial on the performance assessment of stochastic multiobjective optimizers. Tech. Rep., No. 214, Computer Engineering and Networks Laboratory (TIK), Swiss Federal Institute of Technology (ETH) Zurich (February 2006)

An Analysis of the Behaviour of Mutation in Grammatical Evolution

Jonathan Byrne, Michael O'Neill, James McDermott, and Anthony Brabazon

Natural Computing Research & Applications Group
University College Dublin, Ireland
{m.oneill,anthony.brabazon}@ucd.ie

Abstract. This study attempts to decompose the behaviour of mutation in Grammatical Evolution (GE). Standard GE mutation can be divided into two types of events, those that are structural in nature and those that are nodal. A structural event can alter the length of the phenotype whereas a nodal event simply alters the value at any terminal (leaf or internal node) of a derivation tree. We analyse the behaviour of standard mutation and compare it to the behaviour of its nodal and structural components. These results are then compared with standard GP operators to see how they differ. This study increases our understanding of how the search operators of an evolutionary algorithm behave.

1 Introduction

Much attention has been directed towards the behaviour of crossover in Grammatical Evolution due to the traditional importance placed on this search operator in Genetic Programming [1] in general (e.g., [2,3,4]). However, aside from simple studies which examined mutation rates, there has been little analysis of the behaviour of mutation on search in GE. The notable exceptions to this include Rothlauf and Oetzel's locality study on binary mutation [5], a study comparing performance of binary and integer forms of mutation [8] and our first study on standard GE mutation [11]. This study extends this research by examining how each behavioural component of mutation moves the solution through the problem space. Search operators are a key component of any genetic and evolutionary computation representation, and as such it is critical that we understand their behaviour. This study addresses this important research gap by conducting an analysis of the behaviour of GE's mutation operator, focusing on the types of changes that occur when it is applied, and their impact on evolutionary performance.

The remainder of the paper is structured as follows. Firstly, the related research in this area is discussed in Section 2. A brief explanation on the locality of binary mutation is provided in Section 3 before an analysis of the behaviour of mutation in GE is undertaken in Section 4. Three separate experiments are carried out and their results are discussed in Sections 5, 6 and 7. In light of the results further analysis is described in Section 8, before finishing the paper in Section 9 with Conclusions and Future Work.

A.I. Esparcia-Alcazar et al. (Eds.): EuroGP 2010, LNCS 6021, pp. 14–25, 2010.

2   Related Research

In a recent study examining the locality of the mutation operator in Grammatical Evolution it was found that in some cases (less than ten percent of the time) mutation events resulting in small changes to the genotype can result in large changes to the structures generated [5]. More specifically, given a single unit of change at the genotype level (i.e., a bit flip), changes of one unit or greater at the derivation tree level occurred approximately ten percent of the time. 14% of these had a distance of greater than 5 units at the tree level. A unit of change at the phenotypic tree level corresponded to tree edit distance calculations which included deletion (delete a node from the tree), insertion (insert a node into the tree) and replacement (change a node label) change types. It is worth stating that the other 90% of the time mutation has no effect due to the many-to-one mapping adopted in GE which allows multiple values to correspond to the same production rule choice. The genotype change therefore is neutral upon phenotype structure and fitness in these cases.

In this paper we turn our attention to what is occuring that critical 10% of the time when a unit of change arising from mutation at the genotype level does not perfectly correspond with a unit of change at the phenotype level. We wish to establish if it is possible to design a mutation-based search operator that exhibits better properties of locality than the one currently adopted in GE.

3   A Component-Based View of Mutation in GE

In order to expose the impact of mutation on derivation tree structure we design a simple grammar, which uses binary rule choices. This allows us to condense codons (elements in the string representing the individual) to single bits. This simplifies our analysis without loss of generality to more complex grammars with more than two productions for each non-terminal.

Below is a simple binary grammar which might be used in a symbolic regression type problem with two variables (x and y).

```
<e> ::= <o><e><e>   (0)
      | <v>         (1)

<o> ::= +           (0)
      | *           (1)

<v> ::= x           (0)
      | y           (1)
```

We can then construct genomes with binary valued codons to construct sentences in the language described by the above grammar. Consider all genomes of length two codons (2^2 of them) and draw an edge between genomes that are a Hamming distance of one apart. If we then present the corresponding partial derivation trees resulting from those genomes we see the arrangement outlined in

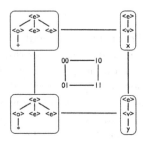

Fig. 1. The 2D neighbourhood for the example grammar (i.e., using the first two codons)

Fig. 1. In this particular example we see that a mutation event at the first codon corresponds to a new derivation tree structure. Here we define a new derivation tree structure as being one that has changed in length, that is, it contains more non-terminal symbols than its neighbour. Mutations from 00 to 10 (and vice versa) and from 01 to 11 (and vice versa) result in these structural changes. Whereas the remaining mutation events result in node relabelling.

Extending the genomes by an additional codon we can visualise the Hamming neighbourhood between the 2^3 genomes both in terms of codon values and partial phenotype structures. These are illustrated in Fig. 2. Again, we see a clear distinction between mutation events that result in structural and non-structural modifications.

Mapping these codons back to the grammar we see that structural mutations occur in the context of a single non-terminal symbol, <e>. We can see from this grammar that this non-terminal alone is responsible for structural changes, as it

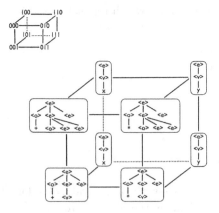

Fig. 2. The 3D neighbourhood for the example grammar (i.e., using the first three codons)

alone can increase the size of the developing structure. The rules for the <o> and <v> non-terminals are non-structural as they simply replace an existing symbol without changing structural length.

Effectively we can now decompose the behaviour of mutation into two types of events. The first are events that are structural in their effect and the second are those which are nodal in their effect. By logical extension we could consider both types of events as operators in their own right, and therefore define a *structural mutation* and a *nodal mutation*. It should be noted, however, that this is a specialisation of standard GE mutation, as it is possible for both types of events to occur during standard application of GE mutation to an individuals genome. *Perhaps the locality of mutation could be improved by simply reducing the number of occurances of the structural form of mutation, or even removing this form of mutation completely?*

If mutation was the sole search operator employed in a GE search, its elimination would have the consequence of removing structural change and structural search. This of course should have detrimental consequences for search as in Genetic Programming we must explore both structures and their contents. Part of the strength of GP approaches as problem solvers is their ability to search variable-length structures, so the removal of this ability would be undesirable. The following analysis and experiments seek to determine the relative importance of these behavioural components of mutation and begin to answer these kinds of questions.

4   An Analysis of Mutation in GE

To show the impact of decomposing mutation into its constituent parts we will look at how well each component of the operator performs on the Max problem. The aim of the Max problem is to generate a tree that returns the largest real value within a set depth limit. The optimal solution to this problem is to have addition operators at the root of the tree so that it creates a large enough variable for multiplication to have an effect. This problem is considered difficult for GP as populations converge quickly on suboptimal solutions that are difficult to escape from, except through a randomised search [7]. As such, this problem should be amenable to the right form of mutation operator. The grammar for this problem is given below:

```
<expr> ::= <op> <expr> <expr> | <var>
<op>   ::= + | *
<var>  ::= 0.5
```

This problem is an interesting application for the new component behaviours of the mutation operator as it highlights the different methods each component uses for exploring the search space. The grammar is suitable for illustrating the mutational differences as it consists of one structural rule(<expr>) and one nodal rule(<op>). Its simplicity also removes any extraneous factors that could complicate the result. The Max problem also requires that every element of the

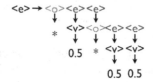

Fig. 3. An Example Max problem parse tree. Total =0.125.

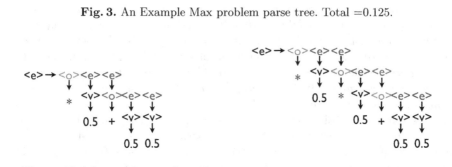

Fig. 4. Nodal mutation performed on parse tree. Total = 0.5.

Fig. 5. Structural mutation performed on parse tree. Total = 0.25.

tree contributes to the final solution. i.e. there are no introns [7], which further removes any confounding factors.

4.1 Experimental Procedure

The experiments described in Sections s 5, 6 and 7 were implemented using GEVA[12,13], this is an open source framework for Grammatical Evolution in Java designed by the NCRA group in UCD. The following properties were kept constant for each experiment execution, these are as follows: Population size = 500, replication rate = 0.1, maximum generations = 50, the Mersenne Twister as the random number generator and fitness proportionate selection using the tournament selection operator with the tournament size set to 3. Generational replacement with an elite size of 1 was used as our replacement operator.

Wrapping was turned off as it could lead to conditions where a codon was both structural and nodal. The experiment was run using mutation exclusively as crossover would have had a confounding effect in combination with the mutation operators. A ramped half and half initialiser was used to create the derivation trees with an initialisation depth of 10. This equates to a phenotype tree of depth 8, the maximum depth allowed for this problem. This was necessary because nodal mutation by itself cannot alter the length of a phenotype and it required trees initialised to the maximum depth for a fair comparison.

5   Analysis of Mutations Effect on Search

This experiment investigates whether there is a statistically significant difference in performance between standard GE mutation and its structural and nodal components. The two component behaviours have been implemented as operators in their own right so that we may measure the relative impact on the overall behaviour of integer mutation. We then examine whether these different components could have a beneficial impact on traversing the search space. Our experiment was carried out on the problem described above. As Nodal and Structural mutation act on subsets of the chromosome, the standard method of mutation had to be altered. Instead of applying the operator to each codon with a certain probability of mutation, only one mutation event was allowed per individual. This meant that each operator produced the same number of mutation events. 500 trial runs were carried out for each operator.

5.1   Experiment Results

The results from this experiment show that selectively altering subsets of codons from the chromosome can have a dramatic effect on how GE navigates the search space. The results are shown in the graphs below, see Figures 6 and 7. The fitness was based on a minimising function (1 over the result), so smaller results are better. As the results were on a logarithmic scale, a Wilcoxon rank-sum test (two-tailed, unpaired) was performed on the nodal and structural distributions that showed they were significantly different. The nodal component behaviour performs the best as it will explore the configurations of the particular tree structure to optimise it, something this problem requires to reach an optimal solution. Conversely structural changes does not explore the contents of the tree but instead explores configurations of derivation tree structures. This leads to poor performance on this problem. This is even more discernible when looking at the average fitness of the population (Figure 7). The fitness of standard mutation matches more closely with structural mutation suggesting it has a damaging effect on the nodal search component, changing the tree structure before it can be fully explored. This result clearly indicates that there are two separate behavioural components operating in standard GE mutation and it also indicates that they might not be complementary behaviours.

6   Comparison with GP Mutation

By splitting GE mutation into its components we now have two operators that are analogous to standard tree-based GP operators, point mutation and subtree mutation. Nodal mutation is identical in behaviour to point mutation so no comparison is needed but while subtree and structural mutation both explore the structure of trees there is a significant difference. There is a dependency on codon placement in GE as it uses a linear genome representation. As the genome is read from left to right, it means a change to a structural codon could change the meaning of the codons that follow it. In the most extreme case a single mutation early on in the genome could generate an entirely different tree. This effect is called 'ripple' mutation, and is similar in effect to ripple crossover [14]. Subtree mutation, on the other hand, replaces a subtree with another randomly

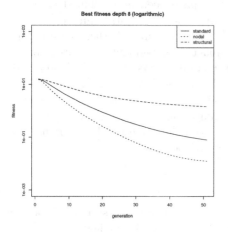
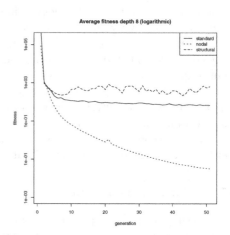

Fig. 6. Log of best fitness for GE operators on Depth 8 Max Problem

Fig. 7. Log of average fitness for GE operators on Depth 8 Max Problem

generated subtree, while leaving the rest of the tree intact [9]. In the following experiment we will apply standard tree-based mutation operators, point and subtree mutation, to the GE derivation tree representation. This allows us to compare a search of the structural space both with and without the ripple effect. We can then determine whether this ripple effect is advantageous to the search process. 500 trial runs were carried out for each operator.

6.1   Experiment Results

This experiment investigated how structural mutation performed against GP subtree mutation and whether the ripple effect was beneficial to the search process. A pairwise Wilcoxon rank-sum test was performed on the final results of both best and average fitness. It showed that all the results were significant except for nodal compared with standard mutation. Figure 8 shows that subtree mutation outperformed structural mutation. When the average individual fitness was examined it showed that despite subtree mutations better performance, most mutations created exponentially worse individuals during the course of the run (Figure 9). This shows that the ripple effect of structural mutation did not have a significantly detrimental effect on the search.

A further experiment was run where the maximum depth was set to 100 while leaving the maximum initialisation depth at 8. This in effect gave nodal mutation a significant disadvantage over the other operators as it cannot increase the derivation tree depth. The results for this experiment are shown in figures 10 and 11. Nodal mutation still performed better than structural and standard mutation but subtree mutation greatly outperformed it. Average fitness in subtree mutation also improved at the greater depth. Upon closer investigation the cause for this was found to be an explosive growth in the derivation tree depth and

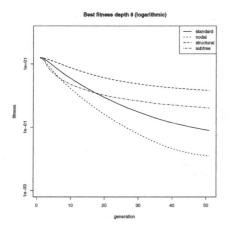

Fig. 8. Log of best fitness results for Depth 8 Max Problem

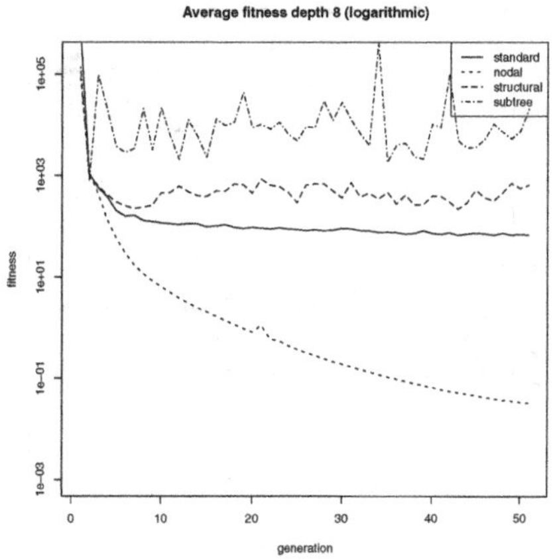

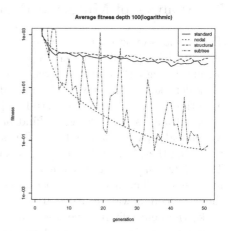

Fig. 9. Log of average fitness results for Depth 8 Max Problem

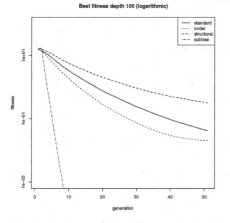

Fig. 10. Log of best fitness results for depth 100 Max Problem

Fig. 11. Log of average fitness results for Depth 100 Max Problem

used codon length. This is shown in figures 12 and 13. Subtree mutation approached the problem by exploiting the fact that it makes larger subtrees. This meant that while it generated better mutations as regards fitness there was also a significant price to be paid in code bloat. Nodal mutation instead took the approach of optimising the structures present in the population to correctly target the position of the terminal set of operators(+,*). This led to the creation of highly efficient trees that could compete with subtree results despite their depth limitation.

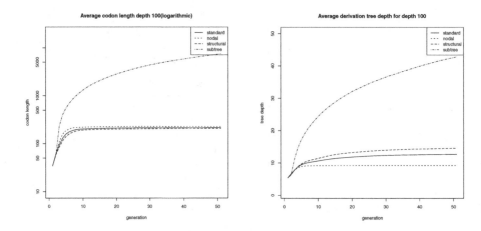

Fig. 12. Average codon length for depth 100 Max Problem (logarithmic)

Fig. 13. Average derivation tree depth for Depth 100 Max Problem

7   Analysis of Mutation Events on Fitness

The previous experiments show how each operator performs during the course of a run but they do not have the granularity to see what was actually happening during each mutation event. Next we conducted an experiment in order to undertake an analysis of the operators' impact on individual independent mutation events. In previous studies [5] changes to the derivation tree were recorded but as we know what kind of phenotypic impact our operators have, we instead look at changes to the fitness of the individual. The experiment was run using the Max Problem with the same settings as described in Section 4.1. The mutation was carried out on a random codon in a randomly initialised individual. When a mutation occurred the change in fitness was recorded and then the codon was returned to its original value. Any mutation events that broke the depth limit were not counted. If a mutation created an invalid individual then this was recorded but no penalty was added to the fitness. This was continued until a sample size of 1,000,000 mutations was gathered for each operator. This experiment does not intend to show how these search operators work in practice. For example the quantity of bad fitness generated by an operator is generally irrelevant as it is bred out of the population(although it reduces the efficiency of the mutation operator). Conversely, a good mutation is always of benefit to a population regardless of its size. There is also a potential interplay of the operators as they are components of standard mutation and multiple codon sites can be mutation during standard application. Instead what these metrics do is focus on some of the mechanics at play during mutation.

7.1   Experiment Results

This experiment attempts to highlight the effects of individual mutation events on the overall fitness of an individual. The results are shown in table 1. It should be noted that over half the time the GE mutation operators generated a neutral mutation. This was because of the structure of the grammar. Each rule had two possible outcomes, mutation would either change the outcome or leave it untouched. Nodal and subtree mutation did not generate any invalids. In nodal mutations case it is because it is incapable of making them whereas it is in the definition of subtree mutation that it cannot generate invalids, so it would keep generating new subtrees until a valid one was produced. This factor also meant that subtree produced a large amount of neutral mutations as many of the alternatives would have made invalid individuals.

Nodal generated the greatest number of beneficial mutation events followed by subtree, standard and structural. As for the quality of these mutations, subtree outperformed the other operators by a factor of three. Nodal also produced the greatest number of bad mutations, followed by standard, and structural with subtree only producing bad mutations 2.9% of the time, unfortunately each bad subtree mutation was massively worse than the others. Overall nodal mutation was the least destructive operator, rarely generating large changes but cumulatively generating the greatest fitness change. Structural performed far worse than nodal but it was still not nearly as destructive as subtree mutation. Upon further investigation into the poor results for average fitness, as shown in Fig 9, it was found that the variance in average fitness increased exponentially at certain points during the run. This would indicate that subtree mutation occasionally produced very unfit subtrees that, depending on the root node of the tree, could make the overall fitness far worse.

Table 1. Results for mutation events on the Max Problem

Mutation Op	Good	Bad	Neutral	Invalid	Avr. Good	Avr. Bad	total Change
Standard	10.1%	26.2%	51.1%	12.6%	9.857	322.648	-138,580,712
Structural	5.2%	24.5%	51.6%	18.6%	11.385	1040.559	-137,691,951
Nodal	18.5%	31%	50.5%	0	10.462	63.106	-17,648,412
Subtree	11.4%	2.9%	85.6%	0	28.865	75461.321	-2,222,353,022

8   Discussion

This study highlighted the two contradictory components of standard GE mutation. The nodal behaviour was more akin to the standard GP point mutation as phenotypic changes consisted of replacing one terminal for another, leaving the derivation tree untouched. This could be beneficial in GE, where the outcome of a particular rule choice is dependent on all the choices that precede it. The behaviour of structural mutation was more explorative, creating variations of the tree structure itself. The results from the comparison with subtree mutation showed that it had a comparable effect on search despite the possibility of the ripple effect changing every codons meaning. Even though it did not perform as well as subtree at the greater depth limit it showed that it was not as susceptible to code bloat as it explored the structure space of the trees.

The point of this paper was not to show which was the best operator, something which is problem dependent anyway. Instead it was to decompose GE's standard mutation operator into it's component behaviours. Despite our intentions, this information could now be used to create a mutation operator that applies these behaviours to a problem as and when they are needed. We have also applied this analysis on a range of other benchmark problems with similar results. The use of intelligent operators might help GE escape local optima as well as find the optimal solution more efficiently. This could be of particular benefit in dynamic environments where an evolutionary algorithm must be able to adjust quickly in response to a changing fitness function [10].

9   Conclusion and Future Work

This study analysed the behavior of mutation in GE. We initially described standard mutation in GE and then broke it into two components which we called Structural and Nodal mutation. We then investigated the effects of these mutation operators as applied to the Max Problem to ascertain if there was any discernible difference between these components. We then compared the operators against GP subtree mutation. Further investigation was carried out on the impact of individual mutation events.

Future work will involve using this information to design a better approach to mutation in GE. This could involve switching from one type of mutation to the other during the course of the run. It is natural to expect that the importance of different types of operators will vary over the course of a run as well as from problem to problem. In this respect we hypothesise that we would observe a greater difference in performance between the different forms of mutation during the end-phase of a run versus the mid and early-phases. In the later phase of a run we would hypothesise that nodal mutation might have a more positive impact than during the early phase, and we would hypothesise the opposite behaviour for structural mutation.

Acknowledgments

I would like to thank Erik Hemberg for his support and I would also like to thank SFI.This research is based upon works supported by the Science Foundation Ireland under Grant No. 08/IN.1/I1868.

References

1. Poli, R., McPhee, N.F., Langdon, W.B.: A Field Guide to Genetic Programming (2008), http://lulu.com, http://www.gp-field-guide.org.uk
2. O'Neill, M., Ryan, C.: Grammatical Evolution: Evolutionary Automatic Programming in an Arbitrary Language. Kluwer Academic Publishers, Dordrecht (2003)

3. O'Neill, M., Ryan, C., Keijzer, M., Cattolico, M.: Crossover in Grammatical Evolution. Genetic Programming and Evolvable Machines 4(1), 67–93 (2003)
4. Harper, R., Blair, A.: A Structure Preserving Crossover in Grammatical Evolution. In: Proc. CEC 2005 IEEE Congress on Evolutionary Computation, vol. 3, pp. 2537–2544. IEEE Press, Los Alamitos (2005)
5. Rothlauf, F., Oetzel, M.: On the Locality of Grammatical Evolution. In: Collet, P., Tomassini, M., Ebner, M., Gustafson, S., Ekárt, A. (eds.) EuroGP 2006. LNCS, vol. 3905, pp. 320–330. Springer, Heidelberg (2006)
6. Langdon, W.B., Poli, R.: An Analysis of the MAX Problem in Genetic Programming. In: Proceedings of the second annual conference, Stanford University, July 13-16, pp. 222–230. Morgan Kaufmann Pub., San Francisco (1997)
7. Langdon, W.B., Poli, R.: An analysis of the MAX problem in genetic programming. Genetic Programming, 222–230 (1997) (Citeseer)
8. Hugosson, J., Hemberg, E., Brabazon, A., O'Neill, M.: An investigation of the mutation operator using different representations in Grammatical Evolution. In: Proc. 2nd International Symposium Advances in Artificial Intelligence and Applications, vol. 2, pp. 409–419 (2007)
9. Koza, J.R.: Genetic programming: on the programming of computers by means of natural selection. The MIT press, Cambridge (1992)
10. Dempsey, I., O'Neill, M., Brabazon, A.: Foundations in Grammatical Evolution for Dynamic Environments. Springer, Heidelberg (2009)
11. Byrne, J., O'Neill, M., Brabazon, A.: Structural and nodal mutation in grammatical evolution. In: Proceedings of the 11th Annual conference on Genetic and evolutionary computation, pp. 1881–1882. ACM, New York (2009)
12. O'Neill, M., Hemberg, E., Gilligan, C., Bartley, E., McDermott, J., Brabazon, A.: GEVA - Grammatical Evolution in Java (v1.0). UCD School of Computer Science Technical Report UCD-CSI-2008-09 (2008), http://ncra.ucd.ie/geva/
13. O'Neill, M., Hemberg, E., Gilligan, C., Bartley, E., McDermott, J., Brabazon, A.: GEVA: Grammatical Evolution in Java. SIGEVOlution 3(2), 17–22 (2009)
14. Keijzer, M., Ryan, C., O'Neill, M., Cattolico, M., Babovic, V.: Ripple crossover in genetic programming. In: Miller, J., Tomassini, M., Lanzi, P.L., Ryan, C., Tetamanzi, A.G.B., Langdon, W.B. (eds.) EuroGP 2001. LNCS, vol. 2038, pp. 74–86. Springer, Heidelberg (2001)

Positional Effect of Crossover and Mutation in Grammatical Evolution

Tom Castle and Colin G. Johnson

School of Computing, University of Kent,
Canterbury, CT2 7NF, UK
{tc33,C.G.Johnson}@kent.ac.uk
http://www.kent.ac.uk

Abstract. An often-mentioned issue with Grammatical Evolution is that a small change in the genotype, through mutation or crossover, may completely change the meaning of all of the following genes. This paper analyses the crossover and mutation operations in GE, in particular examining the constructive or destructive nature of these operations when occurring at points throughout a genotype. The results we present show some strong support for the idea that events occurring at the first positions of a genotype are indeed more destructive, but also indicate that they may be the most constructive crossover and mutation points too. We also demonstrate the sensitivity of this work to the precise definition of what is constructive/destructive.

Keywords: Grammatical Evolution, crossover, mutation, position, bias.

1 Introduction

A desirable trait of the genetic operations of crossover and mutation in evolutionary algorithms, is that they should have high locality; small genotypic changes should result in similarly small changes in the phenotype [1]. This allows the algorithm to more smoothly navigate the search space. Grammatical Evolution (GE) [2] represents programs as a linear genome (genotype) which is then converted to executable code (phenotype), through a mapping operation.

It has been proposed that as a result of the mapping operation, the genetic operators in GE do not maintain high locality [3]. One potential reason for this is that an alteration in the chromosome will change the meaning and context of all following codons, even if those codons remain the same. The expectation therefore, is that mutation and crossover events that occur at points towards the beginning of the genome will on average be far more destructive than those at the end. This paper investigates the extent to which this is true.

The following section gives an introduction to the GE technique and the crossover and mutation operators being considered, followed by a brief review of some existing, similar work. A detailed description of the experiments performed is given, before the results of the experiments are presented along with some discussion as to what they show. Finally, the paper will be concluded with some suggestions for future work.

A.I. Esparcia-Alcazar et al. (Eds.): EuroGP 2010, LNCS 6021, pp. 26–37, 2010.
© Springer-Verlag Berlin Heidelberg 2010

2   Background

2.1   Grammatical Evolution

Grammatical Evolution [2] is an evolutionary approach to generating computer programs which is similar to Genetic Programming (GP) [4]. GE allows the generation of programs in any language definable in Backus Naur Form (BNF). The GE algorithm uses a variable length binary string called a *chromosome* to represent individuals. The chromosome is made up of a sequence of *codons*, which are simply integer values (we use a full range of positive 32-bit integers in this study). During fitness evaluation the chromosome is translated into a phenotype source string, which is valid according to the BNF grammar. This conversion is achieved using the mapping operation.

Mapping is performed by traversing the grammar. At each rule with multiple productions, the production to use is decided by the program's next codon. The integer codon value taken is then divided by the number of available productions with the remainder used as the index of the rule to map to. For example, given the example grammar rule below, the expr may be replaced by any of the 3 productions. The codon C_x is taken from the program to be mapped, and then the rule to use will be decided by: C_x MOD 3, where 3 is the number of productions in this case.

```
expr ::= conditional      {0}
       | loop             {1}
       | assignment       {2}
```

Mapping is complete when all non-terminal grammar rules have been replaced by terminals, or, if the program is deemed to be invalid, which may occur if there are insufficient codons to complete the mapping or some maximum depth/length limit is exceeded. In the case of insufficient codons it is typical to use a wrapping operator whereby mapping continues from the first codon, but this is usually accompanied by a maximum number of wraps.

GE uses the standard genetic operators of crossover and mutation. Mutation is a single point mutation where an individual selected to undergo mutation has a codon selected at random, and this codon is replaced with a new randomly generated codon. Similarly, crossover uses single point crossover, where two parents selected for crossover will have points chosen randomly within each of them, and the two sets of codons following these points exchanged.

A characteristic of the mapping process is the presence of a number of unused codons at the end of an individual. Crossover and mutation events still occur within this unused portion, but the change has no impact on the phenotype or fitness. Throughout the rest of this paper we will only be considering those change events that occur within the *active* region, defined to be those codons that are translated in program code.

2.2   Related Work

Numerous studies have looked into the effect of crossover in various forms of genetic programming. Nordin et al [5] and Johnson [6] independently looked at the fitness change caused by crossover for tree-based GP. Similar studies have also been conducted for linear [7] and graph [8] representations. The consistent conclusion is that most crossover events result in either a reduction in fitness or no change. Our work seeks to confirm whether this is the case in GE too, but in particular is more concerned with the effect crossover position has on this fitness change.

A number of researchers have considered crossover in the grammatical evolution algorithm. Harper and Blair proposed alternatives to the standard one-point crossover, with self-selecting crossover [9] and structure preserving crossover [10], and Keijzer et al. introduced a form of ripple crossover to GE [11]. O'Neill and Ryan [12] sought to identify a homologous crossover for GE. They determined that rather than causing the "mass destruction" expected, the standard one-point crossover operator itself acts as a form of homologous crossover, recombining individuals such that the context of building blocks is preserved.

There has been much less work focusing on the mutation operator in grammatical evolution. Rothlauf and Oetzel [3] examined mutation in relation to locality, determining that the representation used by GE does lead to lower locality. Another study by Hugosson et al. [13] compared a number of mutation operators, leading to the conclusion that the standard bit-flipping mutation is the best choice for locality. They also question whether higher locality in GE is actually beneficial.

3   Method

For each of even-five parity, Santa Fe trail, 6-bit multiplexer and a symbolic regression problem, 1000 runs were carried out to provide a large quantity of crossover and mutation data. The fitness of each individual selected for crossover and mutation was logged before and after the operation, along with the point at which the operation was carried out. The destructive or constructive nature of the operation could then be analysed in relation to the position at which it occurred. If the standardised fitness decreased then this was considered a positive change, if it increased it was negative and no change signalled a neutral effect.

Since crossover operations involve the exchange of material on two candidate solutions, it is more difficult to define what is positive/neutral/negative than for mutation. There are many ways in which to compare the resultant children's fitness to the fitness of the parents:

- average of both children compared to average of both parents
- each child compared to the average fitness of the population
- each child compared to one parent
- each child compared to the average fitness of the parents
- ...

Table 1. Even-five parity parameter tableau for GE

Raw fitness:	Number of inputs producing incorrect outputs, on all 2^5 possible cases.
Standardised fitness:	Same as raw fitness.
Population size:	500
Number of generations:	100
Mutation probability:	0.1
Crossover probability:	0.9

Table 2. Santa Fe trail parameter tableau for GE

Raw fitness:	Number of pieces of food before the ant times out with 600 operations.
Standardised fitness:	Total number of pieces of food, minus the raw fitness.
Population size:	500
Number of generations:	100
Mutation probability:	0.1
Crossover probability:	0.9

None of these definitions are perfect, so two approaches are presented here. In one approach the fitness of each child is compared to one parent program, in the other to the average of both of its parents. These approaches will allow us to consider each crossover operation as two events—one for each crossover point.

Variable length chromosomes make it necessary that some form of normalisation take place in order to compare separate operator events. This was performed by grouping into deciles, so that all crossovers occurring in the first 10% of the chromosome are grouped together, and so forth. Events at points outside the active portion of the chromosome were ignored due to their neutrality and as such, deciles were resolved based upon the position of the change within the active portion of the chromosome.

The parameters used for each run are outlined in tables 1, 2, 3 and 4. Chromosomes were allowed to wrap, but it should be noted that the effects of wrapping were negligible as a result of few individuals requiring it on the given problems.

Table 3. Multiplexer 6-bit parameter tableau for GE

Raw fitness:	Number of inputs producing incorrect outputs, on all 2^6 possible cases.
Standardised fitness:	Same as raw fitness.
Population size:	500
Number of generations:	100
Mutation probability:	0.1
Crossover probability:	0.9

Table 4. Symbolic regression parameter tableau for GE

Raw fitness:	Sum of the error, for a sample of 20 data points in the interval -1.0 to 1.0.
Standardised fitness:	Same as raw fitness.
Population size:	500
Number of generations:	100
Mutation probability:	0.1
Crossover probability:	0.9

4   Results and Discussion

The results of our experiments are presented in this section. We consider firstly mutation, and then crossover (measuring fitness change in two different ways). For each operator, three groups of bar charts are presented. These represent the proportion of positive, neutral and negative changes. Each bar represents one decile, as explained above.

4.1   Mutation

The results of our mutation experiments are presented in figures 1, 2 and 3. The results are not strongly problem-dependent: the same trends can be observed for each problem.

The positive events show the weakest overall pattern in the results: towards the end of the active region, there is typically a declining trend in the proportion of positive events; towards the beginning there is not a strong pattern, though three of the problems show a noticeably lower proportion in the first decile. The neutral events all have an upward trend, and the negatives all demonstrate a rapid downward trend.

Considering the neutral changes, one notable feature is the very high proportion of neutral changes in the later positions in the active region. This suggests that a mutation operator that was biased towards the earlier part of the active region might have a better effect. The results suggest that such an operator would create more movement in the search space; whilst by far the largest proportion of this would be negative, it would also increase the proportion of positive events. Using this alongside a local search operator (e.g. a mutation variant on brood crossover [14]) might help to counteract the number of negatives generated using such a mutation method.

4.2   Crossover

The crossover results are presented using the two different definitions of the positive-neutral-negative classification discussed above.

The results using the first definition, the *averaged parent fitness* where the fitness of the child is compared with the average fitness of its two parents, are presented in figures 4, 5 and 6. As with the mutation results, these results do

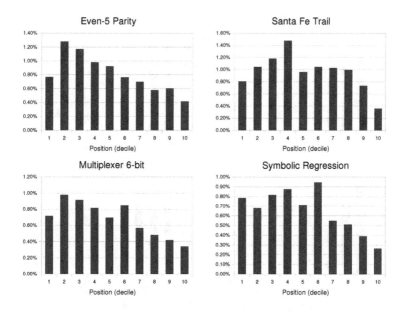

Fig. 1. Proportion of mutations in each decile that had a positive effect on fitness

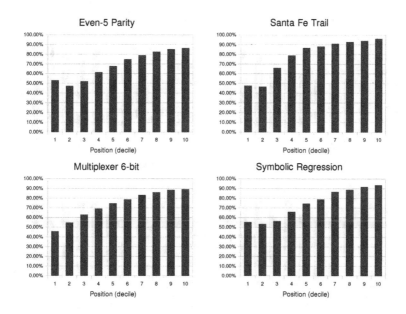

Fig. 2. Proportion of mutations in each decile that had no effect on fitness

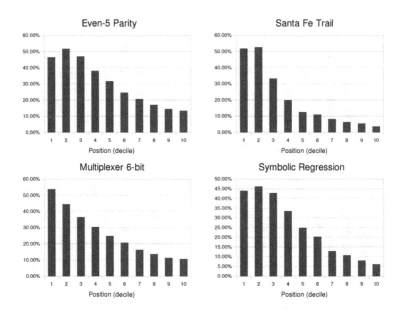

Fig. 3. Proportion of mutations in each decile that had a negative effect on fitness

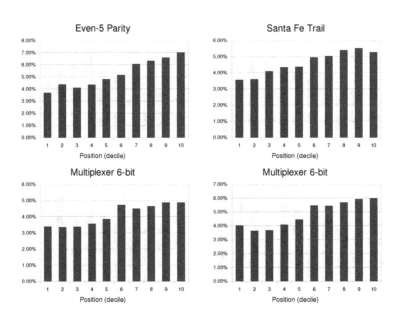

Fig. 4. Proportion of crossover events in each decile that had a positive effect on fitness. Using the *averaged parent fitness* definition of positive crossover.

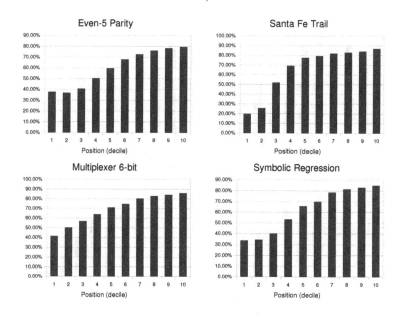

Fig. 5. Proportion of crossover events in each decile that had no effect on fitness. Using the *averaged parent fitness* definition of neutral crossover.

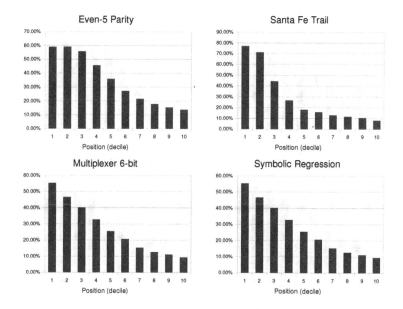

Fig. 6. Proportion of crossover events in each decile that had a negative effect on fitness. Using the *averaged parent fitness* definition of negative crossover.

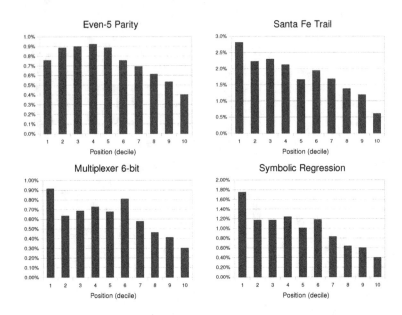

Fig. 7. Proportion of crossover events in each decile that had a positive effect on fitness. Using the *change to first parent* definition of positive crossover.

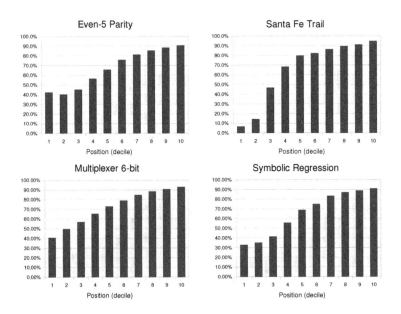

Fig. 8. Proportion of crossover events in each decile that had no effect on fitness. Using the *change to first parent* definition of neutral crossover.

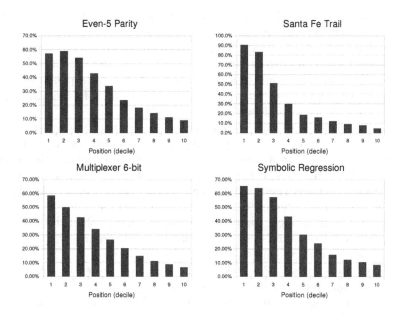

Fig. 9. Proportion of crossover events in each decile that had a negative effect on fitness. Using the *change to first parent* definition of negative crossover.

not show a strong problem-dependence, having similar patterns for all problems. The positive and neutral events both show a strong upwards trend, whereas the negative results show a steep downward trend.

The behaviour of both the negative and neutral events is similar to the behaviour observed in the mutation events. A large proportion of the crossovers towards the end of the active region result in a neutral change to the fitness. This perhaps suggests that these crossovers are placing the crossed over code from the second parent into a region on the first parent that, whilst encoded for, is redundant or inaccessible in the phenotype. One way to address this would be to use a data-flow analysis [15] to ensure that the crossover point is in an accessed part of the code (this idea of choosing a good crossover point has been explored in the technique called *context-aware crossover* [16]). Furthermore, it is possible that phenotypically identical material is being crossed over. This has a positional bias due to shorter regions needing to be equivalent towards the end of the active region.

When compared with the mutation events, the positive crossover events demonstrate a very different pattern of behaviour. Crossover events towards the end of the active region are much more likely to produce a positive effect than those towards the beginning. This suggests that crossover is not simply acting as another form of mutation operator; the code crossed in from the second parent is having a positive effect on the fitness, especially if it makes a smaller change by being towards the end of the active region.

One surprising feature of this analysis is how large a proportion of crossovers are neutral, given that this requires the child to have *exactly* the same fitness as the average of the two parents. This seems unlikely to occur as a result of a crossover event that takes two parents with different fitnesses; it would seem more likely that these are the result of identical or identical-fitness parents crossing over. An interesting piece of future work would be to do a further analysis in which these events were considered separately, as in [6].

By contrast with the mutation results, these suggest that a positional bias in crossover towards the end of the active region would be an obvious improvement, as this should increase the number of positive events and decrease the number of negative events. However, it is perhaps important not to eliminate too many negative events, as otherwise this will simply reduce the search to a hillclimber, which is unlikely to be effective in such a complex search space.

This analysis is made more complex, however, when we look at the alternative definition of positive-neutral-negative events using the *change to first parent* definition, i.e. the child is compared to the first of its parents. The results for this are given in figures 7, 8 and 9. In these results, the effects of crossover have very similar trends to those obtained using mutation, the most notable change being the larger proportion of positives in the first decile for three of the problems. By contrast with the results from the previous definition, these results suggest that crossover is acting as a kind of mutation operator.

Therefore, it is hard to draw any definitive conclusions about crossover from these analyses—it appears that this depends highly on the specific definition of positive/neutral/negative chosen.

5   Future Work

Future work includes examining how these effects change through the generations of the GE run, looking at a wider range of definitions for constructive and destructive operators, and, finally, designing and testing new operators based on what we have learned from our analysis.

References

1. McKay, R.I., Nguyen, X.H., Whigham, P.A., Shan, Y.: Grammars in genetic programming: A brief review. In: Kang, L., Cai, Z., Yan, Y. (eds.) Progress in Intelligence Computation and Intelligence: Proceedings of the International Symposium on Intelligence, Computation and Applications, Wuhan, PRC, China, pp. 3–18. University of Geosciences Press (2005)
2. O'Neill, M., Ryan, C.: Grammatical evolution. IEEE Transactions on Evolutionary Computation 5, 349–358 (2001)
3. Rothlauf, F., Oetzel, M.: On the locality of grammatical evolution. In: Collet, P., Tomassini, M., Ebner, M., Gustafson, S., Ekárt, A. (eds.) EuroGP 2006. LNCS, vol. 3905, pp. 320–330. Springer, Heidelberg (2006)
4. Koza, J.R.: Genetic Programming: On the Programming of Computers by Means of Natural Selection. MIT Press, Cambridge (1992)

5. Nordin, P., Francone, F., Banzhaf, W.: Explicitly defined introns and destructive crossover in genetic programming. In: Rosca, J.P. (ed.) Proceedings of the Workshop on Genetic Programming: From Theory to Real-World Applications, Tahoe City, California, USA, pp. 6–22 (1995)
6. Johnson, C.: Genetic programming crossover: Does it cross over? In: Vanneschi, L., Gustafson, S., Moraglio, A., De Falco, I., Ebner, M. (eds.) EuroGP 2009. LNCS, vol. 5481, pp. 97–108. Springer, Heidelberg (2009)
7. Nordin, P., Banzhaf, W.: Complexity compression and evolution. In: Eshelman, L. (ed.) Genetic Algorithms: Proceedings of the Sixth International Conference (ICGA 1995), Pittsburgh, PA, USA, pp. 310–317. Morgan Kaufmann, San Francisco (1995)
8. Teller, A., Veloso, M.: PADO: A new learning architecture for object recognition. In: Ikeuchi, K., Veloso, M. (eds.) Symbolic Visual Learning, pp. 81–116. Oxford University Press, Oxford (1996)
9. Harper, R., Blair, A.: A self-selecting crossover operator. In: Yen, G.G., et al. (eds.) Proceedings of the 2006 IEEE Congress on Evolutionary Computation, Vancouver, pp. 5569–5576. IEEE Press, Los Alamitos (2006)
10. Harper, R., Blair, A.: A structure preserving crossover in grammatical evolution. In: Corne, D., et al. (eds.) Proceedings of the 2005 IEEE Congress on Evolutionary Computation, Edinburgh, UK, vol. 3, pp. 2537–2544. IEEE Press, Los Alamitos (2005)
11. Keijzer, M., Ryan, C., O'Neill, M., Cattolico, M., Babovic, V.: Ripple crossover in genetic programming. In: Miller, J.F., Tomassini, M., Lanzi, P.L., Ryan, C., Tettamanzi, A.G.B., Langdon, W.B. (eds.) EuroGP 2001. LNCS, vol. 2038, pp. 74–86. Springer, Heidelberg (2001)
12. O'Neill, M., Ryan, C.: Crossover in grammatical evolution: A smooth operator? In: Poli, R., Banzhaf, W., Langdon, W.B., Miller, J.F., Nordin, P., Fogarty, T.C. (eds.) EuroGP 2000. LNCS, vol. 1802, pp. 149–162. Springer, Heidelberg (2000)
13. Hugosson, J., Hemberg, E., Brabazon, A., O'Neill, M.: An investigation of the mutation operator using different representations in grammatical evolution. In: 2nd International Symposium Advances in Artificial Intelligence and Applications, Wisla, Poland, vol. 2, pp. 409–419 (2007)
14. Tackett, W.A.: Greedy recombination and genetic search on the space of computer programs. In: Whitley, L.D., Vose, M.D. (eds.) Foundations of Genetic Algorithms, Estes Park, Colorado, USA, 1994, vol. 3, pp. 271–297. Morgan Kaufmann, San Francisco (1994)
15. Nielson, F., Nielson, H.R., Hankin, C.: Principles of Program Analysis. Springer, Heidelberg (1999)
16. Majeed, H., Ryan, C.: Using context-aware crossover to improve the performance of GP. In: Keijzer, M., et al. (eds.) GECCO 2006: Proceedings of the 8th annual conference on Genetic and evolutionary computation, Seattle, Washington, USA, vol. 1, pp. 847–854. ACM Press, New York (2006)

Sub-tree Swapping Crossover and Arity Histogram Distributions

Stephen Dignum and Riccardo Poli

School of Computer Science and Electronic Engineering,
University of Essex,
Wivenhoe Park, Colchester, CO4 3SQ, UK
{sandig,rpoli}@essex.ac.uk

Abstract. Recent theoretical work has characterised the search bias of GP sub-tree swapping crossover in terms of program length distributions, providing an exact fixed point for trees with internal nodes of identical arity. However, only an approximate model (based on the notion of average arity) for the mixed-arity case has been proposed. This leaves a particularly important gap in our knowledge because multi-arity function sets are commonplace in GP and deep lessons could be learnt from the fixed point. In this paper, we present an accurate theoretical model of program length distributions when mixed-arity function sets are employed. The new model is based on the notion of an *arity histogram*, a count of the number of primitives of each arity in a program. Empirical support is provided and a discussion of the model is used to place earlier findings into a more general context.

Keywords: Genetic Programming, Sub-Tree Swapping Crossover, Program Length, Arity Histograms.

1 Introduction

Understanding how Genetic Programming (GP) explores the space of computer programs requires two things [12, Chapter 11]: a) characterising the search space itself, e.g., in terms of how fitness is distributed in it, and b) explaining how GP explores it, particularly in terms of the search biases of its genetic operators.

Research on the characterisation of the search space has provided evidence of how program functionality and fitness are distributed in program spaces (e.g., showing that beyond a certain minimum program length the distributions of program functionality and, therefore, fitness converge to a limit [6–9]). Research has also characterised the search bias of GP sub-tree swapping crossover in terms of program length distributions, providing an exact fixed point for trees with internal nodes of identical arity [11,13] and an approximate fixed point for the mixed-arity case [1,2].

Understanding the sampling of program length is of particular importance to GP. For example, this has the potential to shed light on the phenomenon of bloat (see [12, Chapter 11] for a recent survey on the topic). Indeed, the work on the fixed-point distributions of program lengths under sub-tree crossover mentioned above has led to a new bloat theory – *crossover-bias* – a number of suggestions for experimental parameter

A.I. Esparcia-Alcazar et al. (Eds.): EuroGP 2010, LNCS 6021, pp. 38–49, 2010.

selection and a new method to control sampling, by length, of GP operators – *operator equalisation.*

One crucial question still open is how to exactly model the limiting distribution of program lengths when mixed-arity function sets are employed. This is particularly interesting because multi-arity function sets are commonplace in GP and important lessons could be learnt from knowing the fixed point.

Note, this is not just a question of better accuracy. Until now, it has not been possible to explain a number of strange empirical findings for mixed arity representations. Why, for instance, are programs with certain compositions of primitives much more likely to be sampled than programs with another composition even if both have exactly the same length? Also, why is it that for smaller lengths, the empirical limiting distribution of program lengths shows a rugged zigzagging profile instead of following the smooth descent, with each succeeding length class sampled with less frequency, seen with common arity function sets? What we need is a model that can explain these phenomena. In this paper we present an accurate theoretical model of program length distributions for mixed-arity function sets which does just that.

The paper is organised as follows. In section 2, we describe a number of models for the prediction of program length based on the repeated application of GP sub-tree swapping crossover, with uniform selection of crossover points, on a flat fitness landscape, i.e., to determine the bias of this operator by removing all other effects. In Section 3, we extend this work and use a number of mathematical generalisations to produce a new model to predict individual occurrence in a population using arity histograms. This is then used to model length class frequencies exactly. Strong empirical evidence is provided in Section 4 to support both models; in particular we show how the length model can be successfully fitted to shorter length classes for mixed arity cases. In Section 5, we discuss the sampling implications of the models and their relationship to the work presented previously in this area notably its implications for program length sampling and GP bloat. Finally, we summarise our findings in Section 6.

2   Background

In [11], a number of models were proposed to predict a limiting distribution of GP tree sizes when sub-tree swapping crossover, with uniform selection of crossover points, was applied on a flat fitness landscape. The limiting distribution of internal nodes for a-ary trees, those whose internal functions have a common arity, a, was shown to be the following Lagrange distribution of the second kind:

$$\Pr\{n\} = (1 - ap_a)\binom{an+1}{n}(1 - p_a)^{(a-1)n+1}p_a{}^n, \tag{1}$$

where $\Pr\{n\}$ is the probability of selecting a tree with n internal nodes and a is the arity of functions that can be used in the creation an individual. The parameter p_a was shown to be related to a and the average size of the individuals in the population at generation 0, μ_0, according to the formula:

$$p_a = \frac{2\mu_0 + (a-1) - \sqrt{((1-a) - 2\mu_0)^2 + 4(1-\mu_0^2)}}{2a(1+\mu_0)}. \tag{2}$$

In [1], Equation (1) was generalised for mixed arity cases with an average internal arity $\bar{a}$ replacing a. $\bar{a}$ can be predicted from experimental parameters for traditional initialisation methods such as GROW and FULL [10] or determined at run time by calculating the average internal arity at generation 0. The Gamma function, Γ, was used to redefine the binomial coefficient (factorials are replaced using $\Gamma(n+1) = n!$) so that the model could accept non-integer average arity values. This resulted in the following equation:

$$\Pr\{n\} = (1 - \bar{a}p_{\bar{a}}) \frac{\Gamma(\bar{a}n+2)}{\Gamma((\bar{a}-1)n+2)\Gamma(n+1)} (1 - p_{\bar{a}})^{(\bar{a}-1)n+1} p_{\bar{a}}^n. \tag{3}$$

Note that this equation is also expressed in terms of internal node counts. Strong empirical support was found in [1] for both Equations (1) and (3).

A further generalisation to length classes,[1] i.e., to also include external nodes, or leaves, was found to be successful for a-ary trees in [2]. However, the generalisation to length classes for mixed-arity trees was found to be less successful, being unable to precisely predict the frequency for the smaller length classes, where a smooth descent was predicted by the models but a more rugged shape was found to occur. As an example, Figure 1 shows experimental and predicted results for sub-tree swapping crossover acting on trees with available arities of 1, 2, 3 and 4 (the experimental set-up is as described in section 4).

In related work [4], empirical evidence was provided to suggest that the probability of the occurrence of an individual in a GP population after repeated application of sub-tree swapping crossover on a flat fitness landscape would be determined by the individual's *arity histogram* – a count of the number of nodes in a tree of each arity (see Figure 2 for an example). Within length classes, programs with certain arity histograms were more likely to be found than others. However, within arity histogram classes there is no bias to sample certain program shapes, indicating that arity histograms represent the lowest level of granularity at which length-related biases occur in the presence of sub-tree swapping crossover.[2]

In the following sections we embrace the idea that if we are to exactly predict length distributions for mixed-arity cases, we will have to incorporate arity histograms in our models. For a-ary trees the arity histogram is, of course, simply the associated internal and external node counts, which explains the earlier success with the a-ary models.

3   Arity Histogram Model

From the work described the previous section, we know that we wish to predict the probability of occurrence of an individual with a particular arity histogram. If we choose n_a to represent a count of arity a nodes, we can define a particular arity histogram of an individual, as the tuple $(n_0, \ldots, n_{a_{max}})$. Note, n_0, is the number of leaves, i.e., nodes with an arity of zero. Using our new notation we can term our target probability, $\Pr\{n_0, \ldots, n_{a_{max}}\}$.

---

[1] Length was derived using the relation $\ell = an + 1$.

[2] Note that unique programs are a subclass of program shapes which are a subclass of arity histogram classes which are in turn a subclass of program lengths.

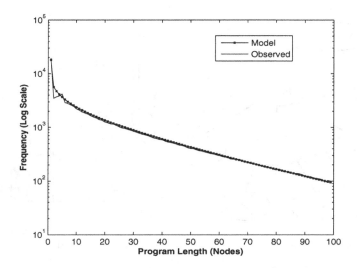

Fig. 1. Comparison between model ($\bar{a} = 2.5$) and empirical program length distributions for trees created with arity 1, 2, 3 and 4 functions and terminals only, initialised with FULL method (depth = 3, initial mean size $\mu_0 = 25.38$, mean size after 500 generations $\mu_{500} = 23.72$). Population size = 100,000.

Below, we will attempt to identify this function by means of generalisation from previous results and intuition. The 'acid test' for the result of our generalisation will be whether or not it fits the empirical data in a variety of conditions.

Let us start by reviewing Equation (1), the original model for a-ary representations. We can see that in order to generalise it, we need to introduce the concept of multiple arities, particularly the associated p_a and n_a values.

First, we postulate that we now have a set of p_a values each associated with a single arity. If we interpret these as forming a probability distribution, we can then imagine that product ap_a in the first term of the equation, actually represents an 'expectation' of a.[3] If this is correct, then the first term $(1 - ap_a)$ should be changed to $(1 - \sum_{a \geq 1} ap_a)$.

The original binomial coefficient term represents the number of ways of choosing internal nodes of the same arity, a, from the length of the resulting tree, $an + 1$. We need to alter this by selecting each arity count, n_a, from the tree length that can be built with this collection of arities, $\sum_{a \geq 1} an_a + 1$. Our binomial coefficient term, therefore, becomes the multinomial coefficient $\binom{\sum_{a \geq 1} an_a + 1}{n_0, \ldots, n_{a_{max}}}$, where n_0 is the count of leaves, n_1 is the count of the functions with arity 1, etc.

The third term, $(1 - p_a)^{(a-1)n+1}$, can be broken into two parts. The superscript is simply the number of terminals for the tree, which we know to be n_0. As with the first term we alter $(1 - p_a)$ to a mixed arity equivalent, which we postulate to be $(1 - \sum_{a \geq 1} p_a)$.

---

[3] In our a-ary model: $E[a] = 0 \times (1 - p_a) + a \times p_a = ap_a$.

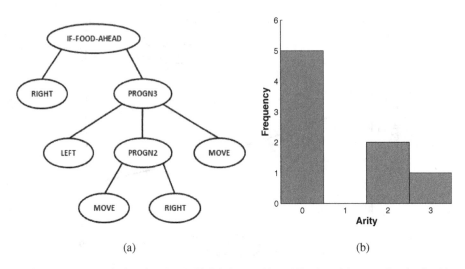

Fig. 2. A proposed solution for the Artificial Ant problem [5] (a) and its associated arity histogram (b)

Continuing this analogy, the final term, p_a^n, represents the value, p_a, to the power of the number of nodes, n. We need to now split out the term so that each value of p_a is associated with the appropriate n_a value. The most natural way to do this is to turn the final term into the product $\prod_{a\geq 1} p_a^{n_a}$.

Putting this altogether, we obtain our mixed-arity model for the limiting distribution of arity histograms created by sub-tree swapping crossover:

$$\Pr\{n_0,\ldots,n_{a_{max}}\} = \left(1 - \sum_{a\geq 1} a p_a\right)\binom{\sum_{a\geq 1} a n_a + 1}{n_0,\ldots,n_{a_{max}}}\left(1 - \sum_{a\geq 1} p_a\right)^{n_0}\prod_{a\geq 1} p_a^{n_a}. \quad (4)$$

This equation has now become a multivariate Lagrange distribution of the second kind. Note, the introduction of counts for program leaves will only affect the second and third terms. On closer inspection we can also see that there is in fact no need to calculate p_0.[4]

Next, we need to create a model that will turn arity histogram probabilities into those of length classes. The set of arity histograms that represent a particular program length ℓ can be defined as:

$$\left\{n_0,\ldots,n_{a_{max}} : \sum_{a\geq 1} a n_a + 1 = \ell\right\}. \quad (5)$$

We can, therefore, calculate the probability of a particular program length by summing the probabilities for each of the associated arity histograms, i.e.,

$$\Pr\{\ell\} = \sum_{n_0,\ldots,n_{a_{max}}:\sum_{a\geq 1} a n_a + 1 = \ell} \Pr\{n_0,\ldots,n_{a_{max}}\}. \quad (6)$$

---

[4] If we define p_0 to be $1 - \sum_{a\geq 1} p_a$ and allow the fourth term to run from $a = 0$, we could also omit the third term.

We term this a *Lagrange distribution of the third kind*. The formula clarifies that the length bias with which sub-tree swapping crossover samples program spaces is, in fact, the result of an even more primitive bias associated with arity histograms.

In the next section we will provide empirical support for our new models of arity-histogram and length distributions, to ensure that they continue to predict a-ary representation length distributions and will now accurately model mixed arity representations.

4   Empirical Validation

In order to verify empirically the models proposed, a number of runs of a GP system in Java were performed. A relatively large population of 100,000 individuals was used in order to reduce drift of average program size and to ensure that enough programs of each length class were available. The FULL initialisation method was used with non-terminals being chosen with uniform probability. Each run consisted of 500 generations. All results were averaged over 20 runs.

To check if the models presented in the previous section match experimental data we need to fit them to the data so as to identify the parameters p_a. This fit was achieved using a hill climber search program that reduced the mean squared error from that observed in the final generation and that predicted by the theoretical distribution, by altering the p_a values.[5]

Our first step was to see if there is evidence that arity histogram occurrence is modeled correctly. In Figure 3, we can see two views of the modeled and empirical data for each experiment. The X-Y plots on the left report the frequency for each arity histogram predicted via Equation (4) vs the corresponding empirical frequency. Note how the data points lie on, or very close to, the diagonal line that represents perfect prediction. Each point in the scatter plots on the right shows either the actual or the predicted frequency for an arity histogram vs the length class it corresponds to. The multiple points at each length are the elements of the set in Equation (5). Of particular interest is that even with a relatively large population size, certain histograms are exceptionally rare. For example, occurrences for a histogram consisting of arity one functions and a single terminal for the 1 & 3 arity experiment, are predicted to be less than 1 by the time we reach a length of 9 nodes and far less in the other experiment.

As we can see in Figures 4 and 5, the model in Equation (6) fits very well the frequencies associated to all length classes for mixed arities. Note in particular how the model, that incorporates the arity histogram model from Equation (4), now captures the fluctuating early values for mixed arity representations.

In order to confirm that Equation (6) is in fact a generalisation of earlier work and accurately predicts a-ary distributions, Figures 6 and 7 show the model and observed data from the final generation for 1-ary and 2-ary trees. In this case the p_a values for the model were calculated using Equation (2).

In essence, we now have evidence that we have isolated the fundamental components of the limiting length distribution for sub-tree swapping crossover. Further work is

---

[5] Initial values of p_a were set uniform randomly between 0 and 0.2. A number of runs were performed and best results were found using small variations (less than 0.001%) with a high number of alternatives at each step (typically 100).

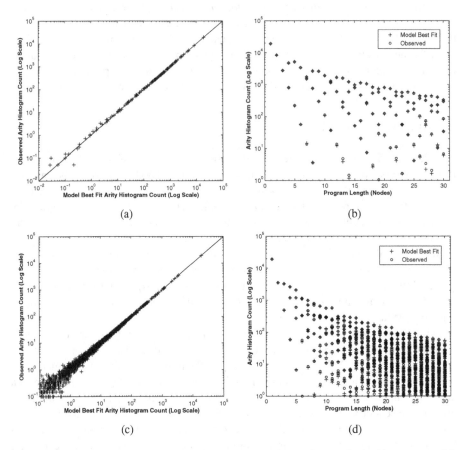

Fig. 3. Comparison between unique arity histogram count observations and arity histogram model predictions obtained by best fit for trees created with arity 1 and 3 functions (a) & (b), arity 1, 2, 3 and 4 functions (c) & (d), and terminals only. Experimental parameters as described in figures 4 and 5 respectively. Diagonal lines added to (a) & (c) represent perfect prediction.

required to make this a complete predictive model, i.e., we need a formula to determine p_a values for mixed arity representations. However, we can now place the findings from earlier work in this area into further context. This is discussed in the next section.

5   Sampling Implications

From our analysis we can now be confident in the assertion that the limiting distribution of program lengths for a GP population after the repeated application of sub-tree swapping crossover, with uniform selection of crossover points, on a flat fitness landscape, is determined solely by the mix of node arities in the initial population.

From the work provided in [4], we know that there is empirical evidence to show that there is no bias for sub-tree swapping crossover to place a particular node label at any

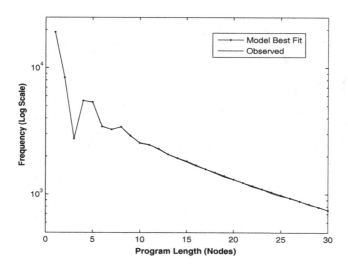

Fig. 4. Comparison between empirical length distributions and an arity histogram model obtained by best fit for trees created with arity 1 and 3 functions and terminals only, initialised with FULL method (depth = 3, initial mean size μ_0 = 15.00, mean size after 500 generations μ_{500} = 15.75). Population size = 100,000. p_1 = 0.2186684078761787, p_3 = 0.15804781356057954.

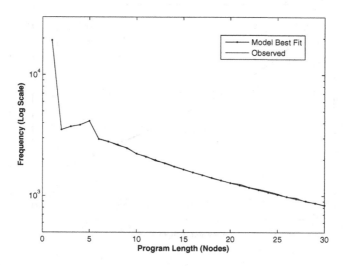

Fig. 5. Comparison between empirical length distributions and an arity histogram model obtained by best fit for trees created with arities 1, 2, 3 and 4 functions and terminals only, initialised with FULL method (depth = 3, initial mean size μ_0 = 25.38, mean size after 500 generations μ_{500} = 23.72). Population size = 100,000. p_1 = 0.09117030091320417, p_2 = 0.08112567496250808, p_3 = 0.0702296050436014, p_4 = 0.0643780797663895.

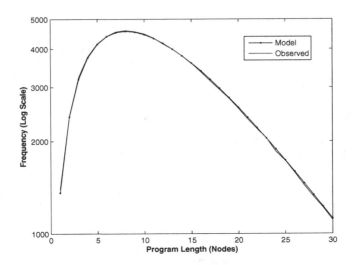

Fig. 6. Comparison between empirical length distributions and an arity histogram model created with arity 1 functions and terminals only, initialised with FULL method (depth = 15, initial mean size μ_0 = 16.00, mean size after 500 generations μ_{500} = 16.15). Population size = 100,000.

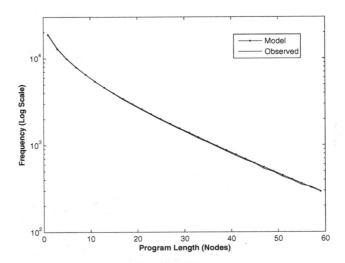

Fig. 7. Comparison between empirical length distributions and an arity histogram model created with arity 2 functions and terminals only, initialised with FULL method (depth = 3, initial mean size μ_0 = 15.00, mean size after 500 generations μ_{500} = 14.19). Invalid even lengths are ignored. Population size = 100,000.

position in a tree. All programs with a particular arity histogram are, therefore, equally likely to be sampled by the application of sub-tree swapping crossover in the absence of other operators. By extension, we can also say that all programs of a certain length are equally likely to be sampled for a-ary trees; this is not true, however, for mixed arity representations. If one wishes to ensure uniform sampling within length classes, alternative variation operators will need to be devised when mixed arity representations are employed with sub-tree swapping crossover.

Looking more closely at Equation (4), we can see that the first term will remain constant for all arity histograms whilst the second term, the multinomial coefficient, will increase the probability for arity histograms that can produce more shapes. The third and final terms decrease rapidly with increasing values of the n_a's producing the eventual smooth curve. Therefore, arity histograms presented to Equation (6), that can produce more shapes than other arity histograms in a particular length class, will have a higher probability of being sampled within that class.

Disregarding the fluctuations shown in earlier length classes for mixed arity classes, Equation (6) is decreasing. The *crossover bias* bloat theory was originally proposed based upon evidence presented by the internal node count models and their decreasing nature, to recap:

I   In each generation selection populates the mating pool with relatively fit programs
II The sub-tree swapping crossover operator will then produce children with a length distribution biased towards smaller programs irrespective of their fitness[6]
III If smaller programs cannot obtain a relatively high fitness, which after the initial generations of any non-trivial GP problem is highly likely, they will be ignored by selection in the next generation
IV Hence, average program size will increase as ever larger programs are placed into the mating pool

Equation (6) and the empirical work provided in Section 4 provide extra evidence to support this theory for sub-tree swapping crossover, in that our more pertinent length model varies only slightly from the smooth descent described for the internal node models presented in Section 2 and used as the basis for the theory in [1]. One can argue that any variation operator that has a bias towards smaller programs will cause bloat in this way and the theory should be renamed to *operator length bias*.

Recent work by Soule [15] has shown empirical evidence of a similar sampling effect for other types of crossover, in addition particular emphasis is placed on variations to sampling caused by altering the nature of the fitness landscape. Future research may look into the speed of convergence to Lagrangian type distributions for different variation operator and problem combinations, i.e., to enable us to gauge which experimental set-ups are likely encounter bloat earlier during an experimental run.

The internal node and length a-ary models presented in Section 2 can be used as predictive models without modification. The length model for mixed arity trees developed

---

[6] It is important to note that there is no change in the average size of programs found in the mating pool from those produced in the resulting child population, i.e., the next generation. However, the distribution has a sampling bias towards smaller programs, with relatively few larger programs.

there remains a strong model for approximation if an exact fit for earlier length classes is not required. One could, for example, use this to implement broad structural convergence measures suggested in [4]. If a more exact model was required, a fit to internal node counts could be used.

The generalised mixed arity internal node model (Equation (3)) is also an interesting starting point to further analyse the arity histogram model proposed here. We can ask how was such a generalised model so successful when only leaves were removed from the investigation? For example, would Equation (6) collapse to Equation (3) with further analysis? This is left to future work.

Finally, recent work using length based *operator equalisation* methods [3, 14], i.e., those that modify selection probabilities according to current and desired length distributions, do not guarantee uniform sampling of unique programs within the length classes desired.[7] One could imagine an extension to the method, however, to sample uniformly within length classes by storing a histogram of arity histograms, possibly using a hashing function as lengths increase. Indeed, as an alternative, it is possible to design an *arity histogram equaliser* to ensure that certain, desired, distributions of arity counts are selected.

6 Conclusions

In this paper we have generalised the Lagrange distribution of the second kind that has recently been shown to represent the limit program length distributions for sub-tree swapping crossover in the presence of single-arity function sets to the important and much more common multi-arity case.

The generalisation has required to express this fixed point via the use of arity histograms which effectively generalise the internal node counts and average arities used in prior work. Arity histograms are the fundamental components of GP sub-tree swapping crossover with regard to program sampling.

This model has allowed us to understand a number of sampling effects and to accurately model not just the smooth descending curves of the internal node models but also those of the more rugged true length distributions, i.e., those that also include leaves. From this, we can now place a number of earlier findings into a more general context. We can also start making use of our new knowledge about the biases of crossover. For example, we can confirm hypotheses about bloat and generalise cures for it.

References

1. Dignum, S., Poli, R.: Generalisation of the limiting distribution of program sizes in tree-based genetic programming and analysis of its effects on bloat. In: Thierens, D., Beyer, H.-G., Bongard, J., Branke, J., Clark, J.A., Cliff, D., Congdon, C.B., Deb, K., Doerr, B., Kovacs, T., Kumar, S., Miller, J.F., Moore, J., Neumann, F., Pelikan, M., Poli, R., Sastry, K., Stanley, K.O., Stutzle, T., Watson, R.A., Wegener, I. (eds.) GECCO 2007: Proceedings of the 9th annual conference on Genetic and evolutionary computation, July 7-11, vol. 2, pp. 1588–1595. ACM Press, New York (2007)

---

[7] Unless only an *a*-ary representation is used.

2. Dignum, S., Poli, R.: Crossover, sampling, bloat and the harmful effects of size limits. In: O'Neill, M., Vanneschi, L., Gustafson, S., Esparcia Alcázar, A.I., De Falco, I., Della Cioppa, A., Tarantino, E. (eds.) EuroGP 2008. LNCS, vol. 4971, pp. 158–169. Springer, Heidelberg (2008)

3. Dignum, S., Poli, R.: Operator equalisation and bloat free GP. In: O'Neill, M., Vanneschi, L., Gustafson, S., Esparcia Alcázar, A.I., De Falco, I., Della Cioppa, A., Tarantino, E. (eds.) EuroGP 2008. LNCS, vol. 4971, pp. 110–121. Springer, Heidelberg (2008)

4. Dignum, S., Poli, R.: Sub-tree swapping crossover, allele diffusion and GP convergence. In: Rudolph, G., Jansen, T., Lucas, S., Poloni, C., Beume, N. (eds.) PPSN 2008. LNCS, vol. 5199, pp. 368–377. Springer, Heidelberg (2008)

5. Koza, J.R.: Genetic Programming: On the Programming of Computers by Means of Natural Selection. MIT Press, Cambridge (1992)

6. Langdon, W.B.: Convergence rates for the distribution of program outputs. In: Langdon, W.B., Cantú-Paz, E., Mathias, K., Roy, R., Davis, D., Poli, R., Balakrishnan, K., Honavar, V., Rudolph, G., Wegener, J., Bull, L., Potter, M.A., Schultz, A.C., Miller, J.F., Burke, E., Jonoska, N. (eds.) Proceedings of the Genetic and Evolutionary Computation Conference, GECCO 2002, New York, July 9-13, pp. 812–819. Morgan Kaufmann Publishers, San Francisco (2002)

7. Langdon, W.B.: How many good programs are there? How long are they? In: De Jong, K.A., Poli, R., Rowe, J.E. (eds.) Foundations of Genetic Algorithms VII, Torremolinos, Spain, September 4-6, 2002, pp. 183–202. Morgan Kaufmann, San Francisco (2003)

8. Langdon, W.B.: Convergence of program fitness landscapes. In: Cantú-Paz, E., Foster, J.A., Deb, K., Davis, L., Roy, R., O'Reilly, U.-M., Beyer, H.-G., Kendall, G., Wilson, S.W., Harman, M., Wegener, J., Dasgupta, D., Potter, M.A., Schultz, A., Dowsland, K.A., Jonoska, N., Miller, J., Standish, R.K. (eds.) GECCO 2003. LNCS, vol. 2724, pp. 1702–1714. Springer, Heidelberg (2003)

9. Langdon, W.B., Poli, R.: Foundations of Genetic Programming. Springer, Heidelberg (2002)

10. Luke, S.: Two fast tree-creation algorithms for genetic programming. IEEE Transactions on Evolutionary Computation 4(3), 274–283 (2000)

11. Poli, R., Langdon, W.B., Dignum, S.: On the limiting distribution of program sizes in tree-based genetic programming. In: Ebner, M., O'Neill, M., Ekárt, A., Vanneschi, L., Esparcia-Alcázar, A.I. (eds.) EuroGP 2007. LNCS, vol. 4445, pp. 193–204. Springer, Heidelberg (2007)

12. Poli, R., Langdon, W.B., McPhee, N.F.: A field guide to genetic programming (with contributions by J.R. Koza) (2008), http://lulu.com, http://www.gp-field-guide.org.uk

13. Poli, R., McPhee, N.F.: Exact schema theorems for GP with one-point and standard crossover operating on linear structures and their application to the study of the evolution of size. In: Miller, J., Tomassini, M., Lanzi, P.L., Ryan, C., Tetamanzi, A.G.B., Langdon, W.B. (eds.) EuroGP 2001. LNCS, vol. 2038, pp. 126–142. Springer, Heidelberg (2001)

14. Silva, S., Dignum, S.: Extending operator equalisation: Fitness based self adaptive length distribution for bloat free GP. In: Vanneschi, L., Gustafson, S., Moraglio, A., De Falco, I., Ebner, M. (eds.) EuroGP 2009. LNCS, vol. 5481, pp. 159–170. Springer, Heidelberg (2009)

15. Soule, T.: Crossover and sampling biases on nearly uniform landscapes. In: Riolo, R.L., Soule, T., Worzel, B. (eds.) Genetic Programming Theory and Practice VI, Genetic and Evolutionary Computation, May 15-17, ch. 6, pp. 75–91. Springer, Ann Arbor (2008)

Novelty-Based Fitness: An Evaluation under the Santa Fe Trail

John Doucette and Malcolm I. Heywood

Faculty of Computer Science, Dalhousie University,
Halifax, NS, Canada
{jdoucett,mheywood}@cs.dal.ca

Abstract. We present an empirical analysis of the effects of incorporating novelty-based fitness (phenotypic behavioral diversity) into Genetic Programming with respect to training, test and generalization performance. Three novelty-based approaches are considered: novelty comparison against a finite archive of behavioral archetypes, novelty comparison against all previously seen behaviors, and a simple linear combination of the first method with a standard fitness measure. Performance is evaluated on the Santa Fe Trail, a well known GP benchmark selected for its deceptiveness and established generalization test procedures. Results are compared to a standard quality-based fitness function (count of food eaten). Ultimately, the quality style objective provided better overall performance, however, solutions identified under novelty based fitness functions generally provided much better test performance than their corresponding training performance. This is interpreted as representing a requirement for layered learning/ symbiosis when assuming novelty based fitness functions in order to more quickly achieve the integration of diverse behaviors into a single cohesive strategy.

1 Introduction

A novelty-based fitness measure is one inspired by inter-species evolution, wherein individuals are awarded *not* for the *quality* of their behavior, but for discovering behaviors in which no/ few individual are presently engaged i.e., phenotypic behavioral diversity [5]. Thus, in a pure novelty-based fitness function individuals are rewarded based only on how different their observed phenotypic behaviors are from the rest of the population. Conversely, an objective or quality based measure of fitness would reward individuals for finding solutions that minimize some concept of 'error'; thus the population as a whole might converge to solutions that are behaviorally very similar e.g., all individuals returning the same classification count.[1] Previous works have considered the utility of niching operators to provoke diversity maintenance, but the utility of such operators under Genetic Programming (GP) is not necessarily straight forward. However,

---

[1] This might imply some diversity relative to the exemplars correctly classified, although this is generally not explicitly articulated in the fitness function.

A.I. Esparcia-Alcazar et al. (Eds.): EuroGP 2010, LNCS 6021, pp. 50–61, 2010.
© Springer-Verlag Berlin Heidelberg 2010

recent work suggests that purely novelty-based evolutionary searches can be particularly effective [5,1,10,9].

Recent research using novelty-based fitness measures for genetic programming include both the aforementioned novelty only formulation and combined novelty–quality fitness functions. Specifically, several authors have employed combined novelty–quality objectives under the domain of classification [7,8]. This is very different from the standard approach to ensemble methods as the novelty objective makes explicit the desire to avoid solely 'cherry picking' the exemplars that are easy to classify. The resulting team of individuals exhibit explicitly non-overlapping behaviors [8]. Other works consider the effects of novelty-based fitness in detail, but have considered post training generalization [5,9,10]. This presents a problem, as the effects directly attributable to novelty-based fitness measures remain unknown, especially the effects on model generalization. With this in mind, we present a detailed empirical study of the effects of various combinations of quality and novelty-based fitness metrics on training and test performance using a classic GP benchmark, the Santa Fe Trail. Two novelty-based fitness measures are considered, as well as a simple combination novelty–quality measure. Particular attention is paid to the effects of novelty-based fitness on generalization performance.

2 Background Concepts

2.1 Generalization

Generalization measures the relative change in behavior of a candidate solution vis-a-vis the environment it was trained on versus an independent set of environments on which testing is performed [3,4]. In maze navigation the navigator often starts in a fixed location and attempts to reach a fixed exit. A system which memorizes the correct sequences of movements and rotations to navigate a specific maze is nearly useless, since it would fail to navigate any maze with an even slightly different structure, starting place, or destination. In contrast, a navigator which has learned a true maze navigating behavior would be capable of 'generalizing' the training scenario to a wide range of previously unseen maze architectures. Needless to say, decisions made regarding representation, credit assignment and cost function all impact on the resulting generalization ability of solutions [4]. Several benchmark problems – e.g., parity and the multiplexer – are frequently deployed without assessing generalization at all [2]. In this work we focus on the contribution of the cost function alone, and keep representation and credit assignment processes constant.

2.2 Novelty Search

Novelty-based search heuristics are those which reward the discovery of unique behaviors, in contrast to quality-based heuristics which reward individuals that are believed to be closer to the domain goal. Thus quality/ goal style objectives tend to reinforce cherry picking of the scenarios that are easier to solve.

The assumption being that this forms a learning gradient from which stronger behavior develops. Conversely, a novelty style objective is more effective at maintaining population diversity and as a consequence might lead to a better supply of building blocks for providing a more general solution. Recent work suggests that novelty-based fitness measures can outperform quality-based fitness measures in maze navigation [5,10,9] since solutions are under no pressure to cluster around local maxima in the search space. Other work has incorporated solution novelty into a Pareto multi-criteria objective function to promote problem decomposition [8], rewarding individuals not for correctly labeling all the data, but for labeling some unique subset of it correctly.

That said, the fact that novelty-based search places less emphasis (or none at all) on finding goal orientated solutions raises concerns about its effects on generalization error. It might be supposed that solutions created without any emphasis on correctness might be correct only coincidentally rather than by virtue of having learned a particular task, and that novelty-based search would produce solutions that fail to generalize.

2.3   The Santa Fe Trail

The Santa Fe Trail is a widely used benchmark in genetic programming [2,3,4]. The problem consists of evolving a controller for an "artificial ant" on a toroidal grid such that the ant correctly follows a trail of food. An ant solves the problem if it eats all of the food on the grid within a certain number of time steps. At each time step the ant can either change the direction it faces by 90 degrees, or move forward one square. As discussed in [4], the ant problem is "deceptive", meaning that there are many local maxima in the space of possible controller programs. These local maxima result from ants which loose the trail and stumble into more food at a later point in the trail. Ants of this type are not very close to solving the problem i.e., they are very unlikely to find the stretch of trail that they missed within the time limit. In contrast, ants that eat more of the trail in order may not eat as much food in total. Consequently, GP does not perform significantly better than random search on this problem, since the most commonly used heuristic (more food = higher fitness) is deceptive [4]. Previous work suggests that novelty-based search should be more effective in deceptive problems [5]. Consequently, the Santa Fe Trail may be a good choice for determining effects of novelty-based search on generalization.

In addition to being a deceptive problem, the ant trail has several advantages. First and foremost is a previously established method of measuring generalization error [3]. This entails generating a set of random trails which share certain properties with the Santa Fe trail, including maximum distance between food, shapes of corners in the trail, and density of food in the trail. The trails may be of different lengths, and may have differing amounts of food. An ant which has successfully learned a general solution to the Santa Fe trail should do well on these trails, while one which has learned specialized strategies (memorizing the turns in the trail) will not. Additionally, the Santa Fe Trail has an easily representable space of program behaviors, namely the order in which the food on the trail is eaten. An ant which follows the trail diligently will thus end up with a very different behavior from one that tessellates the grid, and those behaviors may be concisely represented and quickly compared.

3 Methodology

To test the effects of novelty-based fitness on generalization error, we considered two different methods for determining novelty, hereafter denoted Methods 1 and 2. In this context a novel solution is one in which the ant consumes food on the trail in a sequence that differs from all previously observed behaviors as summarized in terms of a pair-wise similarity metric. Needless to say, the metric employed for the pairwise comparison has a significant impact on the quality of the resulting evaluation [1], with Hamming Distance being assumed in this work i.e., one of the two recommended metrics identified by the earlier study. This also raises the question as to how dissimilar individuals need to be before they are considered novel. Two methods are considered. In Method 1 (Algorithm 1), an archive of fixed size stores "archetypes"; or solutions which represent broad classes of behaviors. Individuals are added to the archive if the behavioral difference between them and all archetypes is larger than the difference between the closest pair of archetypes presently in the archive (line 7). In this case the individual will replace one of the two archetypes which are most similar to each other, causing the inter-archetype difference to increase monotonically over the course of a run (line 11). Archives were fixed at a size of 100 archetypes in all runs. In Method 2 (Algorithm 4), an archive of variable size stores archetypes that differ from each other by at least some constant amount Δ_{min} (as in [5,10]). New individuals are added to the archive if their behavior differs from that of every archetype presently in the archive by at least Δ_{min} (line 10). In the case of both methods, individuals are awarded fitness as a function of how far their behavior is from that of any archetype presently in the archive, with radically different behaviors receiving the highest fitness and those whose behavior is identical to that of some archive member receiving the lowest fitness.

Two additional methods are now introduced to provide a relative baseline on the performance of the purely behavioral performance functions. Method 3 uses the finite archive of Method 1 in a combined equally weighted contribution from novelty and quality objectives, or the average of the fitness returned from the archive method and the fitness returned by the typical "eat most food" fitness evaluation, i.e. $Fitness = \frac{F_{novelty}+F_{quality}}{2}$. Thus, a solution that eats all the pieces of food in a completely unique order will have a fitness of 1; whereas an individual that eats half the food in a previously observed order will have a fitness of 0.25 (0 for having the same behavior as some archive member, 0.25 for eating half the food).

All three of the above methods were implemented with a modified version of the lilgp package [11]. This provides us with the original code for the Santa Fe Trail and therefore a quality-based method for fitness evaluation or items of food eaten (Method 4). The only substantial modification made to the code

Algorithm 1. Novelty-Based Fitness Evaluation with finite archive. Returns the fitness of an individual and adds it to the archive if it qualifies.

1: Let A be an archive storing > 0 individuals.
2: Let I be an individual.
3: **procedure** FITNESS(A,I)
4:     mindiff=$+\infty$
5:     **for all** $a \in A$ **do**
6:         if mindiff $>$ ham(a, I) **then** mindiff $=$ ham(a, I)
7:         **end if**   ▷ ham(. , .) (Algorithm 2)
8:     **end for**
9:     if mindiff $>$ A.current_mindiff **then**
10:         insert I replacing A.minidx
11:         recompute_mindiff(A) ▷ recompute_mindiff(.) (Algorithm 3)
12:     **end if**
        return mindiff
13: **end procedure**

Algorithm 2. Pairwise Hamming Distance Estimation

1: Let i and j be individuals
2: Let $\{i, j\}.foodvect$ be vectors showing the order in which the individual ate food
3: Let $\{i, j\}.foodvect(n) = (x, y)$ iff the nth piece of food eaten was at (x, y)
4: **procedure** HAM(I,J)
5:     **if** $|i.foodvect| < |j.foodvect|$ **then** swap i and j
6:     **end if**
7:     hamsum $= 0$
8:     **for** $z = 1 to |j.foodvect|$ **do**
9:         **if** $i.foodvect \neq j.foodvect$ **then** hamsum++
10:         **end if**
11:     **end for**
12:     hamsum $+ = |i.foodvect| - |j.foodvect|$
        return hamsum
13: **end procedure**

Algorithm 3. Recomputing of the minimum difference between any two members of the archive

1: Let A be an archive storing > 0 individuals.
2: recompute_mindiff(A)
3: **if** $|A| < A.maxsize$ **then**
4:     A.current_mindiff $= 0$
5:     A.minidx $= A$.currentsize
6: **end if**
7: mindiff=$+\infty$
8: **for all** $i, j \in A$; where $i \neq j$ **do**
9:     **if** mindiff $>$ ham(i, j) **then**   ▷ ham(. , .) (Algorithm 2)
10:         A.current_mindiff $=$ ham(i, j)
11:         A.minidx $= i$
12:     **end if**
13: **end for**

Algorithm 4. Novelty-Based Fitness Evaluation with Infinite Archiving. Returns the fitness of an individual and adds it to the archive if it qualifies. $\Delta_{min} = 10$ for all our runs.

```
1: Let A be an archive storing > 0 individuals.
2: Let I be an individual
3: Let Δ_min be a constant s.t. for i and j ∈ A, ham(i,j) >= Δ_min
4: procedure FITNESS(A,I, Δ_min)
5:     mindiff = +∞
6:     for all a ∈ A do
7:         if mindiff > ham(a, I) then mindiff = ham(a, I)
8:         end if                              ▷ ham(. , .) (Algorithm 2)
9:     end for
10:    if mindiff > Δ_min then insert I → A
11:    end if
           return mindiff
12: end procedure
```

other than changing the fitness functions was to allow solutions to be run on test environments after the completion of training.

To compare the four fitness methods, at the end of each run, the individual who had eaten the most food was selected as the champion. We evaluated the champions on a fixed set of 100 test trails generated according to the algorithm in [3], with results measured in terms of the percentage of food eaten on each trail. Each method was run with 500 unique random seeds.

We selected parameters to avoid optimizing any method at the expense of the others. The archive size for Method 1 and Δ_{min} for Method 2 were selected by trying 10 values on single runs with the same random seed and adopting the best performing parameterization. The 10 values were selected at even intervals over (10,200) for archive size, and (5,40) for Δ_{min}. The values of the other parameters are the defaults found in the Santa Fe Trail implementation provided with [11], with the single change of swapping crossover for mutation in the reproduction operators, as in [4]. Table 1 summarizes the complete parameterization.

Table 1. GP Parameters, based on [4,2]

Parameter	Value
Terminal Set	Left, Right, Move_Ahead
Function Set	If_Food_Ahead, Prog2, Prog3
Selection Method	Stochastic Elitism
Max Time steps	400
Max Program Depth	17
Initialization	"Ramped half and half", max depth 6
Reproduction Operators	90% Mutation, 10% Reproduction
Population Size	1000
Maximum Generations	50

4   Results and Analysis

The results have been separated into training, testing, and generalization performance. For simplicity, all results were tested for statistical significance at a confidence level of 95%, with a Bonferroni correction used to compare the means of each pair of samples. A Jarque-Bera test was used to determine whether data were normally distributed. One-way ANOVA tests followed by student t-tests were used to compare normally distributed data, while Kruskal-Wallis tests followed by Wilcoxon Rank-Sum tests were used to compare data which was not normally distributed. In the graphs presented, the limited archive approach of Method 1, the infinite archiving approach of Method 2, the combination novelty–quality formulation of Method 3, and the standard quality-based approach of Method 4 are denoted by the labels "Fixed Archive", "Infinite Archive", "Combination", and "Quality-Based" respectively.

4.1   Training Performance

We gathered training data by measuring the proportion of food eaten by each champion individual in the training enviroment (the Santa Fe Trail). Data from all four methods were normally distributed, and statistically significant differences were returned between all pairs of methods (Figure 1). The quality based function performed best, eating 66% of the food on average, compared with 59%, 56%, and 53% for the combination, infinite archive and fixed archive respectively. Relative to the original Santa Fe study of Koza [2] we note that the level of performance is generally lower. However, this is in part likely due to adopting the 400 time step limit reported by Koza whereas this was apparently 600 in his experiments (see the commentary in [4]).

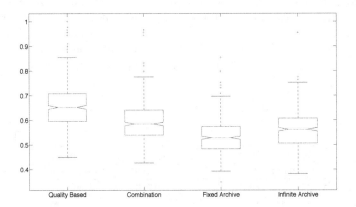

Fig. 1. Plot showing 1st, 2nd, and 3rd quartiles for the distribution of training performance. Whiskers identify the limit of points within 1.5 times the inter quartile distance with crosses marking any outliers.

4.2   Testing Performance

We produced test data by measuring the proportion of food eaten by the champion from each run on 100 test environments. The champions are compared using summary statistics of the collected data, in particular the median, maximum, and minimum proportion of food eaten by each champion on the test environments. The median performance of the champions was normally distributed for all 4 methods. We did not find a statistically significant difference between the performance of the quality-based and combination methods, but did find significant differences between the performance of all other pairs of samples (Figure 2). Both the combination and quality-based methods consumed an average of 35% of the food or more in at least half their runs, while the average was only 32% for the fixed archive method, and 29% for the infinite archive method.

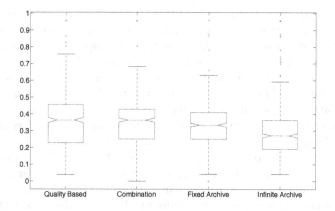

Fig. 2. Plot showing first, second and third quartiles for the distribution of median test performance. See Figure 1 caption for interpretation of the whiskers.

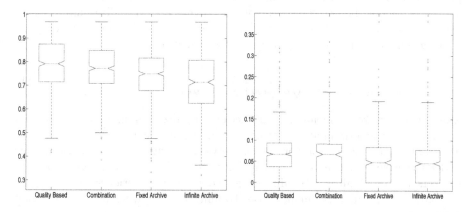

Fig. 3. Plot showing first, second and third quartiles for the distribution of maximum (left) and minimum (right) test performance. See Figure 1 caption for interpretation of the whiskers.

Results for maximum and minimum performance were not normally distributed (Figure 3). We found significant differences between all pairs of samples for maximum performance, with no more than 78% of food being eaten on any test enviroment, on average, for the quality-based method, 77% for the combination method, and only 73% and 71% for the fixed and infinite archive methods. For minimum performance, we found a statistically significant difference between the combination and infinite archive methods, and between the quality-based method and both the fixed and infinite archive methods. On average, champions ate no less than 8% of the food on any test enviroment using the quality-based method, 7% using the combination method, and 6% using the fixed or infinite archiving methods.

4.3   Paired Generalization Error

The final measure considered is paired 'generalization error' or the relative normalized[2] difference between training and test performance of the *same* individual. A drop in performance is generally assumed to appear between training and test performance. However, as this difference increases lack of generalization is a more likely candidate. Hence, higher negative differences are taken as indicating that the model has learned to memorize the Santa Fe Trail in particular; whereas positive values indicate that more food is eaten under the test condition than in training. We found the median generalization error for champions from all four methods to be normally distributed, with statistically significant differences between all pairs of models (Figure 4). The fixed archive method has the lowest median generalization error, with a difference in the proportions of food eaten in the training and median test environments being 21% on average. The combination method has a mean difference of 24%, while the infinite archive has 27%, and the quality based method 31%.

This distribution is further emphasized by considering performance from the perspective an interquartile distance function. Letting training and test performance as a whole be two 'clusters' and comparing the normalized inter cluster distance illustrates the degree to which test and training performance diverge. Thus, given the standard inter cluster distance metric of,

$$\frac{\mu(test) - \mu(train)}{\sqrt{\sigma^2(test) + \sigma^2(train)}} \tag{1}$$

where μ and σ^2 are the mean and variance of normalized 'training' and 'test' performance. Figure 5 summarizes the corresponding inter cluster distance for each fitness function. The strong correlation between training and test performance under the Fixed archive version of novelty objective is immediately apparent. Conversely, the Quality and Infinite archive schemes experience in the region of a 40% decline in performance from training to test; whereas the combined

---

[2] By 'normalized' we imply that the number of food items can vary under test conditions [3], hence both training and test performance are normalized relative to the total of food items available in that scenario.

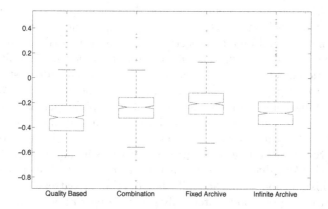

Fig. 4. Plot showing first, second and third quartiles for the distribution of median generalization error. See Figure 1 caption for interpretation of the whiskers.

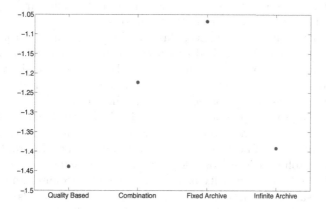

Fig. 5. Plot of inter cluster distance (defined in Eq. (1)) between normalized training and test performance). Negative values express the percent by which food counts under training exceeded that under test.

quality–novelty metric returned an intermediate decline in performance (in the order of 20%).

5 Conclusions and Future Work

Taking as a starting point the Santa Fe trail as a benchmark with known deceptive properties [4] and introducing the test for generalization methodology of Kushchu [3], we evaluated a cross-section of novelty only, combined novelty and quality, and quality only fitness functions. Several general trends are apparent. The classical quality based performance metric provided the strongest training and test performance of all methods; thus, reinforcing the view that if a goal orientated objective can be defined for the domain in question, then assessing performance with such an objective is still very important. A simple linear combination of novelty and quality objectives provided the next best performance under training and test conditions. In the case of the novelty only fitness functions, imposition of a finite archive was generally beneficial under test conditions, but was the worst performing approach under training conditions. We suspect the poor training performance to be the result of rapidly increasing novelty requirements for entry into the archive, such that a solution which follows the trail slightly further than its parent will receive a low fitness value, i.e., on account of having eaten most of its food in the same order as its parent. The higher test performance is likely due to the same factor. Since individuals cannot gain entry into the archive for following the trail, they develop an extremely diverse set of strategies for eating the food, potentially generalizing strategies for any trail. In particular, tessellating strategies were often observed among the solutions from the finite archive method, but rarely observed among solutions from the other methods.

As highlighted above, both the fixed archive and infinite archive methods produce lower quality solutions than the traditional quality only fitness measure. In the case of training performance, this may be in part due to the deceptive nature of the problem. No method produced a true solution which managed to follow the entire trail, but the quality based solutions may not have been any closer to finding a true solution despite eating more of the food. While previous work [5,9,10] suggests novelty-based search may find better solutions sooner than quality based objective approaches in deceptive landscapes, our work suggests that intermediate solutions produced by novelty-based approaches may be of lower quality in terms of both training and test performance. In problems where finding a true solution is impossible or prohibitively expensive, this may be a concern. Indeed, purely novelty based schemes may encounter an overhead in the time necessary to recombine independent solutions (individuals) into a single solution that subsumes the behaviors from multiple individuals.

Future work will continue to look at the role of novelty in evolution. Earlier work using an explicitly Pareto multi-criterion objective composition of novelty and quality objectives indicates that such paradigms are effective at problem decomposition as opposed to forcing solutions to take the form of a single solution [8]. Indeed, evolution through novelty only fitness functions might support multilevel symbiotic/ teaming style models of evolution in GP. In particular, a novelty based phase of evolution might be followed/ combined with a combinatorial style search for the best combinations of solutions from the novelty based search i.e., behaviors can exist symbiotically as independent entities within a 'host' individual at a higher level of representation. Models of this nature in which fitness is shared over a quality style objective have already appeared [6], however, doing so under purely novelty based fitness has not as yet been demonstrated. Likewise, the use of schemes such as NEAT – as was in the case in [5] and [10] – that explicitly support the identification and incorporation of traits from parent individuals into the children may provide a better basis for incorporating initially independent behaviors into a single model. Thus, frameworks such as NEAT and GP teaming – as opposed to canonical GP – might well be in a better position to make use of properties developed under novelty only style fitness functions.

Acknowledgements

J. Doucette was supported in part through an NSERC USRA scholarship and M. Heywood was supported under research grants from NSERC and MITACS.

References

1. Gomez, F.J.: Sustaining diversity using behavioral information distance. In: Proceedings of the Genetic and Evolutionary Computation Conference, pp. 113–120. ACM, New York (2009)
2. Koza, J.: Genetic Programming: On the Programming of Computers by Means of Natural Selection. MIT Press, Cambridge (1992)
3. Kushchu, I.: Genetic programming and evolutionary generalization. IEEE Transactions on Evolutionary Computation 6(5), 431–442 (2002)
4. Langdon, W.B., Poli, R.: Foundations of Genetic Programming. Springer, Heidelberg (2002)
5. Lehman, J., Stanley, K.O.: Exploiting open-endedness to solve problems through the search for novelty. In: Proceedings of the International Conference on Artificial Life XI. MIT Press, Cambridge (2008)
6. Lichodzijewski, P., Heywood, M.I.: Managing team-based problem solving with symbiotic bid-based Genetic Programming. In: Proceedings of the Genetic and Evolutionary Computation Conference, pp. 363–370 (2008)
7. Liu, Y., Yao, X., Higuchi, T.: Evolutionary Ensembles with Negative Correlation Learning. IEEE Transactions on Evolutionary Computation 4(4), 380–387 (2000)
8. McIntyre, A.R., Heywood, M.I.: Cooperative problem decomposition in pareto competitive classifier models of coevolution. In: O'Neill, M., Vanneschi, L., Gustafson, S., Esparcia Alcázar, A.I., De Falco, I., Della Cioppa, A., Tarantino, E. (eds.) EuroGP 2008. LNCS, vol. 4971, pp. 289–300. Springer, Heidelberg (2008)
9. Mouret, J.-B., Doncieux, S.: Overcoming the bootstrap problem in evolutionary robotics using behavioral diversity. In: IEEE Congress on Evolutionary Computation, pp. 1161–1168 (2009)
10. Risi, S., Vanderbleek, S.D., Hughes, C.E., Stanley, K.O.: How novelty search escapes the deceptive trap of learning to learn. In: Proceedings of the Genetic and Evolutionary Computation Conference, pp. 153–160. ACM Press, New York (2009)
11. Zongker, D., Punch, B.: lil-gp 1.0 User's Manual. Michigan State University (1995)

An Analysis of Genotype-Phenotype Maps in Grammatical Evolution

David Fagan, Michael O'Neill, Edgar Galván-López, Anthony Brabazon,
and Sean McGarraghy

Natural Computing Research & Applications Group
University College Dublin, Ireland
{david.fagan,m.oneill,edgar.galvan,anthony.brabazon,
sean.mcgarraghy}@ucd.ie

Abstract. We present an analysis of the genotype-phenotype map in Grammatical Evolution (GE). The standard map adopted in GE is a depth-first expansion of the non-terminal symbols during the derivation sequence. Earlier studies have indicated that allowing the path of the expansion to be under the guidance of evolution as opposed to a deterministic process produced significant performance gains on all of the benchmark problems analysed. In this study we extend this analysis to include a breadth-first and random map, investigate additional benchmark problems, and take into consideration the implications of recent results on alternative grammar representations with this new evidence. We conclude that it is possible to improve the performance of grammar-based Genetic Programming by the manner in which a genotype-phenotype map is performed.

1 Introduction

Within the field of Genetic Programming (GP) [11,19] the use of a genotype-phenotype map is not new [9,1,10,20,13,5,4,8] and a number of variants to the standard tree-based form of GP exist, amongst which some of the most popular are Linear GP [2], Cartesian GP [14] and Grammatical Evolution (GE) [3,18]. GE is a grammar-based form of GP which adopts a mapping from a linear genotype to phenotypic GP trees. O'Neill [15] presented a series of arguments for the adoption of a genotype-phenotype map for GP as it can provide a number of advantages. These include a generalised encoding that can represent a variety of structures allowing GP to generate structures in an arbitrary language, efficiency gains for evolutionary search (e.g. through neutral evolution), maintenance of genetic diversity through many-to-one maps, preservation of functionality while allowing continuation of search at a genotypic level, reuse of genetic material potentially allowing information compression, and positional independence of gene functionality.

For the first time this study presents an examination of the genotype-phenotype map of GE. A number of alternative mappers are proposed and performance is compared against the standard genotype-phenotype map. The remainder of the

A.I. Esparcia-Alcazar et al. (Eds.): EuroGP 2010, LNCS 6021, pp. 62–73, 2010.

paper is structured as follows. A brief overview of the essentials of GE are provided in Section 2 before an example of the standard genotype-phenotype map of GE in Section 3. The next part of the paper describes the experimental setup (Section 4), the results found (Section 5) and a discussion (Section 6) before drawing conclusions and pointing to future work.

2   Grammatical Evolution Essentials

GE marries principles from molecular biology to the representational power of formal grammars. GE's rich modularity gives a unique flexibility, making it possible to use alternative search strategies, whether evolutionary, or some other heuristic (be it stochastic or deterministic) and to radically change its behaviour by merely changing the grammar supplied. As a grammar is used to describe the structures that are generated by GE, it is trivial to modify the output structures by simply editing the plain text grammar. The explicit grammar allows GE to easily generate solutions in any language (or a useful subset of a language). For example, GE has been used to generate solutions in multiple languages including Lisp, Scheme, C/C++, Java, Prolog, Postscript, and English. The ease with which a user can manipulate the output structures by simply writing or modifying a grammar in a text file provides an attractive flexibility and ease of application not as readily enjoyed with the standard approach to GP. The grammar also implicitly provides a mechanism by which type information can be encoded thus overcoming the property of closure, which limits the traditional representation adopted by GP to a single type. The genotype-phenotype mapping also means that instead of operating exclusively on solution trees, as in standard GP, GE allows search operators to be performed on the genotype (e.g., integer or binary chromosomes), in addition to partially derived phenotypes, and the fully formed phenotypic derivation trees themselves. As such, standard GP tree-based operators of subtree-crossover and subtree-mutation can be easily adopted with GE. By adopting the GE approach one can therefore have the expressive power and convenience of grammars, while operating search in a standard GP or Strongly-Typed GP manner. For the latest description of GE please refer to Dempsey et al. [3].

3   GE's Genotype-Phenotype Map

The genotype-phenotype map of GE operates as follows. The process begins from the embryonic start symbol of the grammar. Taking the simple grammar adopted for the Max problem provided in Fig. 6 this is <prog>, which by default is transformed into the non-terminal <expr>. There are two possible transformations which can be applied to <expr>. Either it will be replaced with <op><expr><expr> or with <var>. To decide what happens the next unused codon (an integer in this study) is read from the genome and we mod it's value by the number of choices available (i.e., $choice = integer \% 2$). Lets assume <expr> is transformed into <op><expr><expr>. In this situation there is more than one non-terminal symbol in the current structure which needs to be transformed. The standard mapper in GE always selects the left-most non-terminal, which means in this case `<op>`. In the Max grammar `<op>` can be transformed into one of + or *, again by reading the next codon value and applying the mapping function with modulus 2. Assuming * is selected we end up with the structure `*<expr><expr>`. The mapping continues by taking the left-most non-terminal until we end up with a structure that is comprised exclusively of terminal symbols (i.e., in the case of the Max grammar these are +, *, and 0.5).

A sample grammar is outlined below including an example chromosome. Fig. 1 outlines the depth-first order of expansion of the non-terminal symbols of the standard mapping process in GE. Potentially this introduces a structure bias to the search process as the focus of search is directed towards the left-hand branches and sub-trees of an individual structure. Alternatively if a breadth-first expansion was adopted, Fig. 2 illustrates how the order changes and thus the focus of evolutionary search takes a different direction towards broader tree structures. With the πGE approach [16] the order of expansion is itself evolvable with the genome being consulted as to which non-terminal to expand at each point of the derivation sequence.

```
<e> ::= <e> <o> <e> | <v>
<o> ::= + | -
<v> ::= X | Y
Chromosome ::= 12,2,8,3,5,2,9,14,6,3,8,10,7,12
```

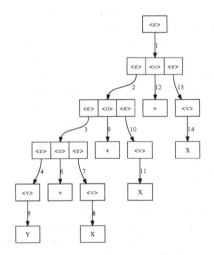

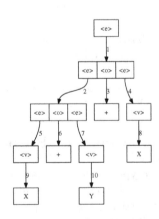

Fig. 1. An illustration of the order of a depth first expansion of the non-terminals in a derivation tree, leading to a solution of Y+X+X+X

Fig. 2. An illustration of the order of a breadth first expansion of the non-terminals in a derivation tree, leading to a solution of X+Y+X

4   Experimental Setup

We wish to test the null hypothesis that there is no difference in performance when alternative mapping strategies are adopted with GE. We will measure performance both in terms of the number of successful solutions found to each problem instance, and by examining the average best fitness.

We adopted GEVA v1.1 [17] for the experiments conducted in this study. The evolutionary parameters adopted on all problems are presented in Table 1. Note that we deliberately use a relatively small population size of 100 compared to the standard 500 that would typically be adopted for these problem instances. This was to make it harder for the mappers to find a perfect solution, and therefore allow us to discriminate more clearly performance differences on these toy benchmark problems.

Table 1. Parameter settings adopted on all problems examined

Parameter	Value
generations	100
population size	100
replacement strategy	generational with elitism (10%)
selection	tournament (tsize=3)
mutation probability	0.01 (integer mutation)
crossover probability	0.9 (ripple)
initial chromosome length	200 codons (random init)
max wrap events	3

4.1   Benchmark Problems

Four standard GP benchmark problems were examined, and 50 independent runs performed for each setup on each problem. The grammar adopted in each case appear in Figs. 3, 4, 5, and 6.

Even-5-parity. This is the classic benchmark problem in which evolution attempts to find the five input even-parity boolean function. The optimal fitness is obtained when the correct output is generated for each of the 32 test cases.

Symbolic Regression. The classic quartic function is used here $x + x^2 + x^3 + x^4$ with 20 input-output test cases drawn from the range -1 to 1. Fitness is simply the sum of the errors. We measure success on this problem using the notion of hits, where a hit is achieved when the error is less than 0.01.

Santa Fe ant trail. The objective is to evolve a program to control the movement of an artificial ant on a toroidal grid of size 32 by 32 units. 89 pieces of food are located along a broken trail, and the ant has 600 units of energy to find all the food. A unit of energy is consumed when the ant uses one of the following operations: `move()`, `right()` or `left()`. The ant also has the capability to look ahead into the square directly facing it to determine if there is food present.

```
<prog> ::= <expr>

<expr> ::= <expr> <op> <expr>
         | ( <expr> <op> <expr> )
         | <var>
         | <pre-op> ( <var> )

<pre-op> ::= not

<op> ::= "|"
       | &
       | ^

<var> ::= d0 | d1 | d2 | d3 | d4
```

Fig. 3. The grammar adopted for the Even-5-parity problem

```
<prog> ::= <expr>

<expr> ::= <expr> <op> <expr>
         | ( <expr> <op> <expr> )
         | <pre-op> ( <expr> )
         | <protected-op>
         | <var>

<op> ::= + | * | -

<protected-op> ::= div( <expr>, <expr>)

<pre-op> ::= sin | cos | exp | inv | log

<var> ::= X | 1.0
```

Fig. 4. The grammar adopted for the Symbolic Regression problem instance

```
<prog> ::= <code>

<code> ::= <line> | <code> <line>

<line> ::= <condition>\n
         | <op>\n

<condition> ::= if(food_ahead()==1){
                    <opcode>
                }
                else { <opcode> }

<op> ::= left(); | right(); | move();

<opcode> ::= <op> | <opcode> <op>
```

Fig. 5. The grammar adopted for the Santa Fe ant trail problem

```
<prog> ::= <expr>

<expr> ::= <op> <expr> <expr>
         | <var>

<op> ::= +
       | *

<var> ::= 0.5
```

Fig. 6. The grammar adopted for the Max problem instance

Max. The aim of the problem is to evolve a tree that returns the largest value within a set depth limit (8 in this study). A minimal function set of addition and multiplication is provided alongside a single constant (0.5). The optimal solution to this problem will have addition operators towards the leaves of the tree to create as large a variable as possible greater than 1.0 in order to exploit multiplication operators towards the root of the tree. This problem is considered difficult for GP as solutions tend to converge on suboptimal solutions which can be difficult to escape from as is shown by Langdon et al [12].

4.2   Mappers

Four alternative mapping strategies are examined in this study. The standard mapper adopted in GE we refer to as **Depth-first**. The name reflects the path this mapper takes through the non-terminal symbols in the derivation tree. The opposite **Breadth-first** strategy was implemented, which maps all of the non-terminal symbols at each successive level of the derivation tree before moving on to the next deepest level. The π**GE** mapper as first described by O'Neill et al. [16] is the third mapper analysed. πGE lets the evolving genome decide which non-terminal to expand at each step in the derivation sequence. Finally we adopt a **Random** control strategy, which randomly selects a non-terminal to expand amongst all of the non-terminals that currently exist in an expanding derivation sequences. This is equivalent to a randomised πGE approach where the order of expansion is not evolved, rather it is chosen at random each time it is performed.

5   Results

The number of runs (out of 50) that successfully found a perfect solution to each problem is presented in Table 2. On three out of the four problems the πGE mapper is the most successful. None of the mappers found a perfect solution to the Max problem with the parameter settings adopted.

Average best fitness plots (over 50 runs) for each problem can be seen in Figs. 7, 8, 9 and 10. Table 3 records the average best fitness and standard deviation at the final generation. The results presented in these figures and table support the success rate data, with the πGE mapper variant outperforming the alternatives on Even-5-Parity, Symbolic Regression and the Santa Fe Ant.

Table 2. Instances of Successful Solution Found over 50 runs

Mapper	Even 5	Santa Fe	Sym Reg	Max
BF	29	1	9	0
DF	31	2	9	0
Rand	13	0	0	0
πGE	38	4	17	0

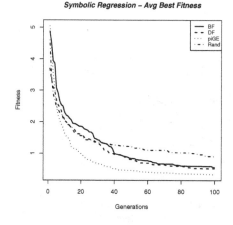

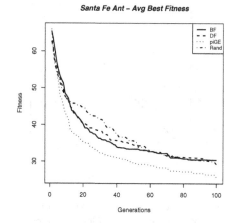

Fig. 7. Average Best Fitness on the Symbolic Regression problem instance

Fig. 8. Average Best Fitness on the Santa Fe ant problem

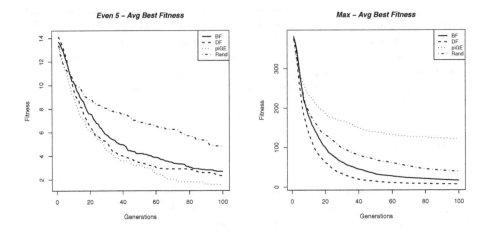

Fig. 9. Average Best Fitness on the Even-5-parity problem

Fig. 10. Average Best Fitness on the Max problem instance

Table 3. Average Best Fitness Values after 100 generations over 50 independent runs

Mapper	Even 5 Avg.Best(std)	Santa Fe Avg.Best(std)	Sym Reg Avg.Best(std)	Max Avg.Best(std)
BF	2.68(3.41)	30.4(13.92)	0.56(0.65)	16.44(14.66)
DF	2.32(3.26)	30.34(14.39)	0.52(0.89)	7.23(10.14)
Rand	4.82(3.29)	29.26(12.07)	0.89(0.76)	121.89(27.45)
πGE	1.52(2.92)	25.64(14.52)	0.33(0.56)	39.31(24.97)

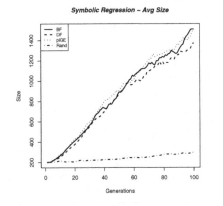

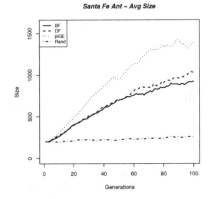

Fig. 11. Average size of individual on the Symbolic Regression problem instance

Fig. 12. Average size of individual on the Santa Fe ant problem

However, on the Max problem instance the standard depth-first mapper has a performance edge.

It is worth noting that the random "control" mapper performs the worst on all of the problems examined in terms of success rates and in terms of the average best fitness attained. A slight exception is on the Santa Fe ant trail where the random mappers performs as well as both depth and breadth-first alternatives, in terms of the average best fitness at the final generation.

We also recorded the size of evolving genomes (Figs. 11, 12, 13 and 14) and derivation trees. Derivation tree size was measured both in terms of the number of nodes in a tree (Figs. 15, 16, 17 and 18) and the depth of a tree (Figs. 19, 20, 21 and 22).

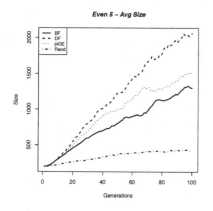

Fig. 13. Average size of individual on the Even-5-Parity problem

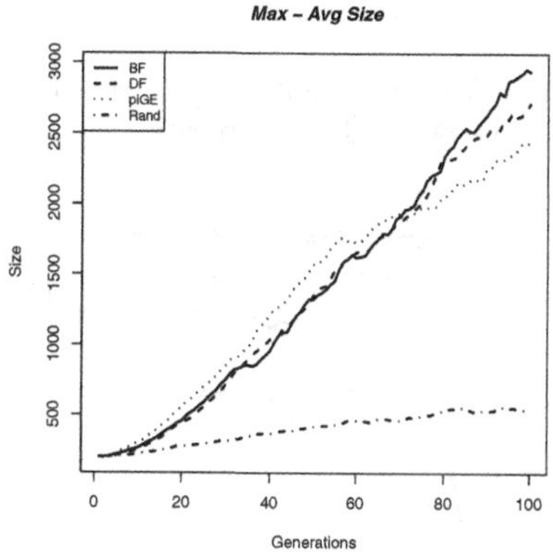

Fig. 14. Average size of individual on the Max problem instance

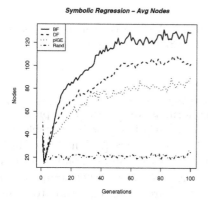
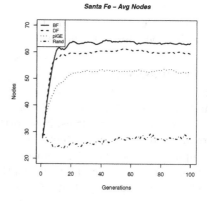

Fig. 15. Average number of Derivation Tree Nodes on the Symbolic Regression problem instance

Fig. 16. Average number of Derivation Tree Nodes on the Santa Fe ant problem

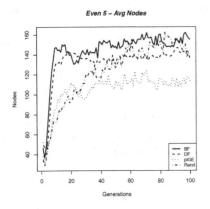

Fig. 17. Average number of Derivation Tree Nodes on the Even-5-parity problem

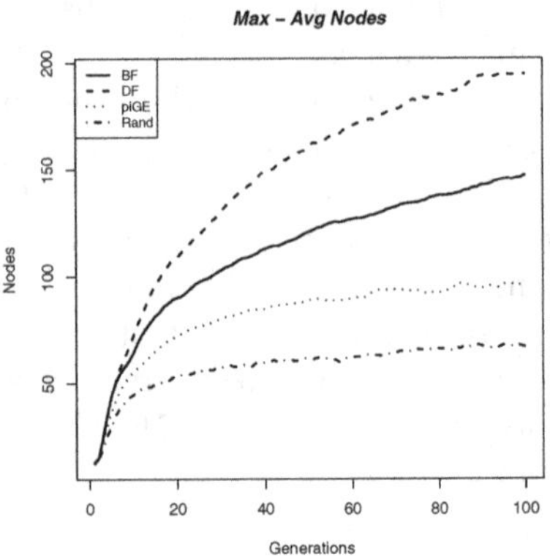

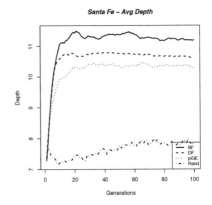

Fig. 18. Average number of Derivation Tree Nodes on the Max problem

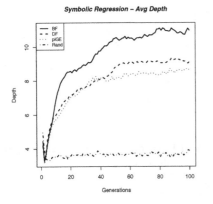

Fig. 19. Average Derivation Tree Depth on the Symbolic Regression problem

Fig. 20. Average Derivation Tree Depth on the Santa Fe ant problem

6   Discussion

While the results show that πGE did not perform as well on the Max problem, relative to the other problems, it is worth noting that solving the Max problem is more about refining the content of the tree not the structure [7]. The Depth-first map appears to be able to generate larger tree structures more rapidly (both in terms of number of nodes and tree depth, see Figs. 18 and 22) when compared to the alternative mapping strategies. This allows search additional time to focus on tree content towards the desired *'s towards the root and +'s towards the function nodes near the leaves. The Max problem is more suited to a systematic pre-order (Depth-first) or level-order (Breadth-first) traversal of the tree, leading to better results faster than the πGE alternative. On all the other problems the

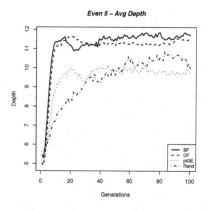

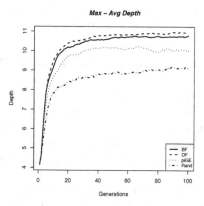

Fig. 21. Average Derivation Tree Depth on the Even-5-parity problem

Fig. 22. Average Derivation Tree Depth on the Max problem instance

Breadth-first map produces larger tree structures both in terms of node count and tree depth (Figs. 15-22).

With respect to the length of the integer genomes it is clear from Figs. 11-14 that the control random mappers lack of order results in the overall lengths of individuals remaining relatively constant over time. The opposite behaviour is observed in the cases of Depth-first, Breadth-first and πGE with the usual GP-bloat behaviour being observed.

In light of the comparison between a Depth-first and Breadth-first mapper presented here, it is interesting to recall the observations made in a study by Hemberg et al. [6]. In the earlier research three grammar variants were examined in the context of Symbolic Regression. The language represented by each of the grammars were all semantically equivalent in terms of the phenotypic behaviour of the solutions that could be generated. The only difference was syntactical. That is, postfix, prefix and infix notations were adopted for the same set of terminal symbols of the language. Performance advantages were observed on the problems examined for the postfix notation over both alternatives. If one examines the behaviour of postfix notation it amounts to a postorder expansion of the tree. In terms of a generative grammar this means that the contents of subtrees are determined before the operator at the root of the subtree.

Effectively the order of the mapping sequence was modified in the Hemberg et al. study to a *Postorder* mapper purely by modifying the syntax of the expressions being evolved. Given that the Breadth-first map adopted in this study is producing similar performance characteristics to the standard Depth-first map, there must be some advantage in conducting the mapping sequence at least partly Breadth-first, and partly in a Depth-first manner. Given the earlier findings on the *Postorder* mapping, there may also be an advantage in reversing the order of expansion between a pre-, post-order, and possibly in-order. It will require further analysis to ascertain if a similar mixture of mapping order is effectively being evolved with the πGE approach, which may go some way to explain the relative advantage πGE has over the other mappers.

7   Conclusions and Future Work

We presented an analysis of the genotype-phenotype map in Grammatical Evolution by comparing performance of the standard *depth-first* approach to *breadth-first*, *πGE*, and *random* variations. Across the benchmark problems analysed we observe an advantage to the adoption of the more flexible πGE map, which is under the control of evolution. Given the additional overhead that the πGE map has, due to the extra degree of freedom which allowing the path of the derivation sequence to be evolvable and the subsequent increase of the overall search space size that this entails, the results are even more impressive. Further research is required to establish Why the more evolvable approach is providing a performance advantage, and this is the current focus of our efforts. With this deeper understanding we can then potentially improve upon the πGE approach and/or develop novel mappers with more evolvable characteristics. We are especially interested in how evolvable genotype-phenotype maps will perform in dynamic environments, and this will form an integral part of the next phase of this research.

Acknowledgments

This research is based upon works supported by the Science Foundation Ireland under Grant No. 08/IN.1/I1868.

References

1. Banzhaf, W.: Genotype-phenotype-mapping and neutral variation – A case study in genetic programming. In: Davidor, Y., Männer, R., Schwefel, H.-P. (eds.) PPSN 1994. LNCS, vol. 866, pp. 322–332. Springer, Heidelberg (1994)
2. Brameier, M.F., Banzhaf, W.: Linear Genetic Programming. Springer, Heidelberg (2007)
3. Dempsey, I., O'Neill, M., Brabazon, A.: Foundations in Grammatical Evolution for Dynamic Environments. Studies in Computational Intelligence. Springer, Heidelberg (2009)
4. Fernandez-Villacanas Martin, J.-L., Shackleton, M.: Investigation of the importance of the genotype-phenotype mapping in information retrieval. Future Generation Computer Systems 19(1) (2003)
5. Harding, S., Miller, J.F., Banzhaf, W.: Evolution, development and learning using self-modifying cartesian genetic programming. In: GECCO 2009: Proc. of the 11th Annual conference on Genetic and evolutionary computation. ACM, New York (2009)
6. Hemberg, E., McPhee, N., O'Neill, M., Brabazon, A.: Pre-, in- and postfix grammars for symbolic regression in grammatical evolution. In: IEEE Workshop and Summer School on Evolutionary Computing (2008)

7. Byrne, J., Mcdermott, J., O'Neill, M., Brabazon, A.: An analysis of the behaviour of mutation in grammatical evolution. In: Esparcia-Alcazar, A.I., Ekart, A., Silva, S., Dignum, S. (eds.) EuroGP 2010. LNCS, vol. 6021, pp. 14–25. Springer, Heidelberg (2010)

8. Kell, D.B.: Genotype-phenotype mapping: genes as computer programs. Trends in Genetics 18(11) (2002)

9. Keller, R.E., Banzhaf, W.: Genetic programming using genotype-phenotype mapping from linear genomes into linear phenotypes. In: Proc. of the First Annual Conference, Genetic Programming 1996. MIT Press, Cambridge (1996)

10. Keller, R.E., Banzhaf, W.: Evolution of genetic code on a hard problem. In: Proc. of the Genetic and Evolutionary Computation Conference (GECCO 2001). Morgan Kaufmann, San Francisco (2001)

11. Koza, J.R., Keane, M.A., Streeter, M.J., Mydlowec, W., Yu, J., Lanza, G.: Genetic Programming IV: Routine Human-Competitive Machine Intelligence. Kluwer Academic Publishers, Dordrecht (2003)

12. Langdon, W., Poli, R.: An analysis of the MAX problem in genetic programming. Genetic Programming (1997)

13. Margetts, S., Jones, A.J.: An adaptive mapping for developmental genetic programming. In: Miller, J., Tomassini, M., Lanzi, P.L., Ryan, C., Tetamanzi, A.G.B., Langdon, W.B. (eds.) EuroGP 2001. LNCS, vol. 2038, p. 97. Springer, Heidelberg (2001)

14. Miller, J.F., Thomson, P.: Cartesian genetic programming. In: Poli, R., Banzhaf, W., Langdon, W.B., Miller, J., Nordin, P., Fogarty, T.C. (eds.) EuroGP 2000. LNCS, vol. 1802, pp. 121–132. Springer, Heidelberg (2000)

15. O'Neill, M.: Automatic Programming in an Arbitrary Language: Evolving Programs with Grammatical Evolution. PhD thesis, University of Limerick (2001)

16. O'Neill, M., Brabazon, A., Nicolau, M., Garraghy, S.M., Keenan, P.: πgrammatical evolution. In: Deb, K., et al. (eds.) GECCO 2004. LNCS, vol. 3103, pp. 617–629. Springer, Heidelberg (2004)

17. O'Neill, M., Hemberg, E., Gilligan, C., Bartley, E., McDermott, J., Brabazon, A.: GEVA: Grammatical evolution in java. SIGEVOlution 3(2) (2008)

18. O'Neill, M., Ryan, C.: Grammatical Evolution: Evolutionary Automatic Programming in a Arbitrary Language. In: Genetic programming. Kluwer Academic Publishers, Dordrecht (2003)

19. Poli, R., Langdon, W.B., McPhee, N.F.: A field guide to genetic programming (2008) (With contributions by J. R. Koza), http://lulu.com, http://www.gp-field-guide.org.uk

20. Stephens, C.R.: Effect of mutation and recombination on the genotype-phenotype map. In: Proc. of the Genetic and Evolutionary Computation Conference, vol. 2. Morgan Kaufmann, San Francisco (1999)

Handling Different Categories of Concept Drifts in Data Streams Using Distributed GP

Gianluigi Folino and Giuseppe Papuzzo

Institute for High Performance Computing and Networking, CNR-ICAR
{folino,papuzzo}@icar.cnr.it

Abstract. Using Genetic Programming (GP) for classifying data streams is problematic as GP is slow compared with traditional single solution techniques. However, the availability of cheaper and better-performing distributed and parallel architectures make it possible to deal with complex problems previously hardly solved owing to the large amount of time necessary. This work presents a general framework based on a distributed GP ensemble algorithm for coping with different types of concept drift for the task of classification of large data streams. The framework is able to detect changes in a very efficient way using only a detection function based on the incoming unclassified data. Thus, only if a change is detected a distributed GP algorithm is performed in order to improve classification accuracy and this limits the overhead associated with the use of a population-based method. Real world data streams may present drifts of different types. The introduced detection function, based on the self-similarity fractal dimension, permits to cope in a very short time with the main types of different drifts, as demonstrated by the first experiments performed on some artificial datasets. Furthermore, having an adequate number of resources, distributed GP can handle very frequent concept drifts.

1 Introduction

In the last few years, many organizations are collecting a tremendous amount of data that arrives in the form of continuous stream. Credit card transactional flows, telephone records, sensor network data, network event logs, urban traffic controls are just some examples of streaming data.

The ever changing nature, the need of storage and the high volume of these data can put in crisis traditional data mining algorithms, as they are not able to capture new trends in the stream. In fact, traditional algorithms assume that data is static, i.e. a concept, represented by a set of features, does not change because of modifications of the external environment. In the above mentioned applications, instead, a concept may drift due to several motivations, for example sensor failures, increases of telephone or network traffic. *Concept drift* (a radical change in the target concept in unforeseen way) can cause serious deterioration of the model performance and thus its detection allows to design a model that is able to revise itself and promptly restore its classification accuracy.

A.I. Esparcia-Alcazar et al. (Eds.): EuroGP 2010, LNCS 6021, pp. 74–85, 2010.

Incremental (online) systems [24] evolve and update a model as new instances of the data arrives and are an approach able to support adaptive ensembles on evolving data streams. These methods build a single model that represents the entire data stream and continuously refine their model as data flows. However, maintaining a unique up-to-date model is not a good solution, as previously trained classifiers would be discarded and an important part of information could be lost. On the contrary, update the model as soon as new data arrive could not be practicable as usually the stream of data is very fast. Furthermore, for many applications, i.e. intrusion detection, user feedback is needed for labeling the data, which also requires time and other resources. A way to overcome this problem is to detect changes and adapt the model only if a concept drift happens.

Ensemble learning algorithms [3,2,7] have been gathering an increasing interest in the research community; these approaches have been applied to many real world problems and they have successfully exploited for the task of classifying data streams [25,22,10], as an example of incremental systems. In particular, coupled with GP demonstrated the improvements that GP obtains when enriched with these methods [9,11,6].

The usage of fractal dimension for keeping into account changes in the distribution of the points of a dataset have been explored in the field of knowledge discovery [1], i.e. in the task of clustering [13] and association rules [21] , because of the fast algorithms existing for computing it and for its capacity to detect concept drifts. However, to the best of our knowledge it has not been applied to the field of classification.

This work presents a general framework based on a distributed GP ensemble algorithm for coping with different types of concept drift for the task of classification of large data streams. The architecture of the framework consists of a distributed GP ensemble classifier used in the training (*stationary*) phase and a fractal dimension-based function for detecting concept drifts in the nonstationary phase. The system is able to detect different kinds of concept drift in a very efficient way. It is worth noticing that the detection function only works on the incoming unclassified data. Thus, only if a change is detected the distributed GP algorithm is performed in order to improve classification accuracy. The GP algorithm builds and updates an ensemble of classifiers, removing the old not-updated classifiers. This latter is one of the many possible choices. A different procedure showed in [25] maintains the classifier having a class distribution similar of that of the current data and it deserves to be investigated in future works.

A previous approach [5] demonstrated that GP ensembles and fractal dimension can be successfully applied for classifying continuous data streams and handling concept drifts. The main strategy used in the above cited paper to detect changes is based on the computing of the fractal dimension of the fitness of incoming data. The limit inherent in this approach is that it needs a continuous phase of training and, in addition, computing the fitness of new data requires that at least a significant sample of these data are pre-classified. In real data streams, this can be very costly, as in many cases it would require a work made by experts or a heavy method for computing real classes of the examples. Furthermore, it is hard to decide when changes may happen. In some cases drift are quite frequent, while in other cases they can require hours, days or months (i.e. the intrusion detection problem).

On the contrary, in our work, changes are detected only on the basis of the fractal dimension computed directly on the new chunks of data. So, labelled training data are necessary only when new drifts are discovered, which can be very rare.

To summarize, the main contributions of this work are that the overhead of handling a population of GP trees is overcome by the usage of a parallel/distributed architecture, that the algorithm detects changes on new not labelled data and that the heavy training phase is executed only when a change is detected and only for a limited number of windows.

The paper is organized as follows. Section 2 introduces the architecture of the system and the main components for training the classifiers and detecting the changes. In Section 3, the different types of drift analyzed and the strategy for detecting changes based on the fractal dimension are discussed in detail. Section 4 presents the experiments performed on some artificial datasets. Finally, Section 5 concludes the paper and presents some interesting future developments.

2   The Streaming Distributed GP Algorithm

In this section, we introduce the ensemble-based GP tool (BoostCGPC) used in the training phase and the framework used to classify the large data streams in presence of drifts.

2.1   The Distributed GP Tool

Ensemble [7,2] is a learning paradigm where multiple component learners are trained for the same task by a learning algorithm, and the predictions of the component learners are combined for dealing with new unseen instances. Let $S = \{(x_i, y_i) | i = 1, \ldots, N\}$ be a training set where x_i, called example or tuple or instance, is an attribute vector with m attributes and y_i is the class label associated with x_i. A predictor (classifier), given a new example, has the task to predict the class label for it.

Ensemble techniques build T predictors, each on a different training set, then combine them together to classify the test set. Boosting was introduced by Schapire [18] and Freund [19] for boosting the performance of any "weak" learning algorithm, i.e. an algorithm that "generates classifiers which need only be a little bit better than random guessing" [19].

The boosting algorithm, called *AdaBoost*, adaptively changes the distribution of the training set depending on how difficult each example is to classify. Given the number T of trials (rounds) to execute, T weighted training sets $S_1, S_2, \ldots, S_T$ are sequentially generated and T classifiers $C^1, \ldots, C^T$ are built to compute a weak hypothesis h_t. Let w_i^t denote the weight of the example x_i

at trial t. At the beginning $w_i^1 = 1/n$ for each x_i. At each round $t = 1, \ldots, T$, a weak learner C^t, whose error ϵ^t is bounded to a value strictly less than $1/2$, is built and the weights of the next trial are obtained by multiplying the weight of the correctly classified examples by $\beta^t = \epsilon^t/(1 - \epsilon^t)$ and renormalizing the weights so that $\Sigma_i w_i^{t+1} = 1$. Thus "easy" examples get a lower weight, while "hard" examples, that tend to be misclassified, get higher weights. This induces AdaBoost to focus on examples that are hardest to classify. The boosted classifier gives the class label y that maximizes the sum of the weights of the weak hypotheses predicting that label, where the weight is defined as $log(1/\beta^t)$. The final classifier h_f is defined as follows:

$$h_f = arg\ max\ (\sum_t^T log(\frac{1}{\beta^t})h_t(x, y))$$

Ensemble techniques have been shown to be more accurate than component learners constituting the ensemble [2,16], thus such a paradigm has gained importance in recent years and has already been successfully applied in many application fields.

A key feature of the ensemble paradigm, often not much highlighted, concerns its ability to solve problems in a distributed and decentralized way.

A GP ensemble offers several advantages over a monolithic GP that uses a single GP program to solve the intrusion detection task. First, it can deal with very large data sets. Second, it can make an overall system easier to understand, modify and implement in a distributed way. Last, it is more robust than a monolithic GP, and can show graceful performance degradation in situations where only a subset of GPs in the ensemble are performing correctly.

Diversity is an important problem that must be considered for forming successful ensembles. Genetic programming does not require any change in a training set to generate individuals of different behaviors. BoostCGPC, presented in [4], builds GP ensembles using a hybrid variation of the classic island model that leads not only to a faster algorithm, but also to superior numerical performance. The pseudocode of this algorithm is reported in figure 1.

It uses a cellular GP algorithm (cGP), presented in [4] to inductively generate a GP classifier as a decision tree for the task of data classification. cGP runs for T rounds; for every round it generates a classifier per node, exchanges it with the other nodes, and updates the weights of the tuples for the next round, according to the boosting algorithm AdaBoost.M2.

Each node is furnished with a cGP algorithm enhanced with the boosting technique AdaBoost.M2 and a population initialized with random individuals, and operates on the local data weighted according to a uniform distribution. The selection rule, the replacement rule and the asynchronous migration strategy are specified in the cGP algorithm. Each node generates the GP classifier by running for a certain number of generations, necessary to compute the number of boosting rounds. During the boosting rounds, each classifier maintains the local vector of the weights that directly reflect the prediction accuracy. At each boosting round the hypotheses generated by each classifier are exchanged among all the processors in order to produce the ensemble of predictors. In this way each node maintains the entire ensemble and it can use it to recalculate the new vector of weights. After the execution of the fixed number of boosting rounds, the classifiers are updated.

Refer to the paper [4] for a more detailed description of BoostCGPC.

Given a network constituted by N nodes,
each having a data set S_j
For j = 1, 2, ..., N (for each island in parallel)
 Initialize the weights associated with each tuple
 Initialize the population Q_j with random individuals
end parallel for
For t = 1,2,3, ..., T (boosting rounds)
 For j = 1, 2, ..., N (for each island in parallel)
  Train cGP on S_j using a weighted fitness
  according to the weight distribution
  Compute a weak hypothesis
  Exchange the hypotheses among the N islands
  Update the weights
 end parallel for
end for t

Output the hypothesis

Fig. 1. The BoostCGPC algorithm based on AdaBoost.M2

2.2   Using BoostCGPC for the Streaming of Data

The streaming algorithm, introduced in this paper, alternates two phases: a nonstationary phase in which a function based on the fractal dimension for detecting changes in new unlabeled data is adopted and a (usually not frequent) stationary phase in which the distributed GP algorithm is run in order to recover from a drift.

The pseudo-code of the algorithm, after an initial phase of training, is shown in figure 2. The initial phase simply consists in the building of the ensemble by means of BoostCGPC. We consider an infinite stream of data composed by unlabeled tuples $T_1, T_2, \ldots, T_\infty$ and an ensemble $E = \{C_1, C_2, \ldots, C_m\}$ previously built by BoostCGPC. A limit is placed on the size of the ensemble, i.e. the maximum number of classifiers is set to M. In order to detect changes, different windows of data are analyzed. The size of each window is set to T_{wind} and, to avoid the overhead associate to the analysis of each tuple, the detection of the change is detected each T_{incr} tuples.

The fractal dimension computed on each window is added to the set of elements to be analyzed by the detection function and the the oldest element is

Given a network constituted by N nodes to train $BoostCGPC$.
Let T_{wind} and T_{incr} be respectively the size of the window
examined and the increment considered.
Given $T_1, T_2, \ldots T_\infty$, the unlabeled tuples composing the stream.
Consider M as the maximum number of classifiers forming the ensemble,
$T_S = \emptyset$ (a set of tuples to analyze),
the boosting ensemble $E = \{C_1, C_2, \ldots, C_m\}$ where $m < M$,
a fractal set $FS = \{Fd_1, Fd_2, \ldots, Fd_K\}$ where $K = \frac{T_{wind}}{T_{incr}}$
while (more_Tuples)
   $TA = \emptyset$ (new tuples to analyze)
   while ($|TA| < T_{incr}$)
      Add new tuples to TA
   end while
   $T_S = T_S \cup TA$ and remove the oldest tuples, until $|T_S| = T_{wind}$
   compute the fractal dimension F_d of the set TS
   Add F_d to the set FS and remove the oldest element
   if (detection_function (FS))
      Generate a set $Tl = \{Tl_1, Tl_2, \ldots, Tl_k\}$ of labeled tuples
      Train $BoostCGPC$ on Tl for T rounds of boosting, using N nodes
      and it outputs $T \times N$ classifiers
      Add these classifiers to the ensemble E
   end if
   if ($| E |> M$)
      prune the ensemble E, removing the oldest $M - |E|$ classifiers
   end if
end while

Fig. 2. The overall algorithm

removed in order to maintain the same size. More details on how the fractal dimension is computed and on how the detection function acts are reported in subsection 3.2.

When a change is detected, a new set of labelled tuples Tl is produced (i.e. taking the labelled tuples from the stream, if they are present or using an automatic/manual classifier). BoostCGPCruns for T rounds on N nodes using this set of tuples and it will produce $T \times N$ classifiers, which will be added to the ensemble removing the oldest classifiers so that the overall number of classifiers remains M. If the size of the ensemble is greater than the maximum fixed size M, the ensemble is pruned by retiring the oldest $T \times N$ predictors and adding the new generated ones.

3 Concept Drifts and Fractal Dimension

In this section, we illustrate the main types of concept drift presented in literature and show how the fractal dimension can be used to detect them.

3.1   Artificial Datasets and Concept Drifts

Concept drifts can be classified on the basis of the speed of the change as gradual or abrupt drifts, or they can be considered recurrent if they are periodic. They are predictable if we can predict when it is likely they occur. Studying different types of concept drift in real world datasets is really hard, as it is not possible to categorize them, to predict their presence and the type and so on; thus using artificial datasets is a better way to analyze this aspect. In [15] a detailed description of the main different types of drift is given. In our work, we use the same categories treated in this paper and modified the dataset generator[1] supplied by the authors.

The datasets simulated comprises the circle function, the sine function, the SEA moving hyperplane [22] and the STAGGER boolean concept [20]. The SEA generator can also be used to generate lines and planes.

In the experiment of the next section, all the data sets contain a noise level of 10% obtained by flipping randomly the class of the tuples from 0 to 1 and vice versa, with probability 0.1. Furthermore, the drifts are ordered by increasing class severity (i.e. the percentage of input space having its target changed after the drift).

The circle data set is a 2-dimensional unit hypercube, thus an example x is a vector of 2 features $x_i \in [0, 1]$. The class boundary is a circle of radius r and center c of coordinates (a, b). If an example x is inside the circle then it is labelled class 1, class 0 otherwise. Drift is simulated moving the radius of the circle. We fixed the center to $(0.5, 0.5)$ and varied the radius from 0.2 to 0.3 (16%), from 0.2 to 0.4(38%) and from 0.2 to 0.5(66%). This simulates drifts more and more abrupt (the class severity is reported in brackets).

The sine function is defined by the formula $a \cdot sin(bx + c) + d$ where $a = b = 1, c = 0$ and d varying from -2 to $1(15\%)$, from -5 to $4(45\%)$, from -8 to $7(75\%)$.

The SEA moving hyperplane in d dimensions is defined by the class boundary $\sum_{i=1}^{d} a_i x_i < a_0$ where $a_1 = a_2 = \cdots = a_d = 0.1$ and a_0 varies from -2 to $-2.7(14\%)$, from -1 to $-3.2(44\%)$ and from -0.7 to $-4.4(74\%)$.

In the STAGGER dataset, each tuple consists of three attribute values: $color \in \{green, blue, red\}$, $shape \in \{triangle, circle, rectangle\}$, and $size \in \{small, medium, large\}$. The drift is simulated changing the target concept, i.e. the boolean function. In our case, as in [15], we simplify the function to $y = (color = / \neq a) \wedge / \vee (shape = / \neq b)$ and it varies from $y = (color = red) \wedge (shape = rectangle)$ to $y = (color = red) \vee (shape = rectangle)(11\%)$, from $y = (color = red) \wedge (shape = rectangle)$ to $y = (color = red) \wedge (shape \neq circle)(44\%)$, and from $y = (color = red) \wedge (shape = rectangle)$ to $y = (color \neq blue) \vee (shape \neq circle)(67\%)$.

3.2   Fractal Dimension and Detection Function

Fractals [14] are particular structures that present *self-similarity*, i. e. an invariance with respect to the scale used. A family of functions, named fractal

---

[1] www.cs.bham.ac. uk/˜flm/opensource/DriftGenerator.zip

dimension (FD)[8], can be usefully adopted to characterize changes in the data. Among the properties of FD is worth to notice that the presence of a noise smaller than the signal does not affect it [23].

We can compute the fractal dimension of a dataset by embedding it in a d-dimensional grid whose cells have size r and computing the frequency p_i with which data points fall in the i-th cell. The fractal dimension is given by the formula $FD = \frac{1}{q-1} \frac{\log \sum_i p_i^q}{\log r}$. Among the fractal dimensions, the *correlation dimension*, obtained when $q = 2$ measures the probability that two points chosen at random will be within a certain distance of each other. Changes in the correlation dimension mean changes in the distribution of data in the data set, thus it can be used as an indicator of concept drift. Fast algorithms exist to compute the fractal dimension. We used the $FD3$ algorithm of [17] that efficiently implements the *box counting method* [12].

Differently from other works, here the fractal dimension is directly computed on the unlabeled data coming from the stream. The application of FD in an adaptive way permits to detect the changes. Fractal dimension is computed on a window of fixed size ($FD_{wind} = 500\ tuples$) with a increment $FD_{incr} = 50$. As the stream goes, we will obtain a fractal set $FS = \{Fd_1, Fd_2, \ldots, Fd_k\}$ where k is the number of elements considered for applying the detection function as described in figure 2. In practice, this detection function, first compute the linear regression of the set FS and then if the absolute value of the angle coefficient is greater than 1 (i.e. an angle of $\frac{\pi}{4}$), a change is detected. Choosing angle coefficients greater (minor) than 1 permits to cope with heavier (lighter) drifts.

4 Performance Evaluation

4.1 Fractal Analysis

In this section, the performance of our framework is analyzed on the artificial datasets described in the subsection 3.1.

The algorithm is run on 30,000 tuples and the concept drifts are simulated each 5,000 steps for a total of 5 drifts, as described in the above cited subsection. It worth remembering that we increased the drift from mild to severe every 5,000 steps.

Figures 3 reports, on the y axis, the fractal dimension for all the datasets and the relative drift detected (vertical lines). The width of the drift shown in the figure is proportional to the number of windows in which the detection function identifies the change. In spite of the different behavior of the datasets generated, our function is able to capture all the drifts, a few windows after they happen. Furthermore, the detection function is quite robust to the noise. In fact, only in the case of the circle and of the sine dataset, two false drifts are detected (and only one in the case of the line and of the hyperplane) because of the presence of the noise and they are very narrow and could be filtered.

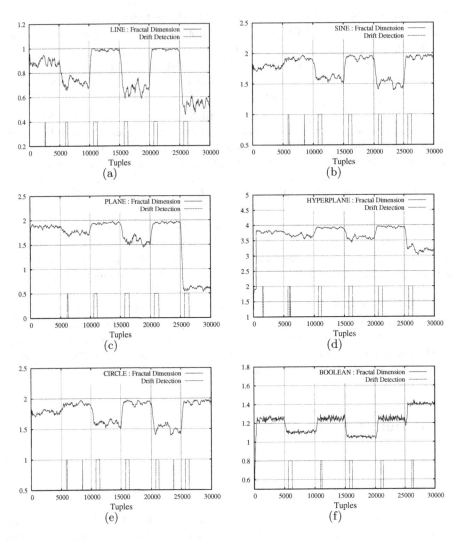

Fig. 3. Fractal Dimension (and Drift Detection) results for (a)Line (b) Sine (c) Plane (d) Hyperplane (e) Circle (f) Boolean with 30,000 tuples, with a concept drift each 5,000 tuples for a total of 5 concept drifts

4.2   Effort Evaluation

The aim of this subsection is to evaluate how quickly BoostCGPC can answer to a concept drift and to understand in which cases it can be applied and in which case it is better to use single-solution traditional techniques that are notoriously faster than GP. If concept drift does not occur too frequently, our algorithm can quickly recover from the drift; even in the case that the frequency is quite high, our distributed algorithm can be used, provided that we have resources sufficient to run it in the time requirements we have to meet. To summarize, we want to evaluate which kind of drifts the ensemble can handle, having a fixed number of nodes or, on the contrary, how many resources we need to reserve (i.e. in a cloud computing environment), in order to handle a very frequent drift. Thus, we run some experiments on different distributed machines using the same standard parameters adopted in [4] and measured the execution times. In the same paper, it is demonstrated that BoostCGPC obtains a good performance using a small sample of the training set. Furthermore, also for very large and complex datasets, a population of 1000 individuals and 5 or 10 rounds of 100 generations of boosting are sufficient to obtain a good accuracy.

Table 1. Environments used in the experiments

Name	CPU	Memory per Node	Number of Nodes
Aleph	Xeon E5520 2,26 GHz	16 GB	16
Spaci	Itanium 2 1.4 GHz	2 GB	64

We fixed a probability of 0.1 for reproduction, 0.8 for crossover and 0.1 for mutation. The maximum depth of the new generated subtrees is 4 for the step of population initialization, 17 for crossover and 2 for mutation. We fixed to 5 the number of rounds for the boosting and we execute 100 generations each round. The dataset is an artificial hypersphere (the circle function extended to a 6-dimensional space) with a noise level of 10% and 100,000 tuples.

Two configurations, consisting respectively of (1) a population of 1280 individuals (2) a population of 320 individuals, are used on the two different environments summarized in table 1. The first, named Aleph, is a modern cluster having 16 nodes, while the second, named Spaci, is an older machine, but having 64 nodes.

The execution times and the standard deviation averaged over 40 tries are reported in table 2. It worth to notice that the algorithm takes about 4 minutes on the modern machine using only one node and 21 seconds on the same machine using 16 nodes. Anyway, if we have very strict time requirements, we can use a smaller population (reducing slightly the accuracy) and obtain a very fast execution time of about 5 seconds both on 64 nodes of Spaci and on 16 nodes of Aleph.

Table 2. Execution times and standard deviation for the two clusters and for (1) a population of 1280 individuals (2) a population of 320 individuals

Nodes	1	2	4	8	16	64
Spaci (1)	817.56 ± 125.8	398.82 ± 59.5	217.18 ± 33.2	121.50 ± 20.8	74.39 ± 17.2	25.07 ± 5.7
Spaci (2)	150.05 ± 22.6	79.61 ± 18.8	43.73 ± 12.2	21.61 ± 3.6	14.31 ± 5.0	4.97 ± 1.3
Aleph (1)	289.15 ± 39.2	141.27 ± 31.7	66.17 ± 21.5	35.63 ± 8.5	21.88 ± 4.4	−
Aleph (2)	56.25 ± 7.4	28.81 ± 6.3	13.29 ± 3.1	6.90 ± 0.8	4.64 ± 1.1	−

Note that, if we need a fast recovery from the drift, GP can be stopped early and the current generated ensemble, generally, maintains a good grade of accuracy.

5   Conclusions

This work provides evidence that Genetic Programming can be profitably applied to the problem of classifying large data streams, coupling fast detection methods and modern distributed architectures. An adaptive method based on the fractal dimension is able to detect both medium and abrupt drifts. The distributed GP algorithm can quickly recover from drifts, provided that we have sufficient resources to run it in the time requirements we have to meet.

Future works aims to evaluate the framework on real world datasets, to explore different concept drift functions that can overcome the limit of the fractal dimension-based function. In fact, the fractal dimension is not able to detect changes that are gradual during a long period of time. To this aim, other functions must be coupled with FD. Furthermore, different pruning strategies apt to reduce the size of ensemble deserve to be explored.

References

1. Barbará, D.: Chaotic mining: Knowledge discovery using the fractal dimension. In: 1999 ACM SIGMOD Workshop on Research Issues in Data Mining and Knowledge Discovery (1999)
2. Breiman, L.: Bagging predictors. Machine Learning 24(2), 123–140 (1996)
3. Dietterich, T.G.: An experimental comparison of three methods for costructing ensembles of decision trees: Bagging, boosting, and randomization. Machine Learning (40), 139–157 (2000)
4. Folino, G., Pizzuti, C., Spezzano, G.: Ensembles for large scale data classification. IEEE Transaction on Evolutionary Computation 10(5), 604–616 (2006)
5. Folino, G., Pizzuti, C., Spezzano, G.: Mining distributed evolving data streams using fractal gp ensembles. In: Ebner, M., O'Neill, M., Ekárt, A., Vanneschi, L., Esparcia-Alcázar, A.I. (eds.) EuroGP 2007. LNCS, vol. 4445, pp. 160–169. Springer, Heidelberg (2007)
6. Folino, G., Pizzuti, C., Spezzano, G.: Training distributed gp ensemble with a selective algorithm based on clustering and pruning for pattern classification. IEEE Trans. Evolutionary Computation 12(4), 458–468 (2008)
7. Freund, Y., Scapire, R.: Experiments with a new boosting algorithm. In: Proceedings of the 13th Int. Conference on Machine Learning, pp. 148–156 (1996)
8. Grassberger, P.: Generalized dimensions of strange attractors. Physics Letters 97A, 227–230 (1983)
9. Iba, H.: Bagging, boosting, and bloating in genetic programming. In: Proc. of the Genetic and Evolutionary Computation Conference GECCO 1999, Orlando, Florida, July 1999, pp. 1053–1060. Morgan Kaufmann, San Francisco (1999)
10. Kolter, J.Z., Maloof, M.A.: Dynamic weighted majority: An ensemble method for drifting concepts. J. Mach. Learn. Res. 8, 2755–2790 (2007)

11. Langdon, W.B., Buxton, B.F.: Genetic programming for combining classifiers. In: Proc. of the Genetic and Evolutionary Computation Conference GECCO 2001, July 2001, pp. 66–73. Morgan Kaufmann, San Francisco (2001)
12. Liebovitch, L., Toth, T.: A fast algorithm to determine fractal dimensions by box counting. Physics Letters 141A(8) (1989)
13. Lin, G., Chen, L.: A grid and fractal dimension-based data stream clustering algorithm. In: International Symposium on Information Science and Engieering, vol. 1, pp. 66–70 (2008)
14. Mandelbrot, B.: The Fractal Geometry of Nature. W.H Freeman, New York (1983)
15. Minku, L.L., White, A.P., Yao, X.: The impact of diversity on on-line ensemble learning in the presence of concept drift. IEEE Transactions on Knowledge and Data Engineering 99(1), 5555
16. Ross Quinlan, J.: Bagging, boosting, and c4.5. In: Proceedings of the 13th National Conference on Artificial Intelligence AAAI 1996, pp. 725–730. MIT Press, Cambridge (1996)
17. Sarraille, J., DiFalco, P.: FD3, http://tori.postech.ac.kr/softwares
18. Schapire, R.E.: The strength of weak learnability. Machine Learning 5(2), 197–227 (1990)
19. Schapire, R.E.: Boosting a weak learning by majority. Information and Computation 121(2), 256–285 (1996)
20. Schlimmer, J.C., Granger Jr., R.H.: Incremental learning from noisy data. Mach. Learn. 1(3), 317–354 (1986)
21. Sousa, E.P.M., Ribeiro, M.X., Traina, A.J.M., Traina Jr., C.: Tracking the intrinsic dimension of evolving data streams to update association rules. In: 3rd International Workshop on Knowledge Discovery from Data Streams, part of the 23th International Conference on Machine Learning, ICML 2006 (2006)
22. Street, W.N., Kim, Y.: A streaming ensemble algorithm (SEA) for large-scale classification. In: Proceedings of the seventh ACM SIGKDD International conference on Knowledge discovery and data mining (KDD 2001), San Francisco, CA, USA, August 26-29, pp. 377–382. ACM, New York (2001)
23. Tykierko, M.: Using invariants to change detection in dynamical system with chaos. Physica D Nonlinear Phenomena 237, 6–13 (2008)
24. Utgoff, P.E.: Incremental induction of decision trees. Machine Learning 4, 161–186 (1989)
25. Wang, H., Fan, W., Yu, P.S., Han, J.: Mining concept-drifting data streams using ensemble classifiers. In: Proceedings of the nineth ACM SIGKDD International conference on Knowledge discovery and data mining (KDD 2003), Washington, DC, USA, August 24-27, pp. 226–235. ACM, New York (2003)

An Indirect Approach to the Three-Dimensional Multi-pipe Routing Problem

Marcus Furuholmen[1], Kyrre Glette[2], Mats Hovin[2], and Jim Torresen[2]

[1] Aker Solutions AS
Snaroyveien 36, P.O. Box 169, 1364 Fornebu, Norway
[2] University of Oslo, Department of Informatics,
P.O. Box 1080 Blindern, 0316 Oslo, Norway
{marcusfu,kyrrehg,jimtoer,matsh}@ifi.uio.no

Abstract. This paper explores an indirect approach to the Three-dimensional Multi-pipe Routing problem. Variable length pipelines are built by letting a virtual robot called a turtle navigate through space, leaving pipe segments along its route. The turtle senses its environment and acts in accordance with commands received from heuristics currently under evaluation. The heuristics are evolved by a Gene Expression Programming based Learning Classifier System. The suggested approach is compared to earlier studies using a direct encoding, where command lines were evolved directly by genetic algorithms. Heuristics generating higher quality pipelines are evolved by fewer generations compared to the direct approach, however the evaluation time is longer and the search space is more complex. The best evolved heuristic is short and simple, builds modular solutions, exhibits some degree of generalization and demonstrates good scalability on test cases similar to the training case.

1 Introduction

Inspired by evolution in natural systems, evolutionary algorithms (EAs) [1] have been successful at optimizing large and complex problems commonly encountered in industry. Examples range from parameter optimization involving a vast number of variables as well as finding near optimal solutions to large and difficult combinatorial problems. However, scalability often becomes challenging as the size of the search space tends to grow exponentially with the problem size. This is commonly caused by the use of a *direct* representation, where every element in the phenotype is represented as an element in the genotype. The field of Artificial Embryogeny (AE) [2] attempt to alleviate this problem by evolving *indirect* representations in the form of e.g. a rule base represented as bit strings, an artificial neural network, or a set of symbolic expressions, which are used to build phenotypes of arbitrary sizes. The computational cost is often higher for evolving indirect solutions, however, once completed it may provide a general solution for a whole class of problems, while a direct approach only provides the solution to the actual problem that was optimized. Furthermore, penalty and repair functions, often necessary for direct approaches, may be avoided since

A.I. Esparcia-Alcazar et al. (Eds.): EuroGP 2010, LNCS 6021, pp. 86–97, 2010.

phenotypes may be built so that feasible solutions are guaranteed. Finally, by carefully selecting a symbolic form of representation, knowledge can be extracted from the process and results may be verified analytically.

The Three-dimensional Multi-pipe Routing (3DMPR) problem is concerned with automating and optimizing pipe routing design involving several pipelines in three dimensions. Pipe routing can be understood as to be a subset of assembly design and is important for several industrial applications such as factory layout, circuit layout, aircraft and ship design. The design is normally done by human experts following a piping and instrumentation diagram (P&ID), as illustrated in figure 1, where the location of various equipment is predetermined. This, however, is a very time consuming process, making it practically impossible for the designer to test several scenarios.

Pipe routing can be seen as a special case of general path planning in robotics in which there are two major families of approaches known as *cell decomposition* and *skeletonization* [3]. Each approach reduces the continuous path-planning problem to a discrete graph search problem. Deterministic shortest path algorithms guarantee an optimal solution given sufficient time; however, pipe routing belongs to a class of optimization problems with very large, multimodal search spaces, where one is more interested in finding feasible solutions in practical time than trying to find the absolute optimal solution. This suggests the 3DMPR problem to be a good candidate for optimization by stochastic search algorithms such as Genetic Algorithms (GAs).

Most research on pipe routing limits the problem to single pipelines in two dimensions [4] [5] [6], multiple pipelines in two dimensions [7] [8] [9] (multiple 2D layers) or single pipelines in three dimensions [10]. GA was compared to deterministic methods in [5] and [6] and it was concluded that GA managed to locate near-optimal solutions in a considerable less time, but that GA's limitation was mainly related to obtaining accurate solutions. Multiple pipes in three dimensions was investigated in [11] and [12], however, in all the reviewed literature the authors implement a direct encoding and test their approach on smaller problems.

The concept of indirect evolution has been proposed for several other application areas. Evolution of heuristics for packing problems [13] [14] [15] [16], scheduling problems [17] [18] [19], and facility layout problems [20] demonstrated that heuristics were generated which in many cases were equal to, or better than, previously known human made heuristics. The Evolutionary Robotics community commonly applies neuroevolution (evolution of neural networks) for automatically generating robot controllers [21] but also Genetic Programming [22] [23] [24], and Gene Expression Programming [25] [26] has been explored for similar applications. A generative representation for the automated design of modular physical robots was proposed by Hornby et al. in [27] while the evolution of structural design through artificial embryogeny was suggested by Kowaliw et al. in [28].

In a previous study we implemented a direct encoding and compared standard GA (SGA), Incremental GA (IGA) and Coevolutionary GA (CGA) on three proposed 3DMPR benchmark problems. In this paper we present and compare, for the first time, an indirect approach which automatically generates 3DMPR heuristics. The heuristics are evolved by a Gene Expression Programming (GEP) based Learning Classifier System (LCS) called GEPLCS. The pipelines are optimized by minimizing material use, minimizing the number of bends as well as minimizing the offset between the pipeline terminals and the goal positions. Collisions are implicitly avoided during the pipeline building process and safety zone requirements are handled by the problem representation.

The next section explains the method, the experimental setup and the results are presented in section 3 and discussed in section 4 while section 5 concludes.

2   Method

This section first explains how the 3DMPR problem is represented and how pipelines are built. Second, we show how heuristics are generated from a set of evolutionary building blocks. Finally, we explain how pipelines are evaluated, and three benchmark problems are presented.

2.1   Building Pipelines

Pipelines are built by letting a virtual robot called a *turtle* [29] move about in a three dimensional Euclidean space from the start position S, as illustrated for two dimensions in figure 2 and described formally in algorithm 1. For each time step t, the turtle moves one step forward unless it collides with an obstacle or has reached the goal position G. When moving forward, the turtle allocates a new pipe segment to the departing location. The turtle senses its environment through a set of sensors and acts in its environment according to an evolved heuristic. For each time step, the heuristic evaluates the sensor data and sets the orientation of the turtle by executing one of the actions in the action set $A = \{R, L, U, D, \#\}$ coding for turn right/left/up/down and do nothing. The turtle rotates around the axis indicated in the illustration while the required safety distance SD is determined by the dimension of the turtle and the pipe diameter PD. The turtle remembers its previous actions by storing what action was actually performed to a build step array. E.g. if the turtle moves one step forward, the symbol f is reported while if the turtle collides, the symbol s is reported. If the "do nothing" command is triggered, no symbol is reported to the build step array.

2.2   Evolving Heuristics by GEPLCS

This section first introduces the concept of a Learning Classifier System (LCS); second, the Gene Expression Programming (GEP) representation and finally, the GEP based LCS system (GEPLCS) which is illustrated in figure 3.

First described by John Holland in [30], a LCS is a Machine Learning system that learns rules (in our case in the form of heuristics), called *classifiers*. The classifiers are used to classify different input states into appropriate actions

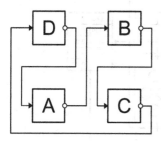

Fig. 1. The P&ID for the "Square" benchmark problem

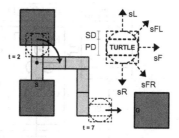

Fig. 2. The turtle leaves pipe segments on its route while navigating from S to G using sensor information

---

Algorithm 1. Pipeline Builder

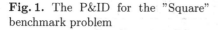

$h \leftarrow$ heuristic
$T \leftarrow$ max number of build step iterations
$P \leftarrow$ number of pipelines
$t \leftarrow 0$
for each pipeline p in P **do**
    Place turtle at the start position S_p
    while last pipe segment in pipeline has not reached goal position G_p and $t < T$ **do**
        if turtle not colliding with any obstacles **then**
            Go forward and leave a pipe segment in departing position
        end if
        Feature vector $\boldsymbol{x} \leftarrow$ get feature vector
        Action vector $\boldsymbol{a} \leftarrow h(\boldsymbol{x})$
        Action $a_{max} \leftarrow MAX(a_1, a_2, ..., a_n)$
        do a_{max}
        $t \leftarrow t + 1$
    end while
end for

---

[31]. The framework has strong links to Reinforcement Learning, however GAs are used to optimize the classifiers. In a Michigan type LCS, a GA focuses on selecting the best classifiers within a single rule set, while in a Pittsburgh type LCS, a GA acts upon a population where each individual codes for an entire rule set. While most LCS implements a binary encoding of the rule sets, Genetic Programming (GP) as well as Artificial Neural Networks have also been used. In this work we implement GEP, which was recently explored in conjunction with LCS by Wilson et al. in [32]. To the authors best knowledge, no papers have been published on the application of LCS for building physical design solutions such as pipelines.

Originally developed by Ferreira [33], GEP is based upon fixed length linear genomes which are translated into executable parse trees of various sizes. The genomes are represented as a collection of symbol strings called *genes* consisting of a head and a tail part. The tail consists of members from a *terminal set* while the head additionally consists of members from a *function set*. The length of the tail t is set by the formula $t = h(n_{max} - 1) + 1$ where h is the length of the head and n_{max} is the arity of the function with the most arguments. The

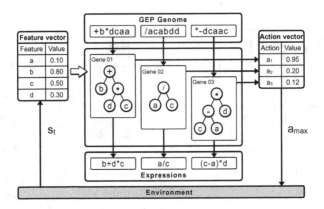

Fig. 3. A Gene Expression Programming based Learning Classifier System (GEPLCS)

linear structure of the genomes enables traditional GA-style crossover and point mutation to be easily implemented. The fixed size of the genomes sets an upper bound on the size of the parse trees, avoiding the problem of bloat, commonly encountered in GP. All solutions generated by GEP are syntactically correct, therefore avoiding the use of repair functions often necessary in GP. For more details on GEP we refer to [33].

In GEPLCS, each individual codes for a complete set of classifiers, thus we may categorize the proposed approach as a Pittsburg type LCS. Each gene in the GEP genome is encoded as a heuristic and corresponds to a single classifier, and each classifier codes for a specific action a. When exposed to a feature vector $\boldsymbol{x}$ sampled from the current state s_t of the phenotype/environment, the classifiers output a real valued action vector $\boldsymbol{a}$. The action with the highest value a_{max} is selected and executed in the environment. The evolved parse trees are easily translated into symbolic expressions examinable by humans.

2.3   Evolutionary Building Blocks

The selected functions and terminals for the 3DMPR problem are listed in table 1. The terminals report values from various sensors as well as selected constants. The turtle is equipped with 13 distance sensors reporting the distance to the closest obstacle. If the ray of a sensor does not hit any obstacle, the value 10^{10} is reported. The turtle is also equipped with sensors monitoring the relative distance to the goal position in each dimension, and the current orientation is monitored in yaw, pitch and roll dimension. The previous action $prev$ is reported as the last entry in the build step array, acting as a memory.

2.4   Fitness Evaluation

A pipeline should reach the goal position G, stay clear from obstacles, minimize the number of bends, and minimize the overall length. Notice the added

Table 1. Functions and Terminals

Functions	Arity	Description
Abs	1	Returns the absolute value
Add	2	Addition
Sub	2	Subtraction
Mult	2	Multiplication
Div	2	Protected Division. Division by zero returns 1
Max	2	Returns the largest of two arguments
IFLTE	4	If first argument is larger than second argument, third argument is returned, else fourth argument is returned

Terminals	Values	Description
sF, sR, sU, sL, sD, sFR, sFU, sFL, sFD, sRU, sRD, sLU, sLD	double	Sensors reporting the distance to closest obstacle in the specified direction (F=Forward, R =Right, L = left, U = Up, D = Down)
dF, dL, dU	double	Manhattan distance to goal in specified direction
yaw, pitch, roll	1/-1	Yaw, pitch and roll orentation
prev	1-6	Previous action
col	1/0	Collide
k0	0.0	Constant
k1	0.5	Constant
k2	1.0	Constant

complexity introduced by the multi-pipe scenario; a pipeline must not collide with the obstacles, with itself or with any other pipeline in the problem. Collision detection during evaluation is unnecessary, since the turtle cannot move forward if it collides with an obstacle. A set of P pipelines are evaluated by the following aggregate scalar error function to be minimized

$$Error = \sum_{i=1}^{P} (w_1 d_i + w_2 b_i + w_3 s_i) \tag{1}$$

where d_i is the Manhattan distance between the outlet of the last pipe segment of the i'th pipeline and the goal position. The variable b_i is the number of bends and s_i the number of segments of pipeline i. The different components are weighted by the values $w_1 = 150$, $w_2 = 10$, and $w_3 = 1$, which were set manually by trial and error.

2.5 Benchmark Problems

To the author's best knowledge, no benchmark problems exist for the 3DMPR problem. We therefore propose three problems in table 2, each problem consisting of four pipelines to be connected. The "Square" problem consists of four equal sized modules to be interconnected, as illustrated in the P&ID in figure 1. The IO points are evenly distributed and located in the horizontal plane; however, the turtle navigates in three dimensions, as illustrated by the evolved solution in figure 5 A). The "Twist" problem consists of two modules to be interconnected by four pipes. Each pipe should connect to the opposite side but at different locations, as illustrated by the evolved solution in 5 B). The "Hub" problem is a common industrial scenario where several modules must connect to a central unit, as illustrated by the evolved solution in 5 C).

Table 2. 3DMPR Benchmark Problems

Square						Twist						Hub					
Modules			Pipelines			Modules			Pipelines			Modules			Pipelines		
ID	Dim	Pos	ID	Start	Goal	ID	Dim	Pos	ID	Start	Goal	ID	Dim	Pos	ID	Start	Goal
A	4,4,4	-5,-5,0	AB	-3,-5,0	3,5,0	A	4,8,8	-5,0,0	AB1	-3,2,-2	3,-2,2	A	6,12,6	0,0,1	BA	-14,0,0	-3,-3,1
B	4,4,4	5,5,0	BC	7,5,0	3,-5,0	B	4,8,8	5,0,0	AB2	-3,-2,-2	3,2,2	B	4,4,4	-16,0,0	CA	-3,15,0	-3,-3,1
C	4,4,4	5,-5,0	CD	7,-5,0	-7,5,0				AB3	-3,2,2	3,-2,-2	C	4,4,4	-5,15,0	DA	12.5,8,0	3,3,1
D	4,4,4	-5,5,0	DA	-3,5,0	-7,-5,0				AB4	-3,-2,2	3,2,-2	D	4,4,4	14.5,0,0	EA	16.5,0,0	3,-3,1
												E	4,4,4	10.5,8,0			

3 Experiments and Results

In this section, the experimental setup is reviewed, the results are presented and compared to a directly encoded GA, and finally, we analyze the best generated heuristic.

10 heuristics were generated by executing 10 independent evolutionary runs with a fixed number of generations $G = 1000$, population size $\mu = 100$, and elitism enabled. The head length $h = 10$ was set by experimentation and the resulting gene length $G_l = 41$ was determined by the formula described in section 2.2. The mutation rate was set to $p_m = 0.1$ while crossover was found to have a destructive effect and was thus not used. Inversion, a common genetic operator in GEP, works by inverting the alleles in a randomly selected region, in either the tail or head region of a gene. The inversion rate $p_i = 0.1$, determines the probability that a single gene will undergo inversion.

The heuristics were trained on only one fitness case, the "Square" problem, a similar approach as e.g. Koza in [24] and Nordin et al. in [34]. In a machine learning paradigm, several fitness cases are usually required in order to generate generalizable solutions. However, since four pipes are built in one fitness case, some generalizable behavior was expected. The training error, computed by function 1, of the best individual for each run, as well as the training error averaged over all runs, is plotted in figure 4 A).

In another study, we applied a Standard GA (SGA) using a direct encoding by letting a "blind" turtle interpret evolved command lines from the symbol set $C = \{F, R, L, U, D, \#\}$, coding for move one step forward, turn right/left/up/down and "do nothing". Figure 4 B) shows 10 runs by applying SGA to the "Square" problem.

Comparing plot A) and B) in figure 4, the average performances of the indirect approach is better than for the direct approach per generation. However, for GEPLCS, several plateaus are encountered and the deviation is larger, indicating a more complex search space. More time is also required (per generation) for evolving the heuristics, mainly due to the building process. The best solution using SGA had an error $E = 1799$, while the best found heuristic generated the solution illustrated in figure 5 A), achieving an error of $E = 268$ which is close to optimal for the "Square" problem. The best found heuristic, which we will call the *3DMPR-H1* heuristic, will be analyzed in the following section.

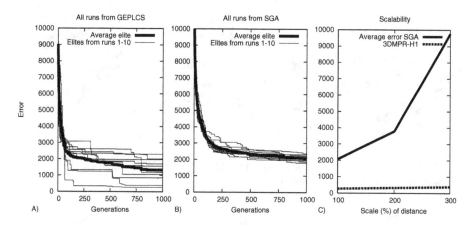

Fig. 4. a) Elites of each evolutionary run for the GEPLCS approach b) Elites of each evolutionary run for the SGA approach c) Comparing the scalability of the 3DMPR-H1 and SGA applied to the "Square" problem

3.1   Analysis of the 3DMPR-H1 Heuristic

As explained in section 2.1; for each time step t in the pipeline building process, the turtle moves one step forward, unless it collides with an obstacle or has reached the goal. The orientation at t is determined by executing the action corresponding to the heuristic expression currently yielding the highest value. The 3DMPR-H1 heuristic is

$Right : prev(sD - 2k_2) - dL$, $Left : sRU$, $Up : yaw(sFR - dF)$, $Down :$ dU and $Nothing : dF + sFD$.

The heuristic is easily interpretable and generates a high-quality solution when applied to the "Square" problem (the problem used for training). All pipelines reaches their respective goals with only 18 bends and 88 pipe segments. Applying the heuristic to the "Twist" problem builds the phenotype in figure 5 B) with error $E = 3432$. Only two pipelines are close to connecting at the goal position, while the other two are "trapped" by the other pipelines. The average error generated by SGA on the "Twist" problem was $E = 773$ after 1000 generations. On the "Hub" problem, the heuristic generated the solution in figure 5 C) with error $E = 1695$, while SGA obtained an average error $E = 1214$ after 1000 generations. Despite a higher error (limited generalizability), the heuristic generates pipelines which avoids obstacles, seeks their individual goals, and have few bends.

The scalability of the heuristic was compared to the scalability of SGA by increasing the distance between the modules in the benchmark problems. The resulting error is plotted in figure 4 C) for the "Square" problem. The error of the solutions generated by the heuristic scales linearly with the problem size, as illustrated for the "Square" in figure 6 A). By applying SGA for a fixed number

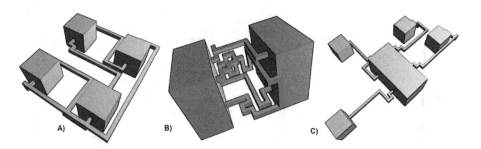

Fig. 5. The 3DMPR-H1 heuristica applied to A) the "Square" problem B) the "Twist" problem and C) the "Hub" problem

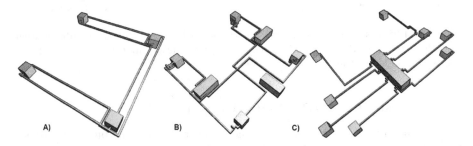

Fig. 6. The 3DMPR-H1 heuristic A) applied to a uniformly scaled verion of the "Square" problem B) avoiding obstacles and C) connecting to a central hub

of generations $G = 1000$, the plot shows that the error (and the evaluation time) scales exponentially with the problem size. The heuristic also manages to avoid obstacles, as illustrated in 6 B), and approximate large scale solutions inspired by the "Hub" problem, as illustrated in figure 6 C).

4   Discussion

The question implicitly asked in this paper is whether it is possible to evolve heuristics in a minimum training environment which are capable of generating high quality solutions to arbitrary large and complex problems. The proposed approach has links to both artificial development as well as machine learning.

We demonstrated the possibility of training a heuristic on a small problem and successfully applying the heuristic on larger, similar problems with a linear scaling of error. The system is capable of building arbitrary large phenotypes independently of the size of the genotype, and the phenotypes are built in close interaction with its environment.

The best found heuristic demonstrated a limited capability of generalization. However, as the size of the problem grows, the cost of optimization by means of direct representations grows exponentially. Thus, when dealing with large scale problems, the evolved heuristic may yield better results. For practical applications, post processing would however be necessary. Better generalization may be obtained by including all benchmarks; however, this would also increase training time.

As discussed by Hornby et al. in [27], indirect approaches are most suitable on problems where regularity, modularity and hierarchy can be exploited. Such features are observable in the evolved solutions in figure 5 and 6 where several pipelines share similar design features. In an engineering perspective, this is an attractive feature enabling standardization and ease of manufacturing.

The evolved 3DMPR-H1 heuristic is simple in its form and possible to understand analytically; it is, however, beyond the scope of present work to give a thorough analysis. Several other, more complex heuristics were also generated which were less interpretable.

Conclusively, we hypothesize that the benefit of using indirect endocings is proportionate to the compressibility of the problem to be solved. High compressibility enables a) the limitation of training time by representing the problem as small scale training cases; b) high generalizability to similar problems; and c) knowledge extraction for human learning. It is, however, unclear how to design the best training environment, as well as how to determine the compressibility of the problem in advance.

5   Conclusions and Future Work

In this paper, for the first time, an approach for evolving heuristics for the Three-dimensional Multi-pipe Routing problem was proposed. A Gene Expression Programming based Learning Classifier System was implemented for evolving the heuristics. The results are encouraging in the sense that the approach managed to automatically generate heuristics for a complex, three dimensional problem, which demonstrated good scalability and reasonable generalization to similar problems. It was found that the error of the best found heuristic scales linearly with the size of the problem (length of pipelines) as compared to a direct encoding where both time and error scales exponentially.

Future research may use the proposed approach for evolving pipe routing heuristics which can be used as part of a fitness function for plant layout optimization. Optionally, pipe routing heuristics and plant layout heuristics may be coevolved in a similar approach as suggested by Furuholmen et al. in [20] and [16]. In this work a scalar aggregate error function describing several (sometimes) conflicting objectives was implemented. This may be addressed by a multi-objective optimization approach by locating the Pareto front and thus being able to choose among several equally good solutions.

Acknowledgement

The authors wish to acknowledge the support of the Norwegian Research Council and the TAIL IO project for their continued funding and support for this research. The TAIL IO project is an international cooperative research project led by StatoilHydro and an R&D consortium consisting of ABB, IBM, Aker Solutions and SKF.

References

1. Eiben, A., Schoenauer, M.: Evolutionary computing. Arxiv preprint cs/0511004 (2005)
2. Stanley, K., Miikkulainen, R.: A Taxonomy for Artificial Embryogeny. Artificial Life 9(2), 93–130 (2003)
3. Norvig, P., Russell, S.: Artificial intelligence: a modern approach. Prentice-Hall, Englewood Cliffs (2003)
4. Ito, T.: A genetic algorithm approach to piping route path planning. Journal of Intelligent Manufacturing 10(1), 103–114 (1999)
5. Ito, T.: Route Planning Wizard: Basic Concept and Its Implementation. In: Hendtlass, T., Ali, M. (eds.) IEA/AIE 2002. LNCS (LNAI), vol. 2358, pp. 547–556. Springer, Heidelberg (2002)
6. Soltani, A., Tawfik, H., Goulermas, J., Fernando, T.: Path planning in construction sites: performance evaluation of the Dijkstra, A*, and GA search algorithms. Advanced Engineering Informatics 16(4), 291–303 (2002)
7. Kim, D., Corne, D., Ross, P.: Industrial plant pipe-route optimisation with genetic algorithms. In: Ebeling, W., Rechenberg, I., Voigt, H.-M., Schwefel, H.-P. (eds.) PPSN 1996. LNCS, vol. 1141, pp. 1012–1021. Springer, Heidelberg (1996)
8. Fan, J., Ma, M., Yang, X.: Path Planning in Pipe System Based on Coevolution[for aero-engines]. Hangkong Dongli Xuebao/Journal of Aerospace Power 19(5), 593–597 (2004)
9. Zhu, D., Latombe, J.: Pipe routing-path planning (with many constraints). In: Proceedings of 1991 IEEE International Conference on Robotics and Automation, pp. 1940–1947 (1991)
10. Sandurkar, S., Chen, W.: GAPRUSgenetic algorithms based pipe routing using tessellated objects. Computers in Industry 38(3), 209–223 (1999)
11. Wang, H., Zhao, C., Yan, W., Feng, X.: Three-dimensional Multi-pipe Route Optimization Based on Genetic Algorithms. International Federation for Information Processing-publications-IFIP 207, 177 (2006)
12. Park, J., Storch, R.: Pipe-routing algorithm development: case study of a ship engine room design. Expert Systems with Applications 23(3), 299–309 (2002)
13. Burke, E., Hyde, M., Kendall, G.: Evolving bin packing heuristics with genetic programming. In: Runarsson, T.P., Beyer, H.-G., Burke, E.K., Merelo-Guervós, J.J., Whitley, L.D., Yao, X. (eds.) PPSN 2006. LNCS, vol. 4193, p. 860. Springer, Heidelberg (2006)
14. Burke, E., Hyde, M., Kendall, G., Woodward, J.: A genetic programming hyperheuristic approach for evolving two dimensional strip packing heuristics. Technical report, Technical report, University of Nottingham, Dept. of Computer Science (2008)
15. Allen, S., Burke, E., Hyde, M., Kendall, G.: Evolving reusable 3d packing heuristics with genetic programming. In: Proceedings of the 11th Annual conference on Genetic and evolutionary computation, pp. 931–938. ACM, New York (2009)
16. Furuholmen, M., Glette, K., Hovin, M., Torresen, J.: Coevolving Heuristics for The Distributors Pallet Packing Problem. In: Proceedings of the IEEE Congress on Evolutionary Computation (2009)
17. Tay, J., Ho, N.: Evolving dispatching rules using genetic programming for solving multi-objective flexible job-shop problems. Computers & Industrial Engineering 54(3), 453–473 (2008)
18. Dimopoulos, C., Zalzala, A.: Investigating the use of genetic programming for a classic one-machine scheduling problem. Advances in Engineering Software 32(6), 489–498 (2001)

19. Jakobovic, D., Budin, L.: Dynamic Scheduling with Genetic Programming. In: Collet, P., Tomassini, M., Ebner, M., Gustafson, S., Ekárt, A. (eds.) EuroGP 2006. LNCS, vol. 3905, p. 73. Springer, Heidelberg (2006)
20. Furuholmen, M., Glette, K., Hovin, M., Torresen, J.: Scalability, generalization and coevolution–experimental comparisons applied to automated facility layout planning. In: Proceedings of the 11th Annual conference on Genetic and evolutionary computation, pp. 691–698. ACM, New York (2009)
21. Floreano, D., Nolfi, S.: Evolutionary Robotics. Springer Handbook of Robotics (2008)
22. Lee, W., Hallam, J., Lund, H.: Applying genetic programming to evolve behavior primitives andarbitrators for mobile robots. In: IEEE International Conference on Evolutionary Computation 1997, pp. 501–506 (1997)
23. Ebner, M.: Evolution of a control architecture for a mobile robot. In: Sipper, M., Mange, D., Pérez-Uribe, A. (eds.) ICES 1998. LNCS, vol. 1478, pp. 303–310. Springer, Heidelberg (1998)
24. Koza, J.: Evolution of subsumption using genetic programming. In: Toward a Practice of Autonomous Systems, Proceedings of the First European Conference on Artificial Life, pp. 110–119. MIT, Cambridge (1992)
25. Furuholmen, M., Hovin, M., Torresen, J., Glette, K.: Continuous Adaptation in Robotic Systems by Indirect Online Evolution. In: Proceedings of Learning and Adaptive Behaviors for Robotic Systems, Lab-Rs 2008, Edinburgh, United Kingdom, August 6-8 (2008)
26. Furuholmen, M., Glette, K., Torresen, J., Hovin, M.: Indirect Online Evolution - A Conceptual Framework for Adaptation in industrial Robotic Systems. In: Hornby, G.S., Sekanina, L., Haddow, P.C. (eds.) ICES 2008. LNCS, vol. 5216, pp. 165–176. Springer, Heidelberg (2008)
27. Hornby, G., Lipson, H., Pollack, J.: Generative representations for the automated design of modular physical robots. IEEE Transactions on Robotics and Automation 19(4), 703–719 (2003)
28. Kowaliw, T., Grogono, P., Kharma, N.: The evolution of structural design through artificial embryogeny. In: Proceedings of the IEEE First International Symposium on Artificial Life (2007)
29. Abelson, H., Disessa, A.: Turtle geometry: The computer as a medium for exploring mathematics. The MIT Press, Cambridge (1986)
30. Holland, J., Reitman, J.: Cognitive systems based on adaptive algorithms. ACM SIGART Bulletin 49 (1977)
31. Dorigo, M., Schnepf, U.: Genetics-based machine learning and behavior-based robotics: a new synthesis. IEEE Transactions on Systems Man and Cybernetics 23(1), 141–154 (1993)
32. Wilson, S.: Classifier conditions using gene expression programming. In: Bacardit, J., Bernadó-Mansilla, E., Butz, M.V., Kovacs, T., Llorà, X., Takadama, K. (eds.) IWLCS 2006 and IWLCS 2007. LNCS (LNAI), vol. 4998, pp. 206–217. Springer, Heidelberg (2008)
33. Ferreira, C.: Gene Expression Programming: a New Adaptive Algorithm for Solving Problems. Arxiv preprint cs.AI/0102027 (2001)
34. Nordin, P., Banzhaf, W., Brameier, M., et al.: Evolution of a world model for a miniature robot using genetic programming. Robotics and Autonomous Systems 25(1), 105–116 (1998)

Phenotypic Diversity in Initial Genetic Programming Populations

David Jackson

Dept. of Computer Science, University of Liverpool
Liverpool L69 3BX, United Kingdom
djackson@liverpool.ac.uk

Abstract. A key factor in the success or otherwise of a genetic programming population in evolving towards a solution is the extent of diversity amongst its members. Diversity may be viewed in genotypic (structural) or in phenotypic (behavioural) terms, but the latter has received less attention. We propose a method for measuring phenotypic diversity in terms of the run-time behaviour of programs. We describe how this is applicable to a range of problem domains and show how the promotion of such diversity in initial genetic programming populations can have a substantial impact on solution-finding performance.

1 Introduction

In genetic programming (GP), the evolutionary process is often characterised by a loss of diversity over time [1,2], with the population settling towards a mixture of just a few high-ranking individuals. This may make it impossible for the process to escape from local optima in the fitness landscape, thereby preventing it from discovering solutions. It is therefore generally accepted that it is important to take steps to instil and subsequently preserve a degree of diversity in GP populations.

One of the difficulties associated with this aim is that there is no general consensus as to how diversity should be measured, and consequently how it should be maintained. Essentially, however, the definitions fall into two camps: *genotypic*, or structural diversity; and *phenotypic*, or behavioural diversity. We shall describe both of these in more depth in Section 2, but the main focus of our paper is on the latter. Existing research on phenotypic diversity has largely concentrated on the fitness values of individuals in a population, and although metrics have been defined to assess its extent, little has been done to promote it.

Our own approach to diversity differs from others in that, rather than involving static analysis or comparisons of fitness, it relies on observations made of the dynamic execution behaviour of individuals. We describe this approach to measuring phenotypic diversity in more detail in Section 3.

In Section 4 we describe experiments which measure phenotypic diversity across a range of problems, and we relate the findings to other diversity metrics. Following this, we investigate the effects of promoting diversity in a population. Another difference from previous work is that we are not concerned here with preserving diversity throughout the lifetime of a run. Instead, we concentrate solely on the role

A.I. Esparcia-Alcazar et al. (Eds.): EuroGP 2010, LNCS 6021, pp. 98–109, 2010.
© Springer-Verlag Berlin Heidelberg 2010

that behavioural diversity can play in the initial population. Studies suggest that the constitution of the population at generation zero can have a significant impact on the dynamics of the remainder of a run [3], and we wish to discover whether that is so for initial populations with altered diversity.

Finally, Section 5 offers some concluding remarks and pointers to future work.

2 Related Work

As it relates to genetic programming, the term 'diversity' has a variety of interpretations, and hence a number of different ways have been proposed for measuring it, creating it and maintaining it. Overviews of diversity measures can be found in [4] and [5], while Burke et al [6] give a more extensive analysis of these measures and of how they relate to fitness.

The most common usage of the term is concerned with differences in the *structure* of individual program trees; that is, in their size, their shape, and in the functions and terminals used at individual nodes. Recognizing the importance of including a wide range of structures in the initial population, Koza [7] proposed the use of a 'ramped half-and-half' algorithm, and many implementations have continued to follow his advice. In this initialisation method, the population is partitioned into a series of tree depths ranging from 2 to some upper value (usually 6). At each of these depths d, half the program trees are created using the so-called 'full' method and half using the 'grow' method. A tree created using the 'full' method has the property that every path from root to terminal node has the same depth d. Creating such a tree involves choosing nodes from the problem function set at each tree level until the maximum depth is reached. In the 'grow' method, on the other hand, nodes at each tree level lower than the maximum are selected randomly from the function and terminal sets. This means that some path lengths may reach the upper value d, but others may be shorter.

The ramped half-and-half approach is claimed to give good diversity in the structure of program fragments which can then be combined and integrated to produce more complex and hopefully fitter programs. What it does not do, however, is to ensure that each member of the initial population is unique in its structure. In his first book [7], Koza therefore recommends that the initialisation code in a GP system should also strive to ensure such uniqueness.

Measurements of structural diversity may involve nothing more than simple node-for-node comparison of program trees; where trees are stored in a 'flattened' character form, this may equate to basic string operations. More sophisticated structural diversity metrics may be based on edit distance [8], where the similarity between two individuals is measured in terms of the number of edit operations required to turn one into the other.

A difficulty with comparing individuals based on their apparent structure is that program trees which are seemingly very different in appearance may in fact compute identical functions. Seeing beyond these surface differences requires the use of graph isomorphism techniques, but these are computationally expensive and become even more so as program trees grow larger over time. A simpler, less costly alternative is to check for pseudo-isomorphism [5], in which the possibility of true isomorphism is assessed based on characteristics such as tree depth and the numbers of terminals and functions present. However, the accuracy of this assessment may be subject to the presence of introns in the code; Wyns et al [9] describe an attempt to improve on this situation through the use of program simplification techniques to remove redundant code.

In contrast, *behavioural* or *phenotypic* diversity metrics are based on the functionality of individuals, i.e. the execution of program trees rather than their appearance. Usually, behavioural diversity is viewed in terms of the spread of fitness values obtained on evaluating each member of the population [10]. One way of measuring such diversity is by considering the fitness distribution as an indicator of entropy, or disorder, in the population [11, 9]. Other approaches consider sets or lists of fitness values and use them in combination with genotypic measures [12, 13]. For certain types of problem it may be possible to achieve the effect of behavioural diversity without invoking the fitness function, via the use of semantic sampling schemes [14].

Semantic analysis of programs is also used in the diversity enhancing techniques described by Beadle and Johnson [15]. In their population initialisation experiments, unique behaviours are generated and converted to the corresponding syntax. The approach seems most applicable to problems in the Boolean domain, although it adds considerably to the initialisation time and is not always an improvement over standard GP at finding solutions (e.g. the 11-multiplexer and Majority-5 problems).

3 Phenotypic Diversity

Our own approach to diversity differs from others in that it does not involve structural considerations, fitness values or semantic analysis of programs. Instead, it focuses on the observed behaviour of individuals when they are executed. To investigate this fully, we have applied it to a variety of problem domains; these comprise two Boolean problems (6-multiplexer and even-4 parity), two navigation problems (Santa Fe and maze traversal), and one numeric problem (symbolic regression of a polynomial).

In the 6-mux problem, the aim is to evolve a program that interprets the binary value on two address inputs (A0 and A1) in order to select which of the four data inputs (D0-D3) to pass onto the output. The function set is {AND, OR, NOT, IF}. Fitness evaluation is exhaustive over all 64 combinations of input values, with an individual's fitness being given in terms of the number of mismatches with expected outputs.

In the even-4 parity problem we search for a program which, given 4 binary inputs, returns TRUE if the number of inputs set to logic 1 is even, and FALSE otherwise. The function set is {AND, OR, NAND, NOR} and fitness is in the range 0-16.

The Santa Fe artificial ant problem consists of evolving an algorithm to guide an artificial ant through a 32x32 matrix in such a way that it discovers as many food pellets as possible. The 89 pellets are laid in a path which frequently changes direction and which contains gaps of varying sizes. The ant can move directly ahead, move left, move right, and determine if food is present in the square immediately ahead of it. These faculties are all encoded in the function and terminal sets of the problem, along with Lisp-like PROGN connectives for joining actions in sequence.

To prevent exhaustive or interminable searching, the ant is allowed a maximum of 600 steps in which to complete the task.

Our other navigation problem is that of finding a route through a maze. Although less well-known than the ant problem, it has been used as the subject for research on introns in several studies [16-18]. The maze is shown in Fig. 1, with the initial position and orientation of the agent to be guided through it indicated by the arrow. The agent can turn left or right, move forward or backward, and test whether there is a wall ahead or not. A no-op terminal does nothing except to expend an instruction cycle. Decision making is via an if-then-else function, whilst iteration is achieved via a while function. Program fitness is measured in terms of how close the agent gets to the exit: zero fitness indicates escape from the maze. Navigation continues until the maze is successfully completed, or an upper bound of 1000 instruction cycles is reached.

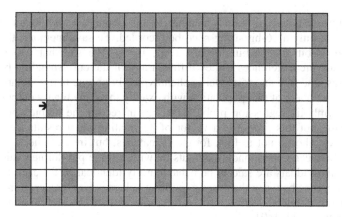

Fig. 1. Pre-defined maze used in the maze navigation problem

Our final problem is symbolic regression of a polynomial. In our version of this, the polynomial we attempt to match through evolution is $4x^4 - 3x^3 + 2x^2 - x$. The only terminal is x, and the function set is $\{+, -, *, /\}$, with the division operator being protected to ensure that divide-by-zero does not occur. The fitness cases consist of 32 x-values in the range [0,1), starting at 0.0 and increasing in steps of 1/32, plus the corresponding y-values. Fitness is calculated as the sum of absolute errors in the y-values computed by an individual, whilst success is measured in terms of the number of 'hits' – a hit being a y-value that differs from the expected output by no more than 0.01 in magnitude.

Aside from the maze traversal problem, all of the above are commonly-used benchmark problems that are described more fully elsewhere (e.g. by Koza [7]). Other parameters as they apply to the experiments described in the remainder of this paper are shown in Table 1.

In the case of the Boolean problems, the behaviour of an individual is measured in terms of the outputs it produces; this is recorded as a string of binary values for each of the test cases used during fitness evaluation. So, for the 6-mux problem, there is a

Table 1. GP system parameters common to all experiments

Population size	500
Initialisation method	Ramped half-and-half
Evolutionary process	Steady state
Selection	5-candidate tournament
No. generations	51 generational equivalents (initial+50)
No. runs	100
Prob. crossover	0.9
Mutation	None
Prob. internal node used as crossover point	0.9

64-bit string associated with each member of the population, while for the even-4 parity problem only a 16-bit string need be recorded. To save memory, these can be packed into 64-bit and 16-bit integers, respectively. We say that two individuals exhibit phenotypic differences if they differ in any of the corresponding bits in their output strings, and that an individual is phenotypically unique in a population if there are no other members of that population with exactly the same binary output string.

For the symbolic regression problem, we again record the outputs produced for each test case, but this time it is a vector of 32 floating point results. In comparing phenotypes we choose not to look for exact matches, but instead check whether the differences between corresponding outputs lie within some pre-defined value epsilon. Hence, two individuals are said to be behaviourally identical if, for each x-value, the absolute difference between the corresponding y-values is less than epsilon. The value for epsilon was arbitrarily chosen to be the same as that used to check for 'hits' in fitness assessment, i.e. 0.01.

For the two navigation problems, the situation is complicated by the fact that the evolving programs do not produce outputs as such: their behaviour is measured in terms of the movements produced by function and terminal execution. Because of this, the record we make of an individual's behaviour is the sequence of moves it makes in the grid or maze during execution. We are not concerned with recording any left or right turns that are executed while remaining on a square, nor with any decision making via execution of statements such as IF_FOOD_AHEAD or WALL_AHEAD.

To record the path histories, we associate with each individual in the population a vector of {north, east, south, west} moves. Each time the executing program moves to a different square, the heading is added to the end of the vector. Since a program times-out after a fixed number of steps (600 for the ant problem, 1000 for the maze), we know that the vector cannot be longer than that number of elements per individual, and so memory occupancy is not a huge issue. Determining behavioural differences between individuals becomes simply a matter of comparing these direction vectors.

4 Diversity Experiments

The first question to be addressed is whether there is in fact a substantial lack of diversity in initial, randomly-generated populations. To determine this, we can count the number of distinct program structures present in the population and, using the methods outlined above, we can also determine the number of distinct behaviours. One other metric we can include is the *fitness diversity*, which represents the spread of fitness values present in the population. Unlike either structural or behavioural diversity, in which every member of the population can be unique, the range of possible fitness values tends to be much smaller than the population size, and varies from problem to problem. We therefore define fitness diversity (FD) to be the number of distinct fitness values found in the population divided by the number of possible values. For example, if a given population in the even-4 parity problem contained a total of 5 different fitness values, then its FD would be 5/17 = 0.294, since the problem allows for 17 possible fitness values (0-16). On this scale, a value of 1.0 would indicate full fitness diversity (which would also imply that the population contained a solution!).

Table 2 presents the structural diversity (SD), the behavioural diversity (BD), and the fitness diversity (FD) for each of our problems. It also shows the best and average fitness of the initial populations, normalised in the range [0, 1], with lower values being better and zero representing a solution. All the figures are averages taken over 100 runs.

Table 2. Diversity and fitness in initial populations

Problem	SD	BD	FD	Best	Av
6-mux	315	257	0.372	0.258	0.46
Even-4	330	170	0.276	0.386	0.5
Regression	326	202	0.153	0.773	0.977
Ant	395	290	0.282	0.603	0.965
Maze	314	29	0.160	0.883	0.998

The first thing to note about this table is that the ramped half-and-half method produces a large number of structural duplicates in the initial population. The number of distinct structures in the population of 500 ranges from 314 in the maze problem to 395 in the ant problem; the other programs are all structural clones of these. To put it another way, 21% to 37% of all population members are copies of other individuals. This suggests that Koza's advice to remove structural duplicates may indeed have some merit.

The situation with regard to behaviour is worse still. At best, the ramped half-and-half algorithm manages to produce 290 distinct behaviours, but that still means there are 210 individuals (42% of the population) behaving in an identical way to other programs. This figure for redundant behaviours rises to a remarkable 94% in the case of the maze problem. Closer investigation reveals that the vast majority of duplicates in this problem are those programs which fail to move the agent from the initial square of the maze, i.e. their recorded path lengths are zero.

In almost all respects, the maze problem seems to come off worst in the make-up of its initial populations. Aside from fitness diversity, in which it is almost as bad as the regression problem, it has the lowest diversity and fitness values of all the problems. By contrast, the 6-mux problem has amongst the highest behavioural and fitness diversity levels and is 'closest' to a solution in terms of its best and average fitness values. In general, however, there appears to be little in the way of correlation between the table columns. The ant problem, for example, has SD and BD levels that are higher than those of 6-mux, but it has a worse FD level and an average fitness that is more than twice as poor.

If we are to attempt to eliminate duplicates being created in the initial population, we need to make alterations to the ramped half-and-half algorithm. We can define the following pseudo-code for this:

```
function duplicated(prog)
    for each member of population created prior to prog
        if member is equivalent to prog
            return TRUE
        endif
    endfor
    return FALSE
endfunction

function initialise_population
    for each prog in the population
        attempts = 0
        depth = assigned depth of this program tree
        do
            create prog tree using ramped half-and-half
                                      at current depth
            attempts = attempts + 1
            if (attempts >= MAX_ATTEMPTS and depth < MAX_DEPTH)
                attempts = 0
                depth = depth + 1
            endif
            test_fitness(prog)
        while (duplicated(prog))
    endfor
endfunction
```

As described earlier, the ramped half-and-half method partitions the population into a sequence of initial depths, usually from 2 up to 6. For each individual, the algorithm above creates a program tree with the assigned depth, then immediately tests its fitness so that its behaviour can be recorded. The program is then compared with previously created members using the duplicated() function, which can be implemented as necessary to check either for genotypic or phenotypic equivalence. If the new program is a duplicate, the tree creation code is executed again and another check made. If a pre-defined number of attempts using the assigned tree depth is ever exceeded, that depth is incremented to give the algorithm a greater chance of finding a program that differs from other members. In our experiments we set MAX_ATTEMPTS to 5.

An interesting question is how much impact the elimination of structural clones (as advocated by Koza) has on phenotypic diversity. Clearly, two programs that are genotypically identical will also be phenotypically identical, and so structural diversity should help to increase behavioural diversity. Table 3 shows the effects produced when the algorithm given above is used to eliminate identical program structures.

Table 3. Diversity and fitness measures when structural clones prevented. Figures in parentheses show differences from Table 2.

Problem	SD	BD	FD	Best	Av
6-mux	500 (+185)	368 (+111)	0.383 (+0.011)	0.249 (-0.009)	0.464 (+0.004)
Even-4	500 (+170)	222 (+52)	0.280 (+0.004)	0.378 (-0.008)	0.5 (0.00)
Regression	500 (+174)	272 (+70)	0.182 (+0.029)	0.789 (+0.016)	0.980 (+0.003)
Ant	500 (+105)	338 (+48)	0.286 (+0.004)	0.603 (0.00)	0.964 (-0.001)
Maze	500 (+186)	29 (0)	0.160 (0.0)	0.85 (-0.033)	0.998 (0.0)

For all problems, our algorithm has managed to eliminate all structural duplicates from the initial population. However, the number of new behaviours introduced in each case falls far short of the number of new structures added. Creating an individual that is genotypically unique does not necessarily mean it will be phenotypically unique. The maze problem again provides the most striking illustration of this: although it adds the most new structures (186) to its population, it adds by far the fewest new behaviours (i.e. none!). We still have 94% of the population exhibiting behaviour that appears elsewhere, and such programs therefore have identical fitness. Even in the best case (6-mux), 26% of the population are still behavioural clones.

The effects on fitness diversity and on best and average fitnesses are fairly minimal. The largest increase in FD is in the regression problem, but even here, this increase is equivalent to moving from 5 distinct fitness vales to 6 values; moreover, the best and average fitness values actually worsen.

The next step is to examine the impact of eliminating behavioural clones, using the algorithm outlined earlier (clearly this will also eliminate structural duplicates). Table 4 shows what happens to fitness diversity and the best and average fitnesses when this is implemented.

Although the increases in fitness diversity are greater than those obtained by removing structural duplicates, they are still small. Even for the maze problem, the increase represents a shift from 4 or 5 distinct fitness values per initial population to only 6 per population. Best and average fitness values also alter little, with average values sometimes even degrading (although not by a statistically significant amount). Again, the biggest improvement in the best fitness value is in the maze problem.

If our measures to promote genotypic and phenotypic diversity have so little effect on fitness diversity and the overall fitness of the initial populations, it must be wondered whether these techniques are sufficient in themselves to improve the performance of a genetic programming system. Table 5 compares the number of solutions found in 100 runs of GP on each of our benchmark problems. A 'standard' GP system with no attempt at duplicate removal is presented alongside a system which removes structural duplicates and one which removes behavioural duplicates.

Table 4. Fitness values when behavioural duplicates prevented. Figures in parentheses give differences from Table 2.

Problem	FD	Best	Av
6-mux	0.395 (+0.023)	0.243 (-0.015)	0.469 (+0.009)
Even-4	0.330 (+0.054)	0.355 (-0.031)	0.5 (0.0)
Regression	0.195 (+0.042)	0.762 (-0.011)	0.983 (+0.006)
Ant	0.312 (+0.030)	0.568 (-0.035)	0.956 (-0.009)
Maze	0.316 (+0.156)	0.652 (-0.231)	0.966 (-0.032)

Table 5. Solution rate for GP systems with and without duplicate prevention. Figures are percentages of solutions found in 100 runs.

Problem	Standard	No Struct Dups	No Behav Dups
6-mux	56	66	79
Even-4	14	11	23
Regression	10	10	24
Ant	13	9	18
Maze	14	18	51

It can be seen from this table that the removal of structural duplicates does not always have a beneficial effect on solution finding performance. However, when behavioural duplicates are eliminated, the performance improves dramatically. This is especially true of the maze problem, in which the solution rate jumps from 14% to 51%. A t-test ($p < 0.05$) performed on the best fitness values found at the end of each run indicates that the improvements are statistically significant.

To make the comparison fair, we have to ask at what cost our improvements are obtained. One commonly used method of comparing cost is Koza's computational effort metric [7], which computes the minimum number of individuals that must be processed to obtain a certain probability (usually 0.99) that a solution will be found. However, Koza's metric assumes a fixed number of fitness evaluations per generation, which for our purposes is not applicable because of the additional effort required to create the initial populations.

Table 6 shows precisely how much extra effort is required for each problem when ensuring that phenotypic duplication is suppressed in generation zero. The metric we have used is a count of the fitness evaluations performed during initialization. In our standard GP system, and in GP systems in which it is only structural uniqueness that is desired, each individual is tested for fitness only once, and so the total number of fitness evaluations is equal to the population size (500 in our example problems). Table 6 shows how much this figure increases when we have to perform repeated

Table 6. Count of fitness evaluations required for initial populations when behavioural duplication prevented. Figures averaged over 100 runs.

Problem	Evaluations
6-mux	1847
Even-4	3759
Regression	2494
Ant	1933
Maze	4232953

evaluations to find behaviourally unique programs. Particularly striking is (as usual) the maze problem, in which it is extremely difficult to discover programs that exhibit behaviour not previously found in the population.

These figures do not tell the whole story, however, since the increased initial effort may be counter-balanced by the reduction of effort required to find solutions in subsequent generations. Hence, to achieve a proper comparison, we count the number of fitness evaluations performed over all runs and divide this figure by the number of solutions found. This gives us measured effort in terms of the number of evaluations per solution. Table 7 compares the results obtained for the various approaches to creating the initial population.

Table 7. Effort (evaluations per solution) for GP systems with and without duplication prevention

Problem	Standard	No Struct Dups	No Behav Dups
6-mux	23263	16416	12140
Even-4	151518	195781	101570
Regression	217612	217486	88430
Ant	158498	240285	118068
Maze	150959	115998	8329286

In all cases except the maze problem, the effort required when behavioural duplicates are prevented in the initial population is significantly lower than that needed for standard GP and for GP with no structural clones. Despite the substantial increase in the number of solutions obtained in the maze problem, this is not enough to counter the large number of fitness evaluations required for initialisation in that problem.

5 Conclusions

While it is generally accepted that it is important to create and maintain diversity in evolving populations, opinions differ as to how such diversity should be assessed, and consequently how it should be enhanced. The usual approach is to base it on static comparisons of program structure, with many GP systems following Koza's advice to prohibit structural duplication in the initial GP population. Our experiments, however, suggest that such approaches are limited in their effectiveness. As an alternative, we have proposed the introduction of phenotypic diversity into populations, this being based on the dynamic behaviour of individuals. We have shown that the approach is not specific to one type of problem, but is applicable to a range of domains, including Boolean problems, numeric problems, and navigation scenarios.

Although the introduction of phenotypic diversity into an initial population does not radically alter its fitness characteristics, the variety of new behaviours is sufficient to encourage more widespread search of the program space, and therefore to improve solution-finding performance in all the problems we investigated. The associated cost is an increase in the number of fitness evaluations required to generate the initial population, but, for most problems, this is outweighed by the overall reduction in the cost per solution. In the case of the maze problem, the difficulty of ensuring uniqueness in the initial population leads to a huge number of fitness evaluations at the creation stage. For problems such as this, it might be better to place an upper limit on the number of new programs that are created for each member that enters the population. This would promote diversity but allow some duplication.

Other avenues for future research concern the ways in which differences in behaviour are measured. At present, two individuals are considered different if their outputs differ in just one test case, or their navigational paths differ by one coordinate. We wish to examine the use of phenotypic diversity metrics which can be 'tuned' to create greater differences between members of a population. We also plan to investigate the use of diversity-promoting algorithms in the post-initialisation stages of the evolutionary process.

References

1. McPhee, N.F., Hopper, N.J.: Analysis of Genetic Diversity through Program History. In: Banzhaf, W., et al. (eds.) Proc. Genetic and Evolutionary Computation Conf., Florida, USA, pp. 1112–1120 (1999)
2. Daida, J.M., Ward, D.J., Hilss, A.M., Long, S.L., Hodges, M.R., Kriesel, J.T.: Visualizing the Loss of Diversity in Genetic Programming. In: Proc. IEEE Congress on Evolutionary Computation, Portland, Oregon, USA, pp. 1225–1232 (2004)
3. Daida, J.M.: Towards Identifying Populations that Increase the Likelihood of Success in Genetic Programming. In: Beyer, H.-G., et al. (eds.) Proc. Genetic and Evolutionary Computing Conf. (GECCO 2005), Washington DC, USA, pp. 1627–1634 (2005)
4. Hien, N.T., Hoai, N.X.: A Brief Overview of Population Diversity Measures in Genetic Programming. In: Pham, T.L., et al. (eds.) Proc. 3rd Asian-Pacific Workshop on Genetic Programming, Hanoi, Vietnam, pp. 128–139 (2006)
5. Burke, E., Gustafson, S., Kendall, G., Krasnogor, N.: Advanced Population Diversity Measures in Genetic Programming. In: Guervós, J.J.M., Adamidis, P.A., Beyer, H.-G., Fernández-Villacañas, J.-L., Schwefel, H.-P. (eds.) PPSN 2002. LNCS, vol. 2439, pp. 341–350. Springer, Heidelberg (2002)
6. Burke, E., Gustafson, S., Kendall, G.: Diversity in Genetic Programming: An Analysis of Measures and Correlation with Fitness. IEEE Transactions on Evolutionary Computation 8(1), 47–62 (2004)
7. Koza, J.R.: Genetic Programming: On the Programming of Computers by Means of Natural Selection. MIT Press, Cambridge (1992)

8. de Jong, E.D., Watson, R.A., Pollack, J.B.: Reducing Bloat and Promoting Diversity using Multi-Objective Methods. In: Spector, L., et al. (eds.) Proc. Genetic Evolutionary Computation Conf., San Francisco, CA, USA, pp. 11–18 (2001)
9. Wyns, B., de Bruyne, P., Boullart, L.: Characterizing Diversity in Genetic Programming. In: Collet, P., Tomassini, M., Ebner, M., Gustafson, S., Ekárt, A. (eds.) EuroGP 2006. LNCS, vol. 3905, pp. 250–259. Springer, Heidelberg (2006)
10. Rosca, J.P.: Genetic Programming Exploratory Power and the Discovery of Functions. In: McDonnell, J.R., et al. (eds.) Proc. 4th Conf. Evolutionary Programming, San Diego, CA, USA, pp. 719–736 (1995)
11. Rosca, J.P.: Entropy-Driven Adaptive Representation. In: Rosca, J.P. (ed.) Proc. Workshop on Genetic Programming: From Theory to Real-World Applications, Tahoe City, CA, USA, pp. 23–32 (1995)
12. D'haeseleer, P., Bluming, J.: Effects of Locality in Individual and Population Evolution. In: Kinnear, K.E., et al. (eds.) Advances in Genetic Programming, ch. 8, pp. 177–198. MIT Press, Cambridge (1994)
13. Ryan, C.: Pygmies and Civil Servants. In: Kinnear, K.E., et al. (eds.) Advances in Genetic Programming, ch. 11, pp. 243–263. MIT Press, Cambridge (1994)
14. Looks, M.: On the Behavioural Diversity of Random Programs. In: Thierens, D., et al. (eds.) Proc. Genetic and Evolutionary Computing Conf. (GECCO 2007), London, England, UK, pp. 1636–1642 (2007)
15. Beadle, L., Johnson, C.G.: Semantic Analysis of Program Initialisation in Genetic Programming. Genetic Programming and Evolvable Machines 10(3), 307–337 (2009)
16. Soule, T.: Code Growth in Genetic Programming. PhD Thesis, University of Idaho (1998)
17. Langdon, W.B., Soule, T., Poli, R., Foster, J.A.: The Evolution of Size and Shape. In: Spector, L., et al. (eds.) Advances in Genetic Programming, vol. 3, pp. 163–190. MIT Press, Cambridge (1999)
18. Jackson, D.: Dormant Program Nodes and the Efficiency of Genetic Programming. In: Beyer, H.-G., et al. (eds.) Proc. Genetic and Evolutionary Computing Conf. (GECCO 2005), Washington DC, USA, pp. 1745–1751 (2005)

A Relaxed Approach to Simplification in Genetic Programming

Mark Johnston[1], Thomas Liddle[1], and Mengjie Zhang[2]

[1] School of Mathematics, Statistics and Operations Research
[2] School of Engineering and Computer Science
Victoria University of Wellington, P.O. Box 600, Wellington, New Zealand
{mark.johnston,liddlethom}@msor.vuw.ac.nz, mengjie.zhang@ecs.vuw.ac.nz

Abstract. We propose a novel approach to program simplification in tree-based Genetic Programming, based upon numerical relaxations of algebraic rules. We also separate proposal of simplifications from an acceptance criterion that checks the effect of proposed simplifications on the evaluation of training examples, looking several levels up the tree. We test our simplification method on three classification datasets and conclude that the success of linear regression is dataset dependent, that looking further up the tree can catch ineffective simplifications, and that CPU time can be significantly reduced while maintaining classification accuracy on unseen examples.

1 Introduction

One problem that limits the effective application of Genetic Programming is *program bloat* [1][2][3][4][5][6][7][8], where program trees tend to grow in size over the generations, causing the GP process to be computationally expensive. Bloat may arise from "model overfitting" (formulating a model that is more complicated than necessary to fit a set of training examples) but equally may occur with no fitness benefit. In addition, program trees sometimes appear contrived to make the best use of the available constant values set in the initial population. Several methods have been proposed to combat bloat: setting a maximum depth or number of nodes of a GP tree [1][4][9]; modifying the fitness function to reward smaller programs (parsimony pressure) [10][11][12]; dynamically creating fitness holes [5]; and operator equalisation [3].

In tree-based GP, program trees in the population may exhibit some algebraic redundancy, i.e., the mathematical expressions that the trees represent can often be directly mathematically simplified during the evolutionary process. This was first proposed by Koza [1] with his editing operation. Two approaches to simplification of programs are the algebraic and numerical approaches. In the *algebraic* approach [13][14][15], the rules of algebra are used (in a bottom-up fashion) to directly simplify the mathematical expression that the tree represents. In the *numerical* approach [16][17], the evaluation of each of the set of training examples is examined to determine if particular subtrees can be approximated by a single constant, removed altogether, or replaced by a smaller subtree. This is

A.I. Esparcia-Alcazar et al. (Eds.): EuroGP 2010, LNCS 6021, pp. 110–121, 2010.
© Springer-Verlag Berlin Heidelberg 2010

similar to "lossy compression" of images and aims for a minimal effect upon the evaluation of training examples.

In this paper, we propose to split the process of simplification into two roles: *proposers* which propose a local change to the program tree; and an *acceptor* which evaluates the proposed local change and determines whether to accept or reject it. The novel aspects are that the proposers use numerical relaxations of algebraic simplification rules, including linear regression, and that the acceptor evaluates the effect of the proposed local change further up the tree. The overall research goal is to determine how simplification affects classification accuracy and computational effort for classification problems. In particular, we wish to balance the number and severity of simplifications proposed (reduction in tree size or wasted proposals that are not accepted) and the additional workload in evaluating them.

The remainder of this paper is structured as follows. Section 2 provides background on algebraic and numerical approaches to simplification in GP programs. Section 3 develops our new approach to simplification of GP programs based upon a relaxation of the algebraic rules and separating the roles of simplification proposer and simplification acceptor. Section 4 describes computational experiments on three datasets and Section 5 discusses the results. Finally, Section 6 draws some conclusions and makes recommendations for future research directions.

2   Algebraic and Numerical Approaches to Simplification

In this section we review some existing algebraic and numerical approaches to the simplification of a program in tree-based GP. We consider a simple GP system which includes the basic arithmetic operators ($+$, $-$, $\times$ and protected division %) together with an `ifpos` operator (which returns the middle child if the left child is positive, and otherwise returns the right child).

2.1   Algebraic Simplification

Algebraic simplification of a GP tree involves the *exact* application of the simple rules of algebra to nodes of the tree in order to produce a smaller tree representing an exactly equivalent mathematical expression. For example, for constants a and c and subtree B, we can replace the subtree $a \times (B \times c)$ with the subtree $b \times B$ where $b = a \times c$ is a new constant node. This can be implemented efficiently using hashing in the finite field $\mathbb{Z}_p$ for prime p [14,15]. The strength of this approach is that any proposed simplification has *no global* effect on the evaluation of any training example. The weakness is that the rules of algebra are applied exactly, i.e., there is no scope for approximate equivalence, nor equivalence across the domain of the training examples. There are also some algebraic simplifications that are difficult for a basic set of locally applied algebraic rules to recognise when applied in a bottom-up fashion.

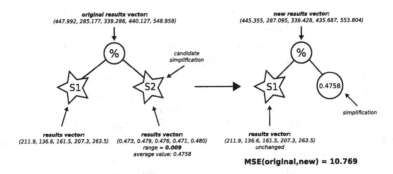

Fig. 1. An example where range simplification causes a (possibly) significant change to the tree one level up. The left subtree (S1) has relatively large values in its results vector (the evaluation of the subtree on the training examples), and is divided by the right subtree (S2) which has relatively small evaluation values. Even though the range of S2 is only 0.009, the division means the simplification potentially magnifies the changes further up the tree.

2.2   Numerical Simplification

Numerical simplification of a GP tree involves the replacement of a subtree with a smaller (possibly *approximate*) substitute based upon the *local* effect on the evaluation of the training examples. Two simple methods recently investigated are:

1. *Range simplification* [16]. In evaluating the training examples, if the range of values a node takes is sufficiently small (less than a *range threshold*), then the node is replaced by a single constant-node (the average value). The strengths of range simplification are that equivalence is based only upon the observed range of the training examples; it also deals with nodes that are calculated from constant values; it allows for features or subtrees with a very small range of values to be simplified; and it is computationally inexpensive. However, the weakness is that local simplifications can have an adverse effect further up the tree in some cases. Figure 1 gives an indication of the potential effect of a local range simplification further up the tree. These changes may have a large effect on the outcome, but could otherwise be swamped by other sources of noise or uncertainty.

2. *Removing redundant children* [17]. In evaluating the training examples, if the difference between the values at a parent node and its child are sufficiently small (less than a *redundancy threshold* in this paper) then the parent can be replaced by the child. Song et al [17] use the criterion that the sum of absolute deviations (SAD) be zero over all training examples, i.e., $\sum_i |p_i - c_i| = 0$ where p_i and c_i are the evaluation of the ith training example at the parent and child respectively. This is a slight relaxation of algebraic simplification to the actual range of values taken by the training examples.

3   New Relaxed Approach to Simplification

We propose a new relaxed approach to simplification. Firstly, we use numerical evaluation of the training examples to determine if the algebraic rules are approximately satisfied. Secondly, we evaluate the numerical effect of any proposed local simplifications further up the tree before accepting them. Hence, we clearly separate the proposal of a local simplification from the acceptance or rejection of the proposal based upon its effect on the numerical evaluation of the training examples. This addresses the weakness of exact algebraic simplification by covering simple algebraic rules and allows for approximate satisfaction of these rules. It also addresses the weakness of local numerical simplification by looking at the effect further up the tree before accepting a proposed simplification.

3.1   Proposers

In this paper we use three numerical simplification operators — range simplification and removal of redundant children (as in Section 2.2), and linear regression (described further below) — to numerically evaluate possible algebraic simplifications, relaxing each equality slightly. Between the three operators, we cover most simple algebraic rules. We make a small modification to each of the first two operators presented before: for simplicity, we use a constant range threshold for range simplification; and we use mean square error (MSE) for redundancy checking (rather than SAD).

Linear regression. Consider the nodes Y and S in a GP tree, where S is a child or grandchild subtree of Y. If we can approximate Y by

$$Y = b \times S + a \tag{1}$$

or

$$Y = b \% S + a \tag{2}$$

sufficiently closely for some constants a and b, then we may be able to significantly reduce the size of the tree. This is an extension of simple algebraic rules and allows for *approximate linearity* of node Y against subtree S (or $\frac{1}{S}$). Figure 2 gives two examples in which linear regression will reduce a tree where other simplification methods do not. A candidate simplification's tree size using this method will be a maximum of $4 + |S|$ nodes, with a possible simplification to $2 + |S|$ under certain conditions on a and b, where $|S|$ is the number of nodes in subtree S. To evaluate linearity, we use Pearson's correlation coefficient. We consider all children and grandchildren of Y as S for simplification and choose the one with the highest value of Pearson's r^2 greater than a *regression threshold*. The proposal is to replace node Y by the simplest version of equation (1) or (2) as appropriate.

3.2   Acceptor

In order to check that a proposed simplification won't cause a significant change further up the tree, we compare the results vectors (the evaluation of the subtree

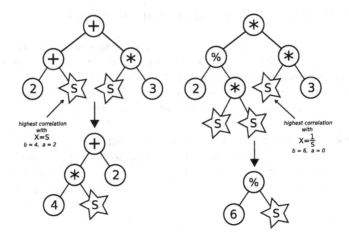

Fig. 2. Simplification examples that are not covered by simple (local) algebraic rules, but are covered by linear regression. Here S represents a particular repeated subtree in each example and Y corresponds to the entire subtree.

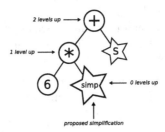

Fig. 3. The acceptor evaluates the effect of a proposed simplification n levels up the tree. Here, arrows point to the node that the MSE calculation applies.

on all training examples) of the old and new (simplified) tree. Figure 3 illustrates which nodes are checked against for different values of n. We go to the ancestor node n levels up and calculate the mean square error (MSE) at that node, i.e., $\sum_i (new_i - old_i)^2$, where old_i and new_i are the original and newly simplified evaluations of the ith training example respectively. If the MSE is less than an *acceptance threshold*, then we accept the simplification and make the change to the tree; if it is not, then we reject the simplification and keep the old tree. In this way we aim to change the tree's fitness as little as possible.

4   Experimental Design

Datasets. To test our simplification system we ran experiments on three different classification datasets: Coins (14 features, 3 classes, [14][16]), Wine (13 features, 3 classes, [18]) and Breast-Cancer Wisconsin (9 features, 2 classes, [19]). Coins consists of 600 images (each 64×64 pixels) of five cent pieces against a random noisy background. Wine gives the result of a chemical analysis of Italian wines from three cultivars (the classes). Each instance of the Breast-Cancer Wisconsin dataset corresponds to a benign or malignant diagnosis.

GP system setup. All experiments were run with the following setup: population size 100, number of generations 100, maximum depth of tree 40, mutation rate 28%, crossover rate 70%, elitism rate 2%. The terminal set consists of the features and random float numbers in the range $[-10, 10]$. We used *static range selection* [20] to choose the class from the tree output and ten-fold cross validation to evaluate each tree in the population.

Simplification frequency. We perform simplification checks on the whole population every k generations, simplifying the population before the selection process occurs for the next generation. We do not simplify the initial population as this may remove too many of the useful "building blocks" present.

Choice of threshold values. For the operators we have implemented there are six different thresholds that we need to test in our experiments: the *proposal thresholds* (range width, redundant MSE and regression r^2); the *acceptance thresholds* (acceptance MSE and the number of levels to look up n); and simplifying the population every k generations. Preliminary experiments suggested a reasonable range of values of each threshold. The set of values for each threshold used in our more extensive experiments can be seen in Table 1, so considering all combinations we have $3^5 \times 4 = 972$ configurations in total, and we ran each configuration on the same set of 100 random seeds.

5   Results and Discussion

Classification accuracy vs computational effort. Table 1 summarises the results for each dataset. The base result is a standard GP with no simplification (and recall that the maximum tree depth is 40), for comparison with all other results. All datasets performed differently in our tests. Regarding average test accuracy, the Coins dataset fluctuated greatly over all configurations, some performing much worse than the base system, but some also a lot better (see Figure 4). On the other hand, the Wisconsin dataset's average test accuracy is virtually unchanged in the range $[95.22\%, 95.71\%]$, while the Wine dataset is at least 8–9% worse than the base system. When considering computational effort (CPU time), all datasets show significant savings. The biggest 'reasonable' time savings (meaning not too much degradation in test accuracy) for the Coins dataset is approximately 75% savings, Wisconsin 60%, and Wine 35%. The Wine dataset runs so quickly, however, that changes in CPU time are difficult to measure accurately, and the time taken across all configurations varies within approximately 0.1 of a second.

Proposal and acceptance thresholds. In general as we increase the value of each of the range width, redundant MSE and acceptance MSE thresholds, CPU time

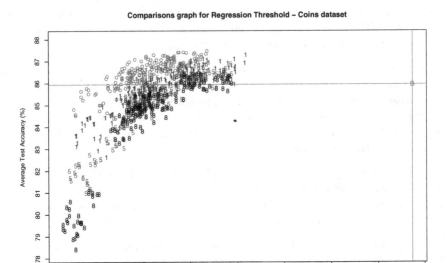

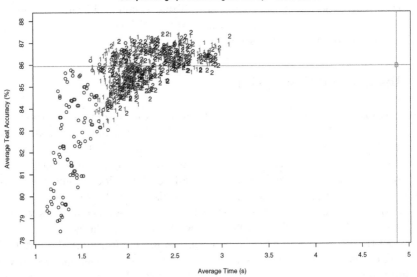

Fig. 4. Two scatter plots showing the average test accuracy vs average CPU time for the Coins dataset. Each point is one of the 972 configurations. The top graph highlights the different values for the regression threshold ('o' = no regression, '1' = 0.99, '5' = 0.95, and '8' = 0.80), and the bottom graph highlights looking n levels up. The lines represent the performance of the base system for comparison.

Table 1. Average CPU time taken (in seconds) and test classification accuracy (as a proportion) grouped by different thresholds for each dataset. Results for each of the three levels of the range threshold are collected over $3^4 \times 4 = 324$ combinations of the other five thresholds, etc.

	Coins				Wine				Wisconsin			
	Time	(s.d.)	T.Acc	(s.d.)	Time	(s.d.)	T.Acc	(s.d.)	Time	(s.d.)	T.Acc	(s.d.)
Base	4.87	1.80	0.8594	0.0314	1.09	0.40	0.7346	0.0379	6.66	2.27	0.9532	0.0063
Range Threshold												
0.1	2.07	0.25	0.8490	0.0205	0.70	0.02	0.6567	0.0305	3.93	0.55	0.9546	0.0020
0.5	1.96	0.22	0.8498	0.0202	0.70	0.02	0.6503	0.0295	3.89	0.53	0.9546	0.0021
1.0	1.89	0.20	0.8489	0.0192	0.70	0.02	0.6466	0.0287	3.84	0.52	0.9545	0.0021
Redundancy Threshold												
0.01	2.11	0.26	0.8540	0.0188	0.70	0.02	0.6531	0.0295	3.92	0.54	0.9546	0.0020
0.05	1.94	0.21	0.8491	0.0203	0.70	0.02	0.6507	0.0294	3.88	0.53	0.9546	0.0021
0.10	1.88	0.20	0.8445	0.0205	0.70	0.02	0.6498	0.0296	3.86	0.53	0.9546	0.0021
Regression Threshold												
none	1.96	0.26	0.8632	0.0210	0.70	0.02	0.6399	0.0295	3.42	0.57	0.9541	0.0024
0.99	2.07	0.25	0.8547	0.0220	0.71	0.02	0.6582	0.0314	4.22	0.61	0.9543	0.0022
0.95	1.96	0.21	0.8446	0.0201	0.70	0.02	0.6548	0.0300	4.04	0.53	0.9549	0.0021
0.80	1.90	0.19	0.8343	0.0175	0.70	0.02	0.6520	0.0280	3.86	0.47	0.9549	0.0018
Levels Up												
0	1.49	0.11	0.8301	0.0192	0.68	0.02	0.6241	0.0215	3.15	0.31	0.9550	0.0019
1	2.18	0.28	0.8585	0.0210	0.71	0.03	0.6630	0.0349	4.35	0.70	0.9543	0.0022
2	2.25	0.29	0.8590	0.0208	0.71	0.03	0.6665	0.0343	4.15	0.61	0.9543	0.0023
Acceptance Threshold												
0.01	2.21	0.29	0.8534	0.0193	0.70	0.02	0.6563	0.0306	3.98	0.56	0.9545	0.0021
0.05	1.90	0.20	0.8485	0.0199	0.70	0.02	0.6499	0.0296	3.87	0.53	0.9546	0.0020
0.10	1.80	0.18	0.8457	0.0201	0.70	0.02	0.6474	0.0285	3.81	0.51	0.9546	0.0020
Simply Every k Generations												
3	2.08	0.24	0.8487	0.0200	0.71	0.02	0.6585	0.0309	4.29	0.60	0.9546	0.0021
4	1.94	0.22	0.8490	0.0194	0.70	0.02	0.6488	0.0290	3.81	0.53	0.9546	0.0022
5	1.89	0.22	0.8499	0.0201	0.70	0.02	0.6463	0.0297	3.55	0.48	0.9545	0.0022

goes down (Wine stays constant however), but so does average test accuracy (except for Coins when the range threshold is 0.5 and Wisconsin which stays fairly constant). It appears that linear regression is causing more computational overhead than it is worth. The Coins dataset shows this most clearly (see the top graph in Figure 4): the time taken with no regression is similar to that with 0.95 and 0.80 values, but the test accuracy stays higher, i.e., additional computational overhead is not offset by the simplifications made. We see similar CPU time savings without regression in the Wisconsin dataset, but test accuracy remains fairly constant. On the Wine dataset, however, using linear regression has higher test accuracy than not using it, but the test accuracy is still significantly less than that of the base system.

How far up the tree to evaluate. In general it seems that as we increase the number of levels we look up before accepting a simplification, the overall average CPU time increases (with the exception of Wisconsin with 2 levels), but so does the test accuracy (Wisconsin's test accuracy remains relatively constant however). This is best displayed in the Coins dataset where both CPU time and test accuracy change significantly (see the bottom graph in Figure 4). In general, looking 0 levels up amounts to a significant time reduction but also a significant reduction in test accuracy, while looking 1 or 2 levels up only is slightly more computationally expensive but maintains a lot higher test accuracy.

How often to simplify. Overall, there doesn't seem to be much change in test accuracy among the different values for k. As we simplify less often, the CPU time reduces significantly on the Coins and Wisconsin datasets, while the time remains unchanged on Wine. This indicates that it might be useful to investigate simplifying even less often.

Comparing number of proposals vs number of acceptances. A central research question is how much computational overhead arises from generating proposals and testing for acceptance. We expect that relaxing the proposal thresholds generates more proposals, each of which must be tested for acceptance. Table 2 compares the number of simplifications proposed and accepted, and percentage accepted, for each proposal operator. It shows the effect of increasing the acceptance threshold within each of these for the Coins dataset (however, the following general observations apply across all datasets) as follows. Unexpectedly, we see *fewer* proposed simplifications (it is apparent that there may be some "repeat proposing" of simplifications, i.e., a candidate gets rejected but is proposed again later on since it is still a good candidate at the local level—this also explains the higher CPU time for more stringent acceptance threshold values). As expected, the number of accepted proposals increases (except for Coins when the regression threshold is in $\{0.99, 0.95\}$, where the number accepted is relatively similar for acceptance threshold in $\{0.05, 0.10\}$). The average percentage of proposals accepted also increases, although at different rates for each dataset and proposal operator (the best acceptance percentage was just over 50%). The CPU time decreases due to a combination of fewer proposals (lower calculation overhead) and higher number of proposals accepted (overhead incurred in our implementation if a simplification proposal is rejected). The Coins dataset shows the largest reduction in CPU time, while none is observed on the Wine dataset. As expected, the average test accuracy decreases—as we accept less accurate approximations of portions of the tree, this causes the tree itself to have poorer accuracy in general. Again, Wisconsin is an exception, showing little change in test accuracy. Coins shows the highest reduction in test accuracy as well as CPU time seen above, so there seems to be a tradeoff. It is interesting to note, however, that some individual combinations of the simplification operators actually increase the average test accuracy compared to the base system (see the top graph in Figure 4). This could mean that simplifications are taking place in an early generation, allowing more of the search space to be covered in less time, but further research would be required to establish this.

How the proposal thresholds affect the number of proposals and acceptances. Across all datasets, for the linear regression operator, decreasing the value of

Table 2. Comparison of number of simplifications proposed vs number accepted for the Coins dataset. Results for each of the three levels of the range threshold by three levels of the acceptance threshold are collected over $3^3 \times 4 = 108$ combinations of the other four thresholds, etc.

	Proposal Thresh.	Accept Thresh.	#Prop	#Acpt	%Acpt	Time (s)	(sd)	T.Acc	(sd)
	Base Sys.	-	-	-	-	4.87	1.8	0.8594	0.0314
Range Thresh.	0.1	0.01	468.37	131.54	28.09	2.29	0.52	0.8531	0.0218
		0.05	340.77	142.53	41.82	2.00	0.35	0.8483	0.0199
		0.10	301.51	147.29	48.85	1.91	0.32	0.8455	0.0193
	0.5	0.01	428.95	111.66	26.03	2.18	0.49	0.8535	0.0208
		0.05	305.13	120.69	39.55	1.89	0.31	0.8492	0.0192
		0.10	270.29	125.77	46.53	1.81	0.28	0.8467	0.0188
	1.0	0.01	422.51	95.31	22.56	2.17	0.65	0.8535	0.0223
		0.05	284.44	103.66	36.44	1.83	0.41	0.8481	0.0197
		0.10	228.95	96.33	42.07	1.68	0.31	0.8450	0.0186
Redundant Thresh.	0.01	0.01	486.03	136.64	28.11	2.27	0.51	0.8566	0.0190
		0.05	370.32	159.29	43.01	2.07	0.38	0.8537	0.0180
		0.10	326.42	162.73	49.85	1.98	0.35	0.8517	0.0175
	0.05	0.01	436.42	109.46	25.08	2.20	0.57	0.8537	0.0215
		0.05	291.89	111.38	38.16	1.84	0.31	0.8477	0.0188
		0.10	255.86	114.56	44.78	1.77	0.27	0.8460	0.0183
	0.10	0.01	397.38	92.41	23.26	2.16	0.60	0.8498	0.0235
		0.05	268.14	96.21	35.88	1.80	0.34	0.8442	0.0207
		0.10	218.47	92.10	42.16	1.66	0.24	0.8394	0.0188
Regression Thresh.	none	0.01				2.13	0.42	0.8653	0.0076
		0.05	–	–	–	1.90	0.30	0.8629	0.0066
		0.10				1.83	0.29	0.8614	0.0066
	0.99	0.01	252.68	78.89	31.22	2.31	0.56	0.8580	0.0124
		0.05	181.62	81.38	44.81	2.00	0.37	0.8539	0.0100
		0.10	157.63	81.11	51.46	1.90	0.32	0.8520	0.0093
	0.95	0.01	517.82	142.15	27.45	2.22	0.59	0.8500	0.0201
		0.05	365.83	151.47	41.40	1.89	0.37	0.8439	0.0161
		0.10	313.79	151.09	48.15	1.78	0.30	0.8399	0.0138
	0.80	0.01	989.28	230.30	23.28	2.18	0.65	0.8401	0.0300
		0.05	693.01	256.32	36.99	1.81	0.40	0.8333	0.0254
		0.10	596.26	260.33	43.66	1.70	0.32	0.8296	0.0231

the threshold increases the number of simplification proposals. Proportionately, the number of proposals accepted increases but on average the percentage of proposals accepted decreases, indicating the acceptance operator is working. Surprisingly, for range simplification and redundancy, as we increase the value of the threshold, we actually see a *reduction* in proposals on average, and therefore a reduction in proposals accepted as well. A possible reason for this reduction could be the nature of the proposal operators: in both cases, once a simplification has occurred, those nodes can no longer be further simplified through these two methods. However, a linear regression simplification could in turn allow for another simplification the next level up the tree, a sort of cascading effect.

6   Conclusions

All configurations of the simplification operators significantly reduced the CPU time for the GP process to run. However, the tradeoff between CPU time and classification accuracy was different for different configurations and different datasets. Range simplification and removing redundant children appear to be useful simplification operators to use because they are simple and computationally efficient. However, the computational tests were inconclusive as to whether the linear regression operator we introduced is worth using (good for Coins, poor for Wine, no change for Wisconsin). Evaluating the effect of proposed simplifications further up the tree (rather than blind acceptance) appears to be very effective (Coins and Wine show that classification accuracy improves); looking one level up seems to be sufficient. As there is little reduction in test accuracy for any of the acceptance MSE threshold values tested in this paper, a more lenient MSE value may be desired for further CPU time reductions. Finally, when simplifying a population, it seems to be better to do so less often because of the high overhead incurred, so the less often you simplify, the faster the GP process runs (our best results were simplifying every five generations).

Avenues for future research include investigating the effect of simplification on tree size and tree depth across different generations, eliminating repeat proposal of the same simplification by the regression operator, applying the linear regression operator on more datasets to see if there is any consistency amongst different types of problems, and further investigating simplifying less often to find the optimal balance between size reduction and computational overhead.

Acknowledgment

This work was supported in part by the University Research Fund (URF09-2399/85608) at Victoria University of Wellington and by the Marsden Fund (08-VUW-014) administrated by the Royal Society of New Zealand.

References

1. Koza, J.R.: Genetic Programming: On the Programming of Computers by Means of Natural Selection. MIT Press, Cambridge (1992)
2. Blickle, T., Thiele, L.: Genetic programming and redundancy. In: Hopf, J. (ed.) Genetic Algorithms within the Framework of Evolutionary Computation, Max-Planck-Institut für Informatik (MPI-I-94-241), pp. 33–38 (1994)
3. Dignum, S., Poli, R.: Operator equalisation and bloat free GP. In: O'Neill, M., Vanneschi, L., Gustafson, S., Esparcia Alcázar, A.I., De Falco, I., Della Cioppa, A., Tarantino, E. (eds.) EuroGP 2008. LNCS, vol. 4971, pp. 110–121. Springer, Heidelberg (2008)
4. Dignum, S., Poli, R.: Crossover, sampling, bloat and the harmful effects of size limits. In: O'Neill, M., Vanneschi, L., Gustafson, S., Esparcia Alcázar, A.I., De Falco, I., Della Cioppa, A., Tarantino, E. (eds.) EuroGP 2008. LNCS, vol. 4971, pp. 158–169. Springer, Heidelberg (2008)

5. Poli, R.: A simple but theoretically-motivated method to control bloat in genetic programming. In: Ryan, C., Soule, T., Keijzer, M., Tsang, E.P.K., Poli, R., Costa, E. (eds.) EuroGP 2003. LNCS, vol. 2610, pp. 204–217. Springer, Heidelberg (2003)
6. Soule, T., Foster, J.A., Dickinson, J.: Code growth in genetic programming. In: Koza, J.R., et al. (eds.) Genetic Programming 1996: Proceedings of the First Annual Conference, Stanford University, CA, USA, pp. 215–223. MIT Press, Cambridge (1996)
7. Soule, T., Heckendorn, R.B.: An analysis of the causes of code growth in genetic programming. Genetic Programming and Evolvable Machines, 283–309 (2002)
8. Streeter, M.J.: The root causes of code growth in genetic programming. In: Ryan, C., Soule, T., Keijzer, M., Tsang, E.P.K., Poli, R., Costa, E. (eds.) EuroGP 2003. LNCS, vol. 2610, pp. 443–454. Springer, Heidelberg (2003)
9. Crane, E.F., McPhee, N.F.: The effects of size and depth limits on tree based genetic programming. In: Yu, T., et al. (eds.) Genetic Programming Theory and Practice III. Genetic Programming, vol. 9, pp. 223–240. Springer, Heidelberg (2005)
10. Nordin, P., Banzhaf, W.: Complexity compression and evolution. In: Eshelman, L. (ed.) Genetic Algorithms: Proceedings of the Sixth International Conference (ICGA 1995), Pittsburgh, PA, USA, pp. 310–317. Morgan Kaufmann, San Francisco (1995)
11. Zhang, B.T., Mühlenbein, H.: Balancing accuracy and parsimony in genetic programming. Evolutionary Computation 3(1), 17–38 (1995)
12. Luke, S., Panait, L.: Lexicographic parsimony pressure. In: Langdon, W.B., et al. (eds.) Proceedings of the 4th Annual Conference on Genetic and Evolutionary Computation (GECCO 2002), New York, pp. 829–836. Morgan Kaufmann, San Francisco (2002)
13. Hooper, D., Flann, N.S.: Improving the accuracy and robustness of genetic programming through expression simplification. In: Koza, J.R., et al. (eds.) Genetic Programming 1996: Proceedings of the First Annual Conference, p. 428 (1996)
14. Wong, P., Zhang, M.: Algebraic simplification of GP programs during evolution. In: Keijzer, M., et al. (eds.) Proceedings of the 8th Annual Conference on Genetic and Evolutionary Computation (GECCO 2006), Seattle, Washington, USA, July 8–12, vol. 1, pp. 927–934. ACM Press, New York (2006)
15. Zhang, M., Wong, P., Qian, D.: Online program simplification in genetic programming. In: Wang, T.-D., Li, X., Chen, S.-H., Wang, X., Abbass, H.A., Iba, H., Chen, G.-L., Yao, X. (eds.) SEAL 2006. LNCS, vol. 4247, pp. 592–600. Springer, Heidelberg (2006)
16. Kinzett, D., Zhang, M., Johnston, M.: Using numerical simplification to control bloat in genetic programming. In: Li, X., Kirley, M., Zhang, M., Green, D., Ciesielski, V., Abbass, H.A., Michalewicz, Z., Hendtlass, T., Deb, K., Tan, K.C., Branke, J., Shi, Y. (eds.) SEAL 2008. LNCS, vol. 5361, pp. 493–502. Springer, Heidelberg (2008)
17. Song, A., Chen, D., Zhang, M.: Bloat control in genetic programming by evaluating contribution of nodes. In: Raidl, G., et al. (eds.) Proceedings of the 11th Annual Conference on Genetic and Evolutionary Computation (GECCO 2009), Montreal, pp. 1893–1894. ACM, New York (2009)
18. Forina, M., Leardi, R., Armanino, C., Lanteri, S.: PARVUS: An Extendable Package of Programs for Data Exploration, Classification and Correlation. Elsevier, Amsterdam (1988)
19. Asuncion, A., Newman, D.J.: UCI Machine Learning Repository (2007), http://www.ics.uci.edu/~mlearn/MLRepository.html
20. Zhang, M., Ciesielski, V.: Genetic programming for multiple class object detection. In: Foo, N.Y. (ed.) AI 1999. LNCS (LNAI), vol. 1747, pp. 180–192. Springer, Heidelberg (1999)

Unsupervised Problem Decomposition Using Genetic Programming

Ahmed Kattan, Alexandros Agapitos, and Riccardo Poli

School of Computer Science and Electronic Engineering
University of Essex, Colchester CO4 3SQ, UK
akatta@essex.ac.uk, aagapi@essex.ac.uk, rpoli@essex.ac.uk

Abstract. We propose a new framework based on Genetic Programming (GP) to automatically decompose problems into smaller and simpler tasks. The framework uses GP at two levels. At the top level GP evolves ways of splitting the fitness cases into subsets. At the lower level GP evolves programs that solve the fitness cases in each subset. The top level GP programs include two components. Each component receives a training case as the input. The components' outputs act as coordinates to project training examples onto a 2-D Euclidean space. When an individual is evaluated, K-means clustering is applied to group the fitness cases of the problem. The number of clusters is decided based on the density of the projected samples. Each cluster then invokes an independent GP run to solve its member fitness cases. The fitness of the lower level GP individuals is evaluated as usual. The fitness of the high-level GP individuals is a combination of the fitness of the best evolved programs in each of the lower level GP runs. The proposed framework has been tested on several symbolic regression problems and has been seen to significantly outperforming standard GP systems.

1   Introduction

Problem decomposition aims to simplify complex real world problems in order to better cope with them. This strategy is regularly used by humans when solving problems. For example, computer programmers often organise their code into functions and classes.

Problem decomposition is important for two reasons. Firstly, it reduces the complexity of a problem and, therefore, makes the problem easier to solve by standard machine learning techniques. Secondly, automated problem decomposition may help researchers to better understand a problem domain by discovering regularities in the problem space. One way to formalise the decomposition process is to assume there exist different patterns in the problem space, each pattern has particular characteristics and therefore it needs a special solution.

Generally, problem decomposition allows a better understanding and control of the problem's complexity. However, while it is not difficult to split a problem into several sub-problems to be solved in cooperation with different methods, using the wrong decomposition may actually increase the problems complexity.

An ideal problem decomposition system would be one that gets the data from the user and identifies different groups in the data; each of these groups should be simpler to solve than the original problem. An intelligent decomposition of problems requires understanding the problem domain and usually can only be carried out by experts. In this

A.I. Esparcia-Alcazar et al. (Eds.): EuroGP 2010, LNCS 6021, pp. 122–133, 2010.

paper, we propose a GP system that can evolve programs that automatically decompose a problem into a collection of simpler and smaller sub-problems while simultaneously solving the sub-problems. This is an area of GP that has not been thoroughly explored thus far.

The structure of the paper is as follows. In the next section we briefly review previous work on problem decomposition. Section 3 provides a detailed description of our proposed framework. This is followed by details on our experimental setting and results in Sections 4 and 5, respectively. Finally, conclusive remarks are given in Section 6.

2 Related Work

The solution to complex problems typically requires the construction of highly complex systems. These systems typically use hierarchical, modular structures to manage and organise their complexity. Modular structures are widespread in engineering and nature. So, it is reasonable to expect that they could be valuable in GP as well. In particular, modularity and hierarchy can be essential tools for problem decomposition. Consequently, starting from Koza's automatically defined functions (ADFs) [1], they have been a subject of substantial empirical exploration from the early days of GP (e.g., see [2,3,4,5,6,7,8]). Due to space limitations, in this section we will review problem decomposition approaches that are based on the notion of dividing up the test cases into (possibly overlapping) subsets, since these are directly relevant to the work reported in this paper.

Rosca *et al.* [9] proposed a system called Evolutionary Speciation Genetic Programming (ESGP) to automatically discover natural decompositions of problems. Each individual consisted of two parts: *condition* and *output*. The *condition* element represents a Boolean function that receives a fitness case presented as an argument and returns feedback on whether the individual chooses to specialise in that case. The *output* element is a standard GP tree, which receives the chosen fitness cases as input. Naturally, some of the fitness cases may be claimed by more than one individual while others are never chosen. Thus, a fitness function was proposed which encourages individuals to fully cover the problem space and minimise the overlap of the claimed fitness cases. The approach was tested with symbolic regression problem and compared with standard GP and with GP(IF), which additionally includes if-then-else in the function set. GP(IF) is selected as it may implicitly split the problem space into different regions. Indeed, experimentation revealed that GP(IF) evolved conditions in such a way as to effectively assign different fitness cases to different pieces of code and, moreover, that GP(IF) outperformed ESGP.

Iba [10] proposed to extend GP using two well-known resampling techniques known as Bagging and Boosting and presented two systems referred to as BagGP and BoostGP. In these systems the whole population is divided into subpopulations. Each subpopulation is evolved independently using a fitness function based on a subset of the fitness cases, which are allocated by the two resampling techniques, i.e., Bagging and Boosting. Later, the best individual from each subpopulation is selected to form a voting scheme to classify unseen data. In both BagGP and BoostGP the number of subpopulations is determined by the user. Experiments on three benchmark problems showed that BagGP and BoostGP outperformed conventional GP. However, when BagGP and BoostGP were applied to a complex real world problem— the prediction of the Japanese stock market– they performed almost identically to standard GP.

More recently, Jackson [11] proposed a hierarchical architecture for GP for problem decomposition based on partitioning the input test cases into subsets. The approach requires a manual partitioning of the test cases. Then, each subset is independently processed in separate evolved branches rooted at a selection node. This node decides which branch to activate based on the given input case. The branches are evolved in isolation and do not interact with each other. The number of branches is determined by the number of subsets into which the test cases have been divided. The proposed architecture has been tested with the 4-, 5- and 10-even-parity problems and polynomial symbolic regression problems with different numbers of branches. In addition, comparisons with standard GP and GP with ADFs have been performed. Experiments showed that this architecture has outperformed conventional GP systems. Its main disadvantage is that the user is required to manually decompose the test cases.

As one can see, none of the previous methods for problem decomposition via test case subdivision is fully automated. Overcoming this limitation is one of the aims of the work presented in this paper.

3   The Approach

Our problem decomposition system works in two main stages: *i) Training*, where the system learns to divide the training cases into different groups based on their similarity and *ii) Testing*, where the system applies what it has learnt to solve unseen data. The training phase is divided into two main steps *i) resampling*, where the system tries to discover the best decomposition for the problem space and *ii) solving*, where the system tries to solve the problem by solving the sub-problems discovered in the resampling stage independently.

In the resampling stage, the system starts by randomly initialising a population of individuals using the ramped half-and-half method (e.g., see [12]). Each individual is composed of two trees: *projector X* and *projector Y*. Each tree receives a fitness case as input and returns a single value as output. The two outputs together are treated as coordinates for a fitness case in a 2-D plane. The process of mapping fitness cases to 2-D points is repeated for all the training examples. For this task, GP has been supplied with a language which allows the discovery of different patterns in the training set. Table 1 reports the primitive set of the system.

Once the training cases are projected via the two components (*projector X* and *Y*), K-means clustering is applied in order to group similar instances in different clusters. Each cluster then invokes an independent GP run to solve cases within its members. Thus, each cluster is treated as an independent problem. The next subsection will describe the clustering process in detail.

3.1   Clustering the Training Examples

We used a standard pattern classification approach on the outputs produced by the two projection trees to discover regularities in the training data. In principle, any classification

Table 1. Primitives set

Function	Arity	Input	Output
+, -, /, *, pow	2	Real Number	Real Number
Sin, Cos, Sqrt, log	1	Real Number	Real Number
Constants 1-6	0	N/A	Real Number
X	0	N/A	Real Number

method can be used with our approach. Here, we decided to use K-means clustering (e.g., see [13]) to organise the training data (as re-represented by their two projection trees) into groups. With this algorithm, objects within a cluster are similar to each other but dissimilar from objects in other clusters. The advantage of this approach is that the experimenter doesn't need to split the training set manually. Also, the approach does not impose any significant constrains on the shape or size of the clusters. Once the training set is clustered, we can use the clusters found by K-means to perform classification of unseen data by simply assigning a new data point to the cluster whose centroid is closest to it.

K-means is a partitioning algorithm that normally requires the user to fix the number of clusters to be formed. However, in our case the optimal number of subdivisions for the problem into sub-problems is unknown. Hence, we use a simple technique to find the optimal number of classes in the projected space based on the density of the samples. Once the system groups the projected samples into classes, it invokes an independent GP search for each cluster.

Since K-means is a very fast algorithm, to find the optimal number of clusters the system repeatedly instructs K-means to divide the data set into k clusters, where $k = 2, 3, ... K_{max}$ ($K_{max} = 10$, in our implementation). After each call the system computes the clusters' quality. The value of k which provided the best quality clusters is then used to split the training set and invoke GP runs on the corresponding clusters.

The quality of the clusters is calculated by measuring cluster *separation* and *representativeness*. Ideal clusters are those that are separated from each other and densely grouped near their centroids.

A modified Davis Bouldin Index (DBI) [14] was used to measure cluster separation. DBI is a measure of the nearness of the clusters' members to their centroids, divided by the distance between clusters' centroids. Thus, a small DBI index indicates well separated and grouped clusters. Therefore, we favour clusters with a low DBI value.

DBI can be expressed as follows. Let C_i be the centroid of the ith cluster and d_i^n the nth data member of the ith cluster. In addition, let the Euclidean distance between d_i^n and C_i be expressed by the function $dis(d_i^n, C_i)$. Furthermore, let again k be the total number of clusters. Finally, let the standard deviation be denoted as $std()$. Then,

$$DBI = \frac{\sum_{i=0}^{k} std[dis(d_i^0, C_i), ..., dis(d_i^n, C_i)]}{dis(C_0, C_1, ..., C_k)}$$

The representativeness of clusters is simply evaluated by verifying whether the formed clusters are representative enough to classify unseen data. In certain conditions, the projection trees may project the data in such a way that it is unlikely to be suitable to classify unseen data. For example, clusters that have few members are unlikely to be representative of unseen data. To avoid pathologies of this kind, the system verifies whether the formed clusters have a sufficiently large number of members. In particular, it penalises the values of k that lead K-mean to form clusters where less than a minimum number of members is present. In this work, the minimum allowed number of members for each cluster was simply set to 10 samples. However, we have not thoroughly investigated whether this was optimal in all conditions. For example, it is likely that the optimum minimum size of the clusters is modulated by the total number of training examples available.

More formally, the quality, Q_k, of the clusters obtained when K-means is required to produce k clusters can be expressed as the follows. Let θ_k be the penalty value applied to the quality if there is a problem with the representativeness of the clusters produced. If any particular cluster has less than a minimum number of members we set $\theta_k = 1000$, while $\theta_k = 0$ if no problem is found. Furthermore, let DBI_k represent the corresponding cluster separation. Then,

$$Q_k = DBI_k + \theta_k$$

After running K-means for all values of k in the range 2 to K_{max}, we choose the optimal k as follows:

$$k_{best} = \arg \min_{2 < k < K_{max}} Q_k$$

The main factor that affects the optimal number of clusters is the density of the projected samples. The method described above effectively analyses the density of the data from this point of view. Algorithm 1, describes the clustering process in details.

A disadvantage of this approach is that the K-means algorithm has to be executed several times per fitness evaluation, which slows down the evolution a little. However, this only needs to be done during evolution. During normal operation we simply apply the previously formed clusters (represented by their centroids) to the unseen data.

As mentioned previously, once the system has identified the optimal k value and the corresponding clusters, it invokes an independent GP search for each cluster. The purpose is to evolve a program that satisfies the fitness cases in the cluster. In the testing phase, unseen data go through the two projector components of the evolved solution and are projected onto a two-dimensional Euclidean space. Then, they are classified based on the closest centroid. Finally, the input data are passed to the evolved program associated to the corresponding cluster.

The advantage of this approach is that it greatly simplifies classification. This is because evolution pushes projection trees to represent the data in such a way as to optimise the performance of the classification algorithm. Here, we used K-means for its simplicity of implementation and its execution speed, but other techniques might work equally well.

3.2   Search Operators

We used tournament selection and the standard genetic operators: sub-tree crossover, sub-tree mutation and reproduction. Naturally, in the top-level GP runs, the genetic operators have to take the multi-tree representation of individuals into account.

```
Project(n, treeX, treeY);
List Qk;
for int k=2; k ≤ KMAX; k++ do
    //call the K-means algorithm
    K-means(k, n);
    int separation = calculate_DBI();
    if check_clusters_representativeness() == true then
        theta = 0
    else
        theta = 1000
    end
    Qk.append(separation + theta, k)
end
//find the best number of clusters
int number_of_clusters = Qk.get_min_k();
```

Algorithm 1. Finding the optimal number of clusters in the projected space

There are several options for applying genetic operators to a multi-tree representation: apply an operator to all trees within an individual, use different operators for different trees, constrain crossover to happen only between trees at the same position in the parents, allow crossover between different trees within the representation, and so on.

It is unclear what technique is best (e.g., see [15] and [16]). So, in preliminary experiments we tried a variety of approaches and found that a good way to guide evolution in our system is to allow crossover to freely pick feature-extractions trees. In other words, the *projector X* tree of one parent can be crossed over with either the *projector X* tree or *projector Y* of the other parent and *vice versa*.

3.3 Fitness Evaluation

We evaluate the top-level GP system's individuals (represented by two projection trees) by measuring how well the whole problem is solved. The clusters formed by K-means represent subsets of training examples. Each cluster invokes a GP search to solve its member's cases. We call this *inner GP search*. For simplicity, each inner GP runs for a small fixed number of generations with a fixed population size. In future research we will study the benefits and drawbacks of letting the system decide the settings of each inner GP run (e.g., based on the size of the associated cluster).

In our system all inner GP systems evolve simultaneously. The fitness of a top-level GP individual depends on the fitness of the best evolved individual in each of the inner GP runs. If k_{best} is the number of clusters found on the projected space using Algorithm 1 and f_i is the fitness of the best evolved program in the ith inner GP run, then the fitness of top-level individuals is:

$$f = \frac{1}{k_{best}} \sum_{i=1}^{k_{best}} f_i.$$

This fitness function encourages the individuals to project the fitness cases in such a way that a solution for the fitness cases in each group can easily be found by the inner GP runs.

4 Experimental Setup

Experiments have been conducted to evaluate the proposed framework. To do this we chose a variety of symbolic regression problems, which we felt were difficult enough to demonstrate the characteristics and benefits of the method.

We used discontinuous functions as symbolic regression target functions. These allow us to study the ability of the system to decompose a complex problem into simpler tasks. Table 2 list the functions as well as the ranges from which we drew samples to create symbolic regression test problems. Function 1 was used in Rosca's experiments in [9] to evaluate his proposed system. Here, we used the same function to ease the comparison against Rosca's system.

In order to evaluate our results, a comparison has been conducted against both canonical GP and GP(IF), where we added an IF-THEN-ELSE primitive to the function set. This primitive has four types of conditions, namely, $<$, $>$, $>=$ and $<=$. The function

Table 2. Test functions

function	Notation	Training interval
1	$f1(x) = \begin{cases} e^{x+5}, & x < 0 \\ 1 - \log(x^2 + x + 1), & x \geq 0 \end{cases}$	[-2,2]
2	$f2(x) = \begin{cases} x + 6, & x < 0 \\ \dfrac{3}{x^2 + 1}, & x \geq 0 \end{cases}$	[-2,2]
3	$f3(x) = \begin{cases} x + \sin(x - 1), & x < 0 \\ 6 * \sin(x) * \cos(x), & 0 \leq x < 1 \\ \sqrt{x}, & x \geq 1 \end{cases}$	[-2,2]
4	$f4(x) = \begin{cases} \dfrac{30\,x}{(x-2)*x}, & x \leq -1 \\ \dfrac{x^4 - x^3 + x^2}{x + 2}, & -1 < x < 0 \\ \dfrac{x}{5}, & 0 \leq x < 1 \\ x^3 * e^x * \cos(x), & x \geq 1 \end{cases}$	[-2,2]
5	$f5(x) = \begin{cases} \dfrac{8}{2 + x^2 + 2x^4}, & x < -2 \\ \dfrac{x^3}{5}, & -2 \leq x < 0 \\ \dfrac{x}{x^2}, & x \geq 0 \end{cases}$	[-4,2]

receives four arguments: the first two are passed to the condition, while the other two represent code to be executed if the condition is true or false, respectively. GP(IF) was selected because, as seen in Rosca's work, it may implicitly split the problem space into different pieces of code and it is, therefore, likely to be competitive for symbolic regression with discontinuous functions.

Our experiments were conducted using the parameter settings in Table 3. The primitive set for both Standard GP and GP(IF) was the same as for our GP system (see Table 1).

Performance has been measured through 100 independent runs for each system (20 runs for each test function). For the training, 100 samples were uniformly selected from the training interval (see Table 2). Evolved solutions were then evaluated using 400 different samples. Each evolved solution has been evaluated with two different test sets. Firstly, we tested performance of the solutions within the training interval (interpolation). Secondly, we evaluated performance on a bigger interval (extrapolation). The extrapolation interval for all test functions was the interval $[-5, 5]$, except for function 5 where we used the interval $[-7, 7]$.

The fitness measurement for GP, GP(IF) and the inner GP runs in our system is the mean absolute error over all training samples. For the top-level GP runs in our system, however, the fitness evaluation described in Section 3.3 has been applied, which averages over the contribution of each cluster in solving the overall problem.

Table 3. Parameters setting

Method	GP Cluster	GP Cluster (inner GP)	GP(IF)	Standard GP
Generations	10	30	30	30
Population	10	100	1000	1000
Crossover	90%	90%	90%	90%
Mutation	5%	5%	5%	5%
Reproduction	5%	5%	5%	5%
Tournament size	2	10	10	10

5   Experimental Results

Table 4 reports the results of the experiments for all five test functions and for standard GP, GP(IF) and our system (GP Cluster). In addition, the average error obtained across 20 independent runs is reported in Table 2, in order to provide information on the stability of each system. Test functions report the best and worst interpolation and extrapolation achieved by each system in all runs and the standard deviation for all runs.

It is clear that our approach has outperformed standard GP by a significant margin in all test functions. It also outperformed GP(IF) in four out of five problems. Furthermore, in all cases standard deviations for Cluster GP were very small, indicating the reliability of the approach. This is the result of the system splitting the relatively complex shape of these discontinuous functions into simpler fragments (i.e., sub-problems). Looking at the number subsets used throughout the test runs, we see that in functions 1, 2 and 5, the system decided to split the training samples into 4 to 10 clusters. In function 3,

Table 4. Experimental results. Statistics are based on 20 independent runs for each function.

Method	Function	GP(IF)	Standard GP	GP Cluster
Worst interpolation		246.36	250.15	**83.64**
Best interpolation		0.52	3.20	**0.15**
Worst extrapolation	1	**342.46**	7.32E+299	44124.30
Best extrapolation		0.73	4.61	**0.11**
Average		27.67	27.22	**6.47**
Std		65.16	53.75	**18.31**
Worst interpolation		40.68	0.84	**0.22**
Best interpolation		0.10	0.26	**0.02**
Worst extrapolation	2	67.79	29353.90	**2.95**
Best extrapolation		0.05	0.41	**0.03**
Average		4.27	0.52	**0.07**
Std		12.32	0.17	**0.05**
Worst interpolation		0.56	2.81	**0.19**
Best interpolation		0.06	0.15	**0.02**
Worst extrapolation	3	1.75	4.4621E+278	3.67
Best extrapolation		0.33	0.37	**0.02**
Average		0.25	0.47	**0.05**
Std		0.11	0.58	**0.04**
Worst interpolation		3.05	2.91	**0.94**
Best interpolation		0.74	1.91	**0.16**
Worst extrapolation	4	3.7E+289	**3128.31**	4780.32
Best extrapolation		**16.54**	21.33	17.20
Average		1.77	2.59	**0.41**
Std		0.64	0.35	**0.23**
Worst interpolation		**1.88**	13.36	2.66
Best interpolation		0.10	0.23	**0.07**
Worst extrapolation	5	**98.99**	2.27E+277	697.28
Best extrapolation		0.10	0.15	**0.06**
Average		**0.40**	2.03	0.74
Std		**0.37**	3.00	0.73

*Numbers in **bold** represent the best achieved result.

the system identified 6 to 10 clusters in the problem space and in function 4, the most complex in our test set, it identified 8 to 10 clusters.

As we mentioned before, function 1 has been used in Rosca's experiments in [9]. The best achieved accuracy reported on the interval [-2,2] was 1.5, while in our system we have a best interpolation error of 0.15.

We summarise the results from Table 4 in Table 5. As one can see our approach comes on the top of the comparison. Moreover, our results also show that GP(IF) is a marginal second, while standard GP comes last.

Table 5. Experimental results summary

Method	GP(IF)	Standard GP	GP Cluster
Worst interpolation Avg.	75.14	54.01	**17.53**
Best interpolation Avg.	0.26	1.15	**0.08**
Worst extrapolation Avg.	1.1912E+289	1.465E+299	**9921.70**
Best extrapolation Avg.	5.20	5.37	**3.48**
Average of Averages	8.32	6.57	**1.55**
Std Avg.	19.78	11.57	**3.87**

Table 6. A Kolmogorov-Smirnov test

Function	Method	Standard GP	GP Cluster
1	GP(IF)	0.001 / 0	0 / 0.275
	Standard GP	N/A	0 / 0
2	GP(IF)	0 / 0.023	0 / 0.771
	Standard GP	N/A	0 / 0.001
3	GP(IF)	0.135 / 0.008	0 / 0.003
	Standard GP	N/A	0 / 0.003
4	GP(IF)	0.135/ 0.008	0 / 0.275
	Standard GP	N/A	0/ 0.135
5	GP(IF)	0 / 0965	0.059 / 0.275
	Standard GP	N/A	0.023 / 0.135

*The results in the table is the P value for Interpolation / Extrapolation

In order to evaluate the statistical significance of our results, a Kolmogorov-Smirnov two-sample test [17] has been performed on the test-case results produced by the best evolved system in each run for all pairs of systems under test and for all five test functions. The test has been repeated for both interpolation and extrapolation. Table 6 reports the P value for the tests. As one can see in 9 out of 10 interpolation cases our system is statistically significantly superior to both standard GP and GP(IF) at the standard 5% significance level. The superior performance of GP(IF) on function 5 observed in Table 4 is not statistically significant (albeit by a very small margin). In the extrapolation results (which are, rather obviously, affected by a much larger variance) our system is statistically significantly superior to the others in 4 out of 10 cases, although as one can infer from Table 5, one might expect that performing more runs would eventually statistically confirm the superiority of our system in more cases.

6   Conclusions

In this paper we presented a new framework to automatically decompose difficult symbolic regression tasks into smaller and simpler tasks. The proposed approach is based on the idea of first projecting the training cases onto a two-dimensional Euclidian space via two evolved projection programs, and then clustering them via the K-means algorithm to better see their similarities and differences. The clustering is guaranteed to be optimal thanks to the use of an iterative process. This process uses a quality measure based on the density of the projected samples. Once the data are clustered, they are passed to separate GP runs which evolve specialised solutions for them. Note that while the projection and clustering steps may seem excessive for scalar domains, they make our problem decomposition technique applicable to much more complex domains.

Experiments have been conducted with symbolic regression problems using five different discontinuous functions as target functions. The proposed approach has outperformed conventional GP systems significantly. Also, experiments showed a remarkable stability for our system across runs.

The main motivation behind this research was to produce an intelligent system that is able to solve complex problems by automatically decomposing the problem space into different classes and thereafter solve each class separately in order to solve the whole problem in cooperation. We feel that we have achieved our aim within the specific domain of input space decomposition, as shown by our experimentation. Of course, there are many other ways of performing problem decomposition and modularisation as mentioned in Section 2. We hope to be able to extend our clustering idea to other forms of decomposition.

This research can be extended in many different ways. In the future we will extend the experimentation by testing the technique on multi-varied problems and non-symbolic-regression problems. In addition, we will investigate the benefits and drawbacks of alternative fitness functions (particularly for the top-level GP system). For example, the fitness function might take the size of the identified clusters into consideration. Moreover, the system should be able to change the settings of each inner GP run according to the difficulty of the given sub-problem. Further, we intend to investigate the relationship between the identified number of clusters and how this affects the solutions' accuracy.

References

1. Koza, J.R.: Genetic Programming II: Automatic Discovery of Reusable Programs. MIT Press, Cambridge (May 1994)
2. Angeline, P.J., Pollack, J.B.: The evolutionary induction of subroutines. In: Proceedings of the Fourteenth Annual Conference of the Cognitive Science Society, Bloomington, Indiana, USA, pp. 236–241. Lawrence Erlbaum, Mahwah (1992)
3. Spector, L.: Evolving control structures with automatically defined macros. In: Siegel, E.V., Koza, J.R. (eds.) Working Notes for the AAAI Symposium on Genetic Programming, November 10–12, pp. 99–105. MIT/AAAI, Cambridge (1995)
4. Rosca, J.P., Ballard, D.H.: Discovery of subroutines in genetic programming. In: Angeline, P.J., Kinnear Jr., K.E. (eds.) Advances in Genetic Programming 2, ch. 9, pp. 177–202. MIT Press, Cambridge (1996)
5. Seront, G.: External concepts reuse in genetic programming. In: Siegel, E.V., Koza, J.R. (eds.) Working Notes for the AAAI Symposium on Genetic Programming, November 10–12, pp. 94–98. MIT/AAAI, Cambridge (1995)
6. Jonyer, I., Himes, A.: Improving modularity in genetic programming using graph-based data mining. In: Sutcliffe, G.C.J., Goebel, R.G. (eds.) Proceedings of the Nineteenth International Florida Artificial Intelligence Research Society Conference, Melbourne Beach, Florida, USA, May 11-13, pp. 556–561. American Association for Artificial Intelligence (2006)

7. Hemberg, E., Gilligan, C., O'Neill, M., Brabazon, A.: A grammatical genetic programming approach to modularity in genetic algorithms. In: Ebner, M., O'Neill, M., Ekárt, A., Vanneschi, L., Esparcia-Alcázar, A.I. (eds.) EuroGP 2007. LNCS, vol. 4445, pp. 1–11. Springer, Heidelberg (2007)
8. McPhee, N.F., Crane, E.F., Lahr, S.E., Poli, R.: Developmental plasticity in linear genetic programming. In: Raidl, G., et al. (eds.) GECCO 2009: Proceedings of the 11th Annual conference on Genetic and evolutionary computation, Montreal, July 8-12, pp. 1019–1026. ACM, New York (2009)
9. Rosca, J., Johnson, M.P., Maes, P.: Evolutionary Speciation for Problem Decomposition (1996) (Available via Citeseer)
10. Iba, H.: Bagging, boosting, and bloating in genetic programming. In: Proceedings of the Genetic and Evolutionary Computation Conference, Orlando, Florida, USA, July 13-17, vol. 2, pp. 1053–1060. Morgan Kaufmann, San Francisco (1999)
11. Jackson, D.: The performance of a selection architecture for genetic programming. In: O'Neill, M., Vanneschi, L., Gustafson, S., Esparcia Alcázar, A.I., De Falco, I., Della Cioppa, A., Tarantino, E. (eds.) EuroGP 2008. LNCS, vol. 4971, pp. 170–181. Springer, Heidelberg (2008)
12. Poli, R., Langdon, W.B., McPhee, N.F.: A Field Guide to Genetic Programming (With contributions by J. R. Koza) (2008), http://lulu.com
13. Han, J., Kamber, M.: Data mining: concepts and techniques. Morgan Kaufmann, San Francisco (2006)
14. Sepulveda, F., Meckes, M., Conway, B.A.: Cluster separation index suggests usefulness of non-motor EEG channels in detecting wrist movement direction intention. In: Proceedings of the 2004 IEEE Conference on Cybernetics and Intelligent Systems, Singapore, pp. 943–947. IEEE Press, Los Alamitos (2004)
15. Muni, D.P., Pal, N.R., Das, J.: A novel approach to design classifier using genetic programming. IEEE Transactions on Evolutionary Computation 8(2), 183–196 (2004)
16. Boric, N., Estevez, P.A.: Genetic programming-based clustering using an information theoretic fitness measure. In: Srinivasan, D., Wang, L. (eds.) 2007 IEEE Congress on Evolutionary Computation, Singapore, September 25-28. IEEE Computational Intelligence Society, pp. 31–38. IEEE Press, Los Alamitos (2007)
17. Peacock, J.A.: Two-dimensional goodness-of-fit testing in astronomy. Royal Astronomical Society, Monthly Notices 202, 615–627 (1983)

GP-Fileprints: File Types Detection Using Genetic Programming

Ahmed Kattan[1], Edgar Galván-López[2], Riccardo Poli[1], and Michael O'Neill[2]

[1] School of Computer Science and Electronic Engineering, University of Essex, Colchester, UK
[2] Natural Computing Research & Applications Group, University College Dublin, Ireland
akatta@essex.ac.uk, edgar.galvan@ucd.ie, rpoli@essex.ac.uk, m.oneill@ucd.ie

Abstract. We propose a novel application of Genetic Programming (GP): the identification of file types via the analysis of raw binary streams (i.e., without the use of meta data). GP evolves programs with multiple components. One component analyses statistical features extracted from the raw byte-series to divide the data into blocks. These blocks are then analysed via another component to obtain a signature for each file in a training set. These signatures are then projected onto a two-dimensional Euclidean space via two further (evolved) program components. K-means clustering is applied to group similar signatures. Each cluster is then labelled according to the dominant label for its members. Once a program that achieves good classification is evolved it can be used on unseen data without requiring any further evolution. Experimental results show that GP compares very well with established file classification algorithms (i.e., Neural Networks, Bayes Networks and J48 Decision Trees).

1 Introduction

From the point of view of an operating system or standard high-level programming languages, a file is normally treated as a sequence of elementary data units, typically bytes. File format is a particular way to encode information for storage in a computer so that the file can be correctly interpreted by the operating system. Unfortunately, there are no universal standards for file types and there are hundreds of file types. This makes file type identification a difficult but increasingly significant problem. Different operating systems have traditionally used different approaches to solve this problem (i.e., file extensions and magic numbers). This, however, is very unreliable given that any user or application can easily change the extension of a file or change the file's meta data. A method is required to identify file's contents. This is useful for applications such as email spam filter, virus detection, forensic analysis and network security.

This paper proposes an application based on the use of Genetic Programming (GP) [7,12] to identify the file contents by analysing the raw binary streams. The question that we investigate is whether it is possible for GP to extract certain regularities from the raw byte-series of files and correlate them with particular data types without the need of any other meta data. The paper is organised as follows. In Section 2 we review previous work related to this research. Section 3 presents the details of the proposed method for file type detection. In Section 4, the experimental setup used to conduct our experiments is presented and in Section 5 we present and discuss our results. Finally, Section 6 draws some conclusions.

A.I. Esparcia-Alcazar et al. (Eds.): EuroGP 2010, LNCS 6021, pp. 134–145, 2010.

2   Previous Work

In [9], McDaniel and Heydari proposed an approach for automatically generating "fingerprints" for files. These fingerprints were then used to recognise the true type of unknown files based on their content instead of using the metadata associated with them. The authors used three algorithms to build these fingerprints: Byte Frequency Analysis (BFA), Byte Frequency Cross-Correlation (BFC) and the File Header/Trailer (FHT) algorithm. The BFA algorithm works by drawing a frequency distribution of the number of occurrences with which each byte value occurs in a file. This frequency distribution is useful in determining the type of a file because many file types have consistent patterns in their frequency distribution. The BFA algorithm presents some limitations related to the fact that it compares overall byte-frequency distributions. This issue is addressed by the BFC algorithm by taking the relationship between byte value frequencies into account. In BFC, two values are calculated: the average difference in frequency between all byte pairs and a correlation strength. Finally, the FHT algorithm works by using file headers and file trailers. These are pattern of bytes that appear in a fixed location of the file: at the beginning and the end of the file. The authors tested the described algorithms and constructed thirty file-type fingerprints using four test files for each file type (i.e., a total library of 120 files). They reported that BFA and BFC showed poor performance (i.e., an accuracy in the range of 27.5% and 45.83%) compared to FHT algorithm (which had an accuracy of 95.83%).

Later, this work has been criticised in [8], by Li et al., who claimed that a single fingerprint is insufficient to represent whole classes of files. Li et al. proposed to analyse the data using n-grams to identify multiple centroids – fingerprints – for each file type. They applied three different techniques: i) Truncation, where part of the file header is analysed and compared with single representative fingerprints; ii) Multi-centroids, where a group of fingerprints is used to form clusters with K-means, each cluster representing a particular file type, then unseen data is classified according to minimal distance; iii) Exemplar files, where unseen data is compared to all fingerprints from all trained data types and classified based on the closest. The authors reported some problems when classifying similar data types such as GIF and JPG. Also, some difficulties appeared when classifying PDF and MS office file types, as some embedded images and figures mislead the algorithms.

Karresand and Shahmehri [6] proposed a method called Oscar that allows classification of data fragments based on their structures without the need of any other meta data (e.g., header information). For this purpose, they used the Byte Frequency Distribution (BFD) of data fragments and calculated the mean and the standard deviation for each byte value. When these measures are put together, they form a model which is used to identify unknown data fragments. In [5], the same authors extended this approach by calculating the rate of change (RoC) (i.e., the absolute value of the difference between two consecutive byte values in a data fragment). RoC allows incorporating the ordering of the bytes into the identification process. The authors reported that their approach, tested using only JPEG files, gave a 99.2% detection rate. The slowest implementation of the algorithm scans a 72.2MB in approximately 2.5 seconds and this scales linearly.

Hall and Wilbon [3] used a sliding window of fixed size and measured the entropy and the data compressibility with LZW compression to identify file types. For each file type, these measurements were averaged from training examples and the standard deviation calculated for each corresponding point. Later, unseen data was compared with these models to predict their contents. The authors reported that entropy was not successful at associating the correct file type with unseen data. Also, this work reported that some file types such as BMP can vary greatly and it is very difficult to correctly classify them based on the proposed method.

Erbacher and Mullholland [1] focused their attention on the location and identification of data types embedded within a file, to offer analysts a technique to more efficiently locate relevant data on a hard drive. For this purpose, the authors used a range of statistical analyses with a variety of file types and were able to identify the types of data embedded within a file. The authors were able to identify five statistics that gave sufficient information to differentiate the different types of data: average, standard deviation, kurtosis, distribution of averages and distribution of standard deviations.

None of the previous methods used evolutionary algorithms, including GP, to solve the problem of identifying file types from their raw binary streams.

3   Approach

An ideal security system would be one that non-invasively reads data from files and detects their contents without the need for human intervention. In this paper we propose a system based on the use of the GP that takes one further step towards the ideal security system. The use of GP to identify file types from their raw binary streams has not been explored thus far. Here, we investigate how to evolve programs that detect the contents of files and inform the user of any suspicious contents according to predefined settings.

Our approach, broadly outlined in Fig. 1, works as follows. We try to spot regularities within the raw byte series and to associate them to different file types (e.g., TXT, PDF, JPG). Each class indicates the contents of the data. The system works in two main stages: i) Training, where the system learns to match different byte-series characteristics with different classes, and ii) Testing, where the system classifies unseen data. The system processes raw byte-series signals and performs three major functions: a) Segmentation of the byte-series based on their statistical features, b) Fileprint creation, and c) Classification of the identified fileprints into their types (e.g., TXT, PDF, JPG). For these tasks, GP has been supplied with a language that allows it to extract statistical features from byte-series. The selection of the primitives of the language was carefully made to avoid unnecessary growth in the search space, while at the same time ensuring that it is rich enough to express the solution. Table 1 reports the primitive set of the system.

The system starts by randomly initialising a population of individuals using ramped half-and-half [7]. As exemplified in Fig. 2, each individual has a multi-tree representation comprising one splitter tree, one fileprint tree and two feature-extraction trees. Multi-tree representations of this kind are common in GP, and have been used, for example, for data classification in [2] and [10].

We used a representation similar to the one proposed by Haynes in [4]. The population is stored into a 2D vector (vector of trees). Each individual is assigned to a fixed position. Thus, individuals components are co-evolved as they are always selected simultaneously.

In the next sections we describe the role of each of the trees in an individual in detail.

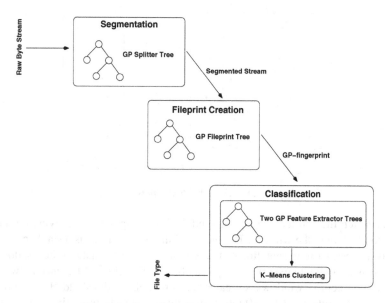

Fig. 1. Outline of our file-type detection process

Table 1. Primitive set used in our experiments

Function	Input
Median, Mean, Average deviation Standard deviation, Variance, Skew, Kurtosis, Entropy, Geometric Mean	Vector of Integers (0-255)
$+, -, /, *, Sin, Cos, Sqrt, log$	Real number

Table 2. Parameters used to conduct our experiments

Parameter	Value
Population Size	100
Generations	30
Crossover Rate	50%
Mutation Rate	50%
Elitism	20%
Tournament Size	5

3.1 Splitter Tree

It is very difficult to extract statistical features from the raw byte-series and directly correlate them with a particular data type. Furthermore, over time there has been an increase in the use of files with complex structures that store data of different types simultaneously. For example, a single game file might contain executable code, text, pictures and background music. Also, many file types, e.g., OpenOffice's ODT, Microsoft's DOCX or a ZIP file, are in fact archives containing inhomogeneous data. This makes the task of recognising file types is today even more difficult and traditional methods unreliable. It is, therefore, necessary to properly handle the fact files may contain multiple data types. The main job of the splitter trees is to split the given raw byte-series into smaller segments based on their statistical features in such a way that each segment is composed of statistically uniform data.

The system moves a sliding window of size L over the given byte-series with steps of S bytes, where, naturally, $S < L$.

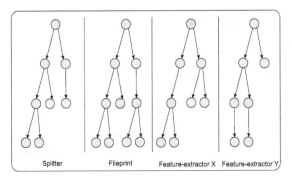

Fig. 2. A typical individual representation

At each step the splitter tree is evaluated. This corresponds to applying a function, f_{splitter}, to the data in the window. The output of the program tree is a single number, λ, which is an abstract representation of the homogeneity of the data in the window. The system then splits the byte-series at a particular position if the difference between the λ's in two consecutive windows is greater than a predefined threshold, θ. The threshold θ has been set arbitrarily ($\theta = 10$ in our implementation). In preliminary experiments we found that small changes in θ did not affect the performance of splitter trees. This is because evolution is free to change the magnitude of the outputs produced by splitter trees to adapt to the threshold. Also, after trying different settings we found that the size of the sliding window L should be large enough to allow the splitter tree to capture useful information regarding the homogeneity of the data and small enough to not conceal statistical differences in the fragments of the data. In our implementation $L = 100$ and $S = 50$.

An effective splitter tree would be able to detect the statistical differences within the data and divide the file into different segments based on the contents of each segment. For example, if the given data was a document file that contains text and graphical charts, a good splitter tree would notice the change in the byte-series values from the text to the pictures and *vice versa*. Moreover, an ideal splitter tree might even detect different fragments within the same data type (e.g., a page full of blank lines within the text or white area in a picture).

3.2   Fileprint Tree

Unlike other techniques where files are processed as single units, our approach attempts to divide the file into smaller segments via the splitter tree and understand the type of each segment separately via the *fileprint* tree before making a final determination about the file type. The main job of the *fileprint* tree is to identify a unique signature for each file. These signatures are meant to be similar for files of the same type and different for files of different types. Hence, the outputs of the fileprint tree are easier to classify into different classes.

As illustrated in Fig. 3, the fileprint tree receives the segments identified by the splitter tree for each file and processes each segment individually. This corresponds to applying a function, $f_{\text{fileprint}}(S_i)$, to the data within each segment, S_i. The output

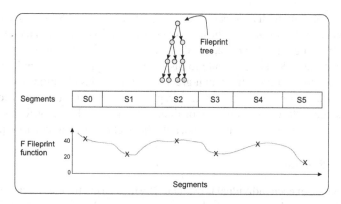

Fig. 3. The fileprint tree processes the segments identified by splitter tree (top). Its output produces a GP-fingerprint for the file (bottom).

of the program is a single number, α, which is an abstract representation of the features of the data within the segments. Thus, the fileprint tree will produce a vector $v = (\alpha_1, \alpha_2, \cdots, \alpha_i)$. Each v contains a series of abstracted numbers that describe the contents of a particular file. Each vector v is referred to as a *GP-fingerprint*. A collection of vectors, $V = (v_1, v_2, \cdots, v_n)$, is obtained after execution of the fileprint tree with all the files in the training set.

3.3   Feature-Extraction Trees

The main job of the feature-extraction trees in our GP representation is to extract features (using the primitives in Table 1) from the GP-fingerprints identified by the fileprint tree and to project them onto a two-dimensional Euclidian space. Here we used two feature extraction trees. In future research we will study the benefits and drawbacks of using a different number.

Each feature-extraction tree represents a transformation formula which maps the original feature set (or more precisely the subset of the features used as terminals in the tree) into a single value output, which can be considered as a composite, higher-level feature. We use an unsupervised pattern classification approach on the outputs produced by the two feature-extraction trees to discover regularities in the training data files. In particular, we used K-means clustering to organise blocks (as represented by their two composite features) into groups. With this algorithm objects within a cluster are similar to each other but dissimilar from objects in other clusters. The advantage here is that the approach does not impose any constrain on the shape of the clusters.

Once the training set is clustered, we can then use the clusters found by K-means to perform classification of unseen data. Naturally, while we can tell K-means to group items in exactly k clusters, being unsupervised, K-means has no way of knowing what each cluster is meant to represent. So, it might produce results that are not useful to classify the files in the training set. For example, at least in principle, K-means might find that text files naturally form two separate groups (judging from their two composite features).

So, how do we convince K-means to group things differently? Simple: we do not act on the K-means algorithm; we act on the composite features. That is, by using evolution, we ask GP to come up with two feature-extraction trees that lead K-means to cluster the file fingerprints in the training set in such a way that all fingerprints in a cluster belong to the same file types and that different file types are associated to different clusters. At the end of evolution, K-means is able to distinguish file types based on their contents. The advantage of this approach is that it greatly simplifies classification. This is because evolution pushes feature-extraction trees to represent the data in such a way to optimise the performance of the classification algorithm. Here, we used K-means for its simplicity of implementation and its execution speed, but other techniques might work equally well.

3.4   Fitness Function

The performance of each individual is evaluated by measuring the classification accuracy of the training examples. Although the system uses a multi-tree representation where each tree has a particular function, this form of performance evaluation is sufficient to encourage each component of a program to perform the particular sub-task assigned to it to its best to achieve good performance in the difficult task of recognising file types.

Fitness is evaluated after performing the clustering of the outputs of the feature-detection trees using K-means. Our fitness evaluation is based on the quality of the clustering in terms of cluster homogeneity and cluster separation.

The homogeneity of the clusters is calculated as follows. As exemplified in Fig. 4, we count the members of each cluster, each data point in the cluster representing the GP-fingerprint of one file in the training set. Since we already know the content type for each fingerprint, we label the clusters according to the dominant data type. The fitness function rates the homogeneity of clusters in terms of the proportion of data points – GP-fingerprints – that are labelled as the file type that labels the cluster.

The system prevents the labelling of different clusters with the same file type even in the cases where the proportions in two or more clusters are equal. Using the information about the GP-fingerprints and their labels we can easily find the total number of data points that belong to the same data type. Any deviations from this optimal value due to clusters containing extra members should be discouraged. Thus, we use a penalty term in the fitness function to penalise extra members in the clusters.

More formally, the clusters homogeneity can be expressed as follows. Let H be a function that calculates the homogeneity of a cluster and CL_i be the ith cluster. Furthermore, let k be the total number of clusters and λ the penalty term. Then,

$$f_{\text{homogeneity}} = \frac{\sum_{i=1}^{k} H(CL_i) - \lambda}{k}$$

The homogeneity of the clusters is not the only measurement of the quality of the classification performed by K-means. Homogenous clusters with objects far apart within a cluster will extend the clusters boundary and may lead to inaccurate classification of unseen objects. Also, clusters that overlap are not suitable. Ideal clusters are separated from each other and densely grouped near their centroids. Therefore, we also measure and reward the separation of the clusters.

The formulation of the Davis Bouldin Index (DBI) proposed in [13] was used to measure cluster quality. DBI is a measure of the nearness of the clusters members to their centroids and the distance between clusters centroids. DBI can be expressed as follows.

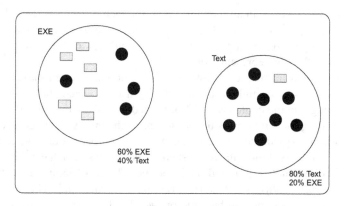

Fig. 4. Homogeneity measure of the clusters

Let C_i be the centroid of the ith cluster and d the nth data member that belongs to the ith cluster. In addition, let the Euclidian distance between d^n and C_i expressed by the function be $dis(d^n, C_i)$. Furthermore, let k be the total number of clusters. Finally, let the standard deviation be denoted as $std()$. Then,

$$DBI = \frac{\sum_{i=1}^{k} std[dis(C_i, d^0), \cdots, dis(C_i, d^n)]}{dis(C_0, C_1, \cdots, C_k)}$$

A small DBI index indicates well separated and grouped clusters. Therefore, we add the negation of the DBI index to the total fitness in order to push evolution to separate clusters (i.e., minimise the DBI). So, the DBI is treated as a penalty value, the lower the DBI the lower penalty applied to the fitness. Thus, the fitness function is as follows:

$$fitness = f_{\text{homogeneity}} - DBI \tag{1}$$

A significant advantage with our method is that the approach does not impose any constraint on the shape of the clusters. Once the training set is clustered, we can then use the clusters found by K-means to perform classification of unseen data.

In the testing phase, unseen data goes through the three components of the evolved solution: blocks are produced by the splitter tree, the GP-fingerprint is obtained by the fileprint tree, and, finally, GP-fingerprints are projected onto a two-dimensional Euclidean space by the two feature-extraction trees. Then, these are classified based on the majority class labels of their K-nearest neighbours. We use a weighted majority voting, where each nearest neighbour is weighted based on its distance from the newly projected data point. More specifically the weight is $w = 1/distance(x_i, z_i,)$, where x_i is the nearest neighbour and z_i is the newly projected data point.

3.5   Search Operators

There are several options for applying genetic operators to a multi-tree representation. For example, we could apply a particular operator that has been selected (based on a predefined probability of application) to all trees within an individual. Alternatively, we could iterate over the trees in an individual and, for each, select a potentially different operator. Another possibility would be to constrain crossover to happen only between trees at the same position in the two parents or we could let evolution freely crossover different trees within the representation.

It is unclear what technique is best. In [10] the authors argued that crossing over trees at different positions might result in swapping useless genetic material resulting in weaker offspring. On the contrary, in [2] suggested that restricting the crossover positions is misleading for evolution as the clusters are indistinguishable during evolution.

In preliminary experiments we tried all of these approaches and we learnt that a good way to guide evolution in our system is as follows. Let the ith individual of the population be denoted as I_i and let T_c^i be the cth tree of individual i, where $c \in \{splitter, fileprint, feature - extraction_x, feature - extraction_y\}$. The system selects an operator with a predefined probability for each T_c^i. In the crossover, a restriction is applied so that splitter and fileprint trees can only be crossed over with their equivalent tree type. However, the system is able to freely crossover feature-extractions trees at any position.

4   Experimental Setup

Experiments were performed on various file types. The main aim of the experiments was to evaluate the performance of the algorithm and to assess the algorithms behaviour under a variety of circumstances.

The results presented in the following section were obtained by using the parameter settings illustrated in Table 2. Evolution halts when 30 generations have elapsed.

Experiments have been divided into four sets. Each set involved 10 independent runs (40 runs in total). In the first set we trained the system to distinguish between two different file types. We increased the number of file types to three in the second set of experiments, to four in the third set, while the last set included five file types. The files types that have been included in the experiments were selected because they are among the most commonly used files types. During the experiments, the algorithm has been trained to distinguish between similar files types (JPG and GIF or TXT and PDF). This allowed us to study the algorithm's ability in distinguishing the files based on their types rather than their contents. The corresponding training sets included 10 different files of each type. Several considerations were taken into account when designing the training set. The training set is processed many times by each individual in each generation. Thus, it has to be small enough to avoid over-fitting and yet big enough to contain enough examples to aid the learning process. Table 3 presents the contents of the training sets for each set of experiments.

To assess the system learning and generalisation we evaluated the accuracy of the evolved programs with a test set. The test set is composed of 30 different files for each type. Table 3 presents the contents of the testing cases for each set of experiments. The test sets are completely independent of the training sets. It should be noticed that the size of test set is bigger than the training set. Also, the test set included complex files such as EXE games, and large PDFs that contain figures and charts. This is to allow us to probe the generalisation capabilities of the evolved solutions.

Table 3. Training and test sets for the experiments

		Training set		Test set	
Function	*File types*	*Total size*	*Number of files*	*Total size*	*Number of files*
2 file types	JPG, GIF	618 KB	20	5.44MB	60
3 file types	JPG, GIF, TXT	987 KB	30	7.9MB	90
4 file types	JPG, GIF, TXT, PDF	1.55 MB	40	16 MB	120
5 file types	JPG, GIF, TXT, EXE, PDF	2 MB	50	17.7MB	150

Table 4. Test-set performance results. Numbers in **boldface** represent the best performance achieved.

Method	*2 file types*	*3 file types*	*4 file types*	*5 file types*
Neural Networks	58.33%	66.67%	74.17%	39.33%
Bayes Nettworks	50.00%	66.67%	83.33%	48.67%
J48	51.67%	51.67%	74.17%	48.67%
GP-fingerprint	**85.00%**	**88.90%**	**85.00%**	**70.77%**

In order to evaluate our approach against other state of the art classification techniques we compared our results with standard Neural Networks [14], Bayes Network [14], and J48 decision trees [14] (a variant of C4.5). For these classification algorithms we used the implementation provided by WEKA [11]. We provided to these algorithms the same training sets and the same primitive sets as our GP system in order to obtain fair comparisons.[1] For each of the Neural Networks and Bayes Network systems we performed 10 different runs for each data set, as we did for our GP system. J48, being a deterministic algorithm, was only executed once for each data set.

5 Results and Analysis

Table 4 summarises the results of our experiments comparing GP with other techniques. For each non-deterministic algorithm we report the best results obtained within independent 10 runs. GP appears to outperform the other classification methods considered by a considerable margin. We believe that the good classification accuracy of our approach is largely attributable to the segmenting the data into smaller parts and obtaining fingerprints.

For all algorithms in we see that performance increases as the number of file types increases from 2 to 4. One might wonder why this happens: recognising two file types would appear to be an easier task than recognising three or four. To understand this, we need to consider that the data in Table 4 represent test-set performance. The reason why performance is lower in the two-file case than in the three- or four-file cases is over-fitting. As one can see in Table 3, the fewer the file types in a data set, the smaller

---

[1] Neural Networks and Bayes Network use deterministic learning models but initial networks are random.

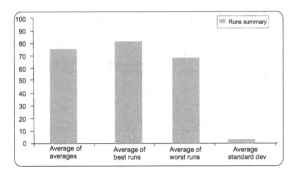

Fig. 5. Summary of results of 40 runs. Ordinates represent percentages.

the data set. Thus, it is easier for a learning algorithm to over fit training sets with 2 and 3 file types than the set with 4. As a result, the fewer the file types the worse the generalisation performance of the corresponding learning systems.

It should be noticed that the lowest performance for all classification algorithms shown in Table 4 occurred when classifying 5 file types. This is due to the fact that the complexity of the problem increases with the number of classes. However, GP performance degraded less than for other approaches indicating that our system may be more robust. The disadvantage of our approach, however, is training time: our GP system entails a learning process of several hours, while other classification techniques only consume a few seconds for the whole learning process. On the other hand, it has to be pointed out that the solution evolved by our system take only a few seconds to predict the files contents. So, they are not only accurate, but also entirely practical.

Although in Table 4 we reported best performance for all systems, including our GP one, in fact our system is remarkably reliable across runs. Fig. 5 summarises the results obtained in our 40 runs. We measured the quality of each experiment set (four sets, each set included 10 runs) by calculating the following statistics: the average classification accuracy across the test files, the corresponding standard deviation, and the best and worst classification accuracies in all runs. The first bar in Fig. 5 shows the average of the resulting four averages. The second bar in the figure is the average of the best evolved program in each set. The third bar represents the quality of the worst evolved program in each set. Finally, the last bar shows the average standard deviation. Note that the average *worst* performance of our GP system is better than the average *best* performance of the other systems in Table 4.

The low standard deviation and reasonably high average performance of our system suggests that one is likely to obtain accurate file-type prediction models within very few GP runs.

6   Conclusions

In this paper we have proposed a system based on genetic programming to evolve programs that can identify file contents without making use of any meta data. This is a novel application of GP.

The classification accuracies obtained by GP were far superior to those obtained by a number of classical algorithms from WEKA [11], namely artificial neural networks, Bayesian networks and J48 decision trees. While evolution is relatively slow with the large training sets required by this application, the resulting programs are entirely practical, being able to process tens of megabytes of data in seconds.

In the future we intend to extend the work to larger and more varied data sets and, hopefully, to turn the best solutions evolved by GP in public-domain stand-alone programs, which could perhaps be integrated in spam filters and anti-virus software.

References

1. Erbacher, R.F., Mulholland, J.: Identification and localization of data types within large-scale file systems. In: SADFE 2007: Proceedings of the Second International Workshop on Systematic Approaches to Digital Forensic Engineering, Washington, DC, USA, pp. 55–70. IEEE Computer Society, Los Alamitos (2007)
2. Boric, N., Estevez, P.A.: Genetic programming-based clustering using an information theoretic fitness measure. In: Proceedings of the IEEE Congress on Evolutionary Computation CEC 2006, pp. 31–38. IEEE, Los Alamitos (2007)
3. Hall, G.A., Davis, W.P.: Sliding window measurement for file type identification. Technical report, Computer Forensics and Intrusion Analysis Group, ManTech. Security and Mission Assurance, Rexas (2006)
4. Haynes, T., Sen, S., Sen, I., Schoenefeld, D., Wainwright, R.: Evolving a team. In: Working Notes of the AAAI 1995 Fall Symposium on Genetic Programming, pp. 23–30. AAAI, Menlo Park (1995)
5. Karresand, M., Shahmehri, N.: File type identification of data fragments by their binary structure. In: Proceedings of the 2006 IEEE Workshop on Information Assurance, NY, pp. 140–147. IEEE Computer Society, Los Alamitos (2006)
6. Karresand, M., Shahmehri, N.: Oscar – file type identification of binary data in disk clusters and ram pages. In: Security and Privacy in Dynamic Environments, pp. 413–424. Springer, Boston (2006)
7. Koza, J.R.: Genetic Programming: On the Programming of Computers by Means of Natural Selection. The MIT Press, Cambridge (1992)
8. Li, W.-J., Stolfo, S.J., Herzog, B.: Fileprints: Identifying file types by n-gram analysis. In: Proceedings of the 2005 IEEE Workshop on Information Assurance, pp. 64–71 (2005)
9. McDaniel, M., Heydari, M.H.: Content based file type detection algorithms. In: HICSS 2003: Proceedings of the 36th Annual Hawaii International Conference on System Sciences (HICSS 2003) - Track 9, Washington, DC, USA, p. 332.1. IEEE Computer Society, Los Alamitos (2003)
10. Muni, D.P., Pal, N.R., Das, J.: A novel approach to design classifiers using genetic programming. IEEE Transactions on Evolutionary Computation 8(2), 183–196 (2004)
11. U. of Waikato. Weka (July 2009), http://www.cs.waikato.ac.nz/ml/weka/
12. Poli, R., Langdon, W.B., McPhee, N.F.: A Field Guide to Genetic Programming (With contributions by J. R. Koza) (2008), http://lulu.com, http://www.gp-field-guide.org.uk
13. Sepulveda, F., Meckes, M., Conway, B.: Cluster separation index suggests usefulness of non-motor eeg channels in detecting wrist movement direction intention. In: IEEE Conference on Cybernetics and Intelligent Systems, pp. 943–947. IEEE Press, Los Alamitos (2004)
14. Witten, I.H., Frank, E.: Data Mining: Practical Machine Learning Tools and Techniques. Morgan Kaufmann, San Francisco (2005)

A Many Threaded CUDA Interpreter for Genetic Programming

W.B. Langdon

CREST centre, Department of Computer Science,
King's College, London, Strand, London, WC2R 2LS, UK

Abstract. A Single Instruction Multiple Thread CUDA interpreter provides SIMD like parallel evaluation of the whole GP population of $\frac{1}{4}$ million reverse polish notation (RPN) expressions on graphics cards and nVidia Tesla. Using sub-machine code tree GP a sustain peak performance of 665 billion GP operations per second (10,000 speed up) and an average of 22 peta GP ops per day is reported for a single GPU card on a Boolean induction benchmark never attempted before, let alone solved.

1 Introduction

There are two main approaches to running genetic programming [10,1,17,20] on highly parallel hardware such as GPUs: 1) compiling evolved programs and running multiple fitness cases in parallel [7,3] 2) interpreting multiple programs in

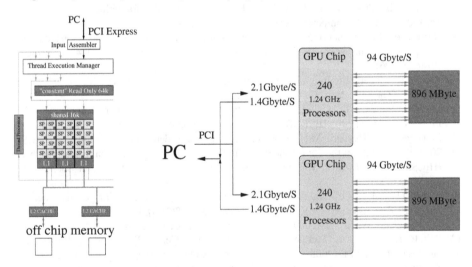

Fig. 1. Left: nVidia G80 GPU multi processor. Right: A GeForce 295 GTX contains 2×10 multi processor on two chips. Each stream processor (SP) obeys the same instruction at the same time. However each has its own registers and its own access to shared and constant memory. For efficiency multi-processors try to coalesce multiple separate access to off chip memory into a single access.

A.I. Esparcia-Alcazar et al. (Eds.): EuroGP 2010, LNCS 6021, pp. 146–158, 2010.

parallel [15,21,16,23,18,4]. The compiled approach suffers from the overhead of running the compiler on the host computer. However Harding [8] has recently demonstrated parallel compilation of the GP population on multiple workstations. Interpreters can run programs immediately but interpreted code is slower than optimised compiler generated machine code. GPU interpreters typically gain their speed by evaluating the whole population in parallel but, as we shall see, GPUs can also run fitness cases in parallel, or mixtures of the two approaches [11].

The essential feature of parallelism in current generation graphic processing units is that they are intended to run programs on multiple data. Graphical applications often require the rapid real time transformation of many data items. This can be performed efficiently in parallel because essentially the same transformation is applied to each datum and the data do not interact. E.g. the two dimensional appearance of a complex three dimensional scene is calculated by using one program to calculate the appearance of the many thousands of three dimensional elements independently. Separate programs are used to deal with cases where elements overlap or obscure each other.

High end GPUs typically contain a few multi-processors, each of which operate in parallel. Each multi-processor is a tightly integrated unit and in some ways resembles the earlier single instruction multiple data (SIMD) parallel computers. Both provide a limited form of parallelism which is convenient to implement in hardware. The hardware gains its speed by having many stream processing units doing the same operation at the same time on different data. See Figure 1. However unlike MasPar SIMD supercomputers of twenty years ago, GPUs are mass market consumer electronics devices for computer games and priced for the hobbyist not the corporation. Hundreds of millions of GPU have been sold rather than approximately 250 MasPar MP-2.

In GPU terminology each stream processor is running a thread. At any instant, all the threads do the same thing. But this raises a problem. What if the program contains branches? E.g. `if(data==0){}` `else {}`. If the contents of `data` are different in different threads, the hardware will decide either to do the `if` or the `else`. It executes all the threads whose instance of `data` puts them down the same route. The hardware stalls all the other threads. This is known as divergence.[1] At some point the hardware will stop the active threads and restart those it stalled. Eventually the whole program will be run. However divergence is a major source of inefficiency.

nVidia's CUDA has a fairly complicated memory hierarchy. However the most important distinction for performance is the small amount of memory ($\approx$1 megabyte) on the GPU chip and the very much bigger memory on the GPU card ($\approx$1 gigabyte). (Currently the GPU has no direct access to the host computer's RAM. Instead data must be explicitly copied to and from the GPU by the PC. See Figure 1) The delay in reading from off-chip memory is hundreds of times more than access to on-chip memory. This is so big that it makes sense

---

[1] Divergence can be avoided by a data flow approach in which the ifs are replaced by evaluating all possibilities and using array indexes to chose from them. However interpreting a single GP individual across multiple test cases can be faster.

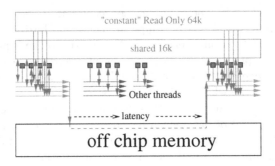

Fig. 2. Reading from onboard GPU memory causes active threads to stall possibly allowing other threads to be active. In contrast access to small areas of read only and shared memory are very much faster. The interpreter stack is placed in shared memory. To reduce bank conflicts stacks can be interleaved to use every 16th memory word.

for the hardware to pause threads which are waiting for off-chip data and start others which are ready to go. See Figure 2. The hardware can seamlessly handle many thousands of threads. (In the case of the 37-Mux we use 262 144 threads.) This all happens transparently for the CUDA programmer.

A single instruction multiple data (SIMD) interpreter for GP was originally proposed by Hugues Juille [9] for the MasPar MP-2 computer. It has recently been used for nVidia GeForce 8800 graphics hardware by ourselves [15] and Robilliard [21]. These SIMD GPU interpreters evaluate each GP tree by treating it as a reverse polish (RPN) expression which is evaluated via a stack in single pass. I.e. without the recursive back tracking normally associated with trees. The stack required careful implementation in RapidMind 2 [15] but is straight forward with nVidia CUDA. For every instruction, SIMD interpreters use cond or if branches to skip through the whole instruction set and only evaluate the current instruction.

The SIMD approach is suitable for use with many types of GP however we demonstrate it on two Boolean benchmark problems (20-multiplexor and 37-multiplexor) where CUDA allows access to another level of parallelism. Sub-machine code GP uses parallel bit or byte level operations, to execute up to 32 (or 64) fitness cases simultaneously [19]. Using pseudo random sampling of test cases with a population of a quarter of a million programs a single GPU is able to solve the 20-multiplexor problem. Peak sustained performance of just over 445 billion GP operations/second was achieved when testing all $2^{37} = 137$ billion fitness cases for solutions to the 37-multiplexor. Probably compiled code would be still faster. When including all activity on the CPU as well as the GPU across the whole run, the single 295 GTX averaged 254 billion GPop/s. In contrast Harding [8] measured, for a compiled approach using a cluster of 14+ workstations each equipped with a low end GPU, a best peak rate of 12.74 billion GP OP/sec for Cartesian GP on a data intensive graphics task.

Table 1. Genetic Programming Parameters for Solving 20 and 37 Multiplexors

Terminals:	20 or 37 Boolean inputs D0–D36
Functions:	AND, OR, NAND, NOR
Fitness:	Pseudo random sample of 2048 of 1 048 576 or 8192 of 137 438 953 472 fitness cases.
Tournament:	4 members run on same random sample. New samples for each tournament and each generation.
Population:	262 144
Initial pop:	Ramped half-and-half 4:5 (20-Mux) or 5:7 (37-Mux)
Parameters:	50% subtree crossover, 5% subtree 45% point mutation. Max depth 15, max size 511 (20-Mux) or 1023 (37-Mux).
Termination:	5 000 generations

2   Genetic Programming Benchmarks

The original intentions was simply to use the 20 Boolean Multiplexor [10] as an impressive demonstration of the GPU. After all it has never been solved by a tree GP before. ([24] used a totally different representation.) The details of our GP are given in Table 1. The choice of population size was motivated by the capacity of the GPU. While the terminal and function sets are those often used for the even parity benchmark [10]. The resulting evolutions are plotted in Figure 3. Solutions are found in generation 423 (20-Mux) and 2866 (37-Mux).

3   RPN GPU Sub-machine-code Genetic Programming

This is the first genetic programming implementation to exploit sub-machine code level parallelism inherent in every GPU. Indeed it is the first time sub-machine-code GP has been used with reverse polish expressions. However it can obviously be used in any Boolean problem. Indeed many non-evolutionary algorithms with a large logic based component could benefit from this approach to exploiting bit-level parallelism. The sub-machine code approach has also been used in the continuous domain (by using 8-bit precision) and in graphics (e.g. 5×5 OCR) [19]. It is straight forward to implement in CUDA compared to other high-level GPGPU languages like RapidMind 2.

4   Genetic Programming on the Host Computer

The GPU is only used for fitness evaluation. When a generation has been interpreted the fitness values of the current individuals are returned to the host. All other operations (crossover, mutation, selection, gathering statistics etc.) are performed by the Linux host computer.

The genetic programming trees are created and manipulated by crossover and mutation as Reverse Polish Notation (RPN) expressions. This is exactly the

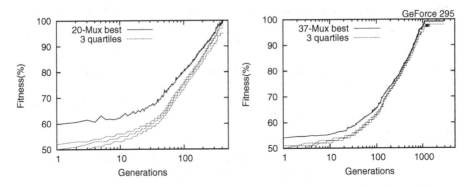

Fig. 3. Evolution of fraction of test cases passed when solving the 20-multiplexor and 37-multiplexor. Dotted lines show three quaters of the population evolves to have fitness near that of the best. (The worst in population, not shown, also starts near 50% but falls towards zero, almost mirroring the best. This may be due to tiny programs being generated by subtree crossover [13, Figure 6] which have poor fitness.) The log-linear rise in fitness over most of the evolution is reminiscent of the coupon collector suggesting major building blocks are equally difficult. This 295 run found a 37-Mux solution in gen 1325 v. 2865 for the Tesla.

same format as is used by the GPU. I.e. the data is not converted between the host CPU and the GPU.

It is common in efficient C++ genetic programming implementations for run time to be totally dominated by the time taken for fitness evaluation and so crossover etc. can be discounted. However for the 37-Mux, due to the speed of the interpreter on the 295 GTX these normally inexpensive operations amount to 43% of the total run time. As fitness evaluation in the 20-Mux is less computationally demanding, this rises to 73%. Since the interpreter has been our focus, no effort has been spent on optimising the host side C++ code. Doubtless some efficiencies could be made to reduce the host side overhead.

Lewis proposed [18] a nice scheme with two GPUs which uses overlapping threads on a quad core computer to ensure both GPUs and CPUs are kept busy and says overlapping execution gave almost a threefold speed increase. He says his twin 112 core super clocked and overclocked GPUs gave up to 4 billion GP operations per second for his cyclic Cartesian GP system.

5   Randomised Test Suite Sub-sampling

The final research area was to use the 20-Mux to demonstrate statistically sound sampling [12,22]. We devised CUDA code which randomly generated samples [14] and tested all members of the same tournament on them. It continued to do this until statistical tests could demonstrate one of the four candidates was better than the other three. While successful, this was eventually abandoned for three reasons. 1) As the population converged, more and more tests would be required to reliably differentiate between the best and second best candidates. Indeed it was even considered adding a statistical test to stop evaluation if it was probably that there was no difference between the best two candidates. 2) The number of random samples needed is highly variable. Since we were using a single thread per program at the time, this lead to many cases where all but the last four programs on a multi-processor had finished. Thus most of the multi-processor was idle. Yet it could not be reassigned to other tasks untill the last four had finished. (Multiple threads will be discussed in Section 7.) 3) However the most compelling reason was we realised that sophisticated eradication of 99% of chance was not needed.

If a fixed number of samples are used, some tournaments are settled by chance. This means sometimes individuals are selected to be parents who would not have won (and so would have died childless) if all test cases had been run. Nevertheless the addition of limited noise in the selection scheme did not prevent solutions from evolving. The size of the sample was set by starting with a power of two and doubling it until a solution was found. For 20-Mux only 2048 samples of 1 048 576 were enough. Whereas for the 37-Mux, 8192 were sufficient.

6 CUDA Code

A fragment showing the main interpreter loop C++ code is given in Figure 4. This CUDA kernel runs in parallel simultaneously in thousands of different threads. Figure 4. shows the main data structures used by sub-machine code GP. Reverse polish expressions are evaluated sequentially from the start to the end (indicated by OPNOP). Terminals are pushed onto the stack (which is in __shared__ memory). In sub-machine code GP the first five inputs correspond to different 32-bit patterns (read from __constant__ train). The other inputs cause either 32 0s or 32 1s to be pushed onto the stack. The binary Boolean functions pop both their 32-bit arguments from the stack and push their 32-bit result back onto the stack. runprog leaves its answer on the top of each thread's stack.

Where there are not enough threads to permit all fitness cases to be run in parallel (i.e. runprog is used serially) it might be advantageous to copy Pop onto the chip itself. E.g. when proving the evolved solution on all 2^n fitness cases, it is copied to constant memory. (All the solutions have also been verified by extracting them and running them in a conventional computer.) Lewis reports [18] success with loading the population into shared memory. However shared memory is very limited and so we use all of it to hold the stacks rather than read-only cache copies of the programs. It appears to be more important to put the stacks close to the stream processors since they are both read and written to and used repeatedly. Indeed, given sufficient threads, the programs are only read once (so a cache is pointless). In cases where the programs are very small (so the stacks are also small) and each is run many times, it might be advantageous to use some of the on chip (i.e. constant or shared) memory to cache the population.

While Koza initially used a tree depth of 17 [10], in order to interpret 256 programs (i.e. 256 stacks) per multi-processor simultaneously, the stack size was

```
__constant__ const unsigned int train[8] =
  {0xAAAAAAAA,0xCCCCCCCC,0xF0F0F0F0,0xFF00FF00,0xffff0000,0,0,0};
extern __shared__ unsigned int shared_array[];
#define stack(sp) Stack[(sp)*blockDim.x+threadIdx.x]
__device__ inline void runprog(unsigned char* const Pop, const unsigned int prog,
                               const unsigned int test32, const int LEN) {

#define AND(A,B)  ((A) & (B))
#define OR(A,B)   ((A) | (B))
#define push(x) {stack(SP) = x; SP++;}
  unsigned int* Stack = shared_array;
  int SP = 0;
  for(unsigned int PC = 0;; PC++){
    const optype opcode = Pop[PC+(prog*LEN)]; //SETOPCODE;
    if(opcode==OPNOP) break;

    const int r = opcode - firstinput;
    if((r & (~7))==0) {push(train[r]);} //OP1
    else {
    const int r5 = opcode-inputd5; //ninputs <= 37bits
    if((r5 & (~31))==0) {
    if(test32 & (1<<r5)) {push(0xffffffff);}
    else                 {push(0x00000000);}
    } else {
    const unsigned int sp1 = stack(SP-1);
    const unsigned int sp2 = stack(SP-2);
    SP -= 2;
    switch(opcode) {
      case OPAND:  push( AND(sp1,sp2)); break;
      case OPOR:   push(  OR(sp1,sp2)); break;
      case OPNAND: push(~AND(sp1,sp2)); break;
      case OPNOR:  push( ~OR(sp1,sp2)); break;
}}}}}
```

Fig. 4. C++ CUDA code fragment for the sub-machine code GP SIMD reverse polish expression tree interpreter

dropped to 15. (Occupying $15 \times 256 = 3840$ of the 4032 available int.) Fortunately there are solutions to both benchmarks which can be evaluated with stacks of only 15 and GP is able to find them.

The interpreter has been used with multiple arity experiments. For GP primitives which take more than two inputs (e.g. if) the maximum stack depth can be more than the maximum tree depth. Either crossover etc. can be modified to enforce a stack limit rather than the conventional tree depth limit. Alternatively the existing tree depth limit can be retained and the corresponding maximum stack depth calculated. The kernel must then be configured to allow this stack size. Typically this means each block can have fewer threads, which will tend to reduce performance.

7 Speed

Performance depends both on the number of fitness cases run in parallel by the interpreter (nparallel) and the the number of copies of the interpreter run in parallel per multiprocessor (block_size). See Figure 5. Each 20-Mux tree is evaluated 64 times on randomly selected inputs. (Remember using sub-machine code GP means each evaluation covers 32 fitness cases, making a total of $32 \times 64 = 2048$.)

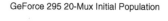

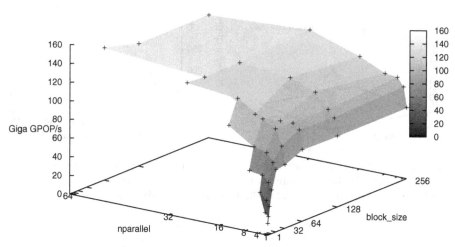

Fig. 5. Speed of interpreter v. number of fitness cases in nparallel threads and number of threads per multi-processor block. (CUDA grid size adjusted so the total number of threads is always $\frac{1}{4}$ million.)

The interpreter allows nparallel=1, 2, 4, 8, 16, 32 or 64 threads to be used per 20-Mux individual. Since all 64 evaluation must be run, each RPN expression in each thread is evaluated by a for loop 64, 32, 16, 8, 4, 2 or 1 times.

We are limited, by shared memory, to at most block_size=256 threads per multiprocessor. This means that if we test each individual with one thread (i.e. run it sequentially in a for loop 64 times) we can test up to 256 programs in parallel in each multi-processor. If we use two threads per program, we can simultaneously test 128 programs in each multi-processor. And so on until with maximum parallelism per 20-Mux program (i.e. nparallel=64) 1, 2 or 4 programs can be run in a single multi-processor block.

With 64, 128 or 256 threads per block, CUDA is approximately twice as fast when interpreting all 64 fitness cases in parallel compared to running them in sequence but interpreting multiple programs in the same block (see Figure 5). Evaluating the same expression in multiple threads should mean they do not diverge, so we expect better performance. However it is gratifying that the original single program-single thread SIMD approach [15] (which was designed for problems with a small number of fitness cases) gets within 50% of the speed where all the fitness cases are run in parallel. The fact that block_sizes 64, 128 and 256 give much the same performance suggests we are not getting any benefit (such as coalesce reads) by running multiple adjacent programs in the same block.

The interpreter tends to speed up in later generations as the trees get bigger (see Figure 7). Nevertheless the initial random population, i.e. Figure 5, is

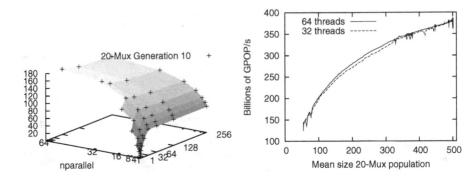

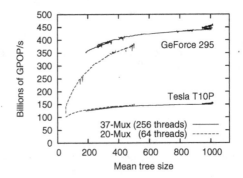

Fig. 6. Left: as Figure 5 but after ten generations. Right: Running all fitness cases in parallel (64 threads) is marginally faster than running each program twice in series with half the fitness cases in parallel (32 threads). Block_size= 64.

Fig. 7. Speed of CUDA Interpreter on GeForce 295 and early engineering 1.08GHz Tesla T10P v. average 20-Mux and 37-Mux tree sizes. The average speed, including selection crossover etc., for the 20-Mux is 96 (Tesla 68) and for 37-Mux it is 254 (Tesla 121) billion GP operation/second.

indicative of the general tradeoff between evaluating trees in parallel and the number of threads per multi-processor (Figure 6).

The slight difference between the two fastest configurations shown in Figure 5 remains small throughout the run. Figure 6 (right) shows maximum parallelism, whereby each program is run only once, is slightly faster (except in generation 0). Hence we use 64 threads per 20-Mux tree. This is consistent with Robilliard *et al.* [21] recommendation to run the interpreter so that each program's fitness cases are run in parallel.

8   Theoretical Performance: Infinite Parallelism Model

For any configuration of the interpreter there is a certain amount of work that must be done. The programs must be transfered to the GPU and their fitness values returned to the host computer and they must be interpreted. The nVidia bandwidthTest program measures the data transfer speeds to and from the GPU. This allows us to estimate the time to copy a 20-Mux population to the GPU: time = $512 \times 262\,144/2170$Mbytes per sec = 62ms. Time to return the (4 byte) fitness values to the host PC: time = $4 \times 262\,144/1433$Mbytes per sec = 0.7ms. (Total 63ms.)

The time taken to transfer data internally within the GPU is very difficult to estimate. It will not only depend upon the number of times each program is executed but also on the degree of coalescing of reads from global memory. This is difficult to estimate. However taking the raw figures from bandwidthTest suggests it can be too short (> 0.2ms) to contribute and global memory latency is much more important.

We estimate the minimum calculation time from when the interpreter gets its best speed. This is when confirming the generality of the evolved 20-Mux solution (507 instructions). Here the whole GPU is devoted to a single program in constant memory, thus removing latency and divergence. Allowing for the time to transfer the answer back to the host gives a minimum calculation time of 53 milliseconds, corresponding to a maximum interpretation rate for the 20-Mux of 573 billion GP operations per second. This gives an estimated minimum time for the initial 20-Mux generation of 115 milliseconds on the 295 GTX.

Figure 8 plots the actual time for all the ways of interpreting the initial population in parallel. We see the wall clock time falls linearly with degree of parallelism. By fitting a least squared error linear regression lines to each we can estimate the infinite parallelism execution time for the initial generation. These seven times are plotted in the right of Figure 8. The vertical intercept of a final regression line says the infinite parallelism execution time would be 223 milliseconds. This is somewhat above our estimate of 115 milliseconds. This suggests that it is not possible to obtain $573\ 10^9$ GP OP/s for the initial population (whose trees have on average only 55 instructions). Using our earlier estimate of transfer time but

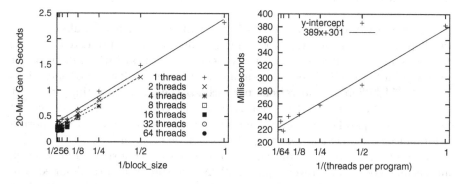

Fig. 8. Left: Elapse time for GeForce 295 GTX to interpret 1/4 million random 20-Mux programs. Right: Elapse time for infinite parallelism v. parallel threads per program. Time for infinite block_size (so 1/block_size=0) is estimated by Y-intercept of linear regression (left).

replacing using the solution (with 507 opcodes) with the new estimate of total time (223 ms) gives a new estimate of 188 billion GP operations per second for the infinite parallelism speed in the initial 20-Mux generation. The best configuration (see Figure 5) is 75% of this. I.e., on the 20-Mux initial population, the 295 GTX is within 25% of the best performance predicted if the interpreter worked with infinite parallelism.

9   Discussion

Modern high performance graphics hardware has a complex parallel hierarchy of memory and processing elements. CUDA exposes this to the programmer in a controlled and somewhat portable way. (I.e. between CUDA capable nVidia hardware.) In contrast other tools try to conceal this and provide a high level obscure view of the hardware. Programming GPUs using either is not easy. For the Mackey-Glass benchmark [15], CUDA is up to 92% faster than RapidMind 2 [21] on similar hardware.

Although we tried to get the best from the T10P Tesla's 192 cores, the CUDA code should run on any modern G80 GPU. In fact no changes to the kernel were needed to run on the GeForce 295 GTX.

For the largest of these problems, our results suggest the interpreter is already within 33% of the best that the current hardware (665 billion GP OP/sec) might deliver in practice.

The interpreter can be used in various models of parallelism. Naturally it is fastest when fitness testing is split across many threads. However when this is not possible individual GP trees can be tested by running fitness cases one after another but the hardware still permits many programs to be run in parallel. The interpreter also allows various intermediate combinations.

10   Conclusions

Ten years ago Koza *et al.* [2] said their Beowulf cluster delivered about a half peta-flop per day on genetic programming runs. We have presented a single office personal computer fitted with a top end graphics card which delivers not floating point but real GP operations at a sustained rate of 22 peta GP operations per day (254 billion GP operations per second). This is twenty times the best reported speed of the fastest previously published GP (obtained by running 14 workstations in parallel [8]) and more than sixty times that of the best reported performance of the next fastest single GPU genetic programming system [21].

The combination of powerful parallel processing in the form of a GPU card, sub-machine code GP, a reverse polish (RPN) interpreter and randomised sub-selection from a test suite has allowed us to solve using tree GP the Boolean 20-multiplexor problem. It has been estimated [24] that it would take more than 4 years. The GPU has consistently done it in less than an hour.

The 37-multiplexor benchmark has 137 billion fitness cases. It has never been attempted before. GP solves it in under a day.

Currently Tesla are available with up to 960 cores, running at up to 1.5 GHz, suggesting a further doubling of performance is possible immediately.

The single GPU code is available via FTP `cs.ucl.ac.uk` directory `genetic/gp-code/gp32cuda.tar.gz`

Acknowledgment

I am greatful for the assistance of Timothy Lanfear and Gernot Ziegler of nVidia, Simon Harding of Memorial, Sean Anderson and Stan Seibert. From King's, I would like to thank Graham Ashton, Don Lokuadassuriyage, Nikolay Korneyev and William Shaw. The initial early engineering Tesla was given by nVidia. Funded by EPSRC grant EP/D050863/1.

References

1. Banzhaf, W., Nordin, P., Keller, R.E., Francone, F.D.: Genetic Programming – An Introduction. Morgan Kaufmann, San Francisco (1998)
2. Bennett III, F.H., Koza, J.R., Shipman, J., Stiffelman, O.: Building a parallel computer system for $18,000 that performs a half peta-flop per day. In: Banzhaf, W., et al. (eds.) GECCO 1999, pp. 1484–1490. Morgan Kaufmann, San Francisco (1999)
3. Chitty, D.M.: A data parallel approach to genetic programming using programmable graphics hardware. In: GECCO 2007, pp. 1566–1573 (2007)
4. Comte, P.: Design & implementation of parallel linear GP for the IBM cell processor. In: Raidl, G., et al. (eds.) GECCO 2009. ACM, New York (2009)
5. Ebner, M., Reinhardt, M., Albert, J.: Evolution of vertex and pixel shaders. In: Keijzer, M., Tettamanzi, A.G.B., Collet, P., van Hemert, J., Tomassini, M. (eds.) EuroGP 2005. LNCS, vol. 3447, pp. 261–270. Springer, Heidelberg (2005)
6. Fok, K.-L., Wong, T.-T., Wong, M.-L.: Evolutionary computing on consumer graphics hardware. IEEE Intelligent Systems 22(2), 69–78 (2007)
7. Harding, S., Banzhaf, W.: Fast genetic programming on GPUs. In: Ebner, M., O'Neill, M., Ekárt, A., Vanneschi, L., Esparcia-Alcázar, A.I. (eds.) EuroGP 2007. LNCS, vol. 4445, pp. 90–101. Springer, Heidelberg (2007)
8. Harding, S.L., Banzhaf, W.: Distributed genetic programming on GPUs using CUDA. In: Hidalgo, I., et al. (eds.) Wks. Paral. Arch. and Bioinspired Algs. (2009)
9. Juille, H., Pollack, J.B.: Massively parallel genetic programming. In: Angeline, P.J., Kinnear Jr., K.E. (eds.) Advances in GP 2, ch.17. MIT Press, Cambridge
10. Koza, J.R.: Genetic Programming. MIT press, Cambridge (1992)
11. Langdon, W.B.: Large scale bioinformatics data mining with parallel genetic programming on graphics processing units. Par. & Dist. Comp. Intelligence
12. Langdon, W.B.: Genetic Programming and Data Structures. Kluwer, Dordrecht (1998)
13. Langdon, W.B.: A SIMD interpreter for genetic programming on GPU graphics cards. Tech. Rep. CSM-470, Computer Science, University of Essex, UK (2007)
14. Langdon, W.B.: A fast high quality pseudo random number generator for nVidia CUDA. In: Wilson, G. (ed.) CIGPU workshop at GECCO, Montreal, July 8, pp. 2511–2513. ACM, New York (2009)

15. Langdon, W.B., Banzhaf, W.: A SIMD interpreter for genetic programming on GPU graphics cards. In: O'Neill, M., Vanneschi, L., Gustafson, S., Esparcia Alcázar, A.I., De Falco, I., Della Cioppa, A., Tarantino, E. (eds.) EuroGP 2008. LNCS, vol. 4971, pp. 73–85. Springer, Heidelberg (2008)
16. Langdon, W.B., Harrison, A.P.: GP on SPMD parallel graphics hardware for mega bioinformatics data mining. Soft Computing 12 12, 1169–1183 (2008)
17. Langdon, W.B., Poli, R.: Foundations of Genetic Programming (2002)
18. Lewis, T.E., Magoulas, G.D.: Strategies to minimise the total run time of cyclic graph based genetic programming with GPUs. In: GECCO 2009, pp. 1379–1386 (2009)
19. Poli, R., Langdon, W.B.: Sub-machine-code genetic programming. In: Spector, L., et al. (eds.) Advances in GP 3, ch. 13, pp. 301–323. MIT Press, Cambridge (1999)
20. Poli, R., Langdon, W.B., McPhee, N.F.: A field guide to genetic programming (With contributions by J. R. Koza) (2008), http://www.gp-field-guide.org.uk
21. Robilliard, D., Marion-Poty, V., Fonlupt, C.: Genetic programming on graphics processing units. Genetic Programming and Evolvable Machines 10(4), 447–471 (2009)
22. Teller, A., Andre, D.: Automatically choosing the number of fitness cases: The rational allocation of trials. In: Koza, J.R. (ed.) GP 1997, July 13-16, pp. 321–328 (1997)
23. Wilson, G., Banzhaf, W.: Linear genetic programming GPGPU on Microsoft's Xbox 360. In: WCCI 2008. IEEE, Los Alamitos (2008)
24. Yanagiya, M.: Efficient genetic programming based on binary decision diagrams. In: 1995 IEEE Conf. Evolutionary Computation, Perth, pp. 234–239 (1995)

Controlling Complex Dynamics with Artificial Biochemical Networks

Michael A. Lones[1], Andy M. Tyrrell[1], Susan Stepney[2], and Leo S. Caves[3]

[1] Department of Electronics
[2] Department of Computer Science
[3] Department of Biology
University of York, Heslington, York YO10 5DD, UK
{mal503,amt}@ohm.york.ac.uk, susan.stepney@cs.york.ac.uk, lsdc1@york.ac.uk

Abstract. Artificial biochemical networks (ABNs) are computational models inspired by the biochemical networks which underlie the cellular activities of biological organisms. This paper shows how evolved ABNs may be used to control chaotic dynamics in both discrete and continuous dynamical systems, illustrating that ABNs can be used to represent complex computational behaviours within evolutionary algorithms. Our results also show that performance is sensitive to model choice, and suggest that conservation laws play an important role in guiding search.

1 Introduction

Biochemical networks are the complex dynamical systems which underlie the functional and structural complexity seen within biological organisms. From an evolutionary computation perspective, biochemical networks are interesting because they describe complex behaviours in a way that is both concise and evolvable. This has led to growing interest in the use of computational models of biochemical networks, particularly within genetic programming. These include artificial genetic regulatory networks [2,12,17,18], computational models of cellular metabolism [1,8,10,19], and those derived from signalling networks [6]. We refer to them collectively as artificial biochemical networks (ABNs).

Traditionally, robotic control has been a popular application area for ABNs [7,17,19]. In principle, it reflects one of the main biological roles of biochemical networks: maintaining correct behaviour when exposed to a complex, dynamic, environment. However, high overheads mean that it is generally not feasible to use large populations or to carry out statistically significant numbers of trials, limiting the use of robotic control as a testbed for studying ABNs. In this paper, we take a different approach: we use ABNs to control numerical dynamical systems. As a testing environment, this has a number of advantages: numerical simulation is relatively fast, the dynamical properties are highly configurable, and test conditions can be replicated between experiments. Control of dynamical systems is also an important problem in its own right, having many applications in science and engineering [15], including those in robotics [3].

A.I. Esparcia-Alcazar et al. (Eds.): EuroGP 2010, LNCS 6021, pp. 159–170, 2010.

The paper is organised as follows: Section 2 introduces the dynamical systems addressed in this paper, Section 3 introduces ABNs, Section 4 describes our models and methodology, Section 5 presents results, and Section 6 concludes.

2 Dynamical Systems

A dynamical system [16] is any system whose subsequent state is determined by a function, or *evolution rule*, of the system's current state. Dynamical systems can be *discrete* or *continuous* time: the evolution rule can be described by a difference equation in the former, and a differential equation in the latter. Starting at a particular point within the system's state space, its *initial conditions*, the path that the system follows through its state space, its *trajectory*, is determined by iterating the evolution rule over a period of time. The set of possible trajectories within the state space are known as the *orbits* of the system. Following initial periods of wandering, *transients*, orbits may converge to limited parts of the state space known as *attractors*. Dynamical systems in which all orbits converge to one or more attractors are *dissipative*. Those which do not converge in this fashion are *conservative*.

Perhaps the most interesting class of dynamical systems are those which display the complex, unpredictable dynamics known as *chaos*. Two of the main hallmarks of a chaotic system are exponential sensitivity to initial conditions and strange attractors. The former entails that small changes in initial conditions can lead to wildly different trajectories through state space (a phenomenon popularly known as the *butterfly effect*), whereas the latter are the complex, typically fractal, regions of state space to which these chaotic orbits converge.

In the following sections, we introduce two dynamical systems, the Lorenz system and Chirikov's standard map. Both of these display chaotic behaviour, but otherwise lie at different ends of the classification spectrum: the former is a continuous dissipative system, the latter is a discrete conservative system.

2.1 The Lorenz System

The Lorenz system [13] is a continuous-time dynamical system whose behaviour is defined by the following set of differential equations:

$$\dot{x} = \sigma\left(y - x\right) \qquad \dot{y} = x(\rho - z) - y \qquad \dot{z} = xy - \beta z \qquad (1)$$

For $\rho \gtrsim 24.74$, the Lorenz system displays chaotic behaviour, with all initial points attracted to a single two-lobed strange attractor (see Fig. 1) which orbits two unstable equilibrium points, which we term ϵ_+ and ϵ_-, located at:

$$\epsilon_+ = (\sqrt{\beta(\rho - 1)}, \sqrt{\beta(\rho - 1)}, \rho - 1) \qquad \epsilon_- = (-\sqrt{\beta(\rho - 1)}, -\sqrt{\beta(\rho - 1)}, \rho - 1) \quad (2)$$

The attractor consists of an infinite number of *unstable periodic orbits*. These are periodic in the sense that they orbit one or both of the fixed points a certain number of times before returning to roughly the same location. The orbits are

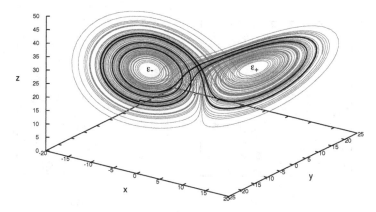

Fig. 1. A trajectory within the Lorenz attractor ($\sigma = 10$, $\rho = 28$, $\beta = \frac{8}{3}$), showing the location of the unstable equilibrium points ϵ_- and ϵ_+. The heavy line shows one of the unstable periodic orbits followed by the trajectory.

unstable in the sense that trajectories will follow them for only a limited period of time before moving to another orbit. The dynamics of the system lead to trajectories which appear to flip unpredictably between the two lobes of the attractor.

2.2   Chirikov's Standard Map

Chirikov's standard map [5] describes a conservative discrete-time dynamical system which iteratively maps points within the unit square[1]:

$$x_{n+1} = (x_n + y_{n+1}) \bmod 1 \qquad\qquad y_{n+1} = y_n - \frac{k}{2\pi} \sin(2\pi x_n) \qquad (3)$$

The map's name follows from its ability to locally capture the behaviour of all systems with co-existing chaotic and ordered dynamics. For low values of k, the dynamics of the system are ordered, with initial points converging to cyclic orbits which remain bounded on the y axis (see Fig. 2a). As k increases, islands of chaotic dynamics begin to appear (see Fig. 2a–d). The map has a critical point at $k_c \approx 0.972$. For $k > k_c$, the chaotic islands are fully connected along the y axis; meaning that, in principle, it is possible to follow a chaotic orbit from $y = 0$ to $y = 1$. However, the permeability of the central region increases only slowly as k moves past k_c [4] (see Fig. 2b–c). As an example of this, when $k = 1.1$, using 1000 randomly chosen initial points and an upper limit of 10^6 iterations, we measured a median transit time of 64000 iterations of equation 3 to move from the bottom to the top of the map, with 27% of trajectories not reaching the target within the upper limit.

---

[1] Following [15], we do not take the modulus of the y co-ordinate, so $y=0$ and $y=1$ are not close, and the unit square as drawn recurs periodically along the y-axis.

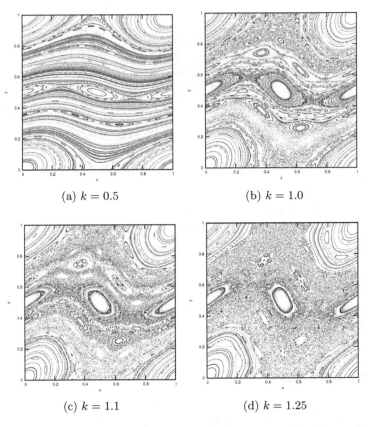

(a) $k = 0.5$ (b) $k = 1.0$

(c) $k = 1.1$ (d) $k = 1.25$

Fig. 2. Sampled orbits of the standard map for various values of k, showing the transition from ordered to chaotic behaviour as k increases. Each plot shows 200 trajectories of length 500, with the same set of initial conditions used for each plot.

2.3 State Space Targeting

Chaos is found in many physical systems. The Lorenz system, for example, is a model of dynamical phenomenon seen in atmospheric, laser, and electronic systems [13]. Chaos leads to complex, unpredictable, behaviour; yet because of its sensitivity to small perturbations, it is also inherently controllable. This has led to considerable interest in methods for controlling trajectories within chaotic dynamical systems, a process which is termed *chaos control*, or *chaos targeting*. This is achieved by adjusting one or more of the system's accessible parameters, with the goal of perturbing the trajectory towards a desired orbit or location within the state space. For dissipative systems such as the Lorenz system, chaos control can be achieved using methods such as OGY [14], which use small perturbations to prevent the trajectory from leaving a particular unstable periodic orbit. For conservative systems, such as Chirikov's standard map, control strategies are somewhat more complicated due to the heterogeneity of the state space.

However, optimal targeting can be achieved by mapping the orbit structure and using perturbations to cross between different regions of the state space [4,15]. For example, in [15], the authors calculate orbits which traverse the standard map in ~ 125 iterations when $k = 1.25$ and ~ 600 iterations when $k = 1.01$.

3   Artificial Biochemical Networks

The structure and function of biological organisms emerges from the orchestrated activities of the biochemical networks operating within individual cells. Broadly speaking, there are three types of biochemical network within a cell: (i) the *metabolic network*, which comprises the protein-mediated chemical reactions that take place within the cell; (ii) the *signalling network*, which represents the protein-mediated responses to chemical messengers received by the cell; and (iii) the *genetic regulatory network*, which determines the proteins that are present in a cell at any given time, and hence the structure of the metabolic and signalling networks. These three types of biochemical network are reflected by three classes of computational model:

Artificial Genetic Networks (AGNs): These model the regulatory interactions which occur between genes in biological cells. The canonical AGN model is the Boolean network (often referred to as a *random* Boolean network, or RBN). In Kauffman's [11] original model, an RBN consists of a set of genes, each of which is either fully on or fully off and whose state is determined by a Boolean function of other genes' states. In effect, they are a generalisation of binary cellular automata in which update rules can reference non-neighbouring cells and functions are heterogenous. In practice, computation can be achieved in the same way as cellular automata: by providing input via the initial activity state of the genes, running an appropriate network for a certain number of time steps, and then reading the output from the final activity states of the genes [7]. AGN models can also be constructed using continuous values for gene expression and continuous-valued regulatory functions [2,12,17].

Artificial Metabolic Networks (AMNs): The best known examples of metabolic-level models are artificial chemistries [1]. An artificial chemistry consists of a set of *chemicals*, a set of rules — which model the transformative agents (such as enzymes) found in natural systems — and an algorithm that determines when these rules are applied. Chemicals may be symbols to which some computational meaning can be associated [19], they may directly encode data structures, they may be overtly computational in nature, e.g. lambda-expressions [10], or they may even be other ABNs [8]. Likewise, rules vary from simple symbolic transformations to functional composition and complex structural modifications. By encoding inputs and outputs in the concentration, internal structure or positioning of chemicals, these artificial chemistries have been applied to a number of computational tasks, including robotics [19].

Artificial Signalling Networks (ASNs): In biology, signalling networks have the role of transducing environmental information to the metabolic and genetic networks. In addition to delivering the information to the correct spatial location(s), they are also responsible for integrating and pre-processing diverse incoming signals; a process which requires a host of cognitive activities [9]. Whilst signalling networks have not yet received the same level of interest as the other classes of biochemical network, artificial signalling networks do show potential as a computational model [6].

4   State Space Targeting with ABNs

In this section, we report our work on using artificial biochemical networks to carry out state space targeting in the Lorenz system and Chirikov's standard map. We use two ABN models: an artificial genetic regulatory network and an artificial metabolic network. The AGN is a continuous-valued version of the Boolean network model. The AMN is an artificial chemistry with continuous-valued chemicals and transition rules. To allow meaningful comparison, both are deterministic and use synchronous updates.

The artificial genetic network (AGN) consists of an indexed set of genes, each of which has an expression level, regulatory inputs, and a regulatory function which maps the expression levels of its regulatory inputs to its own expression level. Formally: $AGN = < G, L_G, I_G, O_G >$, where:

> G is the indexed set of genes $\{g_0, ..., g_n : g_i = < \lambda_i, R_i, f_i >\}$, where:
> > $\lambda_i : \mathbb{R}$ is the expression level of a gene.
> > $R_i \subseteq G$ is the set of regulatory inputs used by a gene.
> > $f_i : R_i \rightarrow \lambda_i$ is a gene's regulatory function.
>
> L_G is an indexed set of initial expression levels, where $|L_G| = |G|$.
> $I_G \subset G$ is the set of genes used as external inputs.
> $O_G \subset G$ is the set of genes used as external outputs.

The AGN is executed as follows:

G1. $\lambda_0 ... \lambda_n$ are initialised from L_G (if AGN not previously executed).
G2. Expression levels of enzymes in I_G are set by the external inputs.
G3. At each time step, each gene g_i applies its regulatory function f_i to the current expression levels of its regulating genes R_i in order to calculate its expression at the next time step, λ_i'.
G4. After a certain number of time steps, execution is halted and the expression levels of enzymes in O_G are copied to the external outputs.

The artificial metabolic network (AMN) comprises an indexed set of enzyme-analogous elements which transform the concentrations of an indexed set of real-valued chemicals. Each enzyme has a set of substrates, a set of products, and a mapping which calculates the concentrations of its products based upon the concentrations of its substrates. Formally: $AMN = < C, E, L_C, I_C, O_C >$, where:

C is the indexed set of chemical concentrations $\{c_0, ..., c_n : \mathbb{R}\}$.
E is the indexed set of enzymes $\{e_0, ..., e_n : e_i =< S_i, P_i, m_i >\}$, where:
    $S_i \subseteq C$ is the set of chemicals used by the enzyme (*substrates*).
    $P_i \subseteq C$ is the set of chemicals produced by the enzyme (*products*).
    $m_i : \mathbb{R}^n \to \mathbb{R}^n$ is the enzyme's substrate-product mapping.

L_C is an indexed set of initial chemical concentrations, where $|L_C| = |C|$.
$I_C \subset C$ is the set of chemicals used as external inputs.
$O_C \subset C$ is the set of chemicals used as external outputs.

Execution of the AMN is similar to that of the AGN:

M1. C is initialised from L_C (if AMN not previously executed).
M2. The concentrations of chemicals in I_C are set by the external inputs.
M3. At each time step, each enzyme e_i applies its mapping m_i to the current concentrations of its substrates S_i in order to determine the new concentrations of its products P_i. Where the same chemical is produced by multiple enzymes, i.e. when $\exists j, k : j \neq k \wedge c_i \in P_j \cap P_k$, the new concentration is the mean output value of all contributing enzymes.
M4. After a certain number of time steps, execution is halted and the concentrations of chemicals in O_C are copied to the external outputs.

We also look at the effect of applying a *mass conservation law*, such that the sum of chemical concentrations remains constant over time. This more closely reflects biological systems, where mass balance results in indirect regulatory interactions between chemical reactions. It is implemented by uniformly scaling concentrations at the beginning of step M3 so that $\sum_{c_i \in C} c_i = 0.5|C|$.

4.1 Mappings

Regulatory (f_i) and enzyme (m_i) mappings are chosen from three parameterisable functions: a Sigmoid, the Michaelis-Menten equation, and the logistic map.

Sigmoids are often used to model the switching behaviour of non-linear biological systems, and are therefore a natural choice for ABNs. For this, we use the logistic function $f(x) = (1 + e^{-sx-b})^{-1}$, where $s \in [0, 20]$ determines the slope and $b \in [-1, 1]$ the slope offset (or *bias*). For multiple inputs, $x = \sum_{j=0}^n i_j w_j$, where $i_0...i_n$ are inputs and $w_0...w_n \in [-1, 1]$ are corresponding input weights (negative values indicating repression).

The Michaelis-Menten equation defines the kinetics of enzyme-mediated reactions, making it particularly interesting from the perspective of AMNs. It is a hyperbolic function, $f(x) = vx(k + x)^{-1}$, where $v \in [0, 1]$ is the asymptotic value of the output and $k \in [0, 1]$ determines the slope. For multiple inputs, $x = \sum_{j=0}^n \frac{i_j w_j}{n}$, truncating negative values.

The logistic map is a discrete dynamical system with both ordered and chaotic regimes, defined $f(x) = rx(1-x)$, where $r \in [0, 4]$ determines whether the system exhibits a periodic or chaotic orbit. In effect, we are interested in whether evolved ABNs can make use of 'pre-packaged' dynamics.

4.2 Methods

ABNs are evolved using a standard generational evolutionary algorithm with tournament selection (size 4), uniform crossover (p=0.15), and point mutation (p=0.06). An ABN is represented as an array of genes (G) or enzymes (E), an array of initial values (L_G or L_C), and an integer in the range $[1, 100]$ specifying the number of time steps for execution. To simplify analysis, the number of genes, enzymes and chemicals are fixed at 10. Crossover points always fall between gene or enzyme boundaries. Inputs and outputs (R_i, S_i and P_i) are represented by absolute references to array positions. Function parameters (e.g. slopes, input weights) and initial values are represented as floating-point values and are mutated using a Gaussian distribution centred around the current value.

For both problems, the ABN is provided with the current state space location at the start of execution and outputs the new value for a specified control parameter at the end of execution. Inputs are copied into the lowest-numbered genes or chemicals and the output is taken from the highest numbered. All runs are terminated after 50 generations.

Lorenz system: The goal is to find an ABN-based controller which can (i) stabilise the system at its equilibrium points and (ii) move between the two points as required. This is tested by requiring it to move from ϵ_- to ϵ_+ and remain there for 5000 time steps, then return to ϵ_-, remaining for another 5000 time steps. In order to do this, the ABN is allowed to modulate the Rayleigh parameter, ρ (see Equ. 1), within the range $[0,100]$. For inputs, the ABN is given the current location, $< x, y, z >$ (values scaled from $[-50, 50]$ to $[0, 1]$), and the distance to the target, d. To make the problem more challenging, exact distance is given only when the Euclidean distance to the target $E < 2.0$. Above this, it is set to the maximum input value, i.e. $d = \min\{1, \frac{E}{2}\}$. The ABN generates a single output, the new value of ρ. The Lorenz equations are numerically integrated using the fourth-order Runge-Kutta method with a step size of $\Delta_t = 0.01$. The ABN is executed every 10 steps to get a new value of ρ. For s time steps, fitness is $\frac{\sum_s 1-d}{s}$, rewarding stability at equilibrium points and short transients. A population size of 500 is used (found to be suitable through trial-and-error).

Standard map: Following the examples of [4] and [15], the goal is to find a controller which can navigate from the bottom to the top of the standard map in the shortest number of steps. In order to do this, the ABN is allowed to modulate parameter k in Equ. 3 within the range $[1.0, 1.1]$. We use the same initial and target regions (shown in Fig. 5) as used in [15]. Inputs to the RBN are the current position $< x, y >$ and the Euclidean distance from the top-centre of the map, and the single output is the new value of k. The evolved ABNs are evaluated on 20 random points within the initial region. Fitness is the mean number of steps required for these trajectories to reach the target region. Trajectories which do not reach the target region within 1000 steps are assigned an arbitrary figure of 2000 steps, biasing search towards controllers effective over all initial conditions. A population size of 200 is used.

5   Results

Results for the Lorenz system and the standard map are shown in Fig. 3. Effective controllers were found for both problems (see Figs. 4 and 5 for examples). However, the two problems appear to need quite different ABN models: for the Lorenz system, best performance comes from AMNs with conserved mass and logistic maps; whereas best performance on the standard map comes from AGNs with Sigmoid functions. Notably, the best solution for one problem is the worst solution for the other; although this is perhaps unsurprising, given that the two problems lie at opposite ends of the dynamical systems spectrum.

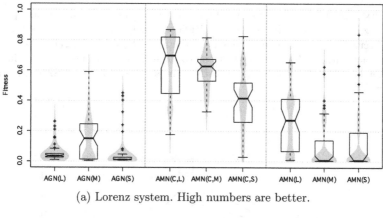

(a) Lorenz system. High numbers are better.

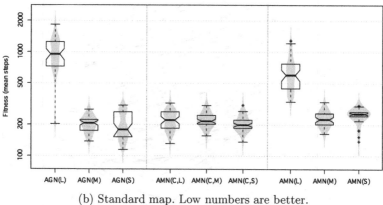

(b) Standard map. Low numbers are better.

Fig. 3. State space targeting using evolved ABNs with (C)onserved mass, (S)igmoids, (M)ichaelis-Menten equations and (L)ogistic maps. Summary statistics of 50 runs are shown as notched box plots. Overlapping notches indicate when median values (thick horizontal bars) are not significantly different at the 95% confidence level. Kernel density estimates of underlying distributions are also given (in grey), showing that some of the fitness distributions are multimodal.

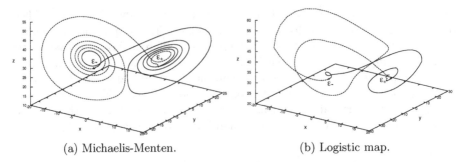

(a) Michaelis-Menten.   (b) Logistic map.

Fig. 4. Example behaviours of evolved controllers moving between unstable points in the Lorenz system via control of the Rayleigh parameter. Both controllers use AMNs with conserved mass. (a) The Michaelis-Menten AMN (fitness 0.821) moves from ϵ_- to a distance within 1.0 of ϵ_+ in 447 steps (broken line), returning to ϵ_- in 454 steps (unbroken line). (b) The logistic map AMN (fitness 0.872) does it in 182 and 170 steps, respectively.

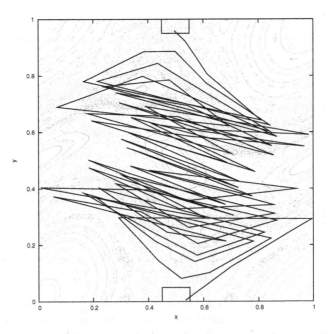

Fig. 5. Example behaviour of an evolved controller guiding a trajectory from a region at the bottom of the standard map, $(0.45,0) \rightarrow (0.55,0.05)$, to a region at the top, $(0.45,0.95) \rightarrow (0.55,1)$, in 83 steps. The standard map is plotted for $k = 1.1$.

Perhaps the most interesting result is the positive effect of conserving mass in the AMN model. In the Lorenz system, this effect is particularly significant and appears critical for good performance. The effect of mass conservation is to force covariance between the chemical concentrations. For example, if the concentration of one chemical increases, the concentrations of all other chemicals are (stoichometrically) decreased. We can hypothesise that this causes a reduction in the number of effective variables of the system, reducing the search effort required to find viable solutions. It also suggests the potentially important role that conservation laws may play in reducing the effective complexity of more biologically-realistic models.

Function choice also has interesting consequences: Michaelis-Menten equations work relatively well on both problems, Sigmoids work well on the standard map, but not so well on the Lorenz system, and logistic maps work well on the Lorenz system but generally perform poorly on the standard map. Whilst the continuous functions offer more consistent performance across the problems, the logistic map did lead to the best overall solutions for the Lorenz system. As demonstrated by Fig. 4, these achieve short paths using eccentric orbits, whereas Michaelis-Menten solutions tend to follow smoother paths. It seems likely that the multimodal, wide distributions of the AMNs using logistic maps reflect a trade-off between expressiveness and evolvability.

6   Conclusions

In this paper, we have demonstrated how evolved artificial biochemical networks (ABNs) can be used to control complex dynamical systems. Our results are promising, showing that relatively simple ABNs are capable of state space targeting within both the Lorenz system and Chirikov's standard map — numerical systems located at opposite ends of the dynamical systems spectrum. Notably, our results on Chirikov's standard map are broadly similar to the analytical methods described in [4] and [15], but without requiring prior knowledge of the system's orbital structure. This supports the notion that ABNs can be used to represent complex computational behaviours in evolutionary algorithms, such as genetic programming, which evolve executable structures.

More generally, we have introduced the notion that dynamical systems are a useful domain for studying ABNs. Our results support their use in comparing the properties of different ABN models, illustrating that different models are suited to different problems. In particular, we have shown the benefit of using a conservation rule in the perturbation of ABN variables to introduce covariance (e.g. masses in the AMN), highlighting the important role constraints may play in guiding search towards viable solutions. Our results also show the sensitivity of ABNs to function choice, and that iterative maps can provide a useful source of pre-packaged dynamics in certain situations.

In future work, we plan to investigate a broader collection of ABN models and dynamical systems, to analyse how the ABNs solve these problems, and to look at how issues of evolvability and representation affect their ability to do so.

References

1. Banzhaf, W.: Artificial chemistries—towards constructive dynamical systems. Solid State Phenomena 97/98, 43–50 (2004)
2. Banzhaf, W.: Artificial regulatory networks and genetic programming. In: Riolo, R.L., Worzel, B. (eds.) Genetic Programming Theory and Practice, ch. 4, pp. 43–62. Kluwer, Dordrecht (2003)
3. Beer, R.D.: Beyond control: The dynamics of brain-body-environment interaction in motor systems. In: Sternad, D. (ed.) Progress in Motor Control V: A Multidisciplinary Perspective, pp. 7–24. Springer, Heidelberg (2009)
4. Bollt, E.M., Meiss, J.D.: Controlling chaotic transport through recurrence. Physica D: Nonlinear Phenomena 81(3), 280–294 (1995)
5. Chirikov, B.V.: Research concerning the theory of nonlinear resonance and stochasticity. Tech. rep., Institute of Nuclear Physics, Novosibirsk (1969)
6. Decraene, J., Mitchell, G.G., McMullin, B.: Evolving artificial cell signaling networks: Perspectives and methods. In: Dressler, F., Carreras, I. (eds.) Advances in Biologically Inspired Information Systems, pp. 167–186. Springer, Heidelberg (2007)
7. Dellaert, F., Beer, R.D.: A developmental model for the evolution of complete autonomous agents. In: Maes, P., et al. (eds.) From Animals to Animats 4: Proc. 4th Int. Conf. Simulation of Adaptive Behavior. MIT Press, Cambridge (1996)
8. Faulconbridge, A., Stepney, S., Miller, J.F., Caves, L.S.D.: RBN-World: A subsymbolic artificial chemistry. In: Proc. ECAL 2009. LNCS. Springer, Heidelberg (2009)
9. Fisher, M.J., Paton, R.C., Matsuno, K.: Intracellular signalling proteins as 'smart' agents in parallel distributed processes. BioSystems 50, 159–171 (1999)
10. Fontana, W.: Algorithmic chemistry. In: Langton, C.G., Taylor, C., Farmer, J.D., Rasmussen, S. (eds.) Artificial Life II, pp. 159–210. Addison-Wesley, Reading (1992)
11. Kauffman, S.A.: Metabolic stability and epigenesis in randomly constructed genetic nets. J. Theor. Biol. 22(3), 437–467 (1969)
12. Kumar, S.: The evolution of genetic regulatory networks for single and multicellular development. In: Keijzer, M. (ed.) GECCO 2004 Late Breaking Papers (2004)
13. Lorenz, E.N.: Deterministic nonperiodic flow. Journal of the Atmospheric Sciences 20(2), 130–141 (1963)
14. Ott, E., Grebogi, C., Yorke, J.A.: Controlling chaos. Phys. Rev. Lett. 64(11), 1196–1199 (1990)
15. Schroer, C.G., Ott, E.: Targeting in Hamiltonian systems that have mixed regular/chaotic phase spaces. Chaos 7, 512–519 (1997)
16. Stepney, S.: Nonclassical computation: a dynamical systems perspective. In: Rozenberg, G., Bäck, T., Kok, J.N. (eds.) Handbook of Natural Computing, vol. 2, ch. 52. Springer, Heidelberg (2009)
17. Taylor, T.: A genetic regulatory network-inspired real-time controller for a group of underwater robots. In: Groen, F., et al. (eds.) Intelligent Autonomous Systems 8 (Proceedings of IAS8), pp. 403–412. IOS Press, Amsterdam (2004)
18. Zhan, S., Miller, J.F., Tyrrell, A.M.: An evolutionary system using development and artificial genetic regulatory networks. In: Wang, J. (ed.) 2008 IEEE CEC. IEEE Press, Los Alamitos (2008)
19. Ziegler, J., Banzhaf, W.: Evolving control metabolisms for a robot. Artificial Life 7, 171–190 (2001)

Geometric Differential Evolution on the Space of Genetic Programs

Alberto Moraglio[1] and Sara Silva[2,3]

[1] School of Computing, University of Kent, Canterbury, UK
`a.moraglio@kent.ac.uk`
[2] INESC-ID Lisboa, Portugal
[3] Center for Informatics and Systems of the University of Coimbra, Portugal
`sara@{kdbio.inesc-id.pt,dei.uc.pt}`

Abstract. Geometric Differential Evolution (GDE) is a very recently introduced formal generalization of traditional Differential Evolution (DE) that can be used to derive specific GDE for both continuous and combinatorial spaces retaining the same geometric interpretation of the dynamics of the DE search across representations. In this paper, we derive formally a specific GDE for the space of genetic programs. The result is a Differential Evolution algorithm searching the space of genetic programs by acting directly on their tree representation. We present experimental results for the new algorithm.

1 Introduction

Differential Evolution (DE) is a population-based stochastic global optimization algorithm [16] that has a number of similarities with Particle Swarm Optimization (PSO) and Evolutionary Algorithms (EAs), and has proven to have robust performance over a variety of difficult continuous optimization problems [16]. The search done by DE has a natural geometric interpretation and can be understood as the motion of points in space obtained by linear combinations of their current positions to determine their new positions.

The original formulation of DE requires the search space to be continuous and the points in space to be represented as vectors of real numbers. There are only few extensions of DE to combinatorial spaces [16] [15] [2] [14] and to the space of genetic programs [13]. Some of these works recast the search in discrete spaces as continuous search via encoding the candidate solutions as vectors of real numbers and then applying the traditional DE algorithm to solve these continuous problems. Other works present DE algorithms defined on combinatorial spaces acting directly on the original solution representation that, however, are only loosely related to the traditional DE in that the original geometric interpretation is lost in the transition from continuous to combinatorial spaces. Furthermore, in the latter approaches every time a new solution representation is considered, the DE algorithm needs to be rethought and adapted to the new representation.

GDE [12] is a very recently devised formal generalization of DE that, in principle, can be specified to any solution representation while retaining the original

A.I. Esparcia-Alcazar et al. (Eds.): EuroGP 2010, LNCS 6021, pp. 171–183, 2010.

geometric interpretation of the dynamics of the points in space of DE across representations. In particular, GDE can be applied to any search space endowed with a distance and associated with any solution representation to derive formally a specific GDE for the target space and for the target representation. GDE is related to Geometric Particle Swarm Optimization (GPSO) [7], which is a formal generalization of the Particle Swarm Optimization algorithm [3]. Specific GPSOs were derived for different types of continuous spaces and for the Hamming space associated with binary strings [8], for spaces associated with permutations [11] and for spaces associated with genetic programs [17].

In previous work [12], GDE was specialized to the space of binary strings endowed with the Hamming distance and produced good experimental results. In this paper, we extend the study of the GDE algorithm and apply it to searching the space of computer programs represented as parse trees. The main purpose of this paper is to show that this is at all possible, and in particular to show that differential mutation, the core search operator of DE that casts it apart from PSO and EAs, can be readily derived for this non-trivial representation. We also present an initial experimental analysis of this new algorithm, which we call GDE-GP.

The remaining part of the paper is organized as follows. Section 2 describes the general GDE algorithm. Section 3 presents specific GDE search operators for parse trees. Section 4 reports an initial experimental analysis for GDE-GP on standard GP benchmark problems. Section 5 presents the conclusions and future work.

2   Geometric Differential Evolution

In this section, we summarize how the general GDE algorithm was derived (Algorithm 2) [12] from the classic DE algorithm (Algorithm 1). The generalization was obtained using a methodology to generalize search algorithms for continuous spaces to combinatorial spaces [12] based on the geometric framework introduced by Moraglio [6]. The methodology is sketched in the following. Given a search algorithm defined on continuous spaces, one has to recast the definition of the search operators expressing them explicitly in terms of Euclidean distance between parents and offspring. Then one has to substitute the Euclidean distance with a generic metric, obtaining a formal search algorithm generalizing the original algorithm based on the continuous space. Next, one can consider a (discrete) representation and a distance associated with it (a combinatorial space) and use it in the definition of the formal search algorithm to obtain a specific instance of the algorithm for this space. Finally, one can use this geometric and declarative description of the search operator to derive its operational definition in terms of manipulation of the specific underlying representation. This methodology was used to generalize PSO and DE to any metric space, obtaining GPSO and GDE, and then to derive their search operators for specific representations and distances. In particular for DE, the specific GDE for the Hamming space associated with binary strings was derived. In Section 3, we derive the specific GDE for the space of parse trees with Structural Hamming Distance (SHD) [9] by plugging this distance in the abstract definition of the search operators.

2.1   Classic Differential Evolution

In the following, we describe the traditional DE [16] (see Algorithm 1). The characteristic that sets DE apart from other Evolutionary Algorithms is the presence of the differential mutation operator (see line 5 of Algorithm 1). This operator creates a mutant vector U by perturbing a vector $X3$ picked at random from the current population with the scaled difference of other two randomly selected population vectors $F \cdot (X1 - X2)$. This operation is considered important because it adapts the mutation direction and its step size to the level of convergence and spatial distribution of the current population. The mutant vector is then recombined with the currently considered vector $X(i)$ using discrete recombination and the resulting vector V replaces the current vector in the next population if it has better or equal fitness (in line 7 of Algorithm 1, higher is better).

Algorithm 1. DE with differential mutation and discrete recombination

---

1: initialize population of N_p real vectors at random
2: **while** stop criterion not met **do**
3:     **for all** vector $X(i)$ in the population **do**
4:         pick at random 3 distinct vectors from the current population $X1, X2, X3$
5:         create mutant vector $U = X3 + F \cdot (X1 - X2)$ where F is the scale factor parameter
6:         set V as the result of the discrete recombination of U and $X(i)$ with probability Cr
7:         **if** $f(V) \geq f(X(i))$ **then**
8:             set the ith vector in the next population $Y(i) = V$
9:         **else**
10:             set $Y(i) = X(i)$
11:         **end if**
12:     **end for**
13:     **for all** vector $X(i)$ in the population **do**
14:         set $X(i) = Y(i)$
15:     **end for**
16: **end while**

2.2   Generalization of Differential Mutation

Let $X1, X2, X3$ be real vectors and $F \geq 0$ a scalar. The differential mutation operator produces a new vector U as follows:

$$U = X3 + F \cdot (X1 - X2) \qquad (1)$$

The algebraic operations on real vectors in Equation 1 can be represented graphically [16] as in Figure 1(a).

Unfortunately, this graphical interpretation of Equation 1 in terms of operations on vectors cannot be used to generalize Equation 1 to general metric spaces because algebraic operations on vectors are not well-defined at this level of generality. However, Equation 1 can be rewritten in terms of only convex combinations of vectors. This allows us to interpret graphically this equation in terms of segments and extension rays, which are geometric elements well-defined on any metric space. Figure 1(b) illustrates the construction of U using convex combination and extension ray. The point E is the intersection point of the segments $[U, X2]$ and $[X1, X3]$. All the distances from E to the endpoints of these segments can be determined from the coefficients of Equation 1 [12]. The point

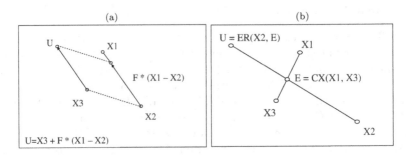

Fig. 1. Construction of U using vectors (a) and construction of U using convex combination and extension ray (b)

U can therefore be determined geometrically in two steps: (i) determining E as convex combination of $X1$ and $X3$; (ii) projecting $X2$ beyond E (extension ray) obtaining a point U at the known required distance from E. In the Euclidean space, the constructions of U using vectors (Figure 1(a)) and convex combinations (Figure 1(b)) are equivalent. For a detailed description of the relationship between the two interpretations see [12].

Segments and extension rays in the Euclidean space can be expressed in terms of distances, hence, these geometric objects can be naturally generalized to generic metric spaces by replacing the Euclidean distance with a generic metric [12]. The differential mutation operator $U = DM(X1, X2, X3)$ with scale factor F can now be defined for any metric space following the construction of U presented in Figure 1(b) as follows:

1. Compute $W = \frac{1}{1+F}$
2. Get E as the convex combination $CX(X1, X3)$ with weights $(1 - W, W)$
3. Get U as the extension ray $ER(X2, E)$ with weights $(W, 1 - W)$

The weight pair of CX can be thought of indicating the intensity of "linear attraction" of E to $X1$ and $X3$ respectively. So, the larger the weight of $X1$ the closer E will be to it. The weight pair of ER has an analogous meaning where the weights refer to attraction of E to $X2$ and U respectively. However, notice that the unknown in the ER case is a point of attraction (U), rather than the point on which the attraction is exerted (E) as it was the case in CX.

After applying differential mutation, the DE algorithm applies discrete recombination to U and $X(i)$ with probability parameter Cr generating V. This operator can be thought as a weighted geometric crossover and readily generalized as follows: $V = CX(U, X(i))$ with weights $(Cr, 1 - Cr)$ [12].

2.3 Definition of Convex Combination and Extension Ray

The notion of convex combination in metric spaces was introduced in the GPSO framework [7]. The convex combination $C = CX((A, W_A), (B, W_B))$ of two points A and B with weights W_A and W_B (positive and summing up to one)

Algorithm 2. Formal Geometric Differential Evolution

```
 1: initialize population of N_p configurations at random
 2: while stop criterion not met do
 3:    for all configuration X(i) in the population do
 4:       pick at random 3 distinct configurations from the current population X1, X2, X3
 5:       set W = 1/(1+F) where F is the scale factor parameter
 6:       create intermediate configuration E as the convex combination CX(X1, X3) with weights
          (1 − W, W)
 7:       create mutant configuration U as the extension ray ER(X2, E) with weights (W, 1 − W)
 8:       create candidate configuration V as the convex combination CX(U, X(i)) with weights
          (Cr, 1 − Cr) where Cr is the recombination parameter
 9:       if f(V) ≥ f(X(i)) then
10:          set the i^{th} configuration in the next population Y(i) = V
11:       else
12:          set Y(i) = X(i)
13:       end if
14:    end for
15:    for all configuration X(i) in the population do
16:       set X(i) = Y(i)
17:    end for
18: end while
```

in a metric space endowed with distance function d returns the set of points C such that $d(A, C)/d(A, B) = W_B$ and $d(B, C)/d(A, B) = W_A$ (the weights of the points A and B are inversely proportional to their distances to C). When specified to Euclidean spaces, this notion of convex combination coincides with the traditional notion of convex combination of real vectors.

The notion of extension ray in metric spaces was introduced in the GDE framework [12]. The weighted extension ray ER is defined as the inverse operation of the weighted convex combination CX, as follows. The weighted extension ray $ER((A, w_{ab}), (B, w_{bc}))$ of the points A (origin) and B (through) and weights w_{ab} and w_{bc} returns those points C such that their convex combination with A with weights w_{bc} and w_{ab}, $CX((A, w_{ab}), (C, w_{bc}))$, returns the point B.

The set of points returned by the weighted extension ray ER can be characterized in terms of distances to the input points of ER, as follows [12]. This characterization may be useful to construct procedures to implement the weighted extension ray for specific spaces.

Lemma 1. *The points C returned by the weighted extension ray $ER((A, w_{ab}), (B, w_{bc}))$ are exactly those points which are at a distance $d(A, B) \cdot w_{ab}/w_{bc}$ from B and at a distance $d(A, B)/w_{bc}$ from A (see [12] for the proof).*

3   GP-Specific Search Operators for GDE

In order to specify the GDE algorithm to the specific space of genetic programs, we need to choose a distance between genetic programs. A natural choice of distance would be a distance (metric) associated to the Koza-style crossover [4]. This would allow us to derive the specific GDE that searches the same fitness landscape seen by this crossover operator. Unfortunately, the Koza-style crossover is provably non-geometric under any metric [10], so there is no distance associated with it[1] we can use as basis for the GDE. Another crossover operator, the homologous crossover [5] is provably geometric under Structural Hamming Distance (SHD) [9] which is a variant of the well-known structural distance for genetic programming trees [1]. We use this distance as basis for the GDE because we will be able to use the homologous crossover as a term of reference. Notice, however, that in principle, we could choose any distance between genetic programming trees as a basis of the GDE.

3.1 Homologous Crossover and Structural Hamming Distance

The common region is the largest rooted region where two parent trees have the same topology. In homologous crossover [5] parent trees are aligned at the root and recombined using a crossover mask over the common region. If a node belongs to the boundary of the common region and is a function then the entire subtree rooted in that node is swapped with it.

The structural distance [1] is an edit distance specific to genetic programming trees. In this distance, two trees are brought to the same tree structure by adding null nodes to each tree. The cost of changing one node into another can be specified for each pair of nodes or for classes of nodes. Differences near the root have more weight. The Structural Hamming Distance [9] is a variant of the structural distance in which, when two matched subtrees have roots of different arities, they are considered to be at a maximal distance (set to 1). Otherwise, their distance is computed as in the original structural distance.

Definition 1. *(Structural Hamming Distance (SHD)). Let T_1 and T_2 be trees, and p and q their roots. Let $hd(p,q)$ be the Hamming distance between p and q (0 if $p = q$, 1 otherwise). Let s_i and t_i be the ith of the m subtrees of p and q.*

$dist(T_1, T_2) = hd(p,q)$ *if* $arity(p) = arity(q) = 0$
$dist(T_1, T_2) = 1$ *if* $arity(p) \neq arity(q)$
$dist(T_1, T_2) = \frac{1}{m+1}(hd(p,q) + \sum_{i=1..m} dist(s_i, t_i))$ *if* $arity(p) = arity(q) = m$

Theorem 1. *Homologous crossover is a geometric crossover under SHD [9].*

3.2 Convex Combination

In the following, we first define a weighted version of the homologous crossover. Then we show that this operator is a convex combination in the space of genetic programming trees endowed with SHD. In other words, the weighted homologous crossover implements a convex combination CX in this space.

Definition 2. *(Weighted homologous crossover). Let P_1 and P_2 be two parent trees, and W_1 and W_2 their weights, respectively. Their offspring O is generated using a crossover mask on the common region of P_1 and P_2 such that for each position of the common region, P_1 nodes appear in the crossover mask with probability W_1, and P_2 nodes appear with probability W_2.*

---

[1] In the sense that there is no distance such that the offspring trees are always within the metric segment between parent trees.

Theorem 2. *The weighted homologous crossover is (in expectation) a convex combination in the space of genetic programming trees endowed with SHD.*

Proof. The weighted homologous crossover is a special case of homologous crossover so it is also geometric under SHD. Therefore, the offspring of the weighted homologous crossover are in the segment between parents as required to be a convex combination. To complete the proof we need to show that the weights W_1 and W_2 of the weighted homologous crossover are inversely proportional to the expected distances $E[SHD(P_1, O)]$, $E[SHD(P_2, O)]$ from the parents P_1 and P_2 to their offspring O, as follows.

Given two trees P_1 and P_2, the SHD can be seen as a weighted Hamming distance on the common region of P_1 and P_2 where the weight w_i on the distance of the contribution of a position i in the common region depends on the arities of the nodes on the path from i to the root node. For each position i of the common region, the expected contribution $SHD_i(P_1, O)$ to the distance $SHD(P_1, O)$ of that specific position is directly proportional to w_i and inversely proportional to the weight W_1 (so, $E[SHD_i(P_1, O)] = w_i/W_1$). This is because, from the definition of weighted homologous crossover, W_1 is the probability that at that position the offspring O equals the parent P_1. So, the higher this probability, the smaller the expected contribution to the distance at that position. Furthermore the contribution to the distance is proportional to the weight w_i of the position i by definition of weighted Hamming distance. From the linearity of the expectation operator, we have that $E[SHD(P_1, O)] = E[\sum_i SHD_i(P_1, O)] = \sum_i E[SHD_i(P_1, O)] = \sum_i w_i/W_1 = 1/W_1$. The last passage holds true because by definition of SHD the sum of the weights on the common region equals 1 (this corresponds to the case of having two trees maximally different on the common region and their distance is 1). Analogously, for the other parent one obtains $E[SHD(P_2, O)] = 1/W_2$. This completes the proof.

3.3 Extension Ray

In the following, we first define two weighted homologous recombinations. Then we show that these operators are extension ray recombinations in the space of genetic programming trees endowed with SHD. The first recombination produces offspring with the same tree structure as the second parent. The second recombination is more general and can produce offspring with tree structure different from both parents. From a geometric viewpoint, these weighted homologous recombinations implement two different versions of extension ray recombination ER in the space of genetic programming trees endowed with SHD, where the first operator produces a subset of the points produced by the second operator.

To determine a recombination that implements an extension ray operator, it is useful to think of an extension ray operator, algebraically, as the inverse operation of a convex combination operator. In the convex combination, the unknown is the offspring C that can be determined by combining the known parents P_1 and P_2. In the extension ray, the distance relationship between P_1, P_2 and C is the same as in the convex combination, but P_1 (the origin of the extension ray) and C (the point the extension ray passes through) are known, and P_2 (the point on the extension ray) is unknown, i.e., $C = CX(P_1, P_2)$ can be equivalently rewritten as $P_2 = ER(P_1, C)$ depending whether C or P_2 is the unknown.

The first weighted extension ray homologous recombination is described in Algorithm 3. The second recombination is the same operator as the first with the following addition before line 6 in Algorithm 3. In the common region, if two subtrees $S_A(i)$ and $S_B(i)$ coincide in structure and contents (not only if their root nodes $T_A(i)$ and $T_B(i)$ coincide), put in the corresponding position i in the offspring T_C a random subtree S_C (with in general different structure and contents from S_A and S_B). Skip the remaining nodes in the common region covered by $S_A(i)$ and $S_B(i)$.

Notice that, in the definition of the second recombination above, any arbitrarily large subtree S_C could be generated to be included in T_C. However, in the implementation, its size should be limited. In the experiment, we generate S_C with the same number of nodes as S_A and S_B.

Algorithm 3. Weighted extension ray homologous recombination 1

Inputs: parent trees T_A (origin point of the ray) and T_B (passing through point of the ray), with corresponding weights w_{AB} and w_{BC} (both weights are between 0 and 1 and sum up to 1)
Output: a single offspring tree T_C (a point on the extension ray beyond T_B on the ray originating in T_A and passing through T_B)
1: compute the Structural Hamming Distance $SHD(T_A, T_B)$ between T_A and T_B
2: set $SHD(T_B, T_C) = SHD(T_A, T_B) \cdot w_{AB}/w_{BC}$ (compute the distance between T_B and T_C using the weights)
3: set $p = SHD(T_B, T_C)/(1 - SHD(T_A, T_B))$ (the probability p of flipping nodes in the common region from T_A and T_B beyond T_B)
4: set $T_C = T_B$
5: **for all** position i in the common region between T_A and T_B **do**
6:     consider the paired nodes $T_B(i)$ and $T_A(i)$ in the common region
7:     **if** $T_B(i) = T_A(i)$ and p > random number between 0 and 1 **then**
8:         set $T_C(i)$ to a random node with the same arity of $T_A(i)$ and $T_B(i)$
9:     **end if**
10: **end for**
11: return tree T_C as offspring

Theorem 3. *The weighted extension homologous ray recombinations 1 and 2 are (in expectation) extension ray operators in the space of genetic programming trees endowed with SHD.*

Proof. First we prove that $T_C = ER(T_A, T_B)$ by showing that $T_B = CX(T_A, T_C)$. Then we prove that the expected distances $E[SHD(T_A, T_B)]$ and $E[SHD(T_B, T_C)]$ are inversely proportional to the weights w_{AB} and w_{BC}, respectively.

Let us consider recombination 1. The offspring T_C has the same structure of T_B. This is because T_C was constructed starting from T_B and then for each node of the common region between T_A and T_B, T_C was not changed or it was randomly chosen but preserving the arity of that node in T_B.

The structures of the common regions $CR(T_A, T_B)$ and $CR(T_A, T_C)$ coincide. This is because the structure of the common region between two trees is only function of their structures. So, since T_B and T_C have the same structure, $CR(T_A, T_B)$ and $CR(T_A, T_C)$ have the same structure.

The tree T_B can be obtained by homologous crossover applied to T_A and T_C (hence, $T_C = ER(T_A, T_B)$). This can be shown considering two separate cases, (i) nodes of T_B inherited from the common region $CR(T_A, T_C)$ and (ii) subtrees of T_B inherited from subtrees of T_A and T_C at the bottom of the common region. Let us consider nodes on the common region. For each node with index i in the common region, the node $T_B(i)$ matches $T_A(i)$ or $T_C(i)$. This is true from the way $T_C(i)$ was chosen on the basis of the values of $T_A(i)$ and $T_B(i)$. We have two cases. First, $T_C(i)$ was chosen at random, when $T_A(i) = T_B(i)$. In this case $T_B(i)$ can be inherited from $T_A(i)$, since it may be $T_B(i) \neq T_C(i)$ but $T_B(i) = T_A(i)$. Second, $T_C(i)$ was chosen to equal $T_B(i)$, when $T_A(i) \neq T_B(i)$. In this case $T_B(i)$ can be inherited from $T_C(i)$. In either cases, for nodes on the common region the corresponding nodes of T_B can be inherited from T_A or T_C. The subtrees of T_B at the bottom of the common region can be inherited all from T_C (both structures and contents). Since by construction T_C inherited those subtrees from T_B without modifying them.

To show that recombination 1 is a weighted extension homologous ray recombination, we are left to show that the expected distances $E[SHD(T_A, T_B)]$ and $E[SHD(T_B, T_C)]$ are inversely proportional to the weights w_{AB} and w_{BC}. The probability p of flipping nodes in the common region away from T_A and T_B beyond T_B was chosen as an appropriate function of w_{AB} and w_{BC} and of $SHD(T_A, T_B)$ to obtain $SHD(T_B, T_C)$ such that the above requirement holds true. It is possible to prove that the chosen p is the correct one using the same argument used in the proof of theorem 2.

Let us consider now recombination 2. In this case, the offspring T_C by construction may have structure different from T_A and T_B. Also, the structures of the common regions $CR(T_A, T_B)$ and $CR(T_A, T_C)$ do not coincide. The structure of $CR(T_A, T_C)$ is covered by the structure of $CR(T_A, T_B)$ ($CR(T_A, T_C)$ is a substructure of $CR(T_A, T_B)$). The part of $CR(T_A, T_B)$ that does not cover $CR(T_A, T_C)$ comprises subtrees that are identical in structures and contents in T_A and T_B.

The tree T_B can be obtained by homologous crossover applied to T_A and T_C (hence, $T_C = ER(T_A, T_B)$). This can be shown similarly as for recombination 1 but with an extra case to consider. Nodes of T_B corresponding to nodes in the common region $CR(T_A, T_C)$ can be inherited from T_A or T_B. The subtrees of T_B at the bottom of the common region $CR(T_A, T_C)$ can be inherited all from T_C (both structures and contents). The extra case is for the subtrees of T_B that are in the part of $CR(T_A, T_B)$ that does not cover $CR(T_A, T_C)$. These subtrees cannot be inherited from T_C, which differs form T_B by construction, but they can always be inherited from T_A.

As for the requirement on the expected distances being inversely proportional to the weights, the probability p can be chosen as the case for recombination 1 due to the recursive definition of SHD that treats nodes and subtrees uniformly.

Now we have operational definitions of convex combination and extension ray for the space of genetic programming trees under SHD. These space-specific operators can be plugged in the formal GDE (Algorithm 2) to obtain a specific GDE for the genetic programming trees space, the GDE-GP.

4   Experiments

This section reports an initial experimental analysis of the GDE-GP behavior on four standard GP benchmark problems: Symbolic Regression of the quartic polynomial, Artificial Ant on the Santa Fe trail, 5-Bit Even Parity, and 11-Bit Multiplexer. In all these problems fitness is calculated so that lower values are better. All the experiments used $F = 0.8$ and $Cr = 0.9$, according to [16]. Both extension ray recombinations 1 and 2 were tested, giving rise to distinct techniques we designate as GDE1 and GDE2. As a baseline for comparison we used standard GP with homologous crossover (70%) and reproduction (30%), always applying point mutation with probability $1/L$, where L is the number of nodes of the individual. We call this baseline HGP. All the experiments were performed using populations of two different sizes (500 and 1000 individuals) initialized with the Ramped Half-and-Half procedure [4] with an initial maximum depth of 8, allowed to evolve for 50 generations. Each experiment was repeated 20 times. Statistical significance of the null hypothesis of no difference was determined with pairwise Kruskal-Wallis non-parametric ANOVAs at $p = 0.05$.

Figure 2 shows the boxplots of the best fitness achieved along the run, using populations of 500 individuals (top row) and 1000 individuals (bottom row). With a population size of 500, in all four problems there is a statistically significant difference between HGP and each of the GDE-GP techniques, and no significant difference between GDE1 and GDE2. GDE-GP is consistently better than HGP, regardless of the extension ray recombination used.

It may be argued that HGP is being crippled by such a small population size, which may reduce diversity along the run. This could be true, because when doubling the population size HGP significantly improves its best fitness of run in all except the Parity problem. However, the GDE-GP techniques also show significant improvements in most cases, and remain consistently better than HGP, regardless of the extension ray recombination used, exactly as before.

However, the observation of diversity, measured as the percentage of genotypically distinct individuals in the population, revealed somewhat unexpected results. Figure 3 (top row) shows the evolution of the median values of diversity along the run, for both population sizes. Not only HGP shows no clear signs of diversity loss, regardless of population size, but GDE-GP exhibits an extraordinarily varied behavior, approaching both extreme values in different problems (in Regression and Artificial Ant it practically reaches 0% while in Parity it reaches 100%), in some cases undergoing large fluctuations along the run (Multiplexer).

Finally, in Figure 3 (bottom row) we look at the evolution of the median values of average program length along the run, for both population sizes. Once again GDE-GP behaves radically differently from HGP, with both GDE1 and GDE2

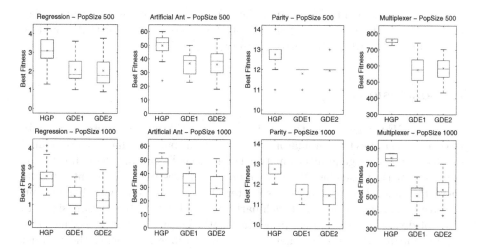

Fig. 2. Boxplots of the best fitness achieved in each problem (× marks the mean). Population sizes of 500 individuals (top row) and 1000 individuals (bottom row).

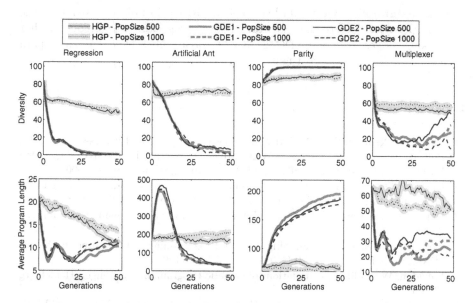

Fig. 3. Evolution of the median values of diversity (top row) and average program length (bottom row) in each problem

presenting large but smooth fluctuations in most problems, when compared to the more constrained but somewhat erratic behavior of HGP. The most interesting case is probably the Artificial Ant, where GDE-GP quickly and steadily increases the average program length until a plateau is reached, followed by a steep decrease to very low values. Curiously, there is no correspondingly interesting behavior in terms of the evolution of fitness (not shown), at least when observed in median terms. Only in the Parity problem GDE-GP exhibits a behavior that would be expected in standard (with subtree crossover) GP runs.

5 Conclusions

Geometric DE is a generalization of the classical DE to general metric spaces. In particular, it applies to combinatorial spaces. In this paper we have demonstrated how to specify the general Geometric Differential Evolution algorithm to the space of genetic programs. We have reported interesting experimental results where the new algorithm performs better than regular GP with homologous crossover in four typical GP benchmarks using different population sizes. In terms of diversity and average program length, neither technique seems to be largely influenced by the population size, most differences being the product of large individual variations. In the future we will deepen our study of the interesting dynamics revealed by the new algorithm.

Acknowledgments. We would like to thank Riccardo Poli for passing us the code of the homologous crossover for genetic programs. The second author also acknowledges project PTDC/EIACCO/103363/2008 from Fundação para a Ciência e a Tecnologia, Portugal.

References

1. Ekart, A., Nemeth, S.Z.: A Metric for Genetic Programs and Fitness Sharing. In: Poli, R., Banzhaf, W., Langdon, W.B., Miller, J., Nordin, P., Fogarty, T.C. (eds.) EuroGP 2000. LNCS, vol. 1802, pp. 259–270. Springer, Heidelberg (2000)
2. Gong, T., Tuson, A.L.: Differential Evolution for Binary Encoding. In: Soft Computing in Industrial Applications, pp. 251–262. Springer, Heidelberg (2007)
3. Kennedy, J., Eberhart, R.C.: Swarm Intelligence. Morgan Kaufmann, San Francisco (2001)
4. Koza, J.R.: Genetic Programming: On the Programming of Computers by Means of Natural Selection. The MIT Press, Cambridge (1992)
5. Langdon, W., Poli, R.: Foundations of Genetic Programming. Springer, Heidelberg (2002)
6. Moraglio, A.: Towards a Geometric Unification of Evolutionary Algorithms, Ph.D. thesis, University of Essex (2007)
7. Moraglio, A., Di Chio, C., Poli, R.: Geometric Particle Swarm Optimization. In: Ebner, M., O'Neill, M., Ekárt, A., Vanneschi, L., Esparcia-Alcázar, A.I. (eds.) EuroGP 2007. LNCS, vol. 4445, pp. 125–136. Springer, Heidelberg (2007)
8. Moraglio, A., Di Chio, C., Togelius, J., Poli, R.: Geometric Particle Swarm Optimization. Journal of Artificial Evolution and Applications, Article ID 143624 (2008)
9. Moraglio, A., Poli, R.: Geometric Landscape of Homologous Crossover for Syntactic Trees. In: Proceedings of CEC-2005, pp. 427–434. IEEE Press, Los Alamitos (2005)

10. Moraglio, A., Poli, R.: Inbreeding Properties of Geometric Crossover and Non-geometric Recombinations. In: Stephens, C.R., Toussaint, M., Whitley, L.D., Stadler, P.F. (eds.) FOGA 2007. LNCS, vol. 4436, pp. 1–14. Springer, Heidelberg (2007)
11. Moraglio, A., Togelius, J.: Geometric PSO for the Sudoku Puzzle. In: Proceedings of GECCO-2007, pp. 118–125. ACM Press, New York (2007)
12. Moraglio, A., Togelius, J.: Geometric Differential Evolution. In: Proceedings of GECCO-2009, pp. 1705–1712. ACM Press, New York (2009)
13. O'Neill, M., Brabazon, A.: Grammatical Differential Evolution. In: Proceedings of ICAI-2006, pp. 231–236. CSREA Press (2006)
14. Onwubolu, G.C., Davendra, D. (eds.): Differential Evolution: A Handbook for Global Permutation-based Combinatorial Optimization. Springer, Heidelberg (2009)
15. Pampara, G., Engelbrecht, A.P., Franken, N.: Binary Differential Evolution. In: Proceedings of CEC 2006, pp. 1873–1879. IEEE Press, Los Alamitos (2006)
16. Price, K.V., Storm, R.M., Lampinen, J.A.: Differential Evolution: A Practical Approach to Global Optimization. Springer, Heidelberg (2005)
17. Togelius, J., De Nardi, R., Moraglio, A.: Geometric PSO + GP = Particle Swarm Programming. In: Proceedings of CEC 2008, pp. 3594–3600. IEEE Press, Los Alamitos (2008)

Improving the Generalisation Ability of Genetic Programming with Semantic Similarity based Crossover

Nguyen Quang Uy[1], Nguyen Thi Hien[2], Nguyen Xuan Hoai[2], and Michael O'Neill[1]

[1] Natural Computing Research & Applications Group, University College Dublin, Ireland
[2] School of Information Technology, Vietnamese Military Technical Academy, Vietnam
quanguyhn@gmail.com, hien_cpqn@yahoo.com, nxhoai@gmail.com, m.oneill@ucd.ie

Abstract. This paper examines the impact of semantic control on the ability of Genetic Programming (GP) to generalise via a semantic based crossover operator (Semantic Similarity based Crossover - SSC). The use of validation sets is also investigated for both standard crossover and SSC. All GP systems are tested on a number of real-valued symbolic regression problems. The experimental results show that while using validation sets barely improve generalisation ability of GP, by using semantics, the performance of Genetic Programming is enhanced both on training and testing data. Further recorded statistics shows that the size of the evolved solutions by using SSC are often smaller than ones obtained from GP systems that do not use semantics. This can be seen as one of the reasons for the success of SSC in improving the generalisation ability of GP.

Keywords: Genetic Programming, Semantics, Generalisation, Crossover.

1 Introduction

Genetic Programming (GP) [23,17] researchers are in recent times paying increasing attention to semantic information, with a dramatic increase in the number of publications (e.g., [11,12,13,15,14,2,21,24,25,3]). Previously, research has focused on syntactic aspects of GP representation. From a programmer's perspective, however, maintaining syntactic correctness is only one part of program construction: not only must programs be syntactically correct but also semantically correct. Thus incorporating semantic awareness in the GP evolutionary process could improve its performance, extending the applicability of GP to problems that are difficult with purely syntactic GP.

In the field of Machine Learning (ML), generalisation has been seen as one of the most desirable properties for learning machines [22]. As GP could be seen as a (evolutionary) machine learning methodology, it is very important to guarantee that the solutions GP finds, not only work well on training data but also on the unseen data [5]. Surprisingly, a lot of GP researchers only report results on training data. While overfitting the training data to get the exact solutions is suitable in some cases, for most of learning problems in reality it would be not enough without considering their generalisation over unseen data. Some recent works (e.g. [5,26,9]) have showed that the ability of GP to generalise could be poor. The awareness of the ability of GP to generalise is also important in the context of performance comparison between different GP systems. It has been recently shown in [5] that an enhanced GP system performance might

A.I. Esparcia-Alcazar et al. (Eds.): EuroGP 2010, LNCS 6021, pp. 184–195, 2010.

be remarkably better than standard GP on training data, but not significantly better on unseen data.

The previous research on improving the ability of GP to generalise is mostly focused on reducing the solution size [26,9,20]. The motivation for such an approach is that GP usually bloats, with solution complexity (size) increasing rapidly during the evolutionary process. The high complexity solutions are often poor in their ability to generalise as they contradict Ockham's razor principles in Machine Learning [22] (simple solutions are prefered). To the best of our knowledge, there has not been any work on the effect of semantic control on the ability of GP to generalise. In this paper, we demonstrate a new and semantic based approach to improve GP in finding solutions that have better properties of generalisation. In particular, we test if a recently proposed semantics based crossover, namely Semantic Similarity based Crossover (SSC) [25], could improve the ability of GP to generalise. The experimental results show the effectiveness of the SSC approach in comparison with both standard GP and the validation set based method. The remainder of the paper is organised as follows. In the next section we review the literature on GP with semantics and GP generalisation. The semantics based crossover (SSC) is described in Section 3 followed by the experimental settings. The experimental results are shown and discussed in Section 5. The last section concludes the paper and highlights some future work.

2   Related Work

Although generalisation of learned solutions is the primary interest of any learning machine [22], it was not seriously considered in the field of GP for a long time. Before Kushchu published his work on the generalisation ability of GP [19], there were rather few research dealing with the GP generalisation aspect. Francone et al. [8] proposed a new GP system called Compiling GP (CGP) and the authors compared its generalisation ability with that of other ML techniques. The results show that the ability of CGP to generalise compares favourably with a number of more traditional ML methods. Furthermore, the influence of using extensive mutation on the ablity of CGP to generalise was investigated and the experimental results show positive effects [1].

Recently, the issue of generalisation in GP is deservedly receiving increased attention. Mahler et al. [20] experimented with Tarpeian Control on some symbolic regression problems and tested the side effects of this method on the generalisation ability of GP. The results were inconsistent and problem dependent, i.e., it can either increase or reduce the generalisation power of solutions found by GP. Gagne et al. [9] investigated two methods to improve generalisation in GP-based learning: the selection of the best of run individuals using a three datasets method (training, validation, and test sets), and the application of parsimony pressure in order to reduce the complexity of the solutions. Their experimental results indicate that using a validation set could slightly improve the stability of the best of run solutions on the test sets. Costa et al. [4] proposed a new GP system called relaxed Genetic Programming (RGP) with generalisation ability better than standard GP.

More recently, Costelloe and Ryan [5] showed the important role of generalisation on GP. They experimentally showed that a technique like Linear Scaling [16] may only be significantly better than standard GP on training data but not superior on testing data. They proposed an approach to improve GP generalisation by combining Linear Scaling and the No Same Mate strategy [10]. Vanneschi and Gustafson [26] improved GP generalisation using a crossover based similarity measure. Their method is to keep a list of over-fitting individuals and to prevent any individual entering the next generation if it is similar (based on structural distance or a subtree crossover based similarity measure) to one individual in the list. The method was then tested on a real-life drug discovery regression problem and the experimental results showed improvements on the ability to generalise. Most research on improving the ability of GP to generalise has been purely focused on reducing the complexity of the solution and semantic control has never been considered as an approach to enhance ability of GP to generalise.

The use of semantics in GP has recently attracted increasing attention by researchers in the field. There are three main approaches to representing, extracting, and using semantics to guide the evolutionary process: (a) using grammar-based approaches [27,3,6], (b) using formal methods [11,13,15], and (c) based on GP s-tree representations [2,21,24]. In [25], a more detailed review of semantics usage and control in GP is given.

Most of previous research on semantics in GP were focused on combinatorial and boolean problems such as the Knapsack problem [3], Boolean problems [2,21], and Mutual Exclusion problems [15]. Recently, researchers have investigated the effect of semantic control in GP for problems in real-valued domains [24,25,18]. Krawiec [18] proposed a way to measure the semantics of an individual that is based on fitness cases. This semantics is then used to guide crossover (*Approximating Geometric Crossover - AGC*). The experiments conducted on both real-valued and boolean regression problems show that AGC is not better than standard subtree crossover (SC) on the tested real-valued problems and only slightly better than SC on the boolean ones. Uy et al. [24] proposed a new crossover operator, namely Semantics Aware Crossover (SAC), based on checking the semantic equivalence of subtrees. SAC was tested on a family of real-valued symbolic regression problems, and was empirically shown to improve GP performance. SAC was then extended to Semantic Similarity based Crossover (SSC) [25]. The experimental results show that the performance of SSC is superior than both of SC and SAC on the tested problems. However, the performance measure was more focused on finding exact solutions (overfitting). It is interesting to see if this semantic based operator could also help to improve the ability of GP to generalise.

3   Semantic Similarity based Crossover

Semantic Similarity based Crossover (SSC) [25] is inspired and extended from earlier research on Semantics Aware Crossover (SAC) [24]. SSC described in this paper is almost identical to that described by Uy et al. [25] with a slightly modified semantic distance measure. Since SSC operates on the semantics of subtrees, first a defintion of subtree semantics is needed. Formally, the *Sampling Semantics* of any (sub)tree is defined as follows:

Let F be a function expressed by a (sub)tree T on a domain D. Let P be a set of points sampled from domain D, $P = \{p_1, p_2, ..., p_N\}$. Then the *Sampling Semantics* of T on P on domain D is the set $S = \{s_1, s_2, ..., s_N\}$ where $s_i = F(p_i), i = 1, 2, ..., N$.

The value of N depends on the problems. If it is too small, the approximate semantics might be too coarse-grained and not sufficiently accurate. If N is too big, the approximate semantics might be more accurate, but more time consuming to measure. The choice of P is also important. If the members of P are too closely related to the GP function set (for example, π for trigonometric functions, or e for logarithmic functions), then the semantics might be misleading. For this reason, choosing them randomly may be the best solution. In this paper, the number of points for evaluating *Sampling Semantics* is set as the number of fitness cases of problems (30 points for $F_1, F3$ and F_5, 60 points for $F_2, F4$ and F_6, see Section 4), and we choose the set of points P uniformly randomly from the problem domain.

Based on *Sampling Semantics* (SS), we define a *Sampling Semantics Distance* between two subtrees. In the previous work [25], *Sampling Semantics Distance* (SSD) was defined as the sum of absolute difference of all values of SS. While the experiments show that this kind of SSD is acceptable, it has undoubted weakness that the value of SSD strongly depends of the number of SS points (N) [25]. To soften this drawback, in this paper we use the mean of absolute distance as the SSD between subtrees. In other words, let $U = \{u_1, u_2, ..., u_N\}$ and $V = \{v_1, v_2, ..., v_N\}$ be the SS of $Subtree_1(St_1)$ and $Subtree_2(St_2)$ on the same set of evaluating values, then the SSD between St_1 and St_2 is defined as follows:

$$SSD(St_1, St_2) = \frac{|u_1 - v_1| + |u_2 - v_2| + ... + |u_N - v_N|}{N} \qquad (1)$$

Thanks to SSD, a relationship known as *Semantic Similarity* is defined. The intuition behind semantic similarity is that exchange of subtrees is most likely to be beneficial if the two subtrees are not semantically identical, but also they are not too semantically dissimilar. Two subtrees are semantically similar on a domain if their SSD on the same set of points in that domain lies within a positive interval. The formal definition of semantic similarity (SSi) between subtrees St_1 and St_2 is as follows:

$$SSi(St_1, St_2) = \textbf{if } \alpha < SSD(St_1, St_2) < \beta$$

$$\textbf{then } \text{true}$$

$$\textbf{else } \text{false}$$

here α and β are two predefined constants, known as the *lower* and *upper bounds* for semantic sensitivity, respectively. Conceivably, the best values for *lower* and *upper bound semantic sensitivity* might be problem dependent. However we strongly suspect that for almost any symbolic regression problem, there is a range of values that is appropriate [25]. The investigation of the effect of different semantic sensitivities on SSC performance is beyond the scope of this paper. In this paper, we set $\alpha = 10^{-4}$ and $\beta = 0.4$ which are good values found in the literature [25].

Inspired from the difficulty in designing an operator with the property of high locality in GP, SSC was proposed with the main objective being to improve the locality of crossover. SSC is in fact an extension of SAC in two ways. Firstly, when two subtrees are selected for crossover, their semantic similarity, rather than semantic equivalence as in SAC, is checked. Secondly, semantic similarity is more difficult to satisfy than semantic equivalence, so repeated failures may occur. Thus SSC uses multiple trials

---

Algorithm 1. Semantic Similarity based Crossover

---

select Parent 1 P_1;
select Parent 2 P_2;
Count=0;
while *Count<Max_Trial* **do**
> choose a random crossover point $Subtree_1$ in P_1;
> choose a random crossover point $Subtree_2$ in P_2;
> generate a number of random points (P) on the problem domain;
> calculate the SSD between $Subtree_1$ and $Subtree_2$ on P
> **if** *$Subtree_1$ is similar to $Subtree_2$* **then**
>> execute crossover;
>> add the children to the new population;
>> return true;
>
> **else**
>> Count=Count+1;

if *Count=Max_Trial* **then**
> choose a random crossover point $Subtree_1$ in P_1;
> choose a random crossover point $Subtree_2$ in P_2;
> execute crossover;
> return true;

---

to find a semantically similar pair, only reverting to random selection after passing a bound on the number of trials. Algorithm 1 shows how SSC operates in detail. In our experiments, the value of Max_Trial was set to 12, with this value having been calibrated by earlier experimental results.

4   Experimental Setup

To investigate the impact of SSC on the ability of GP to generalise, we used six real-valued symbolic regression problems. The tested problems, training and testing data are shown in Table 1. These functions were taken from some other work on GP learning generalisation [5,7,16]. It is noted that the testing sets are often much larger than the

Table 1. Symbolic Regression Functions

Functions	Training Data	Testing Data
$F_1 = x^4 + x^3 + x^2 + x$	30 random points $\subseteq$ [-1,1]	100 $\subseteq$[-1:0.02:1]
$F_2 = x^3 - x^2 - x - 1$	60 random points $\subseteq$ [-1,1]	100 $\subseteq$[-1:0.02:1]
$F_3 = arcsin(x)$	30 random points $\subseteq$ [-1,1]	200 $\subseteq$[-1:0.01:1]
$F_4 = \sqrt{x}$	60 random points $\subseteq$ [0,4]	200 $\subseteq$[0:0.02:4]
$F_5 = 0.3sin(2\pi x)$	30 random points $\subseteq$ [-1,1]	100 $\subseteq$[-0.5:0.02:1.5]
$F_6 = cos(3x)$	60 random points $\subseteq$ [-1,1]	200 $\subseteq$[0:0.01:2]

Table 2. Run and Evolutionary Parameter Values

Parameter	Value
Population size	500
Generations	50
Selection	Tournament
Tournament size	3
Crossover probability	0.9
Mutation probability	0.05
Initial Max depth	6
Max depth	15
Max depth of mutation tree	5
Non-terminals	+, -, *, / (protected version), sin, cos, exp, log (protected version)
Terminals	X, 1
Raw fitness	mean absolute error on all fitness cases
Trials per treatment	100 independent runs for each value

training sets and in some cases they contain values that are not in the training intervals (F_5, F_6). This makes the experimental setting more general.

The GP parameters used for our experiments are shown in Table 2. Despite this being an experiment purely concerned with generalisation ability of crossover, we have retained mutation with a small rate in the system because the aim of the experiment is to study crossover in the context of a normal GP run. Our experiments were conducted on four configurations as follows:

1. Standard Crossover (SC): The fitness is measured as the error rate on the whole training set. The best-of-run individual is the individual with the lowest error rate on the training set in entire evolutionary time. This individual was then tested on the testing data set to give the result for solution generalisation capacity of the run.
2. Standard Crossover with Validation (SCV): The training set is randomly divided into 2 (for each run): 67% is used for training (training set) and the remaining 33% is used for validating (validation set). At each generation the fitness of individuals is measured on the training set and this fitness is used for tournament selection. At the same time, a two-objective trial (fitness and size of an individual) is conducted in order to extract a set of non-dominated individuals (the Pareto front). The individuals in the Pareto front are then evaluated on the validation set, with the best of run individual selected as the one of these with the smallest error rate on the validation set. This configuration is similar to the validation configuration in [9].
3. Semantic Similarity based Crossover (SSC): This configuration is similar to Configuration 1 with only one difference is that SSC is used stead of SC.
4. Semantic Similarity based Crossover with Validation (SSCV): This configuration is similar to Configuration 2 but with SSC rather than SC.

Table 3. Number of solutions of four schemas

Fs	Ms	Training				Validating				Testing			
		GS	MS	BS	US	GS	MS	BS	US	GS	MS	BS	US
F1	SC	22	76	2	0	-	-	-	-	16	72	11	1
	SSC	49	50	1	0	-	-	-	-	39	59	3	1
	SCV	28	71	1	0	29	65	6	0	14	71	14	1
	SSCV	52	48	0	0	56	44	0	0	32	58	9	1
F2	SC	4	81	15	0	-	-	-	-	5	69	26	0
	SSC	15	85	0	0	-	-	-	-	12	86	2	0
	SCV	7	82	11	0	6	76	18	0	3	66	31	0
	SSCV	18	79	3	0	18	79	3	0	13	74	13	0
F3	SC	62	38	0	0	-	-	-	-	37	62	1	0
	SSC	88	12	0	0	-	-	-	-	71	29	0	0
	SCV	65	35	0	0	68	32	0	0	24	74	20	0
	SSCV	90	10	0	0	90	10	0	0	54	46	0	0
F4	SC	22	77	1	0	-	-	-	-	4	88	7	1
	SSC	34	64	0	0	-	-	-	-	9	91	1	0
	SCV	21	78	1	0	24	74	2	0	2	94	4	0
	SSCV	29	70	1	0	38	60	2	0	2	95	3	0
F5	SC	0	99	1	0	-	-	-	-	0	4	94	2
	SSC	5	95	0	0	-	-	-	-	1	5	91	3
	SCV	1	99	0	0	0	94	6	0	0	2	92	6
	SSCV	4	96	0	0	5	91	4	0	0	2	93	5
F6	SC	49	45	6	0	-	-	-	-	40	8	41	11
	SSC	61	38	1	0	-	-	-	-	54	7	34	5
	SCV	47	46	7	0	48	45	7	0	38	7	45	10
	SSCV	59	38	3	0	58	37	5	0	51	4	40	5

5   Results and Discussion

To examine and compare the generalisation performance of these methods, we use a new performance metric to measure the quality of solution of a run. For each run, we select the best individual (based on its fitness on the training data sets or the validating sets) as the final solution of the run. This solution is then tested on the testing sets. We define $\varepsilon = 5.10^{-3}$ as a constant to determine the quality of a solution. For a solution with fitness ft on the training sets (or validating sets or testing sets respectively), we classify it into four categories

1. A good solution (GS) if $ft < \varepsilon$
2. A moderate solution (MS) if $\varepsilon \leq ft < 10\varepsilon$
3. A bad solution (BS) if $10\varepsilon \leq ft < 100\varepsilon$
4. An Unacceptable solution (US) if $100\varepsilon \leq ft$

The number of each category of solutions found on three data sets are shown in Table 3. It can be seen from this table that SSC is consistently better than SC on the training sets.

Table 4. Mean and Standard Deviation of the average of best fitness on three data sets. Note that the values are scaled by 10^2.

Functions	Methods	Training		Validating		Testing	
		Mean	Std	Mean	Std	Mean	Std
F1	SC	1.54	1.23	-	-	6.13	34.1
	SSC	**0.75**	0.99	-	-	**2.17**	9.10
	SCV	1.30	1.09	1.57	1.79	3.86	10.2
	SSCV	**0.67**	0.76	0.80	1.01	**3.19**	9.61
F2	SC	3.07	1.81	-	-	3.88	2.42
	SSC	**1.38**	0.84	-	-	**1.82**	1.27
	SCV	2.92	1.83	3.16	2.27	4.14	2.58
	SSCV	**1.62**	1.32	1.64	1.42	**2.53**	2.45
F3	SC	0.61	0.70	-	-	1.00	1.10
	SSC	**0.25**	0.23	-	-	**0.49**	0.44
	SCV	0.55	0.54	0.54	0.79	1.06	1.01
	SSCV	**0.23**	0.21	0.28	0.60	**0.62**	0.55
F4	SC	1.29	0.99	-	-	1.84	1.50
	SSC	**0.85**	0.75	-	-	**1.37**	1.11
	SCV	1.19	0.94	1.29	1.12	1.86	1.52
	SSCV	**0.99**	1.07	1.17	1.76	**1.56**	1.29
F5	SC	2.40	0.87	-	-	16.2	12.7
	SSC	**1.98**	0.83	-	-	**14.1**	12.6
	SCV	2.35	0.78	3.01	1.19	18.4	19.6
	SSCV	**1.79**	0.84	2.57	1.37	16.1	13.6
F6	SC	1.37	1.77	-	-	20.0	28.5
	SSC	**0.66**	0.98	-	-	**16.2**	22.2
	SCV	1.46	1.83	1.48	2.09	23.3	40.0
	SSCV	**0.84**	1.37	1.19	2.32	**17.8**	25.6

These results are consistent with those in [25] where SSC was shown to be significantly better than both SC and SAC. The results also show that SSC found good solutions more often than SC on all problems. The number of moderate and bad solutions of SSC are also significantly less than ones of SC. It is noted that none of the methods scored unacceptable solutions on the training sets. This means that on the tested problems, it is rather easy for all GP systems to overfit the training data. The table also shows that by using validation sets, the solutions selected at the end of the runs have validation errors almost similar to training errors and the solution quality of SSCV is also consistently better than one of SCV.

The results on test sets show some deterioration in the quality of the solutions for all methods. The table, however, also shows that the performance of SSC on the test sets is still better than SC. SSC generate more good solutions and less bad and unacceptable solution on the test sets regardless of how the test sets are designed. It confirms that the generalisation power of GP is increased when equiped with SSC. In other words, by adding semantic control via SSC, the performance of GP is improved not only on

Table 5. The average size of population and the good solutions on training and testing sets

Fs	ASP				ASGSTr				ASGSTs			
	SC	SSC	SCV	SSCV	SC	SSC	SCV	SSCV	SC	SSC	SCV	SSCV
F1	52.9	43.2	50.1	43.4	64.6	59.8	62.1	60.2	30.8	30.4	20.7	23.1
F2	58.0	55.6	57.6	55.4	83.1	43.1	59.2	77.8	38.5	29.6	38.0	58.0
F3	43.2	40.3	41.8	42.2	58.7	63.5	64.2	62.5	61.5	55.6	48.1	53.0
F4	51.5	48.0	51.7	48.9	65.3	52.3	54.7	49.2	73.8	80.7	53.2	57.0
F5	65.5	63.7	65.7	63.8	NA	50.4	87.5	51.2	NA	90	NA	NA
F6	55.6	42.0	55.8	42.0	64.6	51.5	63.3	41.8	25.9	23.3	31.2	23.3

training data but also on unseen data. On the testing sets, solution quality of SCV and SSCV are slightly worse than SC and SSC respectively. It seems that the generalisation ability of both SC and SSC are not enhanced when the validation sets are used. It is not entirely surprising as it was also shown that the use of a validation set only improves the stability of the best-of-run solutions on the test sets and the improvement was not significant [9].

The second performance metric used here is the mean and standard deviation of the best fitness on three data sets. These results are presented in Table 4 (after the values are scaled by 10^2). A Ranked Wilcoxon Test was also conducted to analyse if the use of SSC results in significantly better solution quality over SC. The confidence interval is 95% and the results are printed bold face if they are statistically significant. The results in this table are consistent with those in Table 3, i.e., SSC is significantly better than SC on all tested functions both on the training and test sets. Unlike some other techniques for improving GP generalisation [5], at least on similar testing problems, SSC does not only improve the solution performance on the traning sets (overfitting) but also on the test sets (generalisation). The table also shows that using validation sets does not help to increase the power of SC or SSC. The superiority of SSCV over SC is mostly related to its semantic control mechanism (with an exception on function F_5).

Since there is a strong correlation between the complexity of solutions and their ability to generalise (Ockham's razor or Minimum Description Length - MDL principle [22], statistics on solution size were also recorded and analysed. This includes the average size of a solution in the population (ASP), the average size of the good solutions on the training sets (ASGSTr) and the average size of the good solutions on the test sets (ASGSTs). These results are depicted in Table 5. In this table, when a method could not find any good solution, NA is printed instead. It can be seen that the average size of a solution in the population for SSC is constantly smaller than SC. It means that SSC not only helps to improve GP solution quality but also to reduce code bloat. This is important as the primary motivation of SSC is to design a crossover operator based on semantic control but not to reduce size or code bloat (i.e., the control exerted on the semantic level seems to have a positive consequence for the syntactic aspects of the evolving programs). While the reason for reducing code bloat of SSC is not investigated in this paper, it seems that the better individuals in SSC tend to be smaller than ones of SC. The results of the average size of the good solutions on the training sets give more evidence for this conclusion. These results show that the ASGSTr of SSC is often smaller than one of SC (with one exception on function F_3). These results can be considered as one of the underlining reasons for the improvement in generalisation power that SSC brings to a GP system.

The results in Table 5, contrary to those in Tables 3 and 4, also show the remarkable effect of the use of validation sets. It shows that the good solutions found by using validation sets (either with SC or SSC), are often smaller in size than without validation. It is understandable as the methods with validation sets tend to select smaller solutions to measure error on the test sets. The results are consistent with Gagne [9], where it was also shown that the use of a validation set helps to reduce the size of the best individuals of runs.

6   Conclusions and Future Work

In this paper, we investigated the impact of semantic control on the ability of GP to generalise by using a recently proposed semantic based crossover, *Semantic Similarity based Crossover* (SSC). The traditional approach for improving generalisation in the field of GP in particular and Machine Learning in general by using validation sets was also examined. Four GP systems were tested on a number of real-valued symbolic regression problems. The empirical results shows a significant positive impact of semantic control in GP on its generalisation ability, and limited effects of using validation sets were observed (except in terms of the average size of good solutions). Further analysis on the average size of individuals in the population and the solutions shows that using semantics (via SSC) also helps to reduce GP code bloat. This leads to both significant GP performance improvement and its ability to find simpler solutions.

Although the experiments provide strong evidence for the important role of semantic control in reducing GP code bloat which leads to the improvement of GP generalisation, it offers no explanation. We are aiming to investigate such causal relationship in the future. It might be very important as it creates a bridge between semantic and syntactic aspects of the GP evolutionary process. Furthermore, and perhap equally important, we are planning to find the answer for the limited impact of validation sets in the GP learning process as found on the problems examined here. Last but not least, we are also intending to do a more comprehensive comparison between SSC generalisation ability with some other generalisation methods in the GP literature (e.g. Tarpeian Control, Relaxed GP, Linear Scaling and No same mate etc).

Acknowledgements

This paper was funded under a Postgraduate Scholarship from the Irish Research Council for Science Engineering and Technology (IRCSET).

References

1. Banzhaf, W., Francone, F.D., Nordin, P.: The effect of extensive use of the mutation operator on generalization in genetic programming using sparse data sets. In: Ebeling, W., Rechenberg, I., Voigt, H.-M., Schwefel, H.-P. (eds.) PPSN 1996. LNCS, vol. 1141, pp. 300–309. Springer, Heidelberg (1996)

2. Beadle, L., Johnson, C.: Semantically driven crossover in genetic programming. In: Proceedings of the IEEE World Congress on Computational Intelligence, pp. 111–116. IEEE Press, Los Alamitos (2008)

3. Cleary, R., O'Neill, M.: An attribute grammar decoder for the 01 multi-constrained knapsack problem. In: Raidl, G.R., Gottlieb, J. (eds.) EvoCOP 2005. LNCS, vol. 3448, pp. 34–45. Springer, Heidelberg (2005)

4. Costa, L.E.D., Landry, J.-A.: Relaxed genetic programming. In: GECCO 2006: Proceedings of the 8th annual conference on Genetic and evolutionary computation, Seattle, Washington, USA, July 2006, vol. 1, pp. 937–938. ACM Press, New York (2006)

5. Costelloe, D., Ryan, C.: On improving generalisation in genetic programming. In: Vanneschi, L., Gustafson, S., Moraglio, A., De Falco, I., Ebner, M. (eds.) EuroGP 2009. LNCS, vol. 5481, pp. 61–72. Springer, Heidelberg (2009)

6. de la Cruz Echeanda, M., de la Puente, A.O., Alfonseca, M.: Attribute grammar evolution. In: Mira, J., Álvarez, J.R. (eds.) IWINAC 2005. LNCS, vol. 3562, pp. 182–191. Springer, Heidelberg (2005)

7. Foreman, N., Evett, M.: Preventing overfitting in GP with canary functions. In: GECCO 2005: Proceedings of the 2005 conference on Genetic and evolutionary computation, Washington DC, USA, June 2005, vol. 2, pp. 1779–1780. ACM Press, New York (2005)

8. Francone, F.D., Nordin, P., Banzhaf, W.: Benchmarking the generalization capabilities of a compiling genetic programming system using sparse data sets. In: Genetic Programming 1996: Proceedings of the First Annual Conference, Stanford University, CA, USA, July 28–31, pp. 72–80. MIT Press, Cambridge (1996)

9. Gagne, C., Schoenauer, M., Parizeau, M., Tomassini, M.: Genetic programming, validation sets, and parsimony pressure. In: Collet, P., Tomassini, M., Ebner, M., Gustafson, S., Ekárt, A. (eds.) EuroGP 2006. LNCS, vol. 3905, pp. 109–120. Springer, Heidelberg (2006)

10. Gustafson, S., Burke, E.K., Krasnogor, N.: On improving genetic programming for symbolic regression. In: Proceedings of the 2005 IEEE Congress on Evolutionary Computation, Edinburgh, UK, vol. 1, pp. 912–919. IEEE Press, Los Alamitos (2005)

11. Johnson, C.: Deriving genetic programming fitness properties by static analysis. In: Foster, J.A., Lutton, E., Miller, J., Ryan, C., Tettamanzi, A.G.B. (eds.) EuroGP 2002. LNCS, vol. 2278, pp. 299–308. Springer, Heidelberg (2002)

12. Johnson, C.: What can automatic programming learn from theoretical computer science. In: Proceedings of the UK Workshop on Computational Intelligence. University of Birmingham (2002)

13. Johnson, C.: Genetic programming with fitness based on model checking. In: Ebner, M., O'Neill, M., Ekárt, A., Vanneschi, L., Esparcia-Alcázar, A.I. (eds.) EuroGP 2007. LNCS, vol. 4445, pp. 114–124. Springer, Heidelberg (2007)

14. Katz, G., Peled, D.: Genetic programming and model checking: Synthesizing new mutual exclusion algorithms. In: Cha, S(S.), Choi, J.-Y., Kim, M., Lee, I., Viswanathan, M. (eds.) ATVA 2008. LNCS, vol. 5311, pp. 33–47. Springer, Heidelberg (2008)

15. Katz, G., Peled, D.: Model checking-based genetic programming with an application to mutual exclusion. In: Ramakrishnan, C.R., Rehof, J. (eds.) TACAS 2008. LNCS, vol. 4963, pp. 141–156. Springer, Heidelberg (2008)

16. Keijzer, M.: Improving symbolic regression with interval arithmetic and linear scaling. In: Ryan, C., Soule, T., Keijzer, M., Tsang, E.P.K., Poli, R., Costa, E. (eds.) EuroGP 2003. LNCS, vol. 2610, pp. 70–82. Springer, Heidelberg (2003)

17. Koza, J.R.: Genetic Programming: On the Programming of Computers by Means of Natural Selection. The MIT Press, Cambridge (1992)

18. Krawiec, K., Lichocki, P.: Approximating geometric crossover in semantic space. In: Rothlauf, F. (ed.) Proceedings of Genetic and Evolutionary Computation Conference, GECCO 2009, Montreal, Québec, Canada, July 8-12, pp. 987–994. ACM, New York (2009)

19. Kushchu, I.: An evaluation of evolutionary generalisation in genetic programming. Artificial Intelligence Review 18(1), 3–14 (2002)
20. Mahler, S., Robilliard, D., Fonlupt, C.: Tarpeian bloat control and generalization accuracy. In: Keijzer, M., Tettamanzi, A.G.B., Collet, P., van Hemert, J., Tomassini, M. (eds.) EuroGP 2005. LNCS, vol. 3447, pp. 203–214. Springer, Heidelberg (2005)
21. McPhee, N., Ohs, B., Hutchison, T.: Semantic building blocks in genetic programming. In: O'Neill, M., Vanneschi, L., Gustafson, S., Esparcia Alcázar, A.I., De Falco, I., Della Cioppa, A., Tarantino, E. (eds.) EuroGP 2008. LNCS, vol. 4971, pp. 134–145. Springer, Heidelberg (2008)
22. Mitchell, T.: Machine Learning. McGraw-Hill, New York (1996)
23. Poli, R., Langdon, W.B., McPhee, N.F.: A Field Guide to Genetic Programming (With contributions by J. R. Koza) (2008), http://lulu.com, http://www.gp-field-guide.org.uk
24. Uy, N.Q., Hoai, N.X., O'Neill, M.: Semantic aware crossover for genetic programming: the case for real-valued function regression. In: Vanneschi, L., Gustafson, S., Moraglio, A., De Falco, I., Ebner, M. (eds.) EuroGP 2009. LNCS, vol. 5481, pp. 292–302. Springer, Heidelberg (2009)
25. Uy, N.Q., O'Neill, M., Hoai, N.X., McKay, B., Lopez, E.G.: Semantic similarity based crossover in GP: The case for real-valued function regression. In: Collet, P. (ed.) 9th International Conference Evolution Artificielle, October 2009. LNCS, pp. 13–24. Springer, Heidelberg (2009)
26. Vanneschi, L., Gustafson, S.: Using crossover based similarity measure to improve genetic programming generalization ability. In: GECCO 2009: Proceedings of the 11th Annual conference on Genetic and evolutionary computation, Montreal, July 8-12, pp. 1139–1146. ACM, New York (2009)
27. Wong, M.L., Leung, K.S.: An induction system that learns programs in different programming languages using genetic programming and logic grammars. In: Proceedings of the 7th IEEE International Conference on Tools with Artificial Intelligence (1995)

Evolving Genes to Balance a Pole

Miguel Nicolau[1], Marc Schoenauer[1], and Wolfgang Banzhaf[2]

[1] INRIA Saclay - Île-de-France
LRI- Université Paris-Sud, Paris, France
{Miguel.Nicolau,Marc.Schoenauer}@inria.fr
[2] Memorial University
Newfoundland, Canada
wolfgang@mun.ca

Abstract. We discuss how to use a Genetic Regulatory Network as an evolutionary representation to solve a typical GP reinforcement problem, the pole balancing. The network is a modified version of an Artificial Regulatory Network proposed a few years ago, and the task could be solved only by finding a proper way of connecting inputs and outputs to the network. We show that the representation is able to generalize well over the problem domain, and discuss the performance of different models of this kind.

1 Introduction

Knowledge of biological systems has come a long way since the inception of the evolutionary computation field [1]. Their remarkable flexibility and adaptivity seems to suggest that more biologically based representations could be applied as representations for program evolution, i.e., Genetic Programming (GP). The objective of this paper is exactly that - to apply a recent biological model as a basis for some GP representations.

We are interested here in a complexification of the genotype-phenotype mapping, a process that seems to contribute to a higher evolvability of genomes [2]. A central piece of this mechanism is the regulation of genes by genes, what has become known as Genetic Regulatory Networks (GRNs).

GRNs are biological interaction networks among the genes in a chromosome and the proteins they produce: each gene encodes specific types of protein, and some of those, termed *Transcription Factors*, regulate (either enhance or inhibit) the expression of other genes, and hence the generation of the protein those genes encode. The study of such networks of interactions provides many interdisciplinary research opportunities, and as a result, GRNs have become an exciting and quickly developing field of research [3].

The question of how to use a GRN approach for GP is a challenge that is being recognized only slowly by GP researchers. While some progress has been made [4,5], there is yet to be proposed a proper unification of the counteracting tendencies of networks to produce dynamics and continuous signals versus the boolean logic and operator-operand-based methodology of traditional GP.

A.I. Esparcia-Alcazar et al. (Eds.): EuroGP 2010, LNCS 6021, pp. 196–207, 2010.

In this contribution, we shall study whether and how the Artificial Gene Regulatory Model proposed in [6] can be used to achieve the function traditionally implemented by control algorithms, by applying it to a classical benchmark problem of control engineering, pole balancing.

Along the way, we hope to learn how to use this type of representation for problems usually solved with less evolvable representations. Our goal is to arrive at a flexible and at the same time very general representation useful in GP in general. While we are not there yet, we have made progress notably by finding ways to couple input and output to artificial GRNs, a feature of utmost importance in Genetic Programming.

This paper is organised as follows. Section 2 describes the GRN model used, along with an analysis of its behaviour and modifications done in order to adapt it to the evolution of solutions for typical GP problems. Section 3 then describes the problem and the evolutionary algorithm we shall use to solve it. Section 4 describes some of the experiments conducted, and finally Section 5 draws conclusions and discusses future work directions.

2 Artificial Gene Regulatory Model

2.1 Representation and Dynamics

The model used in this work [6] is composed of a genome, represented as a binary string, and mobile proteins, which interact with the genome through their binary signatures: they do so at *regulatory sites*, located upstream from genes. The resulting interaction regulates the expression of the associated gene.

Genes are identified within the genome by *Promoter sites*. These consist of an arbitrarily selected 32 bit bit pattern: the sequence XYZ01010101 identifies a gene, with X, Y and Z representing each an arbitrary sequence of 8 bits.

If a promoter site is found, the 160 bits (5×32) following it represent the gene sequence, which encodes a protein. This protein (like all others in the model) is a 32 bit sequence, resulting from a many-to-one mapping of the gene sequence: each bit results from a majority rule for each of the five sets of 32 bits.

Upstream from the promoter site exist two additional 32 bit segments, representing the *enhancer* and *inhibitor* sites: these regulate the protein production of the associated gene. The attachment of proteins to these regulatory sites is what regulates this production. Fig. 1 illustrates the encoding of a gene.

The binding of proteins to the regulatory sites is calculated through the use of the XOR operation, which returns the degree of match as the number of bits set to one (that is, the number of complementary bits between both binary strings).

The enhancing and inhibiting signals regulating the production of protein p_i are calculated by the following equation:

$$e_i, h_i = \frac{1}{N} \sum_{j=1}^{N} c_j \exp(\beta(u_j - u_{max})) \tag{1}$$

where N is the total number of proteins, c_j is the concentration of protein j, u_j is the number of complementary bits between the (enhancing or inhibitory)

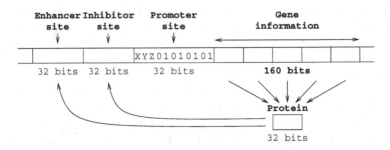

Fig. 1. Bit string encoding of a gene. If a promoter site is found, the gene information is used to create a protein, whose quantity is regulated by the attachment of proteins to the enhancer and inhibitor sites.

regulating site and protein j, u_{max} is the maximum match observed in the current genome, and β is a positive scaling factor. Because of the exponential, only proteins whose match is close to u_{max} will have an influence here.

The production of p_i is calculated via the following differential equation:

$$\frac{dc_i}{dt} = \delta(e_i - h_i)c_i - \Phi(1.0) \tag{2}$$

where δ is a positive scaling factor (representing a time unit), and $\Phi(1.0)$ is a term that proportionally scales protein production, ensuring that $\sum_i c_i = 1.0$, which results in competition between binding sites for proteins.

2.2   Initialisation

Genomes can be initialised either randomly, or by using a duplication and mutation technique [6]: it consists in creating a random 32 bit sequence, followed by a series of length duplications with a typical low mutation rate associated. It has been shown [7,8] that evolution through genome duplication and subsequent divergence (mostly deletion) and specialisation occurs in nature.

In the following, genomes that have been initialized using a sequence of Duplications and Mutations will be termed "DM-genomes" by contrast to the "random genomes".

2.3   Input/Output

Most GP-like problems associate a given set of input values with a set of responses (or outputs), and then measure the fitness of an individual as the difference between the responses obtained and the known correct outputs. However, the model as presented in [6] is a closed world. This Section will now extend it with I/O capabilities, so that it can be applied to typical GP problems.

Model Input. In order to introduce the notation of an input signal, the current model was extended through the insertion of *extra proteins*: regulatory proteins not produced by genes, which are inserted into the model at a given time.

Like the proteins which are produced by the genes in the model, these are also 32-bit binary strings, and like the other regulatory proteins, they cooperate in the regulation of the expression of all genes, through the application of Eq. 1. However, since they are not produced by specific genes, their concentration is always the same across time (unless intentionally modified, see below).

As these are regulatory proteins, their concentration is considered to take up part of the regulatory process. This means that the differential equation used (Eq. 2) to calculate the expression level of TR-genes is changed as follows:

$$\frac{dc_i}{dt} = \delta(e_i - h_i)c_i - \Phi(1.0 - \sum_{j=N+1}^{N_{ep}} c_j) \tag{3}$$

where $N + 1, \ldots, N_{ep}$ are the indices of the extra proteins in the model, and $\Phi(1.0 - \sum_{j=N+1}^{N_{ep}} c_j)$ is a term that proportionally scales protein concentrations, such that the sum of all protein concentrations (gene expression and extra proteins) adds up to 1.0.

These extra proteins can be associated with problem inputs in two ways:

– The binary signatures of the proteins represent the input values;
– The concentrations of the proteins represent the input values.

Each has its advantages and disadvantages. Setting binary signatures allows evolution to exploit binary mutation to find useful matches between binary signatures, but has a low resolution for continuous domains. Setting quantities is more adequate to represent continuous domains, but can be hard to tune - a low extra protein concentration will hardly influence the regulatory process, whereas a high concentration might crush the role of TF-genes.

Model Output. As mentioned before, each gene in the model encodes a transcription factor, which is used in the regulatory process. In nature, however, these are only a subset of the proteins expressed by genes. One could have proteins with different roles in the model, and use some as outputs of the model.

Keeping this idea in mind, the model has been adapted, so that different kinds of promoters can be detected, to identify different types of gene. This allows one to give specific roles to the proteins produced by each type of gene.

In this work, two types of genes were identified in the model: genes encoding transcription factors (*TF-genes*) and genes encoding a *product protein* (*P-genes*). The first ones act just like in the original model [6]: their proteins regulate the production of all genes, regardless of their type. The second ones are only regulated: their actual output signal is left for interpretation to the objective function. In order to identify different types of genes, the genome is scanned for different promoter sites. Dropping the ambiguous sequence used in the original model (see Section 2.1), the following binary sequences were used: XYZ00000000 to identify TF-genes, and XYZ11111111 to identify P-genes, as they have both the same probability of appearing (and no overlapping of their signatures).

Note that a previous approach for extracting an output signal from this model exists [9], where a random site of the genome is used as a regulation site, but despite the results achieved, it does not offer the same degree of flexibility as the technique now presented.

Dynamic Analysis. Several possibilities exist, when choosing the dynamic equation to use when calculating the concentration of P-proteins. In order to keep with the nature of the model, equations based on the calculation of concentration of TF-proteins were tested; the following equation was used:

$$c_i^t = c_i^{t-1} + \delta(e_i - h_i) - \Phi(1.0) \tag{4}$$

where c_i^t is the concentration of the P-protein at time t, c_i^{t-1} its concentration at time $t - 1$, e_i and h_i are calculated as before at time $t - 1$, and $\Phi(1.0)$ is a scaling factor, ensuring the sum of all P-proteins concentrations[1] is 1.0.

This equation was chosen as it seems to give P-genes similar dynamics to TF-genes, for both random genomes and DM-genomes.

3   The Problem: Single-Pole Balancing

The potential of using gene regulatory networks as a representation for an Evolutionary Algorithm lies in their possibly rich, non-linear dynamics [9]. A famous dynamic control benchmark is the pole-balancing problem [10,11], also known as the inverted pendulum problem. It consists in controlling, along a finite one dimensional track, a cart on which a rigid pole is attached. The command is a bang-bang command: the user can apply a constant force to either side of the cart. The objective is to keep the pole balanced on top of the cart, while keeping the cart within the (limited) boundaries of the track.

There are four input variables associated with this problem:

$x \in [-2.4, 2.4]$ m is the position of the cart, relative to the centre;
$\theta \in [-12, 12]$ ° is the angle of the pole with the vertical;
$\dot{x} \in [-1, 1]$ m/s is the velocity of the cart on the track;
$\dot{\theta} \in [-1.5, 1.5]$ °$/s$ is the angular velocity of the pole.

The physical simulation of the cart and pole movements is modelled by the following equations of motion:

$$\ddot{\theta}(t) = \frac{g \sin \theta(t) - \cos \theta(t) \left(\frac{F(t) + ml\dot{\theta}(t)^2 \sin \theta(t)}{m_c + m} \right)}{l \left(\frac{4}{3} - \frac{m \cos^2 \theta(t)}{m_c + m} \right)}$$

$$\ddot{x}(t) = \frac{\frac{F(t) + ml\dot{\theta}(t)^2 \sin \theta(t)}{m_c + m} - ml\ddot{\theta}(t) \cos \theta(t)}{m_c + m}$$

where $g = 9.8$ m/s^2 is the gravity, $l = 0.5$ m the half-pole length, $F(t) = \pm 10$ N is the bang-bang command allowed, $m = 0.1$ kg and $m_c = 1.0$ kg are the masses of the pole and the cart respectively.

---

[1] Concentrations of TF-proteins and P-proteins are normalised independently.

A time step of 0.02s is used throughout the simulations. A failure signal is associated when either the cart reaches the track boundaries ($x = \pm 2.4m$), or the pole falls (i.e., $|\theta| > 12°$).

The resulting controller accepts the four inputs, and outputs one of two answers: push the cart left or right (with constant force $F(t) = \pm 10N$).

3.1   Encoding the Problem

The four inputs were encoded using extra proteins, as explained in Section 2.3. These had the following signatures:

x: 00000000000000000000000000000000 θ: 00000000000000001111111111111111

$\dot{x}$: 11111111111111110000000000000000 $\dot{\theta}$: 11111111111111111111111111111111

They were chosen such that their signatures are as different as possible. Their concentration dictates their value: each of them had the corresponding value of the input variable, scaled to the range $[0.0, 0.1]$. This means that the cumulated regulatory influence of these extra proteins ranged from 0% up to 40%.

The GRN was allowed to stabilize first, and then tested against a random cart state, as seen in the literature. This is thus a very noisy fitness function, as several combinations of the four input variables result in unsolvable states (i.e. the pole cannot be balanced). Success is dictated by a successful series of 120000 time steps without the cart exiting the $\pm 2.4m$ track, or the pole falling beyond the $\pm 12°$ range. The (minimising) fitness is thus:

$$F(x) = \frac{120000}{\text{sucessful time steps}}$$

The output action extracted from the genome is the concentration of a single P-protein: a concentration above 0.5 pushes the cart right, and vice-versa. In the current work, all P-genes that are present in the genome are tested, and the most successful one is used.

As relevant concentration must be close to 0.5, small genomes were used (the higher the number of P-genes, the lower the probability of having a 0.5 P-protein concentration). The genomes were hence initialised with only 7 DM events, with 2% mutation rate, generally leading to very small genomes.

As an alternative to this approach, another technique was used, which consists in extracting the derivative of the chosen P-gene expression: if the derivative is positive between measuring times (i.e. if the concentration of the P-protein increased), then the cart is pushed right; otherwise, it is pushed left. If there was no change in its concentration, then the previous action is repeated.

Another choice lies with the synchronisation between the cart model and the regulatory model, that is, when to extract the current concentration of the elected P-protein and feed it to the cart model. As the interval of update for the cart model is 0.02s, the interval of measurement of the P-gene was set to 2000 time steps. This is however arbitrary, and could become a parameter to optimise, as it could be set differently for different genomes (some genomes have slower reactions, others have faster ones).

3.2   The Evolutionary Algorithm

The evolutionary algorithm used to evolve the binary genomes was an evolution-ary strategy $(250+250)-ES$: 250 parents give birth to 250 offspring, and the best 250 of all 500 are used as the new parent population; a maximum of 50 iterations were allowed. The only variation operator used was a simple bit-flip mutation, set to 1% and adapted by the well-known 1/5 rule of Evolution Strategies [12]: when the rate of successful mutations is higher than 1/5 (i.e. when more than 20% mutation events result in a reduction of the error measure), the mutation rate is doubled; it is halved in the opposite case. However, to avoid stagnation of evolution, if the number of mutation events (i.e. the number of bits flipped per generation) drops below 250, the mutation rate is doubled.

4   Results and Analysis

Fig. 2 shows the average fitness evolution for 50 independent runs, for both expression measurement approaches. Both approaches solve the problem quite fast, but it is obvious that using product tendency gives faster convergence to an optimal solution. This is an expected result: when using P-protein absolute values, the concentration of a P-protein has to be fairly close to 50%, in order to provide a solution. However, when using P-protein tendency, the starting concentration of the P-protein has no influence on the behaviour of the cart.

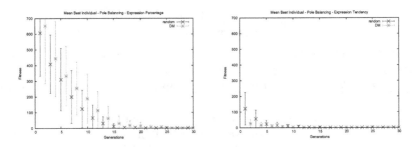

Fig. 2. Mean best individual per generation for the pole-balancing problem, when using P-protein concentration (left) or tendency (right). All results are averaged across 50 runs; error bars plot variance between runs.

4.1   Generalisation Performance

Whitley et al. [11] proposed a generalisation test to assert whether the discovered solution is robust. Once a controller is evolved that can balance the pole for 120000 time steps with a random setup, the evolution cycle is stopped, and this controller is applied to a series of generalisation tests. These consist of combinations of the four input variables, with their normalised values set to the following: 0.05, 0.275, 0.50, 0.725, and 0.95. This results in $5^4 = 625$ initial cases. The generalisation score of the best individual found is thus the number of test

Table 1. Generalisation results. Number of successful attempts to balance the pole for 1000 time steps, out of 625 test cases.

Approach		Best	Worst	Median	Mean	Std. Dev.
Product Percentage	random genomes	422	3	194	202.18	110.01
	DM-genomes	416	23	237	235.68	107.85
Product Tendency	random genomes	359	0	63	85.82	66.99
	DM-genomes	187	7	77	81.40	48.33

cases out of these 625, for which the controller manages to balance the pole for 1000 time steps.

All 50 runs found solutions for this problem, using either P-protein concentrations or P-protein tendencies (for both random and DM-genomes). At the end of each run, the generalisation test was applied to the best individual in the population; Table 1 shows the results obtained.

The results obtained show little difference between random and DM-genomes. However, there is a big difference between using P-proteins concentrations or tendencies, with the former achieving much better results. When using product tendency, the concentration of P-proteins can easily become 0%: the previous move is then repeated, and keeps moving the cart leftwards. This creates a disassociation between the product expression and the cart behaviour, which becomes a handicap when applying the model to some of the harder generalisation tests.

Note that many of the generalisation tests are unsolvable. After an exhaustive search of all possible bang-bang solutions up to 60 steps of simulation, 168 tests were found unsolvable (execution time constrains prevented a deeper search). This means that an ideal controller can only solve 457 (or less) cases. It also shows that

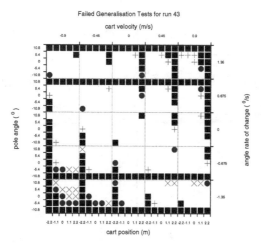

Fig. 3. Generalisation test cases unsolvable at depth 60 (black squares), unsolved by the best random genome ('X'), by the best DM-genome ('+'), and by both (filled circles). Both genomes used P-gene expression levels.

the best result found (422 tests solved), although not as high as one of the best in the literature (446 solved cases [11]), is still quite close to the optimum.

Fig. 3 shows a plot of all the generalisation tests that are not solvable at depth 60, and those that are additionally not solved by the best random and DM-genome. It shows that cases where θ and $\dot{\theta}$ both take large or small values (i.e. a large angle in absolute value, together with a large angular velocity increasing this angle) are unsolvable, and that both genomes additionally fail on cases that are close to these unsolvable cases. It is interesting to see however how the unsolved cases of the DM-genome are mostly symmetric in terms of the matrix of test cases, whereas the random genome is far more unbalanced. This has to do with the sinusoidal nature of the controllers generated by random genomes, as can be seen in the next section.

4.2   Pole Balancing Behaviour of Typical Networks

Fig. 4 shows example behaviours of the 2 best evolved regulatory models (random and DM, using P-protein concentrations), applied to 3 different generalisation cases.

It is interesting to observe the different approaches to solve the same gen-eralisation test. In particular, one can see how the random genome is quite

$$x = 0\ m \qquad \theta = -5.4\ ° \qquad \dot{x} = 0\ m/s \qquad \dot{\theta} = -1.35\ °/s$$

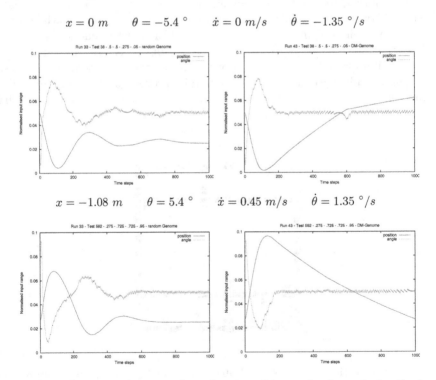

$$x = -1.08\ m \qquad \theta = 5.4\ ° \qquad \dot{x} = 0.45\ m/s \qquad \dot{\theta} = 1.35\ °/s$$

Fig. 4. Example progression over time of cart position and pole angle for the best random genome (left) and the best DM-genome (right), for 2 generalisation tests

sinusoidal in its approach, whereas the DM-genome generates a much more linear behaviour.

4.3   Resulting Networks: A Typical Example

Fig. 5 shows the regulatory networks extracted from the best performing random and DM-genomes, at a threshold of 19 (i.e. only connections with a match larger than 19 are represented, the other ones having a negligible impact on the regulation – see Eq. 1). Even with such a low number of genes, one can see that the regulatory interactions are quite complex. Gene G6 seems to act as a central regulatory node on the random genome, whereas that role is taken up by G1 in the DM-genome. Note also how few connections exist to the chosen P-genes (G1 and G3, respectively); however, the extra protein P4 (representing the rate of change of the pole, $\dot{\theta}$) is directly connected to these on both genomes. This could very well be a mechanism for stronger reaction to changes of $\dot{\theta}$, which has been shown to greatly influence the success rate of a balancing attempt (see Fig. 3).

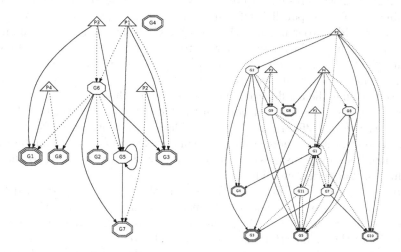

Fig. 5. Regulatory networks extracted from best performing random (left) and DM-genome (right). Hexagon nodes represent TF-genes, double hexagon nodes represent P-genes, the triple hexagon represents the chosen P-gene, and triangles represent the 4 extra proteins. The networks were drawn using a threshold value of 19.

5   Conclusions

One of the main objectives of this paper was to investigate the possibility of using GRNs as a new representation for program synthesis through Genetic Programming. Our motivation was that today's mainstream Evolutionary Computation (EC) approaches are by and large crude simplifications of the biological paradigm of natural evolution, not taking into account many advances of biological knowledge in the recent past [1]. The artificial GRN model used [6] presents an interesting balance between biological accuracy and computational potential, and was proposed as a good basis to introduce more accurate biological basis for EC.

The results obtained show that there is a clear computational potential within the model; it should therefore be possible to use other similar models as basis for EC techniques.

The adaptation of such models to EC is not straightforward. As these are mostly complex systems, a thorough comprehension of their exact dynamics is often not possible. The choice of how to encode inputs and outputs is also not a simple issue, and can greatly influence their computational potential.

Another key issue is the execution speed. While their biological equivalent systems are extremely fast, at the moment these computer models are somewhat slow, and the model used here is no exception. In order to accelerate the regulatory reactions, several tricks were used, such as adapting the sampling time of the differential equation (the δ parameter), and parallelization by distributing the evaluation of genomes across a cluster – the resulting average execution time of a single run was around 25 minutes, when executing the code on 8 recent machines running in parallel. Of course, a fascinating possibility to overcome this issue would be to synthesize the resulting GRN into biological medium.

Regarding this problem, some parameters could be optimized (e.g. by evolution). First, the signature and concentration of the extra proteins: a deeper understanding of their influence on the regulatory process is necessary; it could very well be that their influence is far too strong for the moment.

Second, the synchronisation between the biological and physical models. As mentioned before, different models have different reaction times (for example, stabilization times for genomes of this size may go from a few thousand iterations up to hundreds of thousands); each genome would therefore need to tune its synchronisation period individually.

Future work will now focus on extensive testing of the new extended GRN model on various problem domains. The most promising ones seem to be dynamic control problems, as these might profit the most from the remarkable dynamic properties of the model. But the flexibility of this representation allows one to imagine more GP-like approaches. For example, even though only 2 types of proteins were used, a lot more could be introduced - and potentially represent the equivalent of GP functions or terminals. The change of their concentrations over time could then represent priorities of execution, or even probabilities. Work is under way to explore these new avenues of investigation.

References

1. Banzhaf, W., Beslon, G., Christensen, S., Foster, J.A., Képès, F., Lefort, V., Miller, J.F., Radman, M., Ramsden, J.J.: From artificial evolution to computational evolution: a research agenda. Nature Reviews Genetics 7, 729–735 (2006)
2. Kirschner, M., Gerhart, J.: The plausibility of life: Resolving Darwin's dilemma. Yale University Press, New Haven (2005)

3. Hasty, J., McMillan, D., Isaacs, F., Collins, J.J.: Computational studies of gene regulatory networks: In numero molecular biology. Nature Reviews Genetics 2, 268–279 (2001)
4. Lones, M.A., Tyrrell, A.M.: Modelling biological evolvability: Implicit context and variation filtering in enzyme genetic programming. BioSystems 76(1-3), 229–238 (2004)
5. Zhan, S., Miller, J.F., Tyrrell, A.M.: An evolutionary system using development and artificial genetic regulatory networks. In: Proc. IEEE CEC 2008. IEEE Press, Los Alamitos (2008)
6. Banzhaf, W.: Artificial regulatory networks and genetic programming. In: Riolo, R., Worzel, B. (eds.) Genetic Programming Theory and Practice, ch. 4, pp. 43–62. Kluwer Publishers, Dordrecht (2003)
7. Wolfe, K., Shields, D.: Molecular evidence for an ancient duplication of the entire yeast genome. Nature 387, 708–713 (1997)
8. Kellis, M., Birren, B.W., Lander, E.S.: Proof and evolutionary analysis of ancient genome duplication in the yeast saccharomyces cerevisiae. Nature 428, 617–624 (2004)
9. Kuo, P.D., Banzhaf, W.: Small world and scale-free network topologies in an artificial regulatory network model. In: Pollack, J., et al. (eds.) Artificial Life IX, pp. 404–409. Bradford Books (2004)
10. Barto, A.G., Sutton, R.S., Anderson, C.W.: Neuronlike adaptive elements that can solve difficult learning control problems. IEEE Transactions on Systems, Man and Cybernetics 13, 834–846 (1983)
11. Whitley, D., Dominic, S., Das, R., Anderson, C.W.: Genetic reinforcement learning for neurocontrol problems. Machine Learning 13(2-3), 259–284 (1993)
12. Rechenberg, I.: Evolutionsstrategie 1994. Frommann-Holzboog, Stuttgart (1994)

Solution-Locked Averages and Solution-Time Binning in Genetic Programming

Riccardo Poli

School of Computer Science and Electronic Engineering, University of Essex, UK

Abstract. Averaging data collected in multiple independent runs across generations is the standard method to study the behaviour of GP. We show that while
averaging may represent with good resolution GP's behaviour in the early stages
of a run, it blurs later components of the dynamics. We propose two techniques
to improve the situation: solution-locked averaging and solution-time binning.
Results indicate that there are significant benefits in adopting these techniques.

1 Introduction

In recent work on averaging event-related potentials (ERPs) [5], we highlighted the
fact that while averaging temporal sequences of data points has the beneficial effect
of reducing noise, it also presents a serious drawback. When some of the components
(or waves) of a signal occur at different times in different trials, a blurring effect takes
place as a result of averaging, i.e., averaging may introduce *systematic errors* while it
reduces stochastic ones. This limits how much we can learn from standard temporal
averages. While the problem has been known for a long time in electrophysiology (e.g.,
see [4,2,7]), no easy solution is available. [5] suggested the use of a simple technique
to reduce this blurring effect: subdividing the data into bins based on the time at which
subjects gave their response. Bin optimisation via GP further improved results [1].

The similarity between the averaging of ERPs and standard analysis practise in GP
is striking. Statistics such as mean and best fitness, fitness standard deviation, diversity,
solution size, etc. are routinely recorded during GP runs. Because GP is stochastic, multiple independent runs of the system are performed and the statistics recorded in each
run are then combined, typically by averaging the data corresponding to each generation. So, if averaging of ERPs presents problems of blurring and mis-representation of
statistics, then we may expect averaging to produce similar effects also in GP.

To understand this let us consider the typical dynamics of GP runs. For many problems runs are not homogeneous marches towards a solution. Runs may have different
phases, e.g., an initial period of rapid evolution, followed by one or more periods of
quasi stagnation separated by short transients of rapid evolution when improved solutions are found. While events of this kind will be present in most runs, not all runs will
have the same events. For example, unsuccessful runs will lack the final rush to the solution. Also, even when qualitatively the same events occur in some runs, it is unlikely
that these will always occur at exactly the same time in different runs.

Why is this a problem? Let us imagine the statistics gathered over three independent runs presented a rapid initial increase in the measurements followed by a static

A.I. Esparcia-Alcazar et al. (Eds.): EuroGP 2010, LNCS 6021, pp. 208–219, 2010.

Generation-1 locked   Solution locked

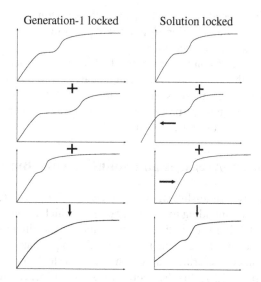

Fig. 1. Example of distortions produced by averaging: standard (generation-1-locked) averaging (left) and solution-locked averaging (right)

period which eventually led to discovering a solution and a final rapid convergence of the population towards it. This is shown in Fig. 1(left). The initial rapid growth is phase locked with the start of the run while the final rapid growth occurs at different generations in different runs. Averaging the data in the traditional way (bottom left) correctly represents the initial rapid growth present in the three runs starting from generation 1. Averaging, however, turns the second phase of rapid increase which occurs at different times in different runs into an inconspicuous slope which is not present in any of the runs and which may be misinterpreted as a slow-down of the initial rapid growth.

This phenomenon is present whenever the temporal data being averaged contain components with different latencies (delays). To understand the nature of the deformations produced by averaging in these conditions, let us consider the simplest possible case: let us imagine that there are only two components in the data recorded in an experiment: a component, $s(t)$, which always starts at generation 1 and continues throughout a run, and a variable-latency component, $r(t)$, which is associated with the final phases of a successful run. For simplicity, let us imagine that the component $r(t)$ starts at random times during a run. However, once it starts, within exactly n generations a solution is found. So, this component is phase-locked with the final generation of a run. Because the conditions which determine the start of $r(t)$ is stochastic, the latency of $r(t)$ is a stochastic variable. Let $\rho(t)$ be the latency distribution of $r(t)$. Let us also assume that $r(t)$ and $s(t)$ are additive, i.e., the statistics of interest is simply the sum of these two components. Under these assumptions it is easy to show [2,7] that the ordinary average of multiple run data is $a_s(t) = s(t) + r(t) \star \rho(t)$, where $\star$ is the convolution operation. Given that latency distribution $\rho(t)$ is non-negative (and typically unimodal), this means that the ordinary average can only show a smoothed (low-pass filtered) version of the variable-latency component $r(t)$. So, averaging introduces systematic errors in the analysis of events that precede (and are related to) the solution of a problem. This blurring is likely to prevent the detection of important phenomena, e.g., related to factors that determine whether a run is successful.

Extending the work in [5] and the response-locked averaging technique used in the ERP literature [4], in this paper we propose and analyse two simple countermeasures one can use to improve the analysis of GP statistics: solution locking and solution-time binning. Both techniques pre-process the data before any generation-by-generation averaging (or other aggregation) is performed.

2 Solution-Locked Averages and Solution-Time Binning

Solution locking involves time-shifting the statistics collected in different runs in such a way that the data corresponding to the generation in which a solution was found are aligned, instead of aligning stats at the first generation.[1] The situation is illustrated in Fig. 1(right). Let us see what averaging these shifted data produces.

For the simple model described above, the solution-locked average is given by $a_r(t) = r(t) + s(t) \star \rho(-t)$ [2,7]. In other words, the solution-locked average will smooth out the component $s(t)$ which is phased locked with the start of the run, but it will not alter $r(t)$. So, this form of averaging can provide very useful information on the late stages in a run, which, as indicated in the previous section, are never well represented in ordinary averages. So, this simple trick can reveal important events which immediately precede (and contribute to) the discovery of solutions. The price to pay is that the early phases of runs will be represented with a low effective resolution.

While this technique is very useful, a researcher will still be presented with two alternative and potentially conflicting representations of the same data: one based on standard averaging and one based on solution-locked averaging. Both for $a_s(t)$ and for $a_r(t)$, the severity of the smoothing effectively depends on how narrow the distribution $\rho(t)$ is. A key problem is that running more experiments and *averaging more data does not help increase the fidelity of the reconstructed statistics* because the convolution with $\rho(t)$ or $\rho(-t)$ introduces a systematic error in the averaging process.

Fortunately, as suggested in [5] for ERPs, a very simple technique can improve the situation: *binning runs based on their recorded solution time and then computing bin averages.* This has the potential of radically reducing the blurring problems of ordinary and solution-locked averages. In particular, solution-time binning can significantly improve the resolution with which variable-latency components of run statistics can be recovered via averaging. The qualitative reason for this is simple to understand.

The idea is that if one selects out of a dataset all those runs which were successful within approximately the same amount of time, it is more likely that similar GP dynamics will have taken place within those runs than if one looked at the whole dataset. So, within those runs, components of statistics that would normally have a widely variable latency might be expected, instead, to present a much narrower latency distribution. In other words, we can expect more homogeneity in binned data. Thus, we should find that, for the runs within a bin, fixed- and variable-latency components are much more

---

[1] Runs where a solution wasn't found can be treated in whatever way they are treated in relation to ordinary averages.

synchronised than if one did not divide the dataset. Averaging such data should, therefore, allows the rejection of noise while at the same time reducing also the undesirable distortions and blurring associated with averaging.

We look at these qualitative ideas more formally in the next section.

3   Analysis of Resolution of Bin Averages

Let us consider in what ways binning by solution time and then averaging would alter the resolution with which fixed latency and variable-latency components of runs statistics can be recovered. Here we will specifically look at the case where runs are aligned at the first generation. However, there are symmetric properties for binned solution-locked averages. For space limitations we omit many intermediate calculations and extensions.

Let us define a function $\delta(x)$ that returns 1 if x is true, and 0 otherwise. It is simple to show that the (ordinary) average of the data in the bin corresponding to the solution-time interval $[r_1, r_2)$ is given by $a_s^{[r_1, r_2)}(t) = s(t) + r(t) \star \rho^{[r_1, r_2)}(t)$ where $\rho^{[r_1, r_2)}(t) = \delta(r_1 \le t < r_2)\rho(t)/\int_{r_1}^{r_2} \rho(t)\,dt$ is the convolution kernel responsible for $r(t)$ appearing blurred in the average. So, in order to see whether $a_s^{[r_1, r_2)}(t)$ provides a better (less blurred) representation of $r(t)$ than $a_s(t)$, we need to analyse the differences between the distributions $\rho^{[r_1, r_2)}(t)$ and $\rho(t)$.

The difference between the two is that $\rho^{[r_1, r_2)}(t)$ is the product of $\rho(t)$ and a rectangular windowing function, $\delta(r_1 \le t < r_2)$. In the frequency domain, therefore, the spectrum of $\rho^{[r_1, r_2)}(t)$ is $\mathcal{R}^{[r_1, r_2)}(f) = \mathcal{R}(f) \star \Delta(f)$, where $\Delta(f)$ is a scaled and rotated (in the complex plane) version of the *sync* function. Therefore, $\mathcal{R}^{[r_1, r_2)}(f)$ is a smoothed and widened version of $\mathcal{R}(f)$. In other words, while $\rho^{[r_1, r_2)}(t)$ is still a low-pass filter, it has a higher cut-off frequency than $\rho(t)$. Thus, *binning by solution time and then averaging improves the resolving power on averages.* Indeed, it is possible to prove that in the limit of very small bins the bin average is an unbiased estimator of the true statistics.

It is possible to generalise these results to the case of multiple additive components in the statistics recorded in a run. The generalisation shows that whenever there is a non-zero correlation between the latency of such components and the solution time, then binning by solution time produces bins where the variability in the latency of all such components is reduced. As a result averaging the data in a bin leads to averages that are less blurred and more representative of reality.

4   Test Problems and Algorithms

To test the ideas proposed in this paper we used a tree-based GP system [3], namely a version of TinyGP [6, appendix B]. The system used tournament selection with a steady state replacement strategy where individuals are replaced with negative tournaments. Both for selection and replacement we used tournaments of size 2. We evolved populations for 100 generations. Programs were initialised using the grow method (see, for example, [6]). Offspring were generated using either sub-tree crossover (with uniform selection of crossover points) or point mutation. When mutation was chosen the nodes in the selected parent program were replaced with random nodes of the same arity with a probability of 5% (per node). Runs were not stopped when a solution was found, but the first time a solution was discovered was recorded.

We considered two problems. The first is the well-known Even-6 parity problem. We used the primitive set: {X1, X2, X3, X4, X5, X6, AND, OR, NOR, NAND, XOR, EQ}. The fitness of a program was the number of entries of the truth table of the even-6 parity function that the program could correctly predict. So, program fitnesses are integers between 0 and 64. We performed 1,000 independent runs of TinyGP with this problem. We used populations of 2,000 individuals. Initial programs had a maximum depth of 6 (counting one-node programs as having a depth of 0). The maximum size programs were allowed to grow during evolution was 1,000 nodes. Crossover was applied with 80% probability, while mutation was applied with 20% probability.

The second problem is the Sine symbolic regression problem, which requires programs to fit the sine function over a full period of oscillation. We used 63 fitness cases obtained by sampling $\sin(x)$ for $x \in \{0.0, 0.1, 0.2, \ldots 6.2\}$. We define a *success* to be a run where the best fitness was less than 3.15, or an average error of less than 0.05 over the 63 test cases. Here we performed 500 independent runs with populations of size 10,000. The primitive set included the functions ADD, SUB, MUL, DIV (protected) plus 100 random constants uniformly distributed in the range $[-5, 5]$ and one input variable. The max initial depth for trees was 5. Crossover and mutation rates (per individual) were 10% and 90%, respectively. Fitness was the sum of absolute errors.

The parameters for each problem were chosen in such a way to obtain approximately a split of one third and two thirds between successful and unsuccessful runs.

5 Results

To exemplify the benefits of our averaging techniques, we will look at best-of-generation and mean fitnesses averaged across multiple runs for the Even-6 parity problem and best-of-generation fitnesses for the Sine symbolic regression (in many symbolic regression problems means vary so much that they are rather uninformative). We will compute averages both with and without solution-locking and solution-time binning.

Before we analyse the data, we would like to stress a few important details about the averaging procedures we adopted. Firstly, when computing solution-locked averages, one needs to *shift runs relatively to one another* in such a way to align their solution time. The method, however, leaves unspecified the *absolute shift* of the solution time with respect to the reference system used to collect or generate the data (which in our case is a Cartesian reference with generations along the abscissas and fitness along the ordinates). By convention, here we have aligned the solution time to the abscissa corresponding to last generation (generation 100). Since most successful runs lasted less that 100 generations, to ensure every point in a plot was an average of the same number of runs, we extended runs as if they started before generation 1, freezing their fitness stats in generation 0, -1, -2, etc. to the value they had at generation 1. Secondly, we should also note that below we will distinguish between successful and unsuccessful runs (see Tab. 1). Finally, note that when computing solution-locked averages involving a mix of successful and unsuccessful runs or only unsuccessful runs, we used the convention that the *solution time* for unsuccessful runs was their last generation.

Table 1. Success rate statistics for the Even-6 parity and the Sine regression problems

Problem	Successful Runs	Total	Success Rate
Even-6 Parity	351	1,000	35.1%
Sine Symbolic Regression	144	500	28.8%

5.1 Ordinary Averages vs. Solution-Locked Averages

Let us first compare ordinary averages and solution-locked averages in the absence of binning. These are shown at the top of Fig. 2. Note that these averages do not distinguish between successful and unsuccessful runs, as it is typically done when reporting fitness statistics in the GP literature.

Looking at ordinary averages and comparing them across the two problems, we see the usual depiction of the dynamics of a GP system: there is a rapid improvement in fitness in the early generations of a run which is followed by a period where improvements are either rarer or smaller or both which eventually leads to a solution. In the Even-6 parity problem effectively the algorithm appears to be almost stagnating in the later phases of a run. What changes across the two problems is the relative slope of the final phases. Other than that, everything seems to confirm the dynamics of the fitness plots we have seen over and over again in the literature.

If we now focus on the solution-locked averages at the top of Fig. 2, however, we get a different picture. Firstly, the plots of such averages are significantly different from those of ordinary averages. For example, we see changes of curvature in the middle of a run. In the case of the Even-6 parity problem we also see an apparent period of stagnation followed by an acceleration in the late stages of runs.

The presence of flexes in the middle of runs and re-accelerations towards the end of runs go against almost every bit of published literature in GP. How is this possible? Which averages should we believe: ordinary or solution-locked? Neither and both.

As we emphasised above we have extended runs before their first generation for the purpose of realigning them at generation 100 and then computing a solution-locked average. So, while we can reasonably trust what's happening near generation 100 (by convention, the solution time), some of the effects we see many generations before generation 100 may be entirely due to our extending runs. This does not mean, however, that solution-locked averages are less reliable than ordinary averages. Indeed, symmetrically, in order to obtain ordinary averages, we have extended runs at the other end, by not stopping them when a solution was first found. So, we should also be very careful in interpreting what we see in ordinary averages when we are many generations away from the first. In some cases the effects we see in such averages in the late stages of a run, e.g., the saturation of best and mean fitnesses, may be entirely artefactual. If we are to believe solution-locked averages (which in principle have the best resolving power in the late stages of a run), in our two problems fitness is still growing significantly when solutions are first found.

To see things more clearly we really need to divide up the successful runs from the unsuccessful ones. This is done in Fig. 2 (middle and bottom, respectively). Note that, since for the unsuccessful runs we conventionally set their solution time to be their final

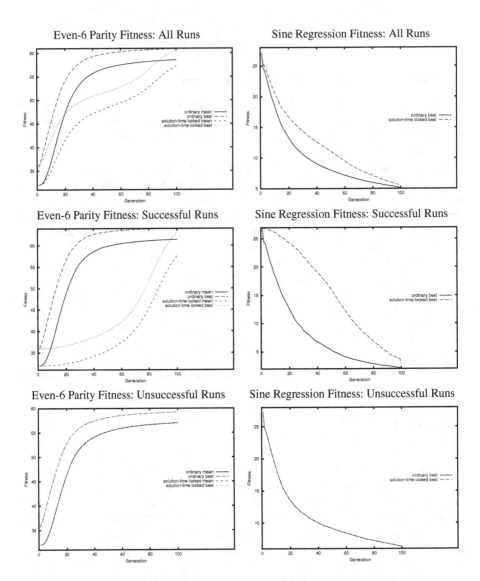

Fig. 2. Comparison between ordinary and solution-locked averages of mean and best population fitnesses for the Even-6 Parity problem (left) and of the mean fitness for the Sine symbolic regression problem (right) when all runs are averaged (top), when only the successful runs are averaged (middle) and when only the unsuccessful runs are considered (bottom)

generation, the plots of ordinary averages and solution-locked averages are on top of each other (see bottom of Fig. 2).

From a qualitative viewpoint the plots of *ordinary* averages of successful and unsuccessful runs are not very different, except, in the fitness values that are reached at the end of a run. Since the plots of averages across all runs are a blend of those for successful and unsuccessful runs, it is then not surprising to see that ordinary averages in the plots at the top of Fig. 2 are also qualitatively identical to the corresponding plots in the middle and bottom of the figure. However, now that successful runs are averaged separately, we can see that for them the differences between ordinary and solution-locked averages are further emphasised (see middle plots in the figure), with both problems showing much bigger end-of-run slopes in their solution-locked averages. In other words, towards the end of successful runs best and average fitnesses either don't saturate or saturate a lot less than we are used to see in ordinary GP averages.

The little step characterising the rightmost points in the solution-locked best fitness plots for the successful runs represents the time where a solution is first visited. So, such a step is present in all plots of this kind, irrespective of problem or system. In problems where fitness is discrete, the variation in best fitness between the last generation and the penultimate generation is an indication of how far (on average) the best of population was from solving the problem.

All of this is not visible in ordinary averages because of the smoothing biases of averaging. As we explained above, both ordinary averages and solution-locked averages are affected by a smoothing effect. The effect influences any component in the statistics which is not phase-locked with the beginning of the run or the end of the run, respectively. Elements which are phase-locked with the solution-time will be smoothed by the kernel $\rho(t)$ — the solution time distribution — in ordinary averages, while elements which are phase-locked with the start of the run will be smoothed by the reflection of that kernel, $\rho(-t)$, in solution-locked averages. Whether or not this smoothing has an effect depends on the width of the solution time distribution (narrower distributions producing less burring than wider ones) and on whether or not the statistics contain components outside the band of the smoothing kernel. In other words, the blurring of statistics that are already smooth is unlikely to produce significant artifacts, while we should expect to see major deformations when statistics present rapid changes.

Thus, to ascertain the potential degree of blur introduced by averaging (whether ordinary or solution-locked), we need to look at the solution time distributions for our two problems. These are shown in Fig. 3. It is clear from these plots that both problems have a wide distribution which can potentially lead to significant blurring effects.

5.2 Solution-Time Binned Averages

To get a clearer picture of what is happening, we need to use solution-time binning on the successful runs. This does not only improve resolution of averages, it also clarifies whether different mechanisms are responsible for different run times.

Figs. 4 and 5 show the results of binning runs and then averaging, for our two problems, using 10 bins of 10 generations each. Naturally, we can align the runs in each bin at generation 1 (as in ordinary averaging) or at the generation where they solved the problem (as in solution-locked averaging). Let us analyse these figures.

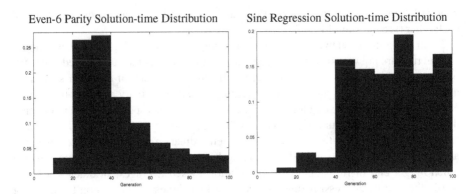

Fig. 3. Distribution of solutions times for the Even-6 Parity and the Sine symbolic regression problems

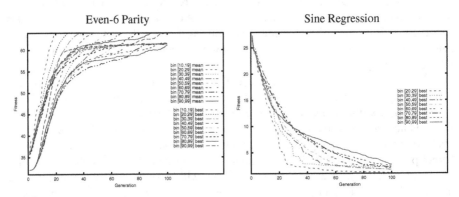

Fig. 4. Results of binning runs with the Even-6 Parity and Sine symbolic regression problems followed by *ordinary averaging* for successful runs

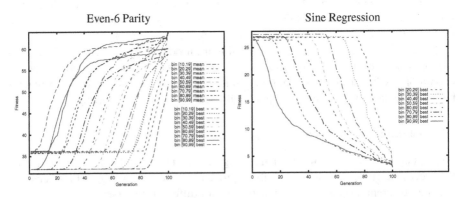

Fig. 5. Results of binning runs with the Even-6 Parity and Sine symbolic regression problems followed by *solution-locked averaging* for successful runs

Let us first focus on the results of solution-time binning in combination with ordinary averaging of the data in the bins shown in Fig. 4. We see here that for the Sine problem the plots of the averages of best fitness are effectively monotonic and featureless, except perhaps for the quickest runs. The plots for different bins are also quite similar, all sharing similar initial trajectories. The only significant differences between bin averages are slight differences in slope after this initial transient: runs which solved the problem sooner present bigger gradients than runs that took many generations to solve the problem. This suggests that GP solves this problem by a progressive and relentless march towards the solution. The difference between the runs that did it quickly and those that took longer appears to be simply a question of the rate at which the march proceeded, which in turn is likely to be due to the natural variability one would expect from stochastic search algorithms. Because run statistics are relatively smooth, the potential blurring effects of averaging (without binning) due to the convolution with the solution-time distribution in Fig. 3 had a limited influence on the averages shown in Fig. 2. This is the reason for their qualitative similarity with corresponding bin averages.

Let us look at the solution-locked averages for the Even-6 Parity problem. In Fig. 4 we see that actually during the generations that precede a solution evolution is still very rapid and only barely showing signs of slowing down. Solution-time bin averages clarify that essentially GP has alternative modes of solution. Firstly, all runs present a rapid initial evolution. During this there seems to be some essential preparation taking place for solving the problem. Indeed, no run solved the problem in less than 10 generations. After this initial transient of 10 to 20 generations, the runs in the first three non-zero bins essentially then continue their march towards the solution without delay (albeit at different speeds). Runs in other bins, instead, tend to slow down significantly (although never completely stagnating) after the transient eventually reaching a solution through a series of rare improvements. In other words, solution-time binning reveals the partial deceptiveness of this problem. Indeed, larger versions of the problem have been known for years to be extremely difficult to solve for GP.

All this makes sense in the light of what we know from a variety of studies with parity functions and continuous symbolic regression. There is, however, one surprising element in the ordinary averages of solution-binned statistics. Namely, in the bins collecting runs that took some time to solve the Even-6 Parity problems, the best fitness appears to speed up its upward motion in the very last stages of a run, which is counter-intuitive. Indeed this is an averaging artifact, as shown by the solution-time binned solution-locked averages shown in Fig. 5. As one can see there, all plots are essentially flat in the generations that precede the solution (which we positioned at generation 100, by convention). It is only at the last generation that a sudden increase in best fitness is present. This is simply associated with the discovery of a solution. The ramps shown in Fig. 4 in the late stages of a run are simply the result of convolving this solution-discovery peak with the kernel $\rho^{[r_1, r_2)}(t)$ associated with each solution-time bin. Although this kernel is typically much narrower than $\rho(t)$, it still has a non-zero width, leading to this residual form of blurring.

Symmetrically, the 10-generation wide sigmoid-like ramps shown in the early parts of each plot in Fig. 5 are artifacts. In fact, they are the result of blurring the initial rapid fitness increase shown in Fig. 4 with the convolution kernel associated with each bin.

So, even with solution-time binning, to get the most and best information (and the least artifacts) out of experimental data, it is essential to compare and analyse both solution-locked averages and ordinary averages. Without these tools, however, relatively little can be learnt from averages.

6   Discussion and Conclusions

Averaging data collected in multiple independent runs across generations is the standard method to study the behaviour of GP. However, as we have illustrated in this paper, standard averaging may suffer from what we could call a key-hole or a magnifying-glass effect. That is, while this technique is able to represent with good resolution the early behaviour of GP, it does so at the cost of putting everything else out of focus. When the dynamics of a GP system (as represented by a statistical descriptor that we want to average across runs) is simple and featureless, this lack of resolution may deform averages to a limited extent. However, when evolution is characterised by multiple rapid transients separated by periods of slow change, then we don't have a way of constructing a clear picture of what happens in a GP system. This may be particular problematic for the late and all-important phases of evolution when a solution is finally constructed.

In this paper we have suggested that solution-locked averaging, i.e., temporally shifting the statistics of successful runs so as to ensure the times at which a solution is first visited are aligned across runs and then averaging, may be a partial solution to these problems. Solution-locked averaging, however, still suffers from a key-hole effect: while it shows the late stages of a run in full resolution, it blurs everything else.

In the paper we have also proposed a second extremely simple technique — binning runs based on solution times and then averaging — that can alleviate the problems of the standard form of averaging mentioned above. The technique is based on one simple and realistic assumption: that roughly the same dynamics takes place in a GP system which is able to solve a problem, when that problem is solved in approximately the same time. For this reason, in such runs, the distribution of latencies of all variable-latency components of the data (including those phase-locked with the solution) should be narrower than if one considered an undivided dataset. As a result, averaging the runs in a solution-time bin should provide a truer picture of the dynamics of GP.

We empirically validated the binning technique by applying a tree-based GP system to two radically different problems. We also provided a theoretical analysis of the resolution of averages with and without binning, which showed that there are benefits in applying solution-time binning even when there is still a substantial variability in the latency of variable-latency components after solution-time binning.

Empirical results and theory points unequivocally in one direction: averaging after solution-time binning produces clearer representations of GP dynamics. When this is further combined with solution-locked averaging, we obtain a much less ambiguous representation of the stages that eventually lead to a solution in successful runs. Much can be learnt from studying such aggregate statistics.

The degree to which ordinary averages deform late-run statistics and the degree to which solution-locked averages smooth the early-run statistics depend on the shape and width of that solution-time distribution. When the distribution is narrow, then effectively runs are already binned. So, solution-time binning cannot be expected to improve resolution by much. Binning is still useful, however, since it clarifies if different run durations are associated with different modes of solution.

In the past, solution-time distributions have frequently been reported and used to compute the computational effort [3]. So, in principle we can now look back at those results to understand to what degree reported average statistics may have been blurred. In new experiments, it seems appropriate to always look at the solution time distribution to decide whether binning and solution-locking should be used. It may also be possible for researchers to retroactively reevaluate, shift and bin results of old experiments, and possibly discover new phenomena or further confirm existing theories.

Given the simplicity of the methods we have proposed, we would like to encourage researchers to adopt them as part of their set of data analysis routines to ensure the best possible use of the evidence contained in experimental results.

In relation to future work, in a sense, we can think of solution-time binning as a spot in the middle ground between single-run analysis and ordinary averages. In the future we would like to further explore this middle ground. For example, we would like to see if binning using gradual membership functions, as we did in [5] for ERPs, can provide even better reconstruction fidelity, if setting bin sizes on the basis of solution time quantiles and/or the noise in the data is beneficial to make best use of the available runs, and if solution-locked and ordinary averages can be jointly used (e.g., in the frequency domain as was done in [7] for ERPs) to further refine the reconstruction of GP's dynamics.

Acknowledgements

This work was supported by the Engineering and Physical Sciences Research Council under grant "Analogue Evolutionary Brain Computer Interfaces" (EP/F033818/1).

References

1. Citi, L., Poli, R., Cinel, C.: High-significance averages of event-related potential via genetic programming. In: Riolo, R.L., O'Reilly, U.-M., McConaghy, T. (eds.) Genetic Programming Theory and Practice VII, Genetic and Evolutionary Computation, May 14-16, vol. 9, pp. 135–157. Springer, Ann Arbor (2009)
2. Hansen, J.C.: Separation of overlapping waveforms having known temporal distributions. Journal of neuroscience methods 9(2), 127–139 (1983)
3. Koza, J.R.: Genetic Programming: On the Programming of Computers by Means of Natural Selection. MIT Press, Cambridge (1992)
4. Luck, S.J.: An introduction to the event-related potential technique. MIT Press, Cambridge (2005)
5. Poli, R., Cinel, C., Citi, L., Sepulveda, F.: Reaction-time binning: a simple method for increasing the resolving power of ERP averages. Psychophysiology (Forthcoming, 2010)
6. Poli, R., Langdon, W.B., McPhee, N.F.: A field guide to genetic programming (With contributions by J. R. Koza) (2008), http://lulu.com, http://www.gp-field-guide.org.uk
7. Zhang, J.: Decomposing stimulus and response component waveforms in ERP. Journal of neuroscience methods 80(1), 49–63 (1998)

Enabling Object Reuse
on Genetic Programming-Based Approaches
to Object-Oriented Evolutionary Testing

José Carlos Bregieiro Ribeiro[1],
Mário Alberto Zenha-Rela[2], and Francisco Fernández de Vega[3]

[1] Polytechnic Institute of Leiria
Morro do Lena, Alto do Vieiro, Leiria, Portugal
jose.ribeiro@estg.ipleiria.pt
[2] University of Coimbra
CISUC, DEI, 3030-290, Coimbra, Portugal
mzrela@dei.uc.pt
[3] University of Extremadura
C/ Sta Teresa de Jornet, 38, Mérida, Spain
fcofdez@unex.es

Abstract. Recent research on search-based test data generation for Object-Oriented software has relied heavily on typed Genetic Programming for representing and evolving test data. However, standard typed Genetic Programming approaches do not allow Object Reuse; this paper proposes a novel methodology to overcome this limitation. Object Reuse means that one instance can be passed to multiple methods as an argument, or multiple times to the same method as arguments. In the context of Object-Oriented Evolutionary Testing, it enables the generation of test programs that exercise structures of the software under test that would not be reachable otherwise. Additionally, the experimental studies performed show that the proposed methodology is able to effectively increase the performance of the test data generation process.

1 Introduction

Software testing is the process of exercising an application to detect errors and to verify that it satisfies the specified requirements. It is an expensive process, typically consuming roughly half of the total costs involved in software development; automating test data generation is thus vital to advance the state-of-the-art in software testing.

The application of Evolutionary Algorithms (EAs) to test data generation is often referred to as *Evolutionary Testing (ET)* [1]. The goal of ET is to find a set of test cases that satisfies a certain test criterion. If structural adequacy criteria are employed, the basic idea is to ensure that all the control elements in a program are executed by a given test set, providing evidence of its quality. Object Reuse is a feature of paramount importance in this context.

A.I. Esparcia-Alcazar et al. (Eds.): EuroGP 2010, LNCS 6021, pp. 220–231, 2010.

Object Reuse (OR) means that one instance can be passed to multiple methods as an argument, or multiple times to the same method as arguments [2]. In the context of Object-Oriented Evolutionary Testing (OOET), it enables the generation of test cases that exercise specific structures of software that would not be reachable otherwise. The `equals` method of Java's `Object` class [3] provides a paradigmatic example. Class `Object` is the root of the Java class hierarchy, and the `equals` method is used to assess if two objects are equivalent; also, several search methods rely on it to verify if an item is present in a collection (e.g., `Vector`'s `indexOf`). However, the `equals` method implements the most discriminating possible equivalence relation on objects: for any non-`null` reference values x and y, this method returns `true` if and only if x and y refer to the same reference. This means that, in order for the method `equals` to return `true`, the same `Object` reference must be passed as an argument twice – in the place of both the implicit parameter (i.e., the `this` parameter) and the explicit parameters. Also, every class has `Object` as a superclass; this means that every class inherits the `equals` method, and uses it internally for equivalence verification. `Object` subclasses may override `equals` in order to implement a less stringent equivalence relation. Still, it is not mandatory; what's more, recent studies have concluded that implementations of the `equals` methods are often faulty [4].

Recent research on ET has relied heavily on typed Genetic Programming (GP) for representing and evolving test data (e.g., [2,5,6]). However, standard GP approaches do not allow node reuse; this paper proposes a novel methodology to overcome this limitation, which involves the definition of novel type of GP nodes – the *At-Nodes* – that "point to" other nodes, thus effectively enabling the creation of edges to nodes that are already part of the tree, and allowing the reuse of sub-trees. The introduction of At-Nodes is performed by means of a custom-made evolutionary operator – the *Object Reuse operator*. This operator acts on an individual by selecting two nodes – the node to be replaced by the At-Node, and the node to be "pointed at" by the At-Node – and by inserting the newly created At-Node into the tree. At-Nodes may be removed from a tree by means of the *Reverse Object Reuse operator* which, in short, searches the tree for At-Nodes, and replaces these nodes with copies of the sub-trees pointed at by the At-Nodes. This particular operator removes the need for the reformulation of other common biology-inspired mechanisms (e.g., Mutation and Crossover [7]). In addition to allowing the search to traverse specific structures, the Object Reuse methodology is able to enhance the performance of the test case generation process: it yields solutions with smaller overall size and lower average structural complexity; and the feasibility of the generated Test Programs is increased as a result of the introduction of a specific heuristic for node selection.

This paper is organised as follows: the next Section starts by providing theoretical background on ET; Section 3 details the proposed Object Reuse methodology; in Section 4, the experimental studies developed in order to validate the approach are described and discussed; related work is contextualised in Section 5; and Section 6 summarises the methodology and emphasises the most relevant contributions.

2   Background and Terminology

ET is an emerging methodology for automatically generating high quality test data for Object-Oriented (OO) software and, in particular, for producing a set of unit-tests that meets a predefined structural adequacy criterion [6]. A unit-test case for OO software consists of an *Method Call Sequence (MCS)*, which defines the test scenario; during test case execution, all participating objects are created and put into particular states through a series of method calls [5]. Each test case focuses on the execution of one particular public method – the *Method Under Test (MUT)*. MUTs may be represented internally by Control-Flow Graphs (CFGs); the aim of the search will then be that of generating a set of Test Programs that traverse all the MUT's CFG nodes, thus achieving full structural coverage. GP is usually associated with the evolution of tree structures, and is particularly suited for representing and evolving Test Programs, which may be represented by *Method Call Trees (MCTs)*. Non-typed GP approaches are, however, unsuitable for representing OO programs, because any element can be a child node in a parse tree for any other element without having conflicting data types; conversely, with *Strongly-Typed Genetic Programming (STGP)* [8], types are defined a priori in the Function Set and define the constraints involved in MCT construction. This feature enables the initialization process and the various genetic operations to only construct syntactically correct MCTs, thus restraining the search-space to the set of compilable Test Programs.

Test case quality evaluation typically involves instrumenting the MUT, and executing it using the generated Test Programs with the intention of collecting trace information with which to derive coverage metrics [6]. Test case execution requires decoding an individual's *genotype* (i.e., the MCT) into its *phenotype* (i.e., the Test Program); Figures 1a, 1b and 1c exemplify this process; Object Reuse has not been introduced at this point. The MUT is the `indexOf` method of the `Vector` class – which corresponds to the root node of the MCT depicted in Figure 1a. Each node's parameters are provided by its children; the MCS (Figure 1b) corresponds to the linearised MCT, with tree linearisation being performed by means of a depth-first traversal algorithm [2]. Each MCS entry contains an *Method Information Object (MIO)*, which encloses: the method signature data necessary for the Test Program's source code to be assembled (e.g., the method's name and class, the parameter types and the return type); and references to other MIOs providing the parameters (if any) for that method (enumerated between square brackets). The Test Program (Figure 1c) is computed with basis on the MCS and corresponds to a syntactically correct translation of the latter.

Compilable Test Programs may still abort prematurely during execution if a runtime exception is thrown [6]. Test cases can thus be separated in two classes: *feasible* test cases are effectively executed, and terminate with a call to the MUT; *unfeasible* test cases terminate prematurely because a runtime exception is thrown before the call to the MUT is reached, and when this happens it is not possible to observe the structural entities traversed in the MUT because the final instruction is not reached. The Test Program depicted in Figure 1c, for example, is unfeasible because a runtime exception it thrown at instruction 6.

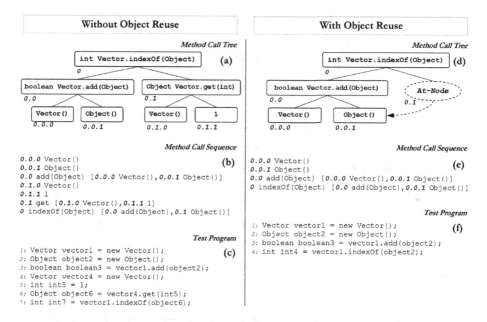

Fig. 1. Example Method Call Trees without and with Object Reuse (*a* and *d*), and corresponding Method Call Sequences (*b* and *e*) and Test Programs (*c* and *f*)

3   An Object Reuse Methodology for OOET

The proposed Object Reuse methodology is based on the introduction of two novel evolutionary operators: the Object Reuse Operator (detailed in the following Subsection), and the Reverse Object Reuse Operator (described in Subsection 3.2). Figure 2 provides an overview of these operators.

3.1   The Object Reuse Operator

The primary goal of the Object Reuse Operator is that of inserting a custom-made type of GP nodes – the At-Nodes – into valid locations of an MCT. The concept of At-Node is, thus, key to the proposed Object Reuse methodology.

At-Nodes. At-Nodes are GP nodes that refer to other (standard) GP nodes, thus enabling the reuse of portions of the tree and, specifically, the reuse of the object references returned by the functions corresponding to the reused sub-trees. This is accomplished by having the node pointed at by the At-Node provide the parameter not only to its parent node, but also to the At-Node's parent node; parameter assignment is performed during the MCT's linearisation by means of the process described in Subsection 3.1.4.

Figure 1d contains an example of a possible MCT resulting from the application of the Object Reuse operator to the tree depicted in Figure 1a. The At-Node labeled 0.1 replaces the node with the same label existing in the original MCT,

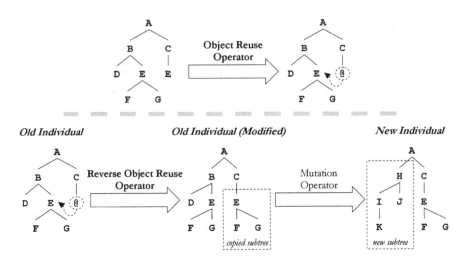

Fig. 2. Object Reuse (*top*) and Reverse Object Reuse (*bottom*) operators overview

whereas node 0.0.1 was selected as the node to be reused. As such, the `Object` instance returned by node 0.0.1 will be used both by its parent (labeled 0.0) and by the At-Node's parent (labeled 0). The MCS and Test Program shown in Figure 1e and 1f mirror this alteration: in the former, the MIO 0.0.1 provides the argument for the explicit parameters of both the 0.0 and 0 MIOs; and in the latter, the reference to the `Object` instance created at instruction 2 is passed to both the `add` and `indexOf` methods (instructions 3 and 4).

The creation of an At-Node for posterior introduction into an MCT requires the Object Reuse operator to select two MCT nodes in the original tree: the *Destination Node* (i.e., the node to which At-Node points to) and the *Replaced Node* (i.e., the root node of the subtree to be truncated and substituted by the At-Node). The first task of the Object Reuse Operator is precisely that of indexing all the valid Replaced-Destination node pairs in an MCT.

Valid Replaced-Destination Node Pairs. A Replaced-Destination node pair is valid if:

- both nodes are distinct non-root standard GP nodes;
- the Replaced Node possesses a type that is swap-compatible with the Destination Node (e.g., a node of type `String` is swap-compatible with a node of type `Object`, because `String` is a sub-type of `Object`);
- the sub-tree rooted at the Replaced Node does not contain a node that is pointed at by an existing At-Node. When an At-Node is inserted into the tree, the sub-tree rooted at the Replaced Node is truncated; if it contains a node that is already being reused, this operation will render the tree invalid;
- the Replaced Node is in a position reached by the linearisation algorithm prior to the Destination Node. This validation ensures that the MIOs only

contain parameter references to elements that precede them in the MCS, and that the corresponding Test Program's method calls have their parameters provided by previously created instances.

After all the valid Replaced-Destination node pairs have been indexed, the Object-Reuse Operator proceeds to select one of those pairs.

Replaced-Destination Node Pair Selection. The node pair selection procedure is performed differently according to the individual's feasibility:

- if the individual is *feasible*, a Replaced-Destination node pair is chosen at random from the set of valid Replaced-Destination node pairs;
- if the individual is *unfeasible*, the Object Reuse operator attempts to select a valid pair so that the Replaced Node belongs to the non-executed portion of the tree, and the Destination Node belongs to the executed portion of the tree. If such pairs exist, one is selected at random; otherwise, a node pair is chosen at random from the set of all valid Replaced-Destination node pairs.

The heuristic described aims to promote Test Program feasibility by favouring the reuse of feasible portions of the MCT. As was mentioned in Section 2, the Test Program depicted in Figure 1c throws a runtime exception at instruction 6; the feasible portion of this program is thus the sequence of instructions 1 to 5, whereas instructions 6 and 7 form the unfeasible sequence. These sequences can be mapped directly to MCS entries which, in turn, can matched to the corresponding MCT node. The valid Replaced-Destination node pairs which fulfil the premise of the heuristic are, thus, the following: {0.1, 0.0.1}; {0.1.0, 0.0.0}; {0.1.0, 0.0}.

Method Call Tree Linearisation. As was referred in Section 2, evaluating the quality of an individual involves its execution which, in turn requires decoding the MCT into the Test Program. However, if At-Nodes exist, a depth-first traversal algorithm does not suffice to linearise a tree; the linearisation algorithm must take into account the fact that certain parameters are supplied not by that node's children, but rather by the node pointed at by an At-Node. The algorithm depicted in Figure 3 describes the polymorphic recursive function utilised to obtain an MCS with basis on an MCT in the presence of At-Nodes.

3.2   The Reverse Object-Reuse Operator

If an MCT contains At-Nodes, some standard evolutionary operators, such as Mutation and Crossover, require the tree to be analysed and possibly modified prior to their application. This necessity is related with the fact that these operators replace subtrees in the original individual by newly created trees (in the case of the former) or by a copy of an another individual's subtree (in the case of the latter); however, if the subtrees truncated in the original individual contain Destination Nodes their elimination will render the MCT inconsistent and disable the possibility of translating it to a syntactically correct Test Program.

Data: Method Call Tree
Result: Method Call Sequence

Global Variables:
Current Node ← Root Node;
isDestinationNode ← false;
Previous MIO ← null;
MCS ← empty sequence;

begin Function linearizeMCT(*Current Node, isDestinationNode*)
     if *Current Node ≠ Root Node and isDestinationNode = false* **then**
       | Previous MIO ← get MIO from from Parent Node of Current Node;
     end
     if *Current Node is an instance of At-Node* **then**
       | Destination Node ← get Destination Node from At-Node;
       | call linearizeMCT(*Destination Node, true*);
     else
        if *Current Node is an instance of Standard Node* **then**
           Current MIO ← get MIO from Current Node;
           if *Previous MIO ≠ null* **then**
          | add Current MIO to Parameter Providers List of Previous MIO;
           end
           if *isDestinationNode = false* **then**
             Child Nodes List ← get Child Nodes List from Current Node;
             foreach *Child Node in Child Nodes List* **do**
            | call linearizeMCT(*Child Node, false*);
             end
             add Current MIO to MCS;
           end
        end
     end
end

Fig. 3. Algorithm for Method Call Tree linearisation in the presence of At-Nodes

The Reverse Object Reuse operator's task is precisely that of pre-processing the individuals to be provided to other well-established operators, thus avoiding their reformulation. It starts by indexing all the At-Nodes in an MCT, and then proceeds to replace each At-Node with a clone copy of the sub-tree rooted at its Destination node. The resulting MCT can then be provided to another evolutionary operator. That is, the Reverse Object Reuse operator's purpose it that of being the first component of a breeding pipeline and acting as a source of individuals; it selects individuals directly from the population (e.g., using Tournament Selection [7]), and provides the (possibly) modified individual to the operator at the end of the breeding pipeline. This process is schematised in Figure 2.

4   Experimental Studies

The Object Reuse methodology described was embedded into *eCrash*, a tool for the ET of OO Java software, with the objective of assessing its impact on both the efficiency and the effectiveness of the evolutionary search; a thorough description of the *eCrash* tool can be found in [6].

Table 1. Sources of Individuals

With Object Reuse	Without Object Reuse
Object Reuse Op. (25%)	Mutation Op. (34%)
Reverse Object Reuse Op. / Mutation Op. (25%)	Crossover Op. (33%)
Reverse Object Reuse Op. / Crossover Op. (25%)	Reproduction Op. (33%)
Reproduction Op. (25%)	

4.1 Targets and Configuration

The Java `TreeMap` (an implementation of Red-Black Tree) and `Vector` classes of JDK 1.4.2 [3] were used as test objects. Their selection is supported by the fact that they are container classes, which are a typical benchmark in software testing of OO programs; Red-Black Trees, in particular, have been empirically shown to be the most difficult to test among containers programs [9]. As MUTs, the 5 most complex public methods (in terms of their Cyclomatic Complexity Number (CCN) [10]) of each class were selected. For each MUT, 2 sets of 20 runs were executed. The Object Reuse and Reverse Object Reuse operators were included in the first, and excluded from the second; Table 1 depicts the sources of individuals selected for each set of runs. The decision of selecting equal probabilities for the Mutation, Crossover and Reproduction operators is supported by previous experiments described in [6]. The remaining evolutionary parameters were common to both sets, and were defined as follows: a single population of 25 individuals was used; the search stopped if an ideal individual was found or after 200 generations; the selection method was Tournament Selection [7] with size 2; the tree builder algorithm was PTC2 [11], with the minimum and maximum tree depths being defined as 4 and 14. The *eCrash* tool was configured in accordance to the setup proposed in [6]. An additional set of 20 runs, in which all individuals were randomly generated using the PCT2 algorithm (with minimum and maximum tree depths of 4 and 14), was performed for comparison purposes; because no evolutionary operators were used, Object Reuse was absent from the process. This random search stopped if an ideal individual was found or after the generation of 5000 individuals. The results were included in Table 2.

4.2 Results and Discussion

The results depicted in Table 2 show that, for both classes, a higher percentage of runs attaining full structural coverage was achieved when including the Object Reuse operator as a source (the only exception being the `putAll(Map)` method of the `TreeMap` class). An average success rate of 62% was achieved with Object Reuse, whereas only 42.5% of the runs were successful without it. What's more, the impossibility of attaining full structural coverage for some of the methods tested is symptomatic of the way in which the lack of the Object Reuse functionality can hinder the evolutionary search. In fact, several search methods – in particular, `Vector`'s `indexOf` and `lastIndexOf`; and `TreeMap`'s `put`, `remove` and `get` – rely on `equals` to verify if an item is contained in a

Table 2. Percentage of runs attaining full coverage (*%f*) and average number of individuals evaluated per run (*#i*); for the *With OR*, *Without OR* and *Random* runs; for the 5 public methods with the highest CCN of the `TreeMap` and `Vector` classes

MUT	CCN	With OR %f	With OR #i	W/out OR %f	W/out OR #i	Random %f	Random #i
TreeMap							
put(Object,Object)	10	10%	4563	0%	5000	0%	5000
putAll(Map)	10	85%	1389	95%	1154	75%	2385
remove(Object)	3	25%	4119	0%	5000	0%	5000
containsValue(Object)	3	100%	501	100%	548	100%	628
get(Object)	2	25%	4000	0%	5000	0%	5000
Vector							
lastIndexOf(Object,int)	10	60%	3203	0%	5000	0%	5000
indexOf(Object,int)	8	40%	4243	0%	5000	0%	5000
removeElementAt(int)	6	85%	1829	75%	2258	70%	2948
addAll(int,Collection)	5	100%	871	95%	1130	80%	1668
remove(int)	4	90%	1904	80%	2545	80%	2815

collection. This means that if instances are not reused, the search for non-`null` arguments of type `Object` will fail. A commonly used workaround (e.g., [6]) is that of including substitute classes into the test cluster, which extend `Object` and override `equals` with a less stringent implementation; this approach, however, does not suffice for the following reasons. Firstly, certain test scenarios may specifically involve using classes that do not override `equals` or the `Object` class itself. Secondly, the decision on which additional classes to include into the test cluster is problem specific and human dependant; to the best of our knowledge, no systematic strategy has been proposed to automate this task. Thirdly, the inclusion of redundant classes into the test cluster will enlarge the search space and will thus have negative consequences on the efficiency of the search [6].

The graphs depicted in Figure 4 provide an overview of the way in which the runs evolved, and on how the Object Reuse methodology affects the test case generation process in terms of coverage, Test Program size and feasibility. The runs in which Object Reuse was employed yield solutions with shorter MCS length (a difference of 20.3%, on average, for `TreeMap`, and 12% for `Vector`). Also, feasibility is significantly promoted, with an average increase of 4% for both the `TreeMap` and `Vector` classes. These observations show that the proposed methodology is not only able to enhance the effectiveness of the test case generation process, but also its efficiency. Firstly, it yields solutions with smaller overall size and lower average structural complexity, thus contributing positively to the area of MCS minimisation. Simpler and shorter test programs do not only reduce the computational effort involved in compilation and execution; they also ease the (mostly human-dependant) task of defining a mechanism for checking that the output of a program is correct given some input (i.e., an oracle). Secondly, the application of the Replaced-Destination Node Pair Selection heuristic is able to increase the average feasibility of the generated Test Programs. Because only feasible Test Programs are concluded with a call to the MUT, a higher level of feasibility will increase the performance of the test case generation process [6].

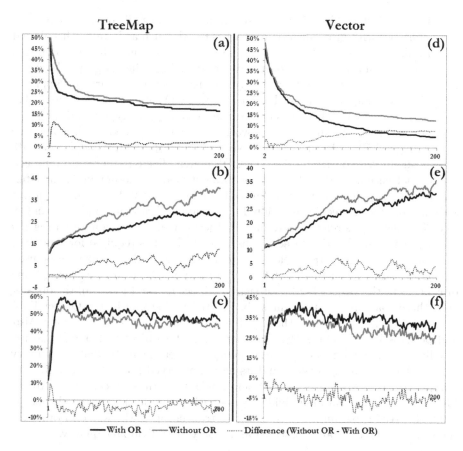

Fig. 4. Average percentage of CFG nodes left to be covered per generation *(a and d)*, average MCS length per generation *(b and e)*, and average percentage of feasible individuals per generation *(c and f)*; for the *With OR* and *Without OR* runs; for the 5 public methods with the highest CCN of the `TreeMap` and `Vector` classes

5   Related Work

The proposed approach to Object Reuse has some similarities with Koza's work on Automatically Defined Functions (ADFs) [12]. ADFs enable GP to solve problems by decomposing them into subproblems, solving the subproblems, and assembling the partial solutions into a solution to the overall problem; an individual's genotype usually consists of a forest of trees (or functions), which are then called repeatedly from the main tree. Therefore, ADFs do enable function reuse, as the possibility of selecting and calling the same function multiple times exists. However, functions in OO languages typically return object references, and each individual function call – even to the same function – returns a distinct reference. As such, ADFs do not enable Object Reuse, as the possibility of utilising the object reference returned by a single function call more than once is not possible. The Object Reuse methodology described also shares some characteristics with graph-based approaches to GP, such as Parallel Distributed GP [13] and Cartesian GP [14], as it also involves loosening the interpretation of the edges of an MCT thus effectively transforming it into a graph. However, to the best of the authors' knowledge, there has been no research on applying any of the above approaches to the generation of OO software and, in particular, to OOET; conversely, STGP has been extended to support type inheritance and polymorphism [15,16], and extensive work has been performed on applying it to OOET (e.g., [2,5,6]). As such, we believe that the proposed methodology constitutes a significant contribution to the OOET area. The only previous approach to Object Reuse known to the authors does not involve a loosening of the interpretation of the edges of an MCT, but rather a loosening of the parameter object assignments during tree linearisation. In [2], Wappler proposes employing an Object Pool that stores references to all the objects created during a Test Program execution; this pool is consulted if a parameter object is required for a method call, and a parameter object selector component selects the instance to be used among all available instances of the required type. There are, however, some drawbacks to the Object Pool approach to Object Reuse. Firstly, all the objects, even those that are not used, must be created and stored in the Object Pool, which will obviously increase the length and complexity of Test Programs. Also, and perhaps most importantly, changing parameter object assignments during tree linearisation will result in a discrepancy between the individual's hereditary information (i.e., its genotype) and its actual observed properties (i.e., its phenotype); in other words, the Test Program might not directly correspond to the MCT. Considering that an individual's evaluation is performed at the phenotype level, the Test Program must be an exact translation of the MCT in order for the fitness to be accurately assessed and reflect an individual's quality.

6   Conclusions

The goal of OOET is to find a set of Test Programs that satisfies a predefined test criterion. Object Reuse means that a single object instance can be passed as an argument multiples times to one or more methods; if structural adequacy criteria are employed it is a feature of the utmost importance, as it enables the generation of test cases that exercise structures of software that would not be reachable otherwise. The main contribution of this work is that of proposing a methodology for enabling Object Reuse on typed GP-based approaches to OOET, which involves the definition of novel type of GP nodes (the At-Nodes) that "point to" other nodes, thus permitting the reuse of portions of the tree and, specifically, the reuse of the object references returned by the functions corresponding to the reused sub-trees. Additionally, At-Nodes may be removed from a tree; this functionality allows avoiding the reformulation of other well-established evolutionary operators, such as Mutation and Crossover. Besides enhancing the effectiveness of the search, the experimental studies performed show that the proposed methodology improves the performance of the test case generation process:

it yields solutions with smaller overall size and lower structural complexity, and it is able to increase the feasibility of Test Programs.

Acknowledgements. The third author acknowledges the support of the following projects: TIN2007-68083-C02-01 (Nohnes project, Spanish Ministry of Science and Education); PDT-08A09 and GRU-09105 (Junta de Extremadura).

References

1. Tonella, P.: Evolutionary testing of classes. In: ISSTA 2004: Proceedings of the 2004 ACM SIGSOFT international symposium on Software testing and analysis, pp. 119–128. ACM Press, New York (2004)
2. Wappler, S.: Automatic Generation of Object-Oriented Unit Tests Using Genetic Programming. PhD thesis, Technischen Universitat Berlin (December 2007)
3. Sun Microsystems: JavaTM 2 Platform, vol. 1.4.2. API Specification (2003), http://java.sun.com/j2se/1.4.2/docs/api/
4. Vaziri, M., Tip, F., Fink, S., Dolby, J.: Declarative object identity using relation types. In: Ernst, E. (ed.) ECOOP 2007. LNCS, vol. 4609, pp. 54–78. Springer, Heidelberg (2007)
5. Wappler, S., Wegener, J.: Evolutionary unit testing of object-oriented software using strongly-typed genetic programming. In: GECCO 2006: Proceedings of the 8th annual conference on Genetic and evolutionary computation, pp. 1925–1932. ACM Press, New York (2006)
6. Ribeiro, J.C.B., Zenha-Rela, M.A., Fernández de Vega, F.: Test case evaluation and input domain reduction strategies for the evolutionary testing of object-oriented software. Inf. Softw. Technol. 51(11), 1534–1548 (2009)
7. Koza, J.R.: Genetic Programming: On the Programming of Computers by Means of Natural Selection (Complex Adaptive Systems). The MIT Press, Cambridge (December 1992)
8. Montana, D.J.: Strongly typed genetic programming. Evolutionary Computation 3(2), 199–230 (1995)
9. Arcuri, A.: Insight knowledge in search based software testing. In: GECCO 2009: Proceedings of the 11th Annual conference on Genetic and evolutionary computation, pp. 1649–1656. ACM, New York (2009)
10. McCabe, T.J.: A complexity measure. IEEE Trans. Software Eng. 2(4), 308–320 (1976)
11. Luke, S.: Two fast tree-creation algorithms for genetic programming. IEEE Transactions on Evolutionary Computation 4(3), 274–283 (2000)
12. Koza, J.R.: Genetic Programming II: Automatic Discovery of Reusable Programs. The MIT Press, Cambridge (1994)
13. Poli, R.: Evolution of graph-like programs with parallel distributed genetic programming. In: Bäck, T. (ed.) ICGA, pp. 346–353. Morgan Kaufmann, San Francisco (1997)
14. Miller, J.F., Thomson, P.: Cartesian genetic programming. In: Poli, R., Banzhaf, W., Langdon, W.B., Miller, J., Nordin, P., Fogarty, T.C. (eds.) EuroGP 2000. LNCS, vol. 1802, pp. 121–132. Springer, Heidelberg (2000)
15. Haynes, T.D., Schoenefeld, D.A., Wainwright, R.L.: Type inheritance in strongly typed genetic programming. In: Angeline, P.J., Kinnear Jr., K.E. (eds.) Advances in Genetic Programming, vol. 2, pp. 359–376. MIT Press, Cambridge (1996)
16. Yu, T.: Polymorphism and genetic programming. In: Miller, J., Tomassini, M., Lanzi, P.L., Ryan, C., Tetamanzi, A.G.B., Langdon, W.B. (eds.) EuroGP 2001. LNCS, vol. 2038, pp. 218–233. Springer, Heidelberg (2001)

Analytic Solutions to Differential Equations under Graph-Based Genetic Programming

Tom Seaton[1], Gavin Brown[2], and Julian F. Miller[1]

[1] Department of Electronics, University of York
[2] School of Computer Science, University of Manchester

Abstract. Cartesian Genetic Programming (CGP) is applied to solving differential equations (DE). We illustrate that repeated elements in analytic solutions to DE can be exploited under GP. An analysis is carried out of the search space in tree and CGP frameworks, examining the complexity of different DE problems. Experimental results are provided against benchmark ordinary and partial differential equations. A system of ordinary differential equations (SODE) is solved using multiple outputs from a genome. We discuss best heuristics when generating DE solutions through evolutionary search.

1 Introduction

Differential equations are ubiquitous throughout the natural sciences, modelling diverse systems from the harmonics of a violin to chemical concentrations in the blood stream. Widely applied finite difference and finite element routines can obtain accurate numerical approximations to DE solutions over prescribed domains [1]. However, the automatic derivation of analytic solutions to many high order or strongly non-linear DE problems remains challenging under standard deterministic approaches. Publicly available symbolic solvers apply analytic techniques such as separation of variables or symmetry reduction, but address specific classes of DE and require extensive supporting libraries for comprehensive support [2].

There has been some interest in the application of machine learning to DE since the advent of genetic algorithms. In this paradigm, the analytic solution can be considered analogous to a search objective, and the equation and any initial or boundary conditions to training data. In 1996 Diver evolved candidate solutions to simple ordinary differential equations (ODE), encoding solutions as strings [3]. Koza briefly addressed learning solutions to ODEs in his seminal work on problems for Tree Genetic Programming (GP) [4]. Cao later used an embedded genetic algorithm to tune parameters of a tree GP based solver [5]. More recently, Tsoulos and Lagaris set out fitness functions using a framework based on Grammar Guided GP [6] and applied them over a comprehensive collection of partial differential equations (PDE) and systems of ODE (SODE). We are also aware of a novel hybrid GP approach to solving DE implemented by Kirstukas et. al [7] for engineering applications.

A.I. Esparcia-Alcazar et al. (Eds.): EuroGP 2010, LNCS 6021, pp. 232–243, 2010.

Given the broad range of techniques historically applied, our goal is to identify general qualities which enable GP frameworks to efficiently explore DE search spaces. One defining characteristic of analytic solutions to differential equations is symbolic symmetry. Where solutions exist, application of the basic rules of differential calculus to trigonometric, polynomial or exponential functions naturally leads to repeated structure. In the present work, we postulate that DE have a higher density of analytic solutions under heuristic search in data-structures which reuse common functional elements. To explore this concept, we carry out an analysis using a variant on an established graph-based approach, Cartesian Genetic Programming (CGP) [8], across a set of benchmark DE. The technique is also examined under simple tree genetic programming, with a view to understanding whether representations reusing repeated structure have an advantage over these particular classes of problem.

Section 2 of this paper outlines some preliminaries of the CGP differential solver, including the specification of appropriate fitness functions and reproduction strategy. Section 3 analyses the corresponding search space composition and describes a method of enumerating DE solutions within CGP data structures. A set of experimental results are presented over benchmark DE in Section 4 and discussed in Section 5. The work concludes with general comments on using evolutionary frameworks for solving DE and a summary of outcomes.

2 CGP Implementation

2.1 Reproduction Strategy

The original implementation of Cartesian Genetic Programming can be classed as a strongly elitist method, since it uses a $1+\lambda$ evolutionary strategy without crossover. The approach selected a single parent from each generation, promoting itself and λ mutated offspring. Our choice of this representation was motivated because the framework provides convenient reuse of previous elements through the evolution of more general directed acyclic graphs (DAG). For this initial analysis, we preclude techniques such as the use of modules [9] or automatically defined functions (see comment in Section 5). The CGP policy adopted in this paper employs a weak form of elitism shown in Figure 1.

1: $g \leftarrow 0$
2: Construct a random starting population of size P. Rank by fitness F.
3: **while** $g < g_{max}$ and $F > tol$ **do**
4:    Select a new parent with the best fitness.
5:    Promote the parent and λ mutated offspring.
6:    Promote one offspring from each of the next $P - (\lambda + 1)$ fittest individuals.

7:    Re-rank using the promoted population.
8:    $g \leftarrow g + 1$
9: **end while**

Mutations are standard point operations on the CGP genotype and *tol* is some minimum error bound on individual fitness. For $\lambda = 1$ the method is random

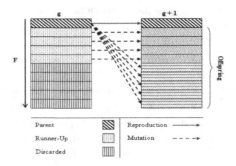

Fig. 1. Strategy for $\lambda = 5$, $P = 10$. The next generation contains the previous parent, five offspring of the parent and four offspring from the next best individuals.

search and $\lambda = P - 1$ is equivalent to conventional CGP. Heuristically, the trade off in selecting lower values of λ is greater diversity in the search, which reduces the risk of stagnation. More generally, the policy is related to a conventional $\mu + \lambda$ search but competes a larger proportion of offspring from the fittest parent. In preliminary experiments, $\lambda = P/2$ was found to be an adequate compromise for all the benchmark ODE and PDE addressed.

2.2 Fitness Functions for Differential Equations

Consider the problem of finding a particular closed analytic solution A to a bounded ODE or PDE, within a domain of interest spanned by the D-dimensional orthogonal basis set $x(x_1...x_D)$. A is an expression in x which

1. Satisfies the defining equality.
2. Meets all boundary or initial conditions.
3. Remains real and finite.

We adopt the approach of Tsoulos and Lagaris [6], evolving a model function $M(x)$, taking a weighted aggregate as the fitness $F(M)$. In general this has the form

$$F(M) = R(M) + \alpha \epsilon(M) \tag{1}$$

where R and ϵ are residual errors calculated for M across the equation and conditions respectively. α is an integer weighting parameter. Table 1 shows $F(M)$ for

Table 1. Fitness Functions for DE bounded on a line and a unit square

Differential Equation	$R(M)$	$\epsilon(M)$
$\frac{dy}{dx} = g(x,y), \quad y(x_0) = c$	$\sum_{i=1}^{N} \left| M(x_i) - \frac{dM(x_i)}{dx} \right|$	$\|M(x_i) - y(x_i)\|_{i=0}$
$\nabla^2 \Psi = g(\Psi, x, y)$ $0 \le x \le 1$ $0 \le y \le 1$	$\sum_{i=1}^{N^2} \|M(x_i, y_i) - \nabla^2(M(x_i, y_i))\|$	$\sum_{i=1}^{N}(\|M(0, y_i) - \Psi(0, y_i)\|$ $+\|M(1, y_i) - \Psi(1, y_i)\|$ $+\|M(x_i, 0) - \Psi(x_i, 0)\|$ $+\|M(x_i, 1) - \Psi(x_i, 1)\|)$

an example 1st order ODE and 2nd order PDE. In the CGP solver, the differential terms are calculated by carrying out $O(N^D)$ centered difference approximations at uniformly sampled training points in the inner domain and $O(N(D-1)+1)$ along each bound. Centered difference approximations are evaluated using two sampling points separated by distance h, contributing error $O(h^2)$.

3   Problem Complexity and Search Space Analysis

3.1   Solving Differential Equations in Evolutionary Search

Abstractly, a DE solver under Graph-based GP searches through a finite, discrete set Ω of representable expressions for members of a subset of solutions, $\omega \subset \Omega$. The solution space ω contains all expressions from Ω which are functionally equivalent to the analytic solution. The concept is illustrated in Figure 2 below. One method of defining the inherent difficulty of a DE problem is to consider the probability p_A of selecting an analytic solution, a member of ω, by blind random search. For convenience we work with $\frac{1}{p_A}$, terming this the 'unguided complexity' κ.

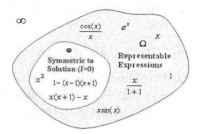

Fig. 2. Depiction of expressions in the search space of an ODE with solution x^2

Definition 1. *Unguided Complexity*

$$\kappa = \frac{1}{p_A} = \frac{|\Omega|}{|\omega|}$$

such that κ is the number of candidates in the total search space per member of the solution set. A genotype representation of a problem where κ is large induces proportionally fewer optimal solutions and is combinatorially harder before the fitness landscape is considered.

3.2   Search Space Ω

Taking a standard case from Koza[4], consider a full bi-arity tree genotype of depth D. The tree is covered by $2^D - 1$ functions (interior vertices) and 2^D terminals (leaves). Hence for function and terminal sets of size f and T respectively, the number of syntactically distinct, labelled trees is given by

$$|\mathbf{\Omega_{TREE}}| = f^{2^D-1} T^{2^D} = T(fT)^{2^D-1} \tag{2}$$

For the CGP genotype, $\mathbf{\Omega_{CGP}}$ is instead defined by combinations of directed graphs. The closest comparison to the bi-arity tree in CGP is a feed-forward bi-arity genotype of the form shown in Figure 3. Here the bounding parameter on $\mathbf{\Omega_{CGP}}$ is the total genotype length, the number of genes C. When $C = 1$ the search space is $\mathbf{\Omega_{CGP}} = fT^2$. Generalising to permit connections to all previous nodes, the size of the total search space is

$$|\mathbf{\Omega_{CGP}}| = f^C \prod_{i=0}^{C-1} (T+i)^2 \tag{3}$$

or more transparently the factorial

$$|\mathbf{\Omega_{CGP}}| = f^C \prod_{i=0}^{C-1} (T+i)^2 = f^C \left(\frac{(T+C-1)!}{(T-1)!} \right)^2 \tag{4}$$

Comparing tree *depth* with CGP *length* is not straightforward, because they may imply a different number of nodes per individual. One method is to consider instead the maximum path length in each graph, such that $C = D$. From Equations 2 and 4, we then have

$$|\mathbf{\Omega_{CGP}}| < |\mathbf{\Omega_{TREE}}| \text{ given that } C, D > 4 \tag{5}$$

using any set of functions and terminals with $f > 1$ or $T > 1$. The feed-forward CGP applied in this experiment explores a smaller space of candidates than the full tree structure, as the maximum path length increases.

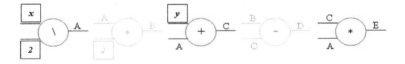

Fig. 3. Example 5 cell bi-arity genome from a single row CGP genotype. Cells 1,3 and 5 are connected to the output. Cells 2 and 4 are redundant.

3.3   Solution Space ω

With increasing genotype length, ω also expands to include increasingly complex symmetry. An alternative strategy to the challenge of enumerating ω directly for DE is to make an estimate by blind random sampling. Consider a number of independent GP runs R on a population size P. Classically the probability of success of an independent run under random search with no evolutionary mechanism is just the binomial product

$$1 - (1 - p_A)^{Pg} \tag{6}$$

$P \times g$ being the number of individuals created by generation g. Therefore a good estimate for p_A can be found by empirically fitting Equation 6 to a cumulative histogram of successes over all runs. Combined with Equations 2 and 4, the experiment gives us κ and ω for each DE problem. We apply this to a set of benchmarks in Section 4.

3.4 Parameter Space

To solve an ODE or PDE with genetic programming, the terminal and functions sets should be specified such that at least one group of elements can be drawn and ordered to give an expression equivalent to the desired analytic solution. Figure 4 illustrates how the unguided complexity can increase with additional functions and terminals. In this simple example, κ tends to grow roughly linearly with T and f. Interestingly, we note that the complexity when searching with both *log* and *exp* operators is lower than with a set precluding one or the other. In practice, the availability of the inverse operation introduces new equivalent solutions within ω and increases the probability of finding an analytic solution under random search. For simplicity, the following experiments use the *minimum* subset of functions under which the analytic forms of all benchmark problems addressed can be represented. Similarly, any constants required by the search are pre-seeded, rather than evolved dynamically. Division by zero is protected, returning one. The full function set included the operators $(+ - * \; / \; sin \; cosine \; log \; exp)$.

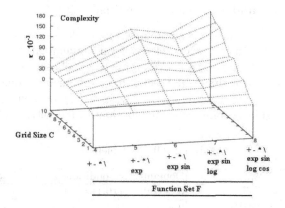

Fig. 4. The parameter space for a one dimensional ODE problem where $\frac{dy}{dx} = \frac{2y}{x}$, with initial condition $y(1) = 1$. $T = 2$ and $C = 4$).

4   Experiment

Exploring the effectiveness of different GP representations for solving DE requires a defined set of benchmark ODE and PDE. To allow ease of comparison, in the following sections we detail a selection of problems drawn from previous publications [3][6][7]. These problems cover a cross-section of different classes, order and domains. Table 2 below describes the parameters used throughout for each algorithm. Values for boundary weighting α and sampling rate N are optimised over the whole problem set. The maximum number of candidate trees or graphs was held constant between each set up ($P \times g_{max} = 10^7$). Candidates in tree GP were selected through a binary tournament strategy, with optimal population size $P = 1000$. Bloat control was introduced by constraining trees to a maximum of 150 nodes.

Table 2. Parameters for CGP and Tree Guided Search

Parameter	CGP	Tree
Population P	10	1000
Max Generations g_{max}	2000	20
Runs	500	500
Weighting α	100	100
Offspring λ	5	-
Sample Rate N	10	10
Mutation Rate	Point	2%
Crossover Rate	-	90%
Reproduction Rate	-	8%

4.1 Complexity and Performance against ODE

The ODE problem set chosen is summarised in Table 3. These consist of linear and non-linear problems for which closed form polynomial, trigonometric and exponential solutions exist. The above problems are chosen to test different aspects of the search algorithms. ODEs [3,9] have similar functional form in their solutions, but treat different equations. These problems should therefore have a comparable unguided complexity, but evaluate differently under the guided

Table 3. ODE Problem Set

No.	ODE	Domain	Conditions	Solution
1	$y' = \frac{2x-y}{x}$	0.1 : 1.0	$y(0.1) = 20.1$	$y = x + \frac{2}{x}$
2	$y' = \frac{1-y\cos(x)}{\sin(x)}$	0.1 : 1.0	$y(0.1) = \frac{2.1}{\sin(0.1)}$	$y = \frac{x+2}{\sin(x)}$
3	$y' = -\frac{1}{5}y + e^{-\frac{x}{5}}\cos(x)$	0.0 : 1.0	$y(0.0) = 0$	$y = e^{-\frac{x}{5}}\sin(x)$
4	$y' + y\cos(x) = 0$	0.0 : 1.0	$y(0.0) = 1$	$y = e^{-\sin(x)}$
5	$y' - \frac{2y}{x} = x$	0.1 : 1.0	$y(1) = 10$	$y = x^2 ln(x) + 10x^2$
6	$y' + y^2 = 0$	0.0 : 1.0	$y(1.0) = 0.5$	$y = \frac{1}{1+x}$
7	$y'' = -100y$	0.0 : 1.0	$y(0) = 0, y'(0) = 10$	$y = sin(10x)$
8	$y'' = 6y' - 9y$	0.0 : 1.0	$y(0) = 0, y'(0) = 2$	$y = 2xe^{3x}$
9	$y'' = -\frac{1}{5}y' - y - \frac{1}{5}e^{-\frac{x}{5}}\cos(x)$	0.0 : 2.0	$y(0) = 0, y'(0) = 1$	$y = e^{-\frac{x}{5}}\sin(x)$
10	$y'' = 4y' - 4y + exp(x)$	0.0 : 1.0	$y(0) = 3, y'(0) = 6$	$y = e^x + 2e^{2x} + xe^{2x}$

search. ODEs [5,8,10] are examples of problems with solutions having more complex functional forms and dependency on several common sub-elements. Figure 5 contrasts the unguided complexity κ of the ODE problem set under tree GP and CGP. Over all known complexity estimates, blind random sampling using the CGP framework achieved a higher success rate than in the Tree framework, by factors ranging between 2 (ODE [4,6]) and 100 (ODE [8]). The solutions to the example ODE are more densely represented under a graph-based framework than in a tree-based representation.

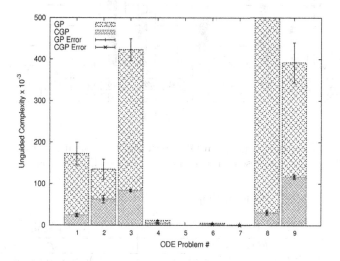

Fig. 5. Estimates of the unguided complexity, κ, on ODEs 1-9. ODES[5] and [10] did not converge under blind random search. All other complexity estimates are lower under CGP.

Figure 6 shows the performance under guided search. The results are presented using a convenient integral metric, such that

$$A_{I_{max}} = \frac{1}{10^7} \int_0^{I_{max}} h(I) dI \qquad (7)$$

($I_{max} = 20000$) where A is the area underneath the probability of success curve $h(I)$, calculated as a discrete sum. $h(I)$ is the chance of having obtained an analytic solution after $I = P \times g$ candidate genomes, taken as an average from 100 runs of the solver. Overall performance for a given number of candidates is greater as $h \rightarrow 1$. The CGP solver converged on a representation of the analytic solution for all cases and performance showed good qualitative correlation with the complexity of each problem. Under guided search, the ODEs having a solution with a simple analytic form were solved more readily by the tree-based representation, but this did not converge for the high complexity case ODE 5. The best guided performance of CGP relative to the bi-arity tree GP occurred

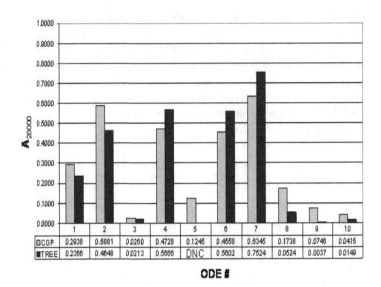

	1	2	3	4	5	6	7	8	9	10
CGP	0.2938	0.5881	0.0260	0.4728	0.1245	0.4658	0.6345	0.1738	0.0746	0.0415
TREE	0.2366	0.4648	0.0213	0.5666	DNC	0.5602	0.7524	0.0524	0.0037	0.0149

ODE #

Fig. 6. Guided solver performance on ODE over 20000 candidate solutions, for CGP and Tree GP. Results are presented using an area metric (Equation 7).

Table 4. Elliptic PDE Problem Set

No.	PDE	Particular Solution
1	$\nabla^2 \Psi(x,y) = 4$	$\Psi(x,y) = x^2 + y^2 + x + y + 1$
2	$\nabla^2 \Psi(x,y) = -2\Psi(x,y)$	$\Psi(x,y) = sin(x)cos(y)$
3	$\nabla^2 \Psi(x,y) = -(x^2 + y^2)\Psi(x,y)$	$\Psi(x,y) = sin(xy)$
4	$\nabla^2 \Psi(x,y) + e^{\Psi} = 1 + x^2 + y^2 + \frac{4}{1+x^{2}+y^{2^2}}$	$\Psi(x,y) = log(1 + x^2 + y^2)$

for problems [1,2,5,8 and 10] which include repeat functional elements in their solutions.

4.2 Partial Differential Equations

An experiment was carried out to demonstrate proof of concept on partial differential equations. A collection of benchmark second order elliptic PDEs were solved using CGP across a Dirichlet bounded unit square, summarised in Table 4.[1] The full general function set was employed.

The full analytic solution was recovered in all cases. On average, the CGP algorithm took longest to recover the more complex functional forms of PDE[1] and PDE[4]. The convergence rate is thought to be slow for these problems because the fitness landscape is dominated by deep local minima near the true

---

[1] A complete specification of the PDE problems and their boundary conditions can be found in Tsoulos et. al. (2006) [6].

solution. Both solutions were often approximated by very fit combinations of nested sine functions, which pre-disposed the search to stagnate.

4.3   CGP and Systems of Differential Equations

An interesting quality of the CGP representation is the intended support for multiple outputs. Solutions are read from different starting nodes on the genotype and evolved simultaneously. We applied this aspect to a simple trigonometric SODE with repeated solutions of the form

$$
\begin{aligned}
y_1' &= cos(x), \ y_1(0) = 0 \\
y_2' &= -y_1, \ y_2(0) = 1 \\
y_3' &= y_2, \ y_3(0) = 0 \\
y_4' &= -y_3, \ y_4(0) = 1 \\
y_5' &= y_4, \ y_5(0) = 0
\end{aligned}
$$

Outputs were obtained from the last n cells in the genome, expanding with one additional node for each extra ODE, repeating for $n > 5$. Figure 7 then shows the corresponding number of candidates I that must be evaluated for a 99% success probability from repeated runs. In this instance, the computational effort is approximately the same as solving a set of equivalent independent ODE. Under the graph-based representation, the new outputs are connected to existing partial solutions. This gives the appearance that solutions with a high degree of symmetry are grown easily, benefiting from 'cross-polination' along the genome.

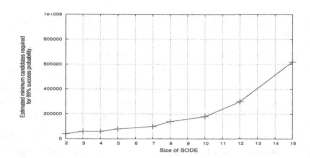

Fig. 7. Average number of individuals required to solve the test SODE, showing the increase with system size. Multiple outputs are read from the CGP genome.

5   Discussion

Section 4 demonstrated that GP search on standard DE problems can show faster convergence when working with representations which support repeated elements. In this instance, the mechanism we used to explore this was to apply a graph-based framework, but we would expect similar improvements when introducing techniques such as modules or ADFs. For the sample problems examined, more compact representations spanned a proportionally higher number of analytic solutions in the search space. It is worth noting that the difficulty of a DE under heuristic search is not strongly dependent on the form of the equation itself, but as in symbolic regression [11], on the length and diversity of the solution and also on boundary conditions.

Common to previous efforts, the main limitation of the approach is the requirement to define a sufficient function and terminal set. Applying prior knowledge of the boundary or initial conditions can provide useful indications of which subset to apply. Throughout all the problems, the boundary weighting condition α played a critical role in the search. It was found that defining a fitness function with strongly weighted boundaries ($\alpha = 100$) generally led to faster convergence on partial solutions, but naturally became dominated by these candidates as the weighting increased. A very low weighting ($\alpha < 1$) skews the population to include candidates which solve the general DE, but with a different functional form to the particular solution.

Differential equations are an interesting area for heuristic search techniques, both as an inductive tool and for engineering applications. In the latter, methods of seeding may be particularly useful, for example incorporating partial solutions based on empirical data. Another natural idea is to apply dimensional constraints, where the metric units of a problem are considered [10]. The approach could also be improved upon by including better techniques for evaluating candidate terms, such as automatic or symbolic differentiation [12].

6   Conclusions

The purpose of this initial work was to explore best heuristics for the evolution of solutions to differential equations under GP. We carried out an analysis of the search space and empirical performance of two GP solvers, conventional CGP and tree GP. It was illustrated that GP structures which automatically reuse common elements, such as graph-based representations, can show improved performance on target DE where solutions have repeated structure. Proof of concept was provided for a CGP solver on PDE and Systems of ODE. We further demonstrated that simple SODE were solvable using multiple outputs from a graph-based genotype and that this approach scaled efficiently with system size. A number of guidelines for solving DEs were inferred, including the selection of compact representations and strongly weighted boundary conditions.

References

1. Sobolob, S.L.: Partial Differential Equations of Mathematical Physics. Pergamen Press, Oxford (1964)
2. Abell, M.L., Braselton, J.P.: Differential Equations with Maple V. Academic Press, London (2000)
3. Diver, D.A.: Applications of genetic algorithms to the solution of ordinary differential equations. J. Phys. A: Math. Gen. 26, 3503–3513 (1993)

4. Koza, J.R.: Genetic Programming, on the Programming of Computers By Means of Natural Selection. MIT Press, Cambridge (1992)
5. Cao, H., Lishan, K., Chen, Y.: Evolutionary Modelling of Systems of Ordinary Differential Equations with Genetic Programming (2000)
6. Tsoulos, I., Lagaris, I.E.: Solving differential equations with genetic programming. Genet. Program. Evolvable Mach. 7, 33–54 (2006)
7. Kirstukas, S.J., Bryden, K.M., Ashlock, D.A.: A hybrid genetic programming approach for the analytical solution of differential equations. International Journal of General Systems 34, 279–299 (2005)
8. Miller, J.F., Thomson, P.: Cartesian Genetic Programming. In: Poli, R., Banzhaf, W., Langdon, W.B., Miller, J., Nordin, P., Fogarty, T.C. (eds.) EuroGP 2000. LNCS, vol. 1802, pp. 121–132. Springer, Heidelberg (2000)
9. Walker, J., Miller, J.F.: Investigating the performance of module acquisition in cartesian genetic programming. In: Genetic and Evolutionary Computation Conference, pp.1649–1655, 25-06 (2005)
10. Durrbaum, A., Klier, W., Hahn, H.: Comparison of Automatic and Symbolic Differentiation in Mathematical Modeling and Computer Simulation of Rigid-Body Systems. Multibody System Dynamics 7, 331–355 (2002)
11. Scmidt, M., Hod, L.: Comparison of Tree and Graph Encodings as Function of Problem Complexity. In: Genetic and Evolutionary Computation Conference, pp. 1674–1679 (2007)
12. Keijzer, M.: Scientific Discovery using Genetic Programming. PhD thesis, Department for Mathematical Modelling, Technical University of Denmark (2001)

Learning a Lot from Only a Little: Genetic Programming for Panel Segmentation on Sparse Sensory Evaluation Data

Katya Vladislavleva[1], Kalyan Veeramachaneni[2], Una-May O'Reilly[2],
Matt Burland[3], and Jason Parcon[3]

[1] University of Antwerp, Belgium
katya@vanillamodeling.com
[2] Massachusetts Institute of Technology, USA
{kalyan,unamay}@csail.mit.edu
[3] Givaudan Flavors Corp., USA
{matt.burland,jason.parcon}@givaudan.com

Abstract. We describe a data mining framework that derives panelist information from sparse flavour survey data. One component of the framework executes genetic programming ensemble based symbolic regression. Its evolved models for each panelist provide a second component with all plausible and uncorrelated explanations of how a panelist rates flavours. The second component bootstraps the data using an ensemble selected from the evolved models, forms a probability density function for each panelist and clusters the panelists into segments that are *easy to please*, *neutral*, and *hard to please*.

Keywords: symbolic regression, panel segmentation, survey data, ensemble modeling, hedonic, sensory evaluation.

1 Introduction

Givaudan Flavours, a leading fragrance and flavour corporation, is currently trying to integrate evolutionary computation techniques into its design of flavours. In one step of its design process, Givaudan conducts a hedonic survey which presents aromas of flavours to a small panel of targeted consumers and queries how much each flavour is liked. Each panelist is asked to sniff roughly 50 flavours.

To best exploit the restricted sample size, Givaudan flavourists first reduce the ingredients they experimentally vary in the flavours to the most important ones. Then they use experimental design to define a set that statistically provides them with the most information about responses to the entire design space.

The specificity of sensory evaluation data is such, that "the panelist to panelist differences are simply too great to ignore as just an inconvenience of the scientific quest," [1], because "taste and smell, the chemical senses, are prime

A.I. Esparcia-Alcazar et al. (Eds.): EuroGP 2010, LNCS 6021, pp. 244–255, 2010.

examples of inter-panelist differences, especially in terms of the hedonic tone (liking/disliking)," [1]. Givaudan employs reliable statistical techniques that regress a single model from the survey data. This model describes how much the panel, as an aggregate, likes any flavour in the space. But since the differences in the liking preferences of the panelists are significant, Givaudan is also using several proprietary methods to deal with the variation in the panel and is interested in alternative techniques.

A goal of our interaction with Givaudan is to generate innovative information about the different panelists and their liking-based responses by developing techniques that will eventually help Givaudan design even better flavours. Here we describe how Genetic Programming (GP) can be used to model sensory evaluation data without suppressing the variation that comes from humans having different flavour preferences. We also describe how GP enables a knowledge mining framework, see Figure 1, that meaningfully segments (i.e. clusters) the panel. With an exemplar Givaudan dataset, we identify the panelists who are "easy to please", i.e. that frequently respond with high liking to flavours, "hard to please" and "neutral". This is, in general, challenging because the survey data is sparse. In this particular dataset there are only 40 flavours in the seven-dimensional sample set and 69 panelist responses per flavour.

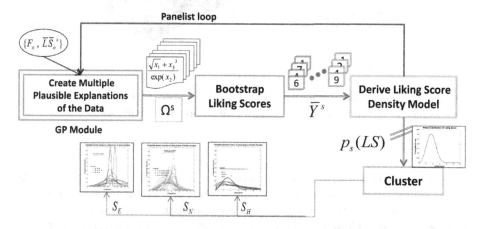

Fig. 1. Knowledge mining framework for sparse sensory data with a focus on panel segmentation. Read clockwise. The top portion is repeated for each panelist.

We proceed as follows: Section 2 introduces our flavour-liking data set. Section 3 discusses why GP model ensembles are well suited for this problem domain and briefly cites related work. Section 4 outlines the 5 steps of our method. Section 5 describes Steps 1 and 2, the ensemble derivation starting from ParetoGP. Section 6 presents Steps 3-5 – how the probability density functions and clusters that ultimately answer the questions are derived from this ensemble, and our experimental results. Section 7 concludes and mentions future work.

2   The Givaudan Flavour Liking Data Set

In this data set, flavour space consists of seven ingredients called *keys*, k_i. A flavour in the flavour space is a mixture by volume of these seven ingredients and the jth flavour is denoted by $\overline{k}^{(b)}$. 69 panelists sniff 40 different flavours and select a rating that is translated to its *liking score*, LS per Figure 2(a). Figure 2(b) illustrates the variation in the liking preferences of 69 panelists for the first ten flavours (for each flavour a histogram of 69 likling scores is depicted using 9 bins). Table 1 gives the notation for different variables used in this paper. Givaudan may pre-process these scores to adjust them for how different panelists use the range of the response scale. We scale all key data to the same range in this study.

LS	Rating
9	Extremely Like
8	Like Very Much
7	Like Moderately
6	Like Slightly
5	Neither Like Nor Dislike
4	Dislike Slightly
3	Dislike Moderately
2	Dislike Very Much
1	Dislike Extremely

(a)   (b)

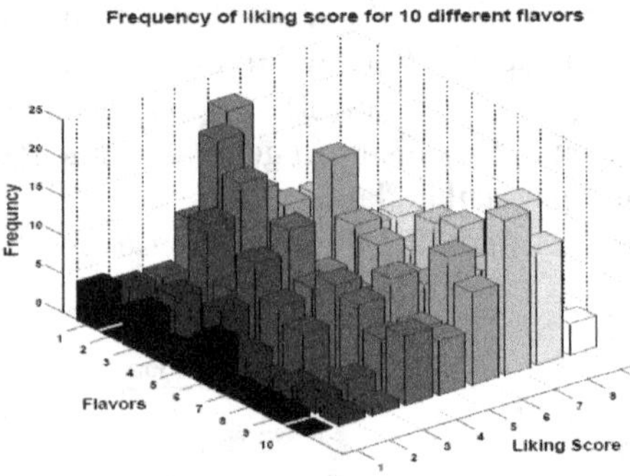

Fig. 2. (a)Category anchoring of the 9 point hedonic scale (b) Liking score frequency for 10 different flavours over all 69 panelists shows preference variance

3   Related Work

Because our data is sparse, it is not justifiable to presume that there is solely one model that explains a panelist's preferences. Thus presuming any structure for a model (which parametric regression requires) is tenuous. Model over-fitting must also be avoided. This makes the non-parametric, symbolic regression modeling capability of GP desirable. GP symbolic regression is also population-based and can be run over the data multiple times with different random seeds to generate multiple, diverse models. Complexity control and interval arithmetics can be used to mitigate data over-fitting. Symbolic regression works without *a priori* assumptions of model structure (except primitive selection).

However, with a few exceptions, GP symbolic regression has been focused on obtaining the most accurate single model from multiple runs. In Section 5, we will describe ParetoGP [2] as one means of explicitly refocusing GP symbolic regression so it generates a robust set of models. The idea of using ensembles for improved generalization of the response prediction is by far not new in regression. It has been extensively used in neural networks (e.g., [3–7]), and even more

Table 1. Problem Specific Variable Description

Variable	Notation	Details
flavour Space	F	The design space of ingredient mixtures
Keys	k_i	$i \in \{1...7\}$
flavour	$\overline{k}$	A mixture of 7 keys, $\overline{k} = \{k_1, ...k_7\}$
A specific flavour	$\overline{k}^{(b)}$	A specific flavour denoted by superscript b
Panelist	s_n	$n \in \{1..69\}$
Set of Panelists	S	$S = \{s_1, s_2, ...s_{69}\}$
Observed flavours	F_o	$F_o = \{\overline{k}^{(1)}....\overline{k}^{(40)}\}$
Bootstrapped flavours	F_B	$F_B = \{\overline{k}^{(1)}......\overline{k}^{(10,000)}\}$
Likability Function	$f^s(\overline{k}^{(j)}) = LS$	Relationship between a $\overline{k}^{(b)}$ and LS
lsd	$p(LS|s)$	Liking score density function for a panelist s
Cumulative density	$P_x(LS \geq x|s)$	Probability of Liking score $\geq x$
Panelist Cluster	S_c	A subset of S, $c \in \{E, N, H\}$
Model	m	Model m for Panelist s
Prediction	$y^{s,b,m}$	Model m's prediction for a $\overline{k}^{(b)}$
Model Ensemble	Ω^s	All models in the ensemble
Prediction Set	$\overline{Y}^{s,b}$	$\overline{Y}^{s,b} = \forall m \in \Omega^s \{y^{s,b,m}\}$
Set of Liking Scores s	$\overline{Y}^s$	$\overline{Y}^s = \forall b \in F_B \{\overline{Y}^{s,b}\}$

extensively in boosting and machine learning in general (albeit, mostly for classification). See [8–14] for examples. [7] presented the idea of using disagreement of ensemble models for quantifying the ambiguity of ensemble prediction for neural networks, but the approach has not been adapted to symbolic regression.

4   Panel Data Mining Steps

Our GP ensemble-based "knowledge mining" method has five steps:

1. Generate a diverse model set for each panelist from the sparse samples.
2. Thoughtfully select an *ensemble* of models meeting accuracy and complexity limits to admit generalization and avoid overfitting and a correlation threshold to avoid redundancy.
3. Use *all* models of the ensemble to generate multiple predictions for many unseen inputs.
4. With minor trimming of the extremes and attention to the discrete nature of liking scores, fit the predictions to a Weibull distribution.
5. Cluster based on the Weibull distribution's probability mass.

It is significant to note that these steps respect the importance of avoiding premature elimination of any plausible information because the data is sparse. The ensemble provides all valid values of the random variable when it is presented with new inputs. This extracts maximum possible information about the random variable, which supports more robust density estimation.

We proceed in Section 5 to detail how we assemble a symbolic regression ensemble, i.e. Steps 1 and 2. In Section 6, we detail Steps 3 through 5.

5   A Symbolic Regression Ensemble

Traditionally symbolic regression has been designed for generating a single model. Researchers have focused on evolving *the* model that best approximates the data and identifies hidden relationships between variables. They have developed multiple competent approaches to over-fitting. There are a number of demonstrably effective procedures for selecting the final model from the GP system. Machine learning techniques such as cross validation and bagging have been integrated. Multiple ways of controlling expression complexity are effective. See [15] for a thorough justification of the above assessment.

Modelers who must provide all and any explanations for the data are not well served by this emphasis upon a single model. Any algorithm variation of symbolic regression, even one that proceeds with attention to avoiding over-fitting, is as fragile as a parametric model with respect to the accuracy of its predictions and the confidence it places in those predictions *if it outputs one model*. The risks are maximal when the best-of-the-run model is selected from the GP system as the solution. Our opinion is supported by the evidence in [16] which shows that symbolic regression performed with complexity control, interval arithmetic, and linear scaling still produces over-fitted best-error-of-the-run models that frequently have extrapolation pathologies.

Symbolic regression can handle dependent and correlated variables and automatically perform feature selection. It is capable of producing hundreds of candidate models that explain sparse data via diverse mathematical structure and parameters. But the combined information of these multiple models has been conventionally ignored. In our framework, we exploit rather than ignore them. During a typical run, GP symbolic regression explores numerous models.

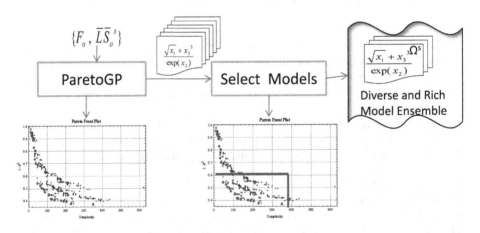

Fig. 3. Ensemble based symbolic regression

We capture the combined explanatory content of fitness-selected models, and pool *as many* explanations as we can from whatever *little data* we have.

An explicit implementation of this strategy, such as ParetoGP, must embed operators and evaluation methods into the GP algorithm to specifically aggregate a rich model set after combining multiple runs. The set will support deriving an ensemble of high-quality but diverse models. Within an ensemble, each model must approximate *all* training data samples well – *high quality*. As an ensemble, the models must collectively diverge in their predictions on unobserved data samples –*diverse*. If a GP symbolic regression system can yield a sufficient quantity of "strong learners" as its solution set, all of them can and should be used to determine both a prediction, and the ensemble disagreement (lack of confidence) at any arbitrary point of the original variable space. In contrast to boosting methods that are intended to improve the prediction accuracy through a combination of weak learners into an ensemble, this ensemble derivation process has the intent of improving prediction robustness and estimating reliability of predictions.

5.1   Model Set Generation

All experiments of this paper use the ParetoGP algorithm which has been specifically designed to meet the goals of ensemble modeling. Any other GP system designed for the same goals would suffice. ParetoGP consists of the tree-based GP with multi-objective model selection optimizing the trade-off between a model's training error and expressional complexity; an elite-preservation strategy (also known as archiving), interval arithmetic, linear scaling and Pareto tournaments for selecting crossover pairs. In each iteration of the algorithm, it tries to closely approximate the (true) Pareto curve trade-offs between accuracy and complexity. It supports a practical rule-of-thumb: "use as many independent GP runs as the computational budget allows", by providing an interface where only the budget has to be stated to control the length of a run. It also has explicit diversity preservation mechanisms and efficiently supports a sufficiently large population size. The training error used in experiments is $1 - R^2$, where R is a correlation coefficient of the scaled model prediction and the scaled observed response. The expressional complexity of models is defined as the total sum of nodes in all subtrees of the tree-based model genome. The following primitives are used for gp trees of maximal arity of four: $\{+, -, *, /, inverse, square, exp, ln\}$. Variables $x_1 - x_7$ corresponding to seven keys and constants from the range $[-5, 5]$ are used as terminals. ParetoGP is executed for 6 independent runs per panelist data before the models from runs are aggregated and combined. The population size equals 500, the archive size is 100. Crossover rate is 0.9, and sub-tree mutation rate is 0.1. ParetoGP collects all models on the Pareto front of each run and for information purposes identifies a "super" Pareto front from among them. All models move forward to ensemble selection. We now have to make a decision about which models will be used to form an ensemble.

5.2   Ensemble Model Selection

In [17], the authors describe an approach to selecting the models which form an ensemble: collect models that differ according to complexity, prediction accuracy and specific predictions. Complexity can be measured by examining some quantity associated with the GP expression tree or by considering how non-linear the expression is. Accuracy is the conventional error measure between actual and predicted observations. Specific predictions are considered to assess correlations and eliminate correlated models. Generally, each ensemble combines:

- A "box" of non-dominated and dominated models in the dual objective space of model prediction error and model complexity.
- A set of models with uncorrelated prediction errors on a designated test set of inputs. Here a model is selected based on a metric which expresses how its error vector correlates with other models' error vector. The correlation must not exceed a value of ρ. The input samples used to compute prediction errors can belong to the training set, test set (if available), or be arbitrarily sampled from the observed region.

The actual ρ and box thresholds for the ensemble selection depend on the problem domain's goals. For this knowledge mining framework, where the next step is to model a probability density function of a liking score, all plausible explanations of the data are desired to acknowledge the variation we expect to see in human preferences. The box thresholds are $accuracy = 0.5$ and $expressional$ $complexity < 400$. This generates models with sufficient generality (since we allowed accuracy as low as 0.5) and restricts any models with unreasonably high complexity with no obvious improvement in accuracy. We chose a value of $\rho = 0.92$ to weed out correlated models. A set of models selected after applying the criteria above is called the $ensemble$, Ω^s.

6   Modeling a Panelist's Propensity to Like

With methods that support refocusing GP based symbolic regression to derive a rich and diverse set of models and the methods [17] that select an ensemble, our GP system becomes a competent cornerstone in our knowledge mining framework. The framework can next use the ensemble, Ω^s designed for a panelist s to answer the question: "How likely is a panelist to answer with a liking score/rating higher than X?". The answer to this question allows us to categorize panelists as: (1) Easy to Please, (2) Hard to Please, (3) Neutral. We accomplish this by modeling the probability density function given by $p(LS|s)$ for a panelist s. To describe our methodology, we rely upon the notations in Table 1.

Density estimation poses a critical challenge in machine learning, especially with sparse data. Even if we assume that we have finite support for the density function and it is discrete, i.e. $LS = \{1, 2, ...8, 9\}$, we need sample sizes of the order of "$supra$-$polynomial$" in the cardinality of support [18]. In addition, if the decision variables are inter-dependent, as they are here, estimating a conditional distribution increases the computational complexity. Most of the research in density estimation has focused on identifying non-parametric methods to estimate distribution of the data. Research on estimation of density from very small sample sizes is limited [18,19].

Figure 4 presents the steps taken to form this liking score probability density model. We first generate 10,000 untested flavours We use the model ensemble Ω^s, which gives us a set of predictions $\overline{Y}^{s,b}$. For each untested flavour we get a set of predictions (*not just one*), which plausibly represents all possible liking scores the panelist would give. We use these to construct the *lsd*, liking score density function, for an individual panelist.

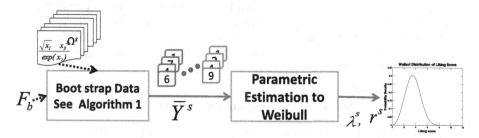

Fig. 4. Bootstrapping the Data and Deriving the Liking Score Probability Density Model

6.1 Deriving Predictions by Bootstrapping the Data

To generate the bootstrapped data of liking scores for the $F_B = \{\overline{k}^{(1)}......\overline{k}^{(10,000)}\}$ we follow the steps described in Algorithm 1.

Algorithm 1. Bootstrapping the LS data for Panelist s

Generate 10,000 flavours randomly, i.e., $F_b = \{\overline{k}^1....\overline{k}^{10,000}\}$ (we use a fixed uniform lattice in the experiments, same for all panelists)

for $(\overline{k}^b \in F_b \; \forall b)$ **do**

(i) Collect all the predictions from Model Ensemble, Ω^s: $\overline{Y}^{s,b}$

(ii) Sort the vector $\overline{Y}^{s,b}$

(iii) Remove the bottom and top 10% of $\overline{Y}^{s,b}$ and call this vector $\overline{R}^{s,j}$

(iv) Append $\overline{R}^{s,j}$ to $\overline{Y}^s$

end for

Fit the $\overline{Y}^s$ to a Weibull distribution. See Section 6.2

6.2 Parametric Estimation of the Liking Score Density Function

We use a parametric Weibull distribution to estimate $p(LS|s)$. The two parameters for the Weibull distribution, λ and r are called scale and shape respectively. A Weibull distribution is an adaptive distribution that can be made equivalent to

an Exponential, Gaussian or Rayleigh distributions as its shape and scale parameters are varied. For our problem this is a helpful capability as a panelist's liking
score follows any one of the three distributions. The derived Weibull distribution
is:

$$p(LS; \lambda, r|s) = \begin{cases} \frac{r}{\lambda}(\frac{LS}{\lambda})^{r-1}e^{-(\frac{LS}{\lambda})^r} & \text{if } LS \geq 0 \\ 0 & \text{if } LS < 0. \end{cases} \quad (1)$$

In addition to steps taken in Section 6.1, we map the bootstrapped data to a
range of the support of Weibull and the hedonic rating scale i.e., $[1, 9]$. There are
some predictions in the $\overline{Y}^s$ which are below 1 or are above 9. We remove 80% of
these predictions as outliers. We assign a liking score of 1 for the remaining 20%
of predictions that are less than '1' in the prediction set. We similarly assign
the liking score of '9' for the ones that are above 9. We use these 20% in $\overline{Y}^s$ to
capture the scores corresponding to the *"extremely dislike"* and *"extremely like"*
condition. Each plot line of Figures 6 (b), (c) and (d) is a *lsd*.

6.3   Clustering Panelists by Propensity to Like

Having estimated the data generated from the models for 10,000 flavours in $F_B = \{\overline{k}^{(1)}......\overline{k}^{(10,000)}\}$ using the methods described in Section 6.2, we can classify the
panelists into three different categories (see Figure 5). We divide the liking score
range $[1..9]$ into three regions as shown in Figure 6. The panelists are then
classified by identifying the region in which the majority (more than 50%) of
their probability mass lies (see Algorithm 2). This is accomplished by evaluating
the cumulative distribution in each of these regions using:

$$P_{(l_1, l_2]}(LS; \lambda, r|s) = e^{-(\frac{l_1}{\lambda})^r} - e^{-(\frac{l_2}{\lambda})^r}. \quad (2)$$

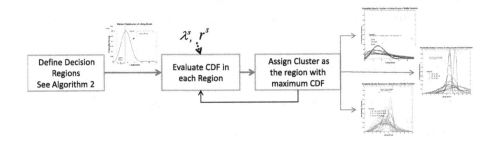

Fig. 5. Clustering the Panelists

6.4   Results on All Panelists

We applied our methodology to the dataset of 66 panelists who can be individually modeled with adequate accuracy. The first cluster is the "hard to please"

Algorithm 2. Clustering the Panelists

---

for $\forall s \in \{S\}$ **do**

  1. Calculate P_{l_1,l_2} using estimated (λ^s, r^s) for $(l_1, l_2] \rightarrow (1, 3.5]$, $(3.5, 6.5]$ and $(6.5, 9.5]$

  2. Assign the panelist s, to the cluster corresponding to the region where he/she has maximum cumulative density

  $s \leftarrow s + 1$

end for

---

panelists. We have 23 panelists in this cluster which is approximately 34.8% of the panel. These panelists have most of their liking scores concentrated between 1-3.5 range. We call these "hard-to-please" since low liking scores might imply that they are very choosy in their liking.

The second cluster is the cluster of "neutral panelists". These panelists rarely choose the liking scores which are *extremely like* or *extremely dislike*. For most of the sampled flavours they choose somewhere in between and hence the name *neutral*. There are 31 panelists in this cluster which is 47% of the total panel.

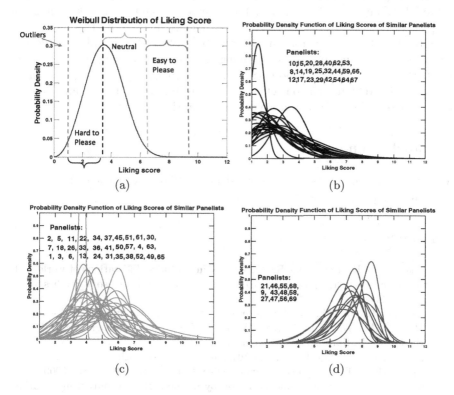

Fig. 6. Liking Score Density Models: (a)Decision regions for evaluating cumulative distribution, (b) Hard to please panelists (c) Neutral Panelists (d) Easy to Please Panelists

The final cluster of panelists is the "easy to please" panelists. This cluster of panelists reports a high liking for most of the flavours presented to them or may report moderate dislike of some. They rarely report "extremely dislike". There are 12 panelists in this cluster which is close to 18% of the total panel.

7 Conclusions and Future Work

This contribution described an ensemble-based symbolic regression approach for knowledge mining from a very small sample of survey measurements. It is only a first small step towards GP-driven flavour optimization and also demonstrates the effectiveness of GP for sparse data modeling. Our goal was to model behavior of panelists who rate flavours. Our methodology postpones decision making regarding a *model*, a *prediction*, and a *decision boundary* until the very end. In Step 1 ParetoGP generates a rich set of models consisting of the multiple plausible explanations for the data from multiple run aggregation of its best models. In Step 2 these are filtered into an efficient and capable ensemble and no valid ex planation is eliminated. In Step 3 *all* the models are consulted, and with minor trimming, their predictions are fit to a probability density function. Finally, in Step 4, when macro-level behaviour has emerged and more is known about the panelists, decision boundaries can be rationally imposed on this probability space to allow their segmentation. Our approach allowed us to robustly identify segments in the panel based on the liking preferences. We conjecture from our results that there are similar potential benefits across any sparse, repeated measure dataset. We will focus our efforts in the future on the theory and practice of efficient techniques for ensemble derivation in the context of GP.

Acknowledgements

We acknowledge funding support from Givaudan Flavors Corp. and thank Guido Smits and Mark Kotancheck.

References

1. Moskowitz, H.R., Bernstein, R.: Variability in hedonics: Indications of world-wide sensory and cognitive preference segmentation. Journal of Sensory Studies 15(3), 263–284 (2000)
2. Smits, G., Kotanchek, M.: Pareto-front exploitation in symbolic regression. In: O'Reilly, U.M., Yu, T., Riolo, R.L., Worzel, B. (eds.) Genetic Programming Theory and Practice II. Springer, Ann Arbor (2004)
3. Liu, Y., Yao, X., Higuchi, T.: Evolutionary ensembles with negative correlation learning. IEEE Transactions on Evolutionary Computation 4(4), 380 (2000)
4. Liu, Y., Yao, X.: Learning and evolution by minimization of mutual information. In: Guervós, J.J.M., Adamidis, P.A., Beyer, H.-G., Fernández-Villacañas, J.-L., Schwefel, H.-P. (eds.) PPSN 2002. LNCS, vol. 2439, pp. 495–504. Springer, Heidelberg (2002)

5. Hansen, L.K., Salamon, P.: Neural network ensembles. IEEE Trans. Pattern Anal. Mach. Intell. 12(10), 993–1001 (1990)
6. Wolpert, D.H.: Stacked generalization. Neural Networks 5(2), 241–259 (1992)
7. Krogh, A., Vedelsby, J.: Neural network ensembles, cross validation, and active learning. In: Tesauro, G., Touretzky, D., Leen, T. (eds.) Advances in Neural Information Processing Systems, vol. 7, pp. 231–238. The MIT Press, Cambridge (1995)
8. Paris, G., Robilliard, D., Fonlupt, C.: Applying boosting techniques to genetic programming. In: Collet, P., Fonlupt, C., Hao, J.-K., Lutton, E., Schoenauer, M. (eds.) EA 2001. LNCS, vol. 2310, pp. 267–278. Springer, Heidelberg (2002)
9. Iba, H.: Bagging, boosting, and bloating in genetic programming. In: Banzhaf, W., Daida, J., Eiben, A.E., Garzon, M.H., Honavar, V., Jakiela, M., Smith, R.E. (eds.) Proceedings of the Genetic and Evolutionary Computation Conference, Orlando, Florida, USA, vol. 2, pp. 1053–1060. Morgan Kaufmann, San Francisco (1999)
10. Schapire, R.E.: The strength of weak learnability. Machine Learning 5(2), 197–227 (1990)
11. Freund, Y., Seung, H.S., Shamir, E., Tishby, N.: Information, prediction, and query by committee. In: Advances in Neural Information Processing Systems [NIPS Conference], vol. 5, pp. 483–490. Morgan Kaufmann Publishers Inc., San Francisco (1993)
12. Sun, P., Yao, X.: Boosting kernel models for regression. In: ICDM 2006: Proceedings of the Sixth International Conference on Data Mining, Washington, DC, USA, pp. 583–591. IEEE Computer Society, Los Alamitos (2006)
13. Freund, Y.: Boosting a weak learning algorithm by majority. Inf. Comput. 121(2), 256–285 (1995)
14. Folino, G., Pizzuti, C., Spezzano, G.: GP ensembles for large-scale data classification. IEEE Trans. Evolutionary Computation 10(5), 604–616 (2006)
15. Vladislavleva, E.: Model-based Problem Solving through Symbolic Regression via Pareto Genetic Programming. PhD thesis, Tilburg University, Tilburg, the Netherlands (2008)
16. Vladislavleva, E.J., Smits, G.F., den Hertog, D.: Order of nonlinearity as a complexity measure for models generated by symbolic regression via pareto genetic programming. IEEE Transactions on Evolutionary Computation 13(2), 333–349 (2009)
17. Kotanchek, M., Smits, G., Vladislavleva, E.: Trustable symoblic regression models. In: Riolo, R.L., Soule, T., Worzel, B. (eds.) Genetic Programming Theory and Practice V. Genetic and Evolutionary Computation, pp. 203–222. Springer, Ann Arbor (2007)
18. Taylor, J.S., Dolia, A.: A framework for probability density estimation. In: Lawrence, N. (ed.) Proceedings of the Eleventh International Conference on Artificial Intelligence and Statistics, Journal of Machine Learning Research, 468–475 (2007)
19. Mukherjee, S., Vapnik, V.: Multivariate density estimation: a support vector machine approach. In: NIPS, vol. 12. Morgan Kaufmann Publishers, San Francisco (1999)

Genetic Programming for Auction Based Scheduling

Mohamed Bader-El-Den and Shaheen Fatima

Department of Computer Science, Loughborough University,
Loughborough LE11 3TU, UK
{M.B.Bader-El-Den,S.S.Fatima}@lboro.ac.uk

Abstract. In this paper, we present a genetic programming (GP) framework for evolving agent's binding function (GPAuc) in a resource allocation problem. The framework is tested on the exam timetabling problem (ETP). There is a set of exams, which have to be assigned to a predefined set of slots and rooms. Here, the exam time tabling system is the seller that auctions a set of slots. The exams are viewed as the bidding agents in need of slots. The problem is then to find a schedule (i.e., a slot for each exam) such that the total cost of conducting the exams as per the schedule is minimised. In order to arrive at such a schedule, we need to find the bidders optimal bids. This is done using genetic programming. The effectiveness of GPAuc is demonstrated experimentally by comparing it with some existing benchmarks for exam timetabling.

1 Introduction

Decentralised scheduling is the problem of allocating resources to alternative possible uses over time, where competing uses are represented by autonomous agents. This scheduling can be done using different methods such as such as first-come first-served, priority-first, and combinations thereof. But, these methods do not generally possess globally efficient solutions. Due to this limitation, considerable research is now focussing on the use of market mechanisms for distributed resource allocation problems [16]. Market mechanisms use prices derived through distributing bidding protocols, such as *auctions*, to determine schedules.

In an auction, there are two types of agents: the *auctioneer* and the *bidders*. The auctioneer could be a seller of a resource and the bidders are buyers that are in need of the resource. The bidders bid for the resource being auctioned and one of them is selected as the *winner*. An agent's bid, in general, indicates the price it is willing to pay to buy the resource. On the basis of the agent's bids, the resource is allocated to the winning agent. The auction *protocol* determines the rules for bidding and also for selecting a winner. There are several protocols such as the *English auction*, the *Dutch auction*, and the *Vickrey* auction protocol [16].

Given an auction protocol, a key problem for the bidders is to find an *optimal bidding function* for the protocol [16]. An agent's bidding function is a mapping from its *valuation* or *utility* or *preference* (for the resource being auctioned) to a *bid*. An agent's valuation is a real number and so is its bid. Since there are several agents bidding for a single resource, an agent must decide how much to bid so that its chance of winning is maximised and the price at which it wins is minimised. Such a bid is called the agent's

A.I. Esparcia-Alcazar et al. (Eds.): EuroGP 2010, LNCS 6021, pp. 256–267, 2010.

optimal bid. An agent's optimal bidding function is then the function that takes the valuation as input and returns its optimal bid.

For a single auction, finding an agent's optimal bidding function is easy. But in the context of the distributed scheduling problem we focus on, there are several auctions that are held sequentially one after another [13]. Furthermore, an agent may need more than one resource and must therefore bid in several auctions. In such cases, an agent's bidding function depends on several parameters such as how many auctions will be held, how many bidders will bid in each of these auctions, and how much the agent and the other bidders value the different resources. This complicates the problem of finding optimal bids. In order to overcome this problem, our objective is to use GP to evolve bidding functions.

We study the distributed scheduling problem in the context of the famous *exam time tabling problem* (ETTP) [8]. The ETTP can be viewed as a decentralised scheduling problem where the exams represent independent entities (users) in need of resources (slots) with possibly conflicting and competing schedule requirements. The problem is then to assign exams to slots (i.e., find a schedule) such that the total cost of conducting the exams as per the schedule is minimised.

Genetic Programming (GP) [15,17,19] is a biologically-inspired search method within the field of Evolutionary Algorithms. These algorithms incorporate some elements of Darwinian evolution in order to discover solutions to difficult problems. This is achieved by evolving a population of individuals, each representing a possible solution. What distinguishes GP from other EA methods is that GP specialises in the discovery of executable computer programs. As mentioned before, one of the key problems in auctions is the design of optimal bidding functions. An agent's bidding function depends on a number of parameters such as the agent's valuation for the resource, the other bidders' valuations for it (it is not always that such information is available), and information regarding related previous auctions. When an auction begins, the agents have little information about these parameters, but as the auction progresses, new information becomes available to the bidders. Thus a key problem for a bidder is to learn this new information and adapt its bidding function accordingly. Given this, the objective of this f is to automate the formulation of optimal bidding functions through the use of genetic programming.

2 The Exam Timetabling Problem

The exam timetabling problem is a common combinatorial optimisation problem which all educational institutions need to face. Although the problem's details tend to vary from one institution to another, the core of the problem is the same: there is a set of exams (tasks), which have to be assigned to a predefined set of slots and rooms (resources).

2.1 Formal Statement of the Problem

We use the following formulation for the exam timetabling problem. The problem consists of a set of n exams $E = \{e_1, \ldots e_n\}$, a set of m students $S = \{s_1, \ldots s_m\}$, a set of q

time slots $P = \{p_1, p_2, \ldots p_q\}$ and a registration function $R : S \to E$, indicating which student is attending which exam. Seen as a set, $R = \{(s_i, e_j) : 1 \leq i \leq m, 1 \leq j \leq n\}$, where student s_i is attending exam e_j. A scheduling algorithm assigns each exam to a certain slot. A solution then has the form $O : E \to P$ or, as a set, $O = \{(e_k, p_l) : 1 \leq k \leq n, 1 \leq l \leq q\}$.

The problem is similar to the graph colouring problem but it includes extra constraints, as shown in [24] (more on this later).

2.2 Timetabling Constraints

Constraints are categorised into two main types:

Hard Constraints: Violating any of these constraints is not permitted since it would lead to an unfeasible solution.

Soft Constraints: These are desirable but not crucial requirements. Violating any of the soft constraints will only affect the solution's quality.

All hard constraints are equally important, while the importance of soft constraints can vary. Most constraints relate to the main entities of the problem: students, exams, rooms and slots.

There is no clear-cut distinction between soft and hard constraints: a constraint that is soft for one institution could be considered hard by another. For example, the constraint that students cannot attend two exams in the same slot is hard for most institutions. However, some other institutions may accept violations of this if only few students are affected, because a special exam session can be set up for those students. Also, an institution with a large number of rooms and a large number of staff relative to the number of students may not care much about the number of exam that could take place in parallel at the same time. On the other hand, a small institution with a limited number of rooms or staff in relation to the student population may give this constraint a much greater importance.

2.3 Cost Functions

Usually a cost function is used to calculate the degree of undesirability of violating each of the soft constraints. This is particularly convenient because, in most cases, changing soft constraint combinations and the importance (weight) of constraints does not require modifications in the timetabling algorithm itself. Only updating the cost function that evaluates the quality of solutions is required.

The following simple function was used in [8] to evaluate the cost of constraint violations:

$$C(t) = \frac{1}{S} \sum_{i=1}^{N-1} \sum_{j=i+1}^{N} [w(|p_i - p_j|)a_{ij}] \tag{1}$$

where N is the total number of exams in the problem, S the total number of students, a_{ij} is the number of students attending both exams i and j, p_i is the time slot where exam i

is scheduled, $w(|p_i - p_j|)$ returns $2^{5-|p_i-p_j|}$ if $|p_i - p_j| \leq 5$, and 0 otherwise.[1] We will adopt this cost function in this work. Of course, solutions with a lower cost are more desirable.

2.4 Related Work

Many different techniques have been used to tackle the timetabling problem. These include: constraint-based methods, graph-based methods, population-based methods, hyper-heuristics, multi-criteria optimisation and techniques based on local search. For space limitations in this section we will focus only on evolutionary based algorithms.

Genetic algorithm (GA) is one of the most frequently used and successful evolutionary algorithms in the area of timetabling. In general, there are two ways of using GAs for timetabling. In the first approach, the GA works directly in the solution space, i.e., each chromosome represents a timetable. One important issue in this approach is how to represent a timetable. Different techniques have been investigated through the years: a recent survey can be found in [22] (which an updated version of [9]). In the second approach, the GA works as a hyper-heuristic framework, i.e., the chromosome represents a sequence of heuristics to be applied for finding solutions rather than simply representing a solution. In most cases the length of the chromosome string is equal to the number of events to be scheduled and each heuristic in the string indicates how the corresponding event should be scheduled. This approach could also be seen as a memetic algorithm. In the remainder of this section we will survey techniques based on the first approach, while the second approach will be further discussed in the next section, alongside other hyper-heuristic techniques.

An investigation on the use of GAs in timetabling was presented in [20], where the differences in the performance of different algorithms around phase-transition regions were studied. The work showed that some simple evolutionary algorithms could outperform hill-climbing-based algorithms in regions associated with certain phase transitions, but not others. A continuation of this study was presented in [21]. This showed that using a direct mapping in a GA for timetabling is not a very good approach. The study highlighted the failure of a number of algorithms, including GAs, in solving some moderately constrained instances, while GAs were able to solve all the lightly and heavily constrained instances.

In [12], a GA representation based on the grouping character of the graph colouring problem was presented. The fitness function used to guide this Grouping GA was defined on the set of partitions of vertices. The algorithm was applied to a set of hard-to-colour graph examples and some real-world timetabling problems. Results were not very competitive with state of the art heuristics. However, the algorithm required much less computation power than other similar methods.

A GA was used in [23]. This was based on a new encoding system, called Linear Linkage Encoding (LLE) [11], which differs from the traditional Number Encoding

---

[1] This means that in the most undesirable situation, i.e., when a student has two exams scheduled one after the other, i will increase the cost function by a large value, namely $2^{5-1} = 16$. This factor rapidly decreases (following a negative exponential profile) as the size of the gap between exams increases.

system for graphs. The authors developed special operators to suit the new LLE encoding. Results showed that LLE is promising for grouping problems such as graph colouring and timetabling.

A hybrid multi-objective evolutionary algorithm was presented in [10]. The framework was used to tackle the uncapacitated exam proximity problem. Traditional genetic operators were replaced by local-search ones, based on a simplified variable neighbourhood descent metaheuristic. A repair operator was introduced to deal with unfeasible timetables. The framework did not require tuning across a number of test cases.

Genetic programming have been widely used in evolving strategies and heuristics. GP been used to evolve Boolean satisfiability heuristics [14,3] and specialised one-dimensional bin packing heuristics [4,5]. Also, in [18] a grammar-based genetic programming system was used to evolve multi-objective induction rules, which could be used in the classification of any data sets.

3   Auction Based Multi-agent for Timetabling

In this section we introduce an auction based multi-agent framework for the ETB problem (GPAuc). In GPAuc, the seller is the exam time tabling system (ETTS) and it auctions the slots one at a time. The exams are the bidders. Every slot could be sold more than once (because one slot could contain more than one non-conflicting exams), but in each auction the slot could be sold only for one exam. Each auction is slightly modified version of the Vickrey auction, which is a type of sealed-bid auction, where bidders submit their bids in "closed envelop" without knowing the bid of the other people in the auction. The highest bidder wins, which is not exactly the case in GPAuc as it will be shown shortly.

The slots are auctioned in a round robin order, in each auction, the slot is sold for no more than one exam, the system keeps looping on all slots till all exams are allocated slots, or until a deadlock is reached (where no more exams could be scheduled without violating a hard constraint). For a GPAuc auction, the winning bid is determined as follows. If the highest bid does not increase the solution's cost[2] beyond a certain limit *AcceptedCost*, the highest bid becomes the winning bid. Otherwise, the same rule is applied to the second highest bid. If the second highest bid causes the cost to increase beyond the Accepted-Cost, the slot is left unsold and the next auction is initiated for the following slot. If no slots have been sold in full round on all available slot, in this case the *Accepted-Cost* are increased. This process is repeated till all exams are scheduled, or reaching a deadlock. A general pseudocode of the algorithm is shown in Algorithm 1.

3.1   Optimisation via Genetic Programming

GP [15,17,19] is an evolutionary algorithm which is inspired by biological evolution. The target of a GP system is to find computer programs that perform a user-defined task. It is a specialisation of genetic algorithms where each individual is a computer program. GP is a machine learning technique used to optimise a population of computer programs

---

[2] An increase of the solution's cost is caused, if allocating the exam to the auctioned slots will violates a one or more of the soft constraints, as shown in the previous section.

Algorithm 1. Algorithm overview

1: $AcceptedCost \leftarrow 0$ {AcceptedCost, is initially 0, this increases if there is a full round and no
    slots have been sold }
2: $RemainingExams \leftarrow NumberOfAllExam$
3: $Deadlock \leftarrow false$
4: **while** $(AvailableExams > 0)$ and $(Deadlock = false)$ **do**
5:     {keep going while there are still exams to schedule}
6:     $ExamSoldLastRound \leftarrow false$
7:     **for** $i \leftarrow 1$ to $NumberOfSlots$ **do**
8:         {start of new round}
9:         Offer slot i for sale
10:        collect bids from exams for slot i
11:        **if** $CostHighestBid \leq AcceptedCost$ **then**
12:
13:            Assign the Exam with the $HighestBid$ to slot i to
14:            $RemainingExams - -$
15:            $ExamSoldLastRound \leftarrow true$
16:            InformExams() {This function informs the exams about the new schedule so they
                can know the available slots and so on, any exam with zero available slots will raise
                the $Deadlock$ flag }
17:        **else if** $CostSecondHighestBid \leq AcceptedCost$ **then**
18:            {otherwise, check the second highest bid exam}
19:            Assign the Exam with the $SecondHighestBid$ to slot i to
20:            $RemainingExams - -$
21:            $ExamSoldLastRound \leftarrow true$
22:        **else**
23:            Do not sell exam i now
24:        **end if**
25:    **end for**
26:    **if** $ExamSoldLastRound = false$ **then**
27:        increase $AcceptedCost$ {if one round finished without assigning any exams to any slots
            increase the accepted rate}
28:    **end if**
29: **end while**

---

depending on a fitness function that measures the program's performance on a given
task. Tree presentation of the individuals is the most common presentation which also
we will be using here. GP applies a number of operators such as crossover, mutation
and reproduction to transform the current populations of programs into new, hopefully
better, populations of programs.

– Crossover: Given two parents (in a tree presentation), a random point is selected
  in each parent tree. Then, offspring are created by replacing the sub-tree rooted at
  the crossover point in one of the parents a copy of the sub-tree rooted at the second
  crossover point.
– Mutation: one of the most used form of mutation in GP is the following, Given one
  parents (in a tree presentation), a random point is selected in this parent, the tree
  rooted by this point is then deleted and another new sub-tree is created.

Table 1. GP function and terminal sets

Function Set	Terminal Set
$add(d_1, d_2)$: returns the sum of d_1 and d_2	slt : total number of available slots for the currently bidding exam e
$sub(d_1, d_2)$: subtracts d_2 from d_1	std : the total number of students attending the bidding exam e
$mul(d_1, d_2)$: returns the multiplication of d_1 by d_2	$conf$: the total number of all exams (scheduled and not scheduled yes) in conflict with exam e
$div(d_1, d_2)$: protected division of d_1 by d_2	$cSched$: number of already scheduled exams till now that are in conflict with e
$abs(d_1)$: returns the absolute value of d_1	$cPendd$: number of not scheduled exams that are in conflict with e
$neg(d_1)$: multiplies d_1 by -1	$cost$: current increase in the cost if e to current slot
$fneg(d_1)$: $abs(d_1)$ multiplied by -1, to force negative value	
$sqrt(d_1)$: returns the a protected square root of d_1	

The GP's function and terminal sets are shown in Table 1, the terminal set parameters are inspired by a number of graph-coloring heuristic which have been used in exam timetabling [8], which are the following:

- Largest Degree first (LD): Two exams are considered to be in conflict with each other if they cannot be scheduled in the same slot. In this study we consider two exams conflicting if they have one or more students registered in both exams. LD of exam x is total number exams in conflict with x, in general one can say that exams with high LD are more difficult to schedule than exams with lower LD value, so it is preferred to schedule exams with high LD first.
- Largest Enrolment first (LE): In our case, LE depends on the number of student registered in exam x, in general, the more students the more the exam is expecting to bid for a slot.
- least Saturation Degree first (SD): Most important one. selects exams with least number of available slots to schedule first. This is the only heuristic that entails updating. That is, assigning an exam to a slot will make this slot unavailable for all other slots in conflict with this exam and the count of their available slots will be decreased by one.
- Largest Weighted Degree first (LWD): is the same as the LD heuristic but if there is more than one exam with the same number of conflicts, the tie is broken in favour of the exam with more students.

Table 2. Characteristics of benchmark exam timetabling problems we are using. For each case we show: total number of exams, number of students registered in at least one exam, maximum number of slots available, maximum number of students registered in one exams, maximum number of exams registered by one student and matrix density.

Name	Exams	Std.	Slots	Max. S. Reg.	Max. E. Reg.	Matrix Density
car91	682	16925	35	1385	9	0.128
car92	543	18419	32	1566	7	0.138
ear83	190	1125	24	232	10	0.267
hec92	81	2823	18	634	7	0.421
kfu93	461	5349	20	1280	8	0.055
lse91	381	2726	18	382	8	0.063
sta83	139	611	13	237	11	0.144
tre92	261	4360	23	407	6	0.181
uta93	184	21266	35	1314	7	0.126
york83	181	941	21	175	14	0.289

Fitness Function. The fitness function we used is the following:

$$f(inv_i) = [\frac{1}{S} \sum_{i=1}^{M-1} \sum_{j=i+1}^{M} w(|p_i - p_j|)a_{ij}] + (N - M) \times C \qquad (2)$$

where: N is the total number of exams in the problem, M is the total number of exams that have been successfully scheduled, $(N - M) \geq 0$ is the number of unscheduled exams, C is constant. The objective is to minimise this equation, so the lower the fitness value the better the individual is.

The first part of the fitness function in Equation (2) is almost the same as the cost function (1). The second part adds extra penalty for each exam the heuristic (individual) has not been able to schedule. Even though solutions with unscheduled exams are considered to be invalid solutions, this extra penalty for unscheduled exams is introduced to give GP better ability to differentiate between individuals.

3.2   Experimental Results

We tested our method for timetabling by applying it to one of the most widely used benchmarks in exam timetabling, against which many state-of-the-art algorithms have been compared in the past. The benchmark was first presented in [8]. Its characteristics are shown in Table 2. The size of the problems varies from 81 to 682 exams and from 611 to 18419 students. In Table 2 Max. S. Reg. is the maximum number of students registered in one exam; Max. E. Reg. is the maximum number of exams registered by one student; matrix density is the density of the conflict matrix, which is given by the ratio of the number of conflicting exams over the total number of all possible pair exam combinations.

We did run a number of experiments using different GP parameters, with population size varying between 50 to 1000, number of generations range between 50 and 100, the

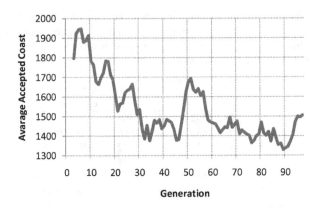

Fig. 1. The average value of the final *Accepted cost* of the best evolved functions

reproduction and mutation rate is 5% or 10% of the total population, and 80% for the crossover rate. The selection is done using tournament selection of 5.

Tables 3 shows the cost (using equation number (1)) of the GPAuc compared to a number of other construction techniques, as it could be noticed the GPAuc is very competitive with other methods taking in consideration that GPAuc does not use back-tracking. Moreover, GPAuc is as distributed methods and that all bidding functions are automatically evolved without human interaction.

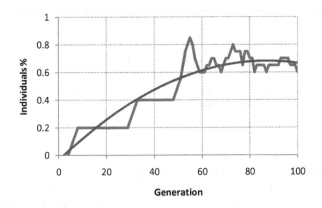

Fig. 2. Percentage of individuals that have been able to schedule all exams in the best evolved function

Figures 1, 2, 3 and 4 provide some analysis into the behaviour of the best performing individuals throughout the generations. These graphs are drawn from evolving bidding functions on the York83 instance, with population size 500, number of generations 100, mutation and reproduction rate 10% and crossover rate of 90%.

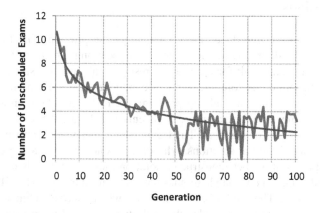

Fig. 3. Average number of remaining exams in all best behaving individuals

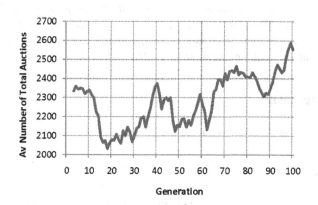

Fig. 4. Average number of all auction taking place in best performing heuristics through out all the generations

Table 3. Initial Experimental Results

	car91	car92	ear83	hec92	kfu93	lse91	sta83	tre92	uta93	york83
GPAuc	7.03	5.80	41.2	13,01	15.90	13.01	157.3	9.32	3.82	45.60
Asmuni et al [1]	5.20	4.52	37.02	11.78	15.81	12.09	160.42	8.67	3.57	40.66
Bader-El-Den et al [2]	5.12	4.15	37.20	11.96	14.54	11.17	158.63	8.63	3.43	40.05
Burke et al [6]	5.41	4.84	38.19	12.72	15.76	13.15	141.08	8.85	3.88	40.13
Carter et al [8]	7.10	6.20	36.40	10.80	14.00	10.50	161.50	9.60	3.50	41.70
Multi-stage [6]	5.41	4.84	38.84	13.11	15.99	13.43	142.19	9.2	4.04	44.51

4 Conclusions

In this paper we have introduced the GPAuc a genetic programming framework for evolving agent's binding function in an resource allocation problem, GPAuc is the first phase of general framework for multi-agent resource allocation system, which is designed to construct initials solutions through conducting auction. The framework was customised for the exam time tabling problem, the ETP could be seen as a resource allocation problem where the exams are the agents and slot are the resources.

The GPAuc is a part of a general The framework consists of two main phases, construction for building initial solutions, while the second phase is concerned with improving the quality of the bets constructed solution (here we will only discuss the first phase in details). Graph coloring heuristics have been used to guide the GP in evolving the bidding function. The framework is tested on a widely used benchmarks in the field of exam time-tabling and compared with highly-tuned state-of-the-art approaches. Results shows that the framework is very competitive with other constructive techniques, and have been able to outperform some methods for constructing exam timetables. As it could be seen, the results are not the best among all other frameworks, and this for two main reason, in the GPAuc no backtracking is used, the second which is more important that the GPAuc is considered as a more distributed approach and that the bidding functions are automatically generated using GP.

Acknowledgements

This research was undertaken as part of the EPSRC (EP/G000980/1) project.

References

1. Asmuni, H., Burke, E.K., Garibaldi, J.M., McCollum, B.: Fuzzy multiple heuristic orderings for examination timetabling. In: Burke, Trick [7], pp. 334–353
2. Bader-El-Den, M., Poli, R., Fatima, S.: Evolving timetabling heuristics using a grammar-based genetic programming hyper-heuristic framework. Memetic Computing 1, 205–219 (2009)
3. Bader-El-Den, M.B., Poli, R.: Generating sat local-search heuristics using a gp hyper-heuristic framework. In: Monmarché, N., Talbi, E.-G., Collet, P., Schoenauer, M., Lutton, E. (eds.) EA 2007. LNCS, vol. 4926, pp. 37–49. Springer, Heidelberg (2008)
4. Burke, E.K., Hyde, M.R., Kendall, G.: Evolving bin packing heuristics with genetic programming. In: Runarsson, T.P., Beyer, H.-G., Burke, E.K., Merelo-Guervós, J.J., Whitley, L.D., Yao, X. (eds.) PPSN 2006. LNCS, vol. 4193, pp. 860–869. Springer, Heidelberg (2006)
5. Burke, E.K., Hyde, M.R., Kendall, G., Woodward, J.: Automatic heuristic generation with genetic programming: evolving a jack-of-all-trades or a master of one. In: GECCO 2007: Proceedings of the 9th annual conference on Genetic and evolutionary computation, pp. 1559–1565. ACM, New York (2007)
6. Burke, E.K., McCollum, B., Meisels, A., Petrovic, S., Qu, R.: A graph-based hyper-heuristic for educational timetabling problems. European Journal of Operational Research 176(1), 177–192 (2007)
7. Burke, E.K., Trick, M.A. (eds.): PATAT 2004. LNCS, vol. 3616. Springer, Heidelberg (2005)

8. Carter, M.W., Laporte, G., Lee, S.Y.: Examination timetabling: Algorithmic strategies and. Journal of Operational Research Society 47, 73–83 (1996)
9. Corne, D., Ross, P., Ian Fang, H.: Evolutionary timetabling: practice, prospects and work in progress. In: Proceedings of the UK Planning and Scheduling SIG Workshop, Strathclyde (1994)
10. Côté, P., Wong, T., Sabourin, R.: A hybrid multi-objective evolutionary algorithm for the uncapacitated exam proximity problem. In: Burke, Trick [7], pp. 294–312
11. Du, J., Korkmaz, E., Alhajj, R., Barker, K.: Novel clustering approach that employs genetic algorithm with new representation scheme and multiple objectives. In: Kambayashi, Y., Mohania, M., Wöß, W. (eds.) DaWaK 2004. LNCS, vol. 3181, pp. 219–228. Springer, Heidelberg (2004)
12. Erben, W.: A grouping genetic algorithm for graph colouring and exam timetabling. In: Burke, E., Erben, W. (eds.) PATAT 2000. LNCS, vol. 2079, pp. 132–158. Springer, Heidelberg (2001)
13. Fatima, S.S.: Bidding strategies for multi-object auctions. In: Negotiation, Auctions and Market Engineering. LNBIP, vol. 2, pp. 200–212. Springer, Heidelberg (2008)
14. Fukunaga, A.S.: Automated discovery of composite sat variable-selection heuristics. In: Eighteenth national conference on Artificial intelligence, Menlo Park, CA, USA. American Association for Artificial Intelligence, pp. 641–648 (2002)
15. Koza, J.R.: Genetic Programming: On the Programming of Computers by Means of Natural Selection. MIT Press, Cambridge (1992)
16. Krishna, V.: Auction Theory. Academic Press, London (2002)
17. Langdon, W.B., Poli, R.: Foundations of Genetic Programming. Springer, Heidelberg (2002)
18. Pappa, G., Freitas, A.: Evolving rule induction algorithms with multi-objective grammar-based genetic programming. Knowledge and information systems 19(3), 283–309 (2009)
19. Poli, R., Langdon, W.B., McPhee, N.F.: A field guide to genetic programming (2008) (With contributions by J. R. Koza) Published via, http://lulu.com and freely available at, http://www.gp-field-guide.org.uk
20. Ross, P., Corne, D., Terashima-Marín, H.: The phase-transition niche for evolutionary algorithms in timetabling. In: Selected papers from the First International Conference on Practice and Theory of Automated Timetabling, London, UK, pp. 309–324. Springer, Heidelberg (1996)
21. Ross, P., Hart, E., Corne, D.: Some observations about ga-based exam timetabling. In: Burke, E.K., Carter, M. (eds.) PATAT 1997. LNCS, vol. 1408, pp. 115–129. Springer, Heidelberg (1998)
22. Ross, P., Hart, E., Corne, D.: Genetic algorithms and timetabling, pp. 755–771. Springer-Verlag New York Inc., New York (2003)
23. Ülker, Ö., Özcan, E., Korkmaz, E.E.: Linear linkage encoding in grouping problems: Applications on graph coloring and timetabling. In: Burke, E.K., Rudová, H. (eds.) PATAT 2007. LNCS, vol. 3867, pp. 347–363. Springer, Heidelberg (2007)
24. Welsh, D., Powell, M.: An upper bound for the chromatic number of a graph and its application to timetabling problems. The Computer Journal 10(1), 85–87 (1967)

Bandit-Based Genetic Programming

Jean-Baptiste Hoock and Olivier Teytaud

TAO (Inria), LRI, UMR 8623(CNRS - Univ. Paris-Sud),
bat 490 Univ. Paris-Sud 91405 Orsay, France
hoock@lri.fr

Abstract. We consider the validation of randomly generated patterns in a Monte-Carlo Tree Search program. Our bandit-based genetic programming (BGP) algorithm, with proved mathematical properties, outperformed a highly optimized handcrafted module of a well-known computer-Go program with several world records in the game of Go.

1 Introduction

Genetic Programming (GP) is the automatic building of programs for solving a given task. In this paper, we investigate a bandit-based approach for selecting fruitful modifications in genetic programming, and we apply the result to our program MoGo.

When testing a large number of modifications in a stochastic algorithm with limited ressources in an uncertain framework, there are two issues:

- which modifications are to be tested now ?
- when we have no more resources (typically no more time), we must decide which modifications are accepted.

The second issue is often addressed through statistical tests. However, when many modifications are tested, it is a problem of multiple simultaneous hypothesis testing: this is far from being straightforward; historically, this was poorly handled in many old applications. Cournot stated that if we consider a significance threshold of 1% for differences between two sub-populations of a population, then, if we handcraft plenty of splittings in two sub-populations, we will after a finite time find a significant difference, whenever the two populations are similar. This was not for genetic programming, but the same thing holds in GP: if we consider 100 random mutations of a program, all of them being worst than the original program, and if we have a 1% risk threshold in the statistical validation of each of them, then with probability $(1 - 1/100))^{100} \simeq 37\%$ we can have a positive validation of at least one harmful mutation. Cournot concluded, in the 19th century, that this effect was beyond mathematical analysis; nonetheless this effect is clearly understood today, with the theory of multiple hypothesis testing - papers cited below clearly show that mathematics can address this problem.

The first issue is also non trivial, but a wide literature has been devoted to it: so-called bandit algorithms. This is in particular efficient when no prior information on the modifications is available, and we can only evaluate the quality of a modification through statistical results.

A.I. Esparcia-Alcazar et al. (Eds.): EuroGP 2010, LNCS 6021, pp. 268–277, 2010.

Usually the principles of a Bernstein race are as follows:

- decide a risk threshold δ_0;
- then, modify the parameters of all statistical tests so that all confidence intervals are *simultaneously* true with probability $\geq 1 - \delta_0$;
- then, as long as you have computational resources, apply a *bandit* algorithm for choosing which modification to test, depending on statistics; typically, a bandit algorithm will choose to spend computational resources on the modification which has the best statistical upper bound on its average efficiency;
- at the end, select the modifications which are significant.

A main reference, with theoretical justifications, is [22]. A main difference here is that we will not assume that all modifications are cumulative: here, whenever two modifications A and B are statistically good, we can't select both modifications - maybe, the baseline + A + B will be worse than the baseline, whenever both baseline+A and baseline+B are better than the baseline.

In section 2, we present non-asymptotic confidence bounds. In section 3 we present racing algorithms. Then, section 4 presents our algorithm and its theoretical analysis. Section 5 is devoted to experiments.

2   Non-asymptotic Confidence Bounds

In all the paper, we consider fitness values between 0 and 1 for simplifying the writing. The most classical bound is Hoeffding's bound. Hoeffding's bound states that with probability at least $1 - \delta$, the empirical average $\hat{r}$ verifies $|\hat{r} - \mathbb{E}r| \leq deviation_{\text{Hoeffding}}(\delta, n)$ where n is the number of simulations and where

$$deviation_{\text{Hoeffding}}(\delta, n) = \sqrt{\log(2/\delta)/n}. \tag{1}$$

[1,22] has shown the efficiency of using Bernstein's bound instead of Hoeffding's bound, in some settings. The bound is then $deviation_{\text{Bernstein}} = \hat{\sigma}\sqrt{2\log(3/\delta)/n} + 3\log(3/\delta)/n$, where $\hat{\sigma}$ is the empirical standard deviation. Bernstein's version will not be used in our experiments, because the variance is not small in our case; nonetheless, all theoretical results also hold with Bernstein's variant.

3   Racing Algorithms

Racing algorithms are typically (and roughly, we'll be more formal below) as follows:

Let S be equal to S_0, some given set of admissible modifications.
while $S \neq \emptyset$ **do**
    Select $s = select() \in S$ with some algorithm
    Perform one Monte-Carlo evaluation of s.
    if s is statistically worse than the baseline **then**
        $S \leftarrow S \setminus \{s\}$ // s is discarded

else if s is statistically better than the baseline **then**
  Accept s; $S \leftarrow S \setminus \{s\}$ s is accepted
end if
end while

With relevant statistical tests, we can ensure that this algorithm will select all "good" modifications (to be formalized later), reject all bad modifications, and stop after a finite time if all modifications have a non-zero effect. We refer to [22] for more general informations on this, or [18,15] for the GP case; we will here focus on the most relevant (relevant for our purpose) case. In genetic programming, it's very clear that even if two modifications are, independently, good, the combination of these two modifications is not necessarily good. We will therefore provide a different algorithm in section 4 with a proof of consistency.

4   Theoretical Analysis for Genetic Programming

We will assume here that for a modification s, we can define:

- $e(s)$, the (of course unknown) expected value of the reward when using modification s. This expected value is termed the efficiency of s. We will assume in the sequel that the baseline is 0.5 - an option is good if and only if it performs better than 0.5, and the efficiency is the average result on experiments.
- $n(s)$, the number of simulations of s already performed.
- $r(s)$ the total reward of s, i.e. the sum of the rewards of the $n(s)$ simulations with modification s.
- $ub(s)$, an upper bound on the efficiency of s, to be computed depending on the previous trials ($ub(s)$ will be computed thanks to Bernstein bounds or Hoeffding bounds).
- $lb(s)$, a lower bound on the efficiency of s (idem).

The two following properties will be proved for some specific functions lb and ub; the results around our BGP (bandit-based genetic programming) algorithm below hold whenever lb and ub verify these assumptions.

- **Consistency:** with probability at least $1 - \delta_0$, for all calls to ub and lb, the efficiency of s is between $lb(s)$ and $ub(s)$:

$$e(s) \in [lb(s), ub(s)]. \tag{2}$$

- **Termination:** when the number of simulations of s goes to infinity, then

$$ub(s) - lb(s) \to 0. \tag{3}$$

These properties are exactly what is ensured by Bernstein's bounds or Hoeffding's bounds. They will be proved for some variants of ub and lb defined below (Lemma 1, using Hoeffding's bound); they will be assumed in results about the BGP algorithm below. Therefore, our results about BGP (Theorem 1) will hold for our variants of lb and ub. Our algorithm and proof do not need a specific function ub or lb, provided that these assumptions are verified. However, we precise below a classical form of ub and lb, in order to point out that there exists such ub and lb; moreover, they are easy to implement. lb and ub are computed by a function with a memory (*i.e.* with static variables):

Function *computeBounds(s)*   (variant 1)
Static internal variable: $nbTest(s)$, initialized at 0.
Let n be the number of times s has been simulated.
Let r be the total reward over those s simulations.
$nbTest(s) = nbTest(s) + 1$
Let $lb(s) = r/n - deviation_{\text{Hoeffding}} \left(\delta_0/(\#S \times 2^{nbTest(s)}), n \right)$.
Let $ub(s) = r/n + deviation_{\text{Hoeffding}} \left(\delta_0/(\#S \times 2^{nbTest(s)}), n \right)$.

What is important in these formula is that the sum of the $\delta_0/(\#S \times 2^{nbTests(s)})$, for $s \in S$ and $nbTest(s) \in \{1, 2, 3 \dots \}$, is at most δ_0. By union bound, this implies that the overall risk is at most δ_0. The proof of the consistency and of the termination assumptions are therefore immediate consequences of Hoeffding's bounds (we could use Bernstein's bounds if we believed that small standard deviations matter). A (better) variant, based on $\sum_{n \geq 1} 1/n^2 = \pi^2/6$ is

---
Function *computeBounds(s)*   (variant 2)
Static internal variable: $nbTest(s)$, initialized at 0.
Let n be the number of times s has been simulated.
Let r be the average reward over those s simulations.
$nbTest(s) = nbTest(s) + 1$
Let $lb(s) = r/n - deviation_{\text{Hoeffding}} \left(\delta_0/(\#S \times \left(\frac{\pi^2 nbTest(s)^2}{6} \right)), n \right)$.
Let $ub(s) = r/n + deviation_{\text{Hoeffding}} \left(\delta_0/(\#S \times \left(\frac{\pi^2 nbTest(s)^2}{6} \right)), n \right)$.

We show precisely the consistency of *computeBounds* below.

Lemma 1 (Consistency of *computeBounds*.). *For all S finite, for all algorithms calling computeBounds and simulating modifications in arbitrary order, with probability at least $1 - \delta_0$, for all s and after each simulation, $lb(s) \leq e(s) \leq ub(s)$.*

The proof is removed due to length constraints.   □

Our algorithm, BGP (Bandit-based Genetic Programming), based on the *computeBounds* function above, is as follows:
BGP algorithm.
$S = S_0 =$ some initial set of modifications.
while $S \neq \emptyset$ **do**
    Select $s \in S$ // the selection rule is not specified here
                                        // (the result is independent of it)
    Let n be the number of simulations of modification s.
    Simulate s n more times (*i.e.* now s has been simulated $2n$ times).

$$//\text{this ensures } nbTests(s) = O(\log(n(s)))$$

$computeBounds(s)$
if $lb(s) > 0.501$ **then**
    Accept s; exit the program.
else if $ub(s) < 0.504$ **then**
    $S \leftarrow S \setminus \{s\}$ // s is discarded.
end if
end while

We do not specify the selection rule. The result below is independent of the particular rule.

Theorem 1 (Consistency of BGP). *When using variant 1 or variant 2 of computeBounds, or any other version ensuring consistency (Eq. 2) and termination (Eq. 3), BGP is consistent in the sense that:*

1. *if at least one modification s has efficiency $> .504$, then with probability at least $1 - \delta_0$ a modification with efficiency $> .501$ will be selected (and the algorithm terminates).*
2. *if no modification has efficiency $> .504$, then with probability at least $1 - \delta_0$ the algorithm will*
   (a) either select a modification with efficiency $> .501$ (and terminate);
   (b) or select no modification and terminate.

Remark. The constants 0.501 and 0.504 are arbitrary provided that the latter is greater or equal to the former. The proof is removed due to length constraints.   □

We have only considered $|S| < \infty$. The extension to $S = \{s_1, s_2, s_3, \dots\}$ countable is straightforward but removed due to length constraints.

5   Experiments

Life is a Game of Go in which rules have been made unnecessarily complex, according to an old proverb. As a matter of fact, Go has very simple rules, is very difficult for computers, is central in education in many Asian countries (part of school activities in some countries) and has NP-completeness properties for some families of situations[12], and PSPACE-hardness for others[21], and EXPTIME-completeness for some versions [23]. It has also been chosen as a testbed for artificial intelligence by many researchers. The main tools, for the game of Go, are currently MCTS/UCT (Monte-Carlo Tree Search, Upper Confidence Trees); these tools are also central in many difficult games and in high-dimensional planning. An example of nice Go game, won by MoGo as white in 2008 in the GPW Cup, is given in Fig. 1 (left). Since these approaches have been defined [7,10,17], several improvements have appeared like First-Play Urgency [25], Rave-values [5,14] (see ftp://ftp.cgl.ucsf.edu/pub/pett/go/ladder/mcgo.ps for B. Bruegman's unpublished paper), patterns and progressive widening [11,8], better than UCB-like (Upper Confidence Bounds) exploration terms [20], large-scale

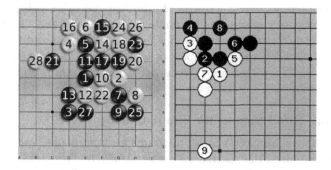

Fig. 1. Left: A decisive move (number 28) played by MoGo as white, in the GPW Cup 2008. Right: An example from Senseis of good large pattern in spite of a very bad small pattern. The move 2 is a good move.

parallelization [13,9,6,16], automatic building of huge opening books [2]. Thanks to all these improvements, our implementation MoGo already won even games against a professional player in 9x9 (Amsterdam, 2007; Paris, 2008; Taiwan 2009), and recently won with handicap 6 against a professional player (Tainan, 2009), and with handicap 7 against a top professional player, Zhou Junxun, winner of the LG-Cup 2007 (Tainan, 2009). Besides impressive results for the game of Go, MCTS/UCT have been applied to non-linear optimization [4], optimal sailing [17], active learning [24]. The formula used in the bandit is incredibly complicated, and it is now very hard to improve the current best formula [20].

Here we will consider only mutations consisting in adding patterns in our program MoGo. Therefore, accepting a mutation is equivalent to accepting a pattern. We experiment random patterns for biasing UCT. The reader interested in the details of this is referred to [20]. Our patterns contain jokers, black stones, empty locations, white stones, locations out of the goban, and are used as masks over all the board: this means that for a given location, we consider patterns like "there is a black stone at coordinate +2,+1, a stone (of any color) at coordinate +3,0, and the location at coordinate -1,-1 is empty". This is a very particular form of genetic programming. We consider here the automatic generation of patterns for biasing the simulations in 9x9 and 19x19 Go. Please note that: (1) When we speak of good or bad shapes here, it is in the sense of "shapes that should be more simulated by a UCT-like algorithm", or "shapes that should be less simulated by a UCT-like algorithm". This is not necessarily equivalent to "good" or "bad" shapes for human players (yet, there are correlations). (2) In 19x19 Go, MoGoCVS is based on tenths of thousands of patterns as in [8]. Therefore, we do not start from scratch. A possible goal would be to have similar results, with less patterns, so that the algorithm is faster (the big database of patterns provides good biases but it is very slow). (3) In 9x9 Go, there are no big library of shapes available; yet, human expertise has been encoded in MoGo, and we are far from starting from scratch. Engineers have spent hundreds of hours manually optimizing patterns. The goals are both (i) finding shapes that should be more simulated (ii) finding shapes that should be less simulated.

Section 5.1 presents our experiments for finding good shapes in 9x9 Go. Section 5.2 presents our experiments for finding bad shapes in 9x9 Go. Section 5.3 presents our unsuccessful experiments for finding both good and bad shapes in 19x19, from MoGoCVS and its database of patterns as in [8]. Section 5.4 presents results on MoGoCVS with patterns removed, in order to improve the version of MoGoCVS without the big database of pattern.

5.1   Finding Good Shapes for Simulations in 9x9 Go

Here the baseline is MoGo CVS. All programs are run on one core, with 10 000 simulations per move. All experiments are performed on Grid5000. The selection rule, not specified in BGP, is the upper bound as in UCB[19,3]: we simulate s such that $ub(s)$ is maximal. We here test modifications which give a positive bias to some patterns, *i.e.* we look for shapes that should be simulated more often.

For each iteration, we randomly generate some individuals, and test them with the BGP algorithm. For the three first iterations, 10 patterns were randomly generated; the two first times, one of these 10 patterns was validated; the third time, no pattern was validated. Therefore, we have three version of MoGo: MoGoCVS, MoGoCVS+P1, and MoGoCVS+P1+P2, where P1 is the pattern validated at the first iteration and P2 is the pattern validated at the second iteration. We then tested the relative efficiency of these MoGos as follows:

Tested code	Opponent	Success rate
MoGoCVS + P1	MoGoCVS	$50.78\% \pm 0.10\%$
MoGoCVS + P1 + P2	MoGoCVS +P1	$51.2\% \pm 0.20\%$
MoGoCVS + P1 + P2	MoGoCVS	$51.9\% \pm 0.16\%$

We also checked that this modification is also efficient for 100 000 simulations per move, with success rate $52.1 \pm 0.6\%$ for MoGoCVS+P1+P2 against MoGoCVS. There was no pattern validated during the third iteration, which was quite expensive (one week on a cluster). We therefore switched to another variant; we tested the case $|S_0| = 1$, *i.e.* we test one individual at a time. We launched 153 iterations with this new version. There were therefore 153 tested patterns, and none of them was validated.

5.2   Finding Bad Shapes for Simulations in 9x9 Go

We now switched to the research of negative shapes, *i.e.* patterns with a negative influence of the probability, for a move, to be simulated. We kept $|S_0| = 1$, i.e. only one pattern tested at each iteration. There were 173 iterations, and two patterns P3 and P4 were validated. We verified the quality of these negative patterns as follows, with mogoCVS the version obtained in the section above:

Tested code	Opponent	Success rate
MoGoCVS + P1 + P2 + P3	MoGoCVS + P1 + P2	$50.9\% \pm 0.2\%$
MoGoCVS + P1 + P2 + P3	MoGoCVS	$52.6\% \pm 0.16\%$
MoGoCVS + P1 + P2 + P3 + P4	MoGoCVS + P1 + P2 + P3	$50.6\% \pm 0.13\%$
MoGoCVS + P1 + P2 + P3 + P4	MoGoCVS	$53.5\% \pm 0.16\%$

This leads to an overall success of 53.5% against MoGoCVS, obtained by BGP.

5.3   Improving 19x19 Go with Database of Patterns

In 19x19 Go, all tests are performed with 3500 simulations per move. Here also, we tested the case $|S_0| = 1$, *i.e.* we test one individual at a time. We tested only positive biases. The algorithm was launched for 62 iterations. Unfortunately, none of these 62 iterations was accepted. Therefore, we concluded that improving these highly optimized version was too difficult. We switched to another goal: having the same efficiency with faster simulations and less memory (the big database of patterns strongly slowers the simulations and takes a lot of simulations), as discussed below.

5.4   Improving 19x19 Go without Database of Patterns

We therefore removed all the database of patterns; the simulations of MoGo are much faster in this case, but the resulting program is nonetheless weaker because simulations are far less efficient (see *e.g.* [20]). Fig. 1 (right) presents a known (from Senseis `http://senseis.xmp.net/?GoodEmptyTriangle#toc1`) difficult case for patterns: move 2 is a good move in spite of the fact that locally (move 2 and locations at the east, north, and north east) form a known very bad pattern (termed empty triangle), termed empty triangle, and is nonetheless a good move due to the surroundings.

We keep $|S_0| = 1$, 127 iterations. There were six patterns validated, validated at iterations 16, 22, 31, 57, 100 and 127. We could validate these patterns Q1,Q2,Q3,Q4,Q5,Q6 as follows. MoGoCVS+AE means MoGoCVS equipped with the big database of patterns extracted from games between humans.

Tested code	Opponent	Success rate
MoGoCVS + Q1	MoGoCVS	50.9% ± 0.13%
MoGoCVS + Q1 + Q2	MoGoCVS + Q1	51.2% ± 0.28%
MoGoCVS + Q1 + Q2 + Q3	MoGoCVS + Q1 + Q2	56.7% ± 1.50%
MoGoCVS + Q1 + ... + Q4	MoGoCVS + Q1 + Q2 + Q3	52.1% ± 0.39%
MoGoCVS + Q1 + ... + Q5	MoGoCVS + Q1 + ... + Q4	51.1% ± 0.20%
MoGoCVS + Q1 + ... + Q6	MoGoCVS + Q1 + ... + Q5	54.1% ± 0.78%
MoGoCVS + Q1 + Q2	MoGoCVS	53.4% ± 0.50%
MoGoCVS + Q1 + Q2 + Q3	MoGoCVS	57.3% ± 0.49%
MoGoCVS + Q1 + ... + Q4	MoGoCVS	59.4% ± 0.49%
MoGoCVS + Q1 + ... + Q5	MoGoCVS	58.6% ± 0.49%
MoGoCVS + Q1 + ... + Q6	MoGoCVS	61.7% ± 0.49%
MoGoCVS	MoGoCVS + AE	26.6% ± 0.20%
MoGoCVS + Q1	MoGoCVS + AE	27.5% ± 0.49%
MoGoCVS + Q1 + Q2	MoGoCVS + AE	28.0% ± 0.51%
MoGoCVS + Q1 + Q2 + Q3	MoGoCVS + AE	30.9% ± 0.46%
MoGoCVS + Q1 + ... + Q4	MoGoCVS + AE	32.1% ± 0.43%
MoGoCVS + Q1 + ... + Q5	MoGoCVS + AE	30.9% ± 0.46%
MoGoCVS + Q1 + ... + Q6	MoGoCVS + AE	32.8% ± 0.47%

An important property of BGP is that all validated patterns are confirmed by these independent experiments. We see however that in 19x19, we could reach roughly 30% of success rate against the big database built on human games (therefore our BGP version uses far less memory than the other version); we will keep this experiment running, so that maybe we can go beyond 50 %. Nonetheless, we point out that we already have 60 % against the version without the database, and the performance is still increasing (improvements were found at iterations 16,22,57,100,122,127, with regular improvements - we have no plateau yet) - therefore we successfully improved the version without patterns, which is lighter (90% of the size of MoGoCVS is in the database).

6   Conclusions

We proposed an original tool for genetic programming. This tool is quite conservative: it is based on a set of admissible modifications, and has strong theoretical guarantees. Interestingly, the application of this theory to GP was successful, with in particular the nice property that all patterns selected during the GP run could be validated in independent experiments. We point out that when humans test modifications of MoGo, they usually test their algorithms based on simple confidence intervals, without taking into account the fact that, as they test multiple variants, one of these variants might succeed just by chance - it happened quite often that modifications accepted in the CVS were later removed, causing big delays and many non-regression tests. This is in particular true for this kind of applications, because the big noise in the results, the big computational costs of the experiments, imply that people can't use p-values like 10^{-10} - with BGP, the confidence intervals can be computed at a reasonnable confidence level, and the algorithm takes care by itself of the risk due to the multiple simultaneous hypothesis testing. In 9x9 Go, BGP outperformed human development, and the current CVS of MoGo is the version developped by BGP. In 19x19 Go, we have an improvement over the default version of MoGo, but not against the version enabling the use of big databases - we nonetheless keep running the experiments as the success rate is still increasing and we had a big improvement for light versions.

References

1. Audibert, J.-Y., Munos, R., Szepesvari, C.: Use of variance estimation in the multi-armed bandit problem. In: NIPS 2006 Workshop on On-line Trading of Exploration and Exploitation (2006)
2. Audouard, P., Chaslot, G., Hoock, J.-B., Perez, J., Rimmel, A., Teytaud, O.: Grid coevolution for adaptive simulations; application to the building of opening books in the game of go. In: Proceedings of EvoGames (2009)
3. Auer, P., Cesa-Bianchi, N., Fischer, P.: Finite time analysis of the multiarmed bandit problem. Machine Learning 47(2/3), 235–256 (2002)
4. Auger, A., Teytaud, O.: Continuous lunches are free plus the design of optimal optimization algorithms. Algorithmica (2009)
5. Bruegmann, B.: Monte carlo go (1993)
6. Cazenave, T., Jouandeau, N.: On the parallelization of UCT. In: Proceedings of CGW 2007, pp. 93–101 (2007)

7. Chaslot, G., Saito, J.-T., Bouzy, B., Uiterwijk, J.W.H.M., van den Herik, H.J.: Monte-Carlo Strategies for Computer Go. In: Schobbens, P.-Y., Vanhoof, W., Schwanen, G. (eds.) Proceedings of the 18th BeNeLux Conference on Artificial Intelligence, Namur, Belgium, pp. 83–91 (2006)
8. Chaslot, G., Winands, M., Uiterwijk, J., van den Herik, H., Bouzy, B.: Progressive strategies for monte-carlo tree search. In: Wang, P., et al. (eds.) Proceedings of the 10th Joint Conference on Information Sciences (JCIS 2007), pp. 655–661. World Scientific Publishing Co. Pte. Ltd., Singapore (2007)
9. Chaslot, G., Winands, M., van den Herik, H.: Parallel Monte-Carlo Tree Search. In: van den Herik, H.J., Xu, X., Ma, Z., Winands, M.H.M. (eds.) CG 2008. LNCS, vol. 5131, pp. 60–71. Springer, Heidelberg (2008)
10. Coulom, R.: Efficient selectivity and backup operators in monte-carlo tree search. In: van den Herik, H.J., Ciancarini, P., Donkers, H.H.L.M(J.) (eds.) CG 2006. LNCS, vol. 4630, pp. 72–83. Springer, Heidelberg (2007)
11. Coulom, R.: Computing elo ratings of move patterns in the game of go. In: Computer Games Workshop, Amsterdam, The Netherlands (2007)
12. Crasmaru, M.: On the complexity of Tsume-Go. In: van den Herik, H.J., Iida, H. (eds.) CG 1998. LNCS, vol. 1558, pp. 222–231. Springer, Heidelberg (1999)
13. Gelly, S., Hoock, J.B., Rimmel, A., Teytaud, O., Kalemkarian, Y.: The parallelization of monte-carlo planning. In: Proceedings of the International Conference on Informatics in Control, Automation and Robotics ICINCO 2008, pp. 198–203 (2008) (To appear)
14. Gelly, S., Silver, D.: Combining online and offline knowledge in UCT. In: ICML 2007: Proceedings of the 24th international conference on Machine learning, pp. 273–280. ACM Press, New York (2007)
15. Holland, J.H.: Genetic algorithms and the optimal allocation of trials. SIAM J. Comput. 2(2), 88–105 (1973)
16. Kato, H., Takeuchi, I.: Parallel monte-carlo tree search with simulation servers. In: 13th Game Programming Workshop (GPW 2008) (November 2008)
17. Kocsis, L., Szepesvari, C.: Bandit-based monte-carlo planning. In: Fürnkranz, J., Scheffer, T., Spiliopoulou, M. (eds.) ECML 2006. LNCS (LNAI), vol. 4212, pp. 282–293. Springer, Heidelberg (2006)
18. Koza, J.R.: Genetic Programming: On the Programming of Computers by means of Natural Evolution. MIT Press, Massachusetts (1992)
19. Lai, T., Robbins, H.: Asymptotically efficient adaptive allocation rules. Advances in Applied Mathematics 6, 4–22 (1985)
20. Lee, C.-S., Wang, M.-H., Chaslot, G., Hoock, J.-B., Rimmel, A., Teytaud, O., Tsai, S.-R., Hsu, S.-C., Hong, T.-P.: The Computational Intelligence of MoGo Revealed in Taiwan's Computer Go Tournaments. IEEE Transactions on Computational Intelligence and AI in games (2009)
21. Lichtenstein, D., Sipser, M.: Go is polynomial-space hard. J. ACM 27(2), 393–401 (1980)
22. Mnih, V., Szepesvári, C., Audibert, J.-Y.: Empirical Bernstein stopping. In: ICML 2008: Proceedings of the 25th international conference on Machine learning, pp. 672–679. ACM, New York (2008)
23. Robson, J.M.: The complexity of go. In: IFIP Congress, pp. 413–417 (1983)
24. Rolet, P., Sebag, M., Teytaud, O.: Optimal active learning through billiards and upper confidence trees in continous domains. In: Proceedings of the ECML conference (2009)
25. Wang, Y., Gelly, S.: Modifications of UCT and sequence-like simulations for Monte-Carlo Go. In: IEEE Symposium on Computational Intelligence and Games, Honolulu, Hawaii, pp. 175–182 (2007)

Using Imaginary Ensembles to Select GP Classifiers

Ulf Johansson[1], Rikard König[1], Tuve Löfström[1], and Lars Niklasson[2]

[1] School of Business and Informatics, University of Borås, Sweden
{ulf.johansson,rikard.konig,tuve.lofstrom}@hb.se
[2] Informatics Research Centre, University of Skövde, Sweden
lars.niklasson@his.se

Abstract. When predictive modeling requires comprehensible models, most data miners will use specialized techniques producing rule sets or decision trees. This study, however, shows that genetically evolved decision trees may very well outperform the more specialized techniques. The proposed approach evolves a number of decision trees and then uses one of several suggested selection strategies to pick one specific tree from that pool. The inherent inconsistency of evolution makes it possible to evolve each tree using all data, and still obtain somewhat different models. The main idea is to use these quite accurate and slightly diverse trees to form an imaginary ensemble, which is then used as a guide when selecting one specific tree. Simply put, the tree classifying the largest number of instances identically to the ensemble is chosen. In the experimentation, using 25 UCI data sets, two selection strategies obtained significantly higher accuracy than the standard rule inducer J48.

Keywords: Classification, Decision trees, Genetic programming, Ensembles.

1 Introduction

Only comprehensible predictive models make it possible to follow and understand the logic behind a prediction or, on another level, for decision-makers to comprehend and analyze the overall relationships found. When requiring comprehensible predictive models, most data miners will use specialized techniques producing either decision trees or rule sets. Specifically, a number of quite powerful and readily available decision tree algorithms exist. Most famous are probably Quinlan's C4.5/C5.0 [1] and Breiman's CART [2].

Although evolutionary algorithms are mainly used for optimization, Genetic Algorithms (GA) and Genetic Programming (GP) have also proved to be valuable data mining tools. The main reason is probably their very general and quite efficient global search strategy. Unfortunately, for some basic data mining problems like classification and clustering, finding a suitable GA representation tends to be awkward. Using GP, however, it is fairly straightforward to specify an appropriate representation for the task at hand, just by tailoring the function and terminal sets.

Remarkably, GP data mining results are often comparable to, or sometimes even better than, results obtained by the more specialized machine learning techniques. In particular, several studies show that decision trees evolved using GP often are more

A.I. Esparcia-Alcazar et al. (Eds.): EuroGP 2010, LNCS 6021, pp. 278–288, 2010.

accurate than trees induced by standard techniques like C4.5/C5.0 and CART; see e.g. [3] and [4]. The explanation is that while decision tree algorithms typically choose splits greedily, working from the root node down, the GP performs a global optimization. Informally, this means that the GP often chooses some locally sub-optimal splits, but the overall model will still be more accurate and generalize better to unseen data.

The inherent inconsistency (i.e. that runs on the same data using identical settings can produce different results) of GP is sometimes cited as a disadvantage for data mining applications. Is it really possible to put faith in one specific evolved tree when another run might produce a different tree, even disagreeing on a fairly large number of instances? The answer to this question is not obvious. Intuitively, most data miners would probably want one accurate and comprehensible model, and having to accept several different models from the same data is confusing. We, however, argue that consistency is a highly overvalued criterion, and showed in [5] that most of the decision trees extracted (from neural networks) using GP had higher accuracy than corresponding CART trees. Why should using a tree inducer to get one specific model be considered better than obtaining several, slightly different models, each having high accuracy? In that study, we also used the fact that we had several, slightly different, trees available to produce probability estimation trees, in a similar way to Provost and Domingos [6]. In a later study we utilized the inconsistency to achieve implicit diversity between base classifiers in ensemble models, contrasting our approach with standard bagging [8]. Bagging obtains diversity among the base classifiers in an ensemble by training them on different subsets of the data, thus resulting in less data being available to each base classifier.

Nevertheless, there are situations where a decision-maker wants to make use of only one comprehensible model. Naturally, this model should then be "the best possible". Exactly what criterion this translates to is not obvious, but, as always, test accuracy, i.e., the ability to generalize to novel data, must be considered very important. So, the overall question addressed in this study is whether access to a number of evolved decision tree models will make it easier to produce one, single model, likely to have good test accuracy.

Given a pool of independently trained (or evolved) models, there are two basic strategies to produce one model; either you pick one of the available models, or you somehow use the trained models to create a brand new model. In this paper, we will investigate the first strategy, i.e., how do we pick a specific model from the pool. The most straightforward alternative is, of course, to compare all models and pick the one having the highest accuracy on either training data or on an additional (validation) data set. The hypothesis tested in this study is, however, that we can do better by somehow using the fact that we have a number of models available.

2 Background

An *ensemble* is a composite model aggregating multiple base models, making the ensemble prediction a function of all included base models. The most intuitive explanation for why ensembles work is that combining several models using averaging will eliminate uncorrelated base classifier errors; see e.g., [9]. Naturally, there is nothing to gain by combining identical models, so the reasoning requires that base classifiers commit their errors on different instances. Informally, the key term diversity therefore means that the base classifiers make their mistakes on different instances. The important result that ensemble error depends not only on the average accuracy of the base models, but also on their diversity was, for regression problems, formally derived by Krogh and Vedelsby in [10]. The result was Equation (1), stating that the ensemble error, E, can be expressed as:

$$E = \bar{E} - \bar{A} \tag{1}$$

where $\bar{E}$ is the average error of the base models and $\bar{A}$ is the ensemble diversity (ambiguity), measured as the weighted average of the squared differences in the predictions of the base models and the ensemble. Since diversity is always positive, this decomposition proves that the ensemble will always have higher accuracy than the average accuracy obtained by the individual classifiers.

It must be noted, however, that with a zero-one loss function, there is no clear analogy to the bias-variance-covariance decomposition. Consequently, the overall goal of obtaining an expression where the classification error is decomposed into error rates of the individual classifiers and a diversity term is currently beyond the state of the art. Nevertheless, several studies have shown that sufficiently diverse classification ensembles, in practice, almost always will outperform even the strongest single base model.

So, the key result that we hope to utilize is the fact that an ensemble most often will be a very accurate model, normally generalizing quite well to novel data. In this specific setting, when we are ultimately going to pick one specific model (base classifier), we will investigate whether it is better to pick a model that agrees as much as possible with the (imaginary) ensemble instead of having the highest possible individual training accuracy.

3   Method

This section will first describe the different selection strategies evaluated in the study. The second part gives an overview of the GP used and the last part, finally, gives the details for the experimentation.

3.1   Selection Strategies

As described above, an ensemble is normally a very accurate model of the relationship between input and target variables. In addition, an ensemble could also be used to generate predictions for novel instances with unknown target values, as they become available. In the field of semi-supervised learning, this is referred to as *coaching*. Specifically, ensemble predictions could be produced even for the test instances, as long as the problem is one where predictions are made for sets of instances, rather than one instance at a time. Fortunately, in most real-world data mining projects, bulk predictions are made, and there is no shortage of unlabeled instances. As an example, when a predictive model is used to determine the recipients of a marketing campaign, the test set; i.e., the data set actually used for the predictions, could easily contain thousands of instances.

It must be noted that it is not "cheating" to use the test instances in this way. Specifically, we do not assume that we have access to values of the target variable on test instances. Instead, we simply produce a number of test set predictions, and then utilize these for selecting one specific model. Naturally, only the selected model is then actually evaluated on the test data.

In the experimentation, we will evaluate four different selection strategies. Three of these use imaginary ensembles and the concept *ensemble fidelity*, which is defined as the number of instances classified identically to the ensemble.

- **TrAcc:** The tree having the highest *training accuracy* is selected.
- **TrFid:** The tree having the highest *ensemble fidelity* on *training data* is selected.
- **TeFid:** The tree having the highest *ensemble fidelity* on *test data* is selected.
- **AllFid:** The tree having the highest *ensemble fidelity* on both *training data* and *test data* is selected.

In addition, we will also report the average accuracies of the base classifiers (which corresponds to evolving only one tree, or picking one of the trees at random) and results for the J48 algorithm from the Weka workbench [11]. J48, which is an implementation of the C4.5 algorithm, used default settings.

Some may argue that most data miners would not select a model based on high training accuracy, but instead use a separate validation set; i.e., a data set not used for training the models. In our experience, however, setting aside some instances to allow the use of fresh data when selecting a model will normally not make up for the lower average classifier accuracy, caused by using fewer instances for training. Naturally, this is especially important for data sets with relatively few instances to start with, like most UCI data sets used in this study. Nevertheless, we decided to include a preliminary experiment evaluating the selection strategy *ValAcc* which, of course, picks the tree having the highest accuracy on a validation set.

3.2 GP Settings

When using GP for tree induction, the available functions, F, and terminals, T, constitute the literals of the representation language. Functions will typically be logical or relational operators, while the terminals could be, for instance, input variables or constants. Here, the representation language is very similar to basic decision trees. Fig. 1 below shows a small but quite accurate (test accuracy is 0.771) sample tree evolved on the Diabetes data set.

```
if (Body_mass_index > 29.132)
  |T: if (plasma_glucose < 127.40)
  |    |T: [Negative] {56/12}
  |    |F: [Positive] {29/21}
  |F: [Negative] {63/11}
```

Fig. 1. Sample evolved tree from Diabetes data set

The exact grammar used internally is presented using Backus-Naur form in Fig. 2 below.

```
F = {if, ==, <, >}
T = {i₁, i₂, ..., iₙ, c₁, c₂, ..., cₘ, ℜ}

DTree      :-    (if RExp Dtree Dtree) | Class
RExp       :-    (ROp ConI ConC) | (== CatI CatC)
ROp        :-    < | >
CatI       :-    Categorical input variable
ConI       :-    Continuous input variable
Class      :-    c₁ | c₂ | ... | cₘ
CatC       :-    Categorical attribute value
ConC       :-    ℜ
```

Fig. 2. Grammar used

The GP parameter settings used in this study are given in Table 1 below. The length penalty was much smaller than the cost of misclassifying an instance. Nevertheless, the resulting parsimony pressure was able to significantly reduce the average program size in the population.

Table 1. GP parameters

Parameter	Value	Parameter	Value
Crossover rate	0.8	Creation depth	6
Mutation rate	0.01	Creation method	Ramped half-and-half
Population size	1000	Fitness function	Training accuracy
Generations	100	Selection	Roulette wheel
Persistence	50	Elitism	Yes

3.3 Experiments

For the experimentation, 4-fold cross-validation was used. The reported test set accuracies are therefore averaged over the four folds. For each fold, 15 decision trees were evolved. If several trees had the best score (according to the selection strategy), the result for that strategy was the *average test set accuracy of these trees*.

All selection strategies except *ValAcc* used the same pool of trees, where each tree was evolved using all available training instances. When using *ValAcc*, 75% of the available training instances were used for the actual training and the remaining 25% for validation.

The 25 data sets used are all publicly available from the UCI Repository [12]. For a summary of data set characteristics, see Table 2 below. *Classes* is the number of classes, *Instances* is the total number of instances in the data set, *Con.* is the number of continuous input variables and *Cat.* is the number of categorical input variables.

Table 2. Data set characteristics

Data set	Instances	Classes	Con.	Cat.
Breast cancer (BreastC)	286	2	0	9
CMC	1473	3	2	7
Colic	368	2	7	15
Credit-A	690	2	6	9
Credit-G	1000	2	7	13
Cylinder bands (Cylinder)	512	2	20	20
Diabetes	768	2	8	0
Glass	214	7	9	0
Haberman	306	2	3	0
Heart-C	303	2	6	7
Heart-S	270	2	6	7
Hepatitis	155	2	6	13
Iono	351	2	34	0
Iris	150	3	4	0
Labor	57	2	8	8
Liver	345	2	6	0
Lung cancer (LungC)	32	3	0	56
Lymph	148	4	3	15
Sonar	208	2	60	0
TAE	151	3	1	4
Vote	435	2	0	16
Wisconsin breast cancer (WBC)	699	2	9	0
Wine	178	3	13	0
Zoo	100	7	0	16

4 Results

Table 3 below shows the results from the preliminary experiment. The main result is that it is clearly better to use all data for actual training, compared to reserving some instances to be used as a validation set. Comparing *TrAcc* to *ValAcc*, *TrAcc* wins 15 of 25 data sets, and also obtains a higher mean accuracy over all data sets.

The explanation is obvious from the fact that using all available instances (*Rand All*) results in considerably higher average classifier accuracy, compared to using only 75% of the instances for the training (*Rand 75%*). As a matter of fact, *Rand All* (i.e. using a random tree trained on all instances) even outperforms the *ValAcc* selection strategy, both when comparing average accuracy over all data sets, and when considering wins and losses.

Table 4 below shows the results from the main experiment. The overall picture is that all selection strategies outperform both J48 and *Rand*; i.e., picking a random tree. The best results were obtained by the selection strategy utilizing the imaginary ensemble only on the test instances, which of course is an interesting observation.

Table 3. Preliminary experiment: test accuracies

Data set	TrAcc	ValAcc	Rand All	Rand 75%
BreastC	**72.7**	70.6	**74.2**	70.3
Cmc	**55.0**	53.7	51.9	51.6
Colic	83.6	**84.9**	**84.5**	83.4
Credit-A	84.5	85.5	84.7	**85.1**
Credit-G	**72.6**	69.3	71.0	69.4
Cylinder	**69.4**	67.6	67.3	65.5
Diabetes	73.4	**74.3**	73.8	73.3
Ecoli	**81.3**	80.2	79.0	78.0
Glass	65.4	**66.6**	64.9	63.6
Haberman	73.3	73.6	73.4	**74.9**
Heart-C	76.7	**77.4**	76.3	75.7
Heart-S	77.3	**77.7**	77.0	75.2
Hepatitis	**82.5**	81.1	81.5	81.2
Iono	**89.0**	86.7	87.3	87.1
Iris	**96.0**	94.2	94.3	94.4
Labor	85.0	84.8	**86.3**	83.8
Liver	60.9	**63.6**	62.9	60.7
LungC	67.0	57.3	**67.7**	57.9
Lymph	75.7	73.5	**76.0**	76.0
Sonar	**76.0**	72.1	73.2	71.7
Tae	54.3	52.5	**55.4**	54.2
Vote	93.2	94.0	94.7	**94.8**
WBC	**96.2**	95.8	95.7	95.3
Wine	88.4	**90.9**	90.4	90.0
Zoo	**93.4**	90.9	91.9	88.4
Mean	77.7	76.8	77.4	76.1
# Wins	15	10	20	4

To determine if there are any statistically significant differences, we use the statistical tests recommended by Demšar [13] for comparing several classifiers over a number of data sets; i.e., a Friedman test [14], followed by a Nemenyi post-hoc test [15]. With six classifiers and 25 data sets, the critical distance (for α=0.05) is 1.51, so based on these tests, *TeFid* and *AllFid* obtained significantly higher accuracies than J48 and *Rand*. Furthermore, the difference between *TeFid* and *TrAcc* is very close to being significant at α=0.05. All in all, it is obvious that basing the selection on fidelity to the imaginary ensemble is beneficial, especially when also considering the ensemble predictions on test instances.

Since the most common and straightforward alternative is to simply use a decision tree, it is particularly interesting to compare the suggested approach to J48. As seen in Table 5 below, all selection strategies clearly outperform J48. A standard sign test requires 18 wins for α=0.05, so the difference in performance between the selection strategies *TeFid* and *AllFid* and J48 are significant, also when using pair-wise comparisons. In addition, both *TrFid*, and to a lesser degree, *TrAcc* clearly outperform J48. Interestingly enough, this is despite the fact that *J48* wins almost half of the data sets when compared to a random tree. So, the success of the suggested approach must be credited to the selection strategies, rather than having only very accurate base classifiers.

Table 4. Main experiment: test accuracies

Data set	J48	TrAcc	TrFid	TeFid	AllFid	Rand.
BreastC	69.9	72.7	**74.8**	**74.8**	**74.8**	74.2
Cmc	50.6	**55.0**	51.7	51.7	51.7	51.9
Colic	**85.6**	83.6	84.3	84.2	84.2	84.5
Credit-A	85.5	84.5	**86.0**	85.1	**86.0**	84.7
Credit-G	**73.0**	72.6	71.5	72.4	71.9	71.0
Cylinder	57.8	69.4	67.4	**70.0**	67.6	67.3
Diabetes	73.3	73.4	73.4	73.4	73.4	**73.8**
Ecoli	78.6	81.3	81.6	**81.9**	81.3	79.0
Glass	66.8	65.4	**68.7**	68.2	67.8	64.9
Haberman	73.9	73.3	74.0	**74.5**	74.2	73.4
Heart-C	75.9	76.7	76.8	**77.6**	76.7	76.3
Heart-S	77.0	77.3	76.7	**78.1**	77.8	77.0
Hepatitis	80.6	82.5	**83.0**	81.7	81.6	81.5
Iono	90.0	89.0	**90.7**	90.2	90.4	87.3
Iris	95.3	**96.0**	94.8	94.7	94.7	94.3
Labor	73.7	85.0	85.0	**87.6**	**87.6**	86.3
Liver	62.0	60.9	**68.1**	**68.1**	**68.1**	62.9
LungC	65.6	67.0	67.0	**78.1**	**78.1**	67.7
Lymph	73.0	75.7	**77.7**	76.4	**77.7**	76.0
Sonar	75.5	**76.0**	74.5	72.8	74.8	73.2
Tae	55.0	54.3	55.0	55.0	55.0	**55.4**
Vote	95.6	93.2	95.1	**95.7**	95.5	94.7
WBC	95.6	96.2	**96.6**	96.4	96.5	95.7
Wine	91.6	88.4	89.9	**93.8**	93.0	90.4
Zoo	93.1	93.4	91.4	**97.0**	96.5	91.9
Mean	**76.6**	**77.7**	**78.2**	**79.2**	**79.1**	**77.4**
# Wins	**2**	**3**	**8**	**13**	**6**	**2**
Mean rank	**4.34**	**3.98**	**3.12**	**2.48**	**2.76**	**4.28**

Table 5. Wins, draws and losses against J48

	TrAcc	TrFid	TeFid	AllFid	Rand.
Wins/Draws/Losses	15/0/10	16/1/8	**19/1/5**	**19/1/5**	13/0/12

Another interesting comparison is to look specifically at selection strategies not considering test instances. After all, not all predictions are performed in bulks. Table 6 below therefore compares J48 to *TrAcc* and *TrFid*. Even now the picture is quite clear; the best choice is to select a tree based on ensemble fidelity.

Table 6. Comparing strategies not using test instances

Strategy	J48	TrAcc	TrFid
TrAcc	15/0/10	TrAcc	
TrFid	16/1/8	15/3/7	TrFid
Rand	13/0/12	12/0/13	9/0/16

Table 7 below, finally, presents the results in a slightly different way. Here, the ta-bulated numbers represent the average rank (based on test accuracy) of the selected tree among the 15 available trees. As an example, a rank of 1.00 would indicate that the suggested strategy picked the best possible tree on each fold. Here, it must be noted that when several trees obtained identical accuracies, they all got the best rank-ing, instead of an average rank. If, as an example, three trees obtained the best accura-cy, a selection strategy picking either of these trees would get a rank of 1 on that fold. A strategy picking the second best tree would then receive a rank of 4, and so on. In addition, if a selection strategy picked several trees (because they had identical scores) the ranking on that fold, for that strategy, would be the average rank of the selected trees.

Table 7. Comparing trees selected by the strategies

Data set	TrAcc	TrFid	TeFid	AllFid	Rand.
BreastC	8.23	**1.00**	**1.00**	**1.00**	2.78
Cmc	**1.50**	2.75	2.75	2.75	3.55
Colic	8.42	**3.33**	3.50	3.50	3.80
Credit-A	7.13	**3.75**	6.13	**3.75**	7.22
Credit-G	**4.25**	7.25	**4.25**	5.75	7.65
Cylinder	**5.75**	7.25	4.75	6.75	7.67
Diabetes	8.75	6.50	6.50	6.50	**4.82**
Ecoli	4.00	3.00	**2.75**	3.50	7.10
Glass	7.75	**2.50**	**2.50**	3.00	7.02
Haberman	6.09	4.56	**3.25**	4.00	5.57
Heart-C	6.75	7.17	**5.50**	7.38	7.07
Heart-S	7.33	6.50	**5.28**	5.50	7.00
Hepatitis	**4.25**	4.54	4.83	5.38	5.95
Iono	6.00	**2.63**	3.17	3.25	7.23
Iris	3.13	**1.73**	1.75	1.75	3.23
Labor	6.42	6.42	**3.75**	**3.75**	5.35
Liver	10.75	**3.75**	**3.75**	**3.75**	7.32
LungC	6.50	6.50	**2.50**	**2.50**	6.20
Lymph	5.63	4.33	4.50	**3.75**	5.55
Sonar	**3.75**	5.00	7.42	4.75	7.18
Tae	5.25	5.50	5.50	5.50	**4.82**
Vote	10.59	5.69	**3.50**	4.25	6.73
WBC	3.83	**1.50**	3.00	2.38	6.78
Wine	9.00	8.25	**2.00**	3.50	6.43
Zoo	4.54	5.68	**1.50**	1.75	6.18
Mean	6.22	4.68	3.81	3.99	6.01
#Wins	5	8	13	6	2

There are several interesting observations in Table 7. First of all, no strategy suc-ceeds in always picking one of the best trees. This is a clear message that it is still very hard to estimate performance on unseen data based on results on available data. Picking the most accurate tree on training data (*TrAcc*), is sometimes the best option (5 wins) but, based on this comparison, it is still the worst choice overall. *TeFid* is again the best selection strategy, with a mean value indicating that the tree picked by *TeFid* is, on average, ranked as one of the best four.

5 Conclusions

This paper shows that the predictive performance of genetically evolved decision trees can compete successfully with trees induced by more specialized machine learning techniques, here J48.

The main advantage for an evolutionary approach is the inherent ability to produce a number of decision trees without having to sacrifice individual accuracy to obtain diversity. Here, each tree was evolved based on all available training data, which is in contrast to standard techniques, which normally have to rely on some resampling technique to produce diversity.

The proposed method, consequently, evolves a collection of accurate yet diverse decision trees, and then uses some selection strategy to pick one specific tree from that pool. The key idea, suggested here, is to form an imaginary ensemble of all trees in the pool, and then base the selection strategy on that ensemble. Naturally, the assumption is that individual trees that, to a large extent, agree with the ensemble are more likely to generalize well to novel data.

In the experimentation, the use of several selection strategies produced evolved trees significantly more accurate than the standard rule inducer J48. The best performance was achieved by selection strategies utilizing the imaginary ensemble on actual predictions, thus limiting the applicability to problems where predictions are made for sets of instances. Nevertheless, the results also show that even when bulk predictions are not possible, the suggested approach still outperformed J48.

6 Discussion and Future Work

First of all, it is very important to recognize the situation targeted in this paper, i.e., that for some reason models must be comprehensible. If comprehensibility is not an issue, there is no reason to use decision trees or rule sets, since these will almost always be outperformed by opaque techniques like neural networks, support vector machines or ensembles.

A potential objection to the suggested approach is that using evolutionary algorithms to produce decision trees is much more computationally intense, and therefore slower, than using standard techniques. This is certainly true, but the novel part in this paper, i.e., the evolution of several trees just to pick one, could easily be run in parallel, making the entire process no more complex and time consuming than evolving just one tree.

Regarding the use of the same instances later used for the actual prediction when selecting a specific model, it must be noted that it is not very complicated, and definitely not cheating. All we do is give each model the opportunity to vote, and then the voting results are used for the model selection. Correct test target values are, of course, not used at all during the model building and selection part.

In this study, we used GP to evolve all decision trees. The suggested approach is, however, also potentially applicable to standard algorithms like C4.5 and CART. The most natural setting would probably be quite large data sets, where each tree would have to be induced using a sample of all available instances, thereby introducing some implicit diversity.

Acknowledgments. This work was supported by the INFUSIS project (www.his.se/infusis) at the University of Skövde, Sweden, in partnership with the Swedish Knowledge Foundation under grant 2008/0502.

References

1. Quinlan, J.R.: C4.5: Programs for Machine Learning. Morgan Kaufmann, San Francisco (1993)
2. Breiman, L., Friedman, J.H., Olshen, R.A., Stone, C.J.: Classification and Regression Trees. Wadsworth International Group (1984)
3. Tsakonas, A.: A comparison of classification accuracy of four genetic programming-evolved intelligent structures. Information Sciences 176(6), 691–724 (2006)
4. Bojarczuk, C.C., Lopes, H.S., Freitas, A.A.: Data Mining with Constrained-syntax Genetic Programming: Applications in Medical Data Sets. In: Intelligent Data Analysis in Medicine and Pharmacology - a workshop at MedInfo-2001 (2001)
5. Johansson, U., König, R., Niklasson, L.: Inconsistency - Friend or Foe. In: International Joint Conference on Neural Networks, pp. 1383–1388. IEEE Press, Los Alamitos (2007)
6. Provost, F., Domingos, P.: Tree induction for probability-based ranking. Machine Learning 52, 199–215 (2003)
7. Johansson, U., Sönströd, C., Löfström, T., König, R.: Using Genetic Programming to Obtain Implicit Diversity. In: IEEE Congress on Evolutionary Computation, pp. 2454–2459. IEEE Press, Los Alamitos (2009)
8. Breiman, L.: Bagging Predictors. Machine Learning 24(2), 123–140 (1996)
9. Dietterich, T.G.: Machine learning research: four current directions. The AI Magazine 18, 97–136 (1997)
10. Krogh, A., Vedelsby, J.: Neural network ensembles, cross validation, and active learning. In: Advances in Neural Information Processing Systems, San Mateo, CA, vol. 2, pp. 650–659. Morgan Kaufmann, San Francisco (1995)
11. Witten, I.H., Frank, E.: Data Mining: Practical machine learning tools and techniques, 2nd edn. Morgan Kaufmann, San Francisco (2005)
12. Blake, C.L., Merz, C.J.: UCI Repository of machine learning databases, University of California, Department of Information and Computer Science (1998)
13. Demšar, J.: Statistical Comparisons of Classifiers over Multiple Data Sets. Journal of Machine Learning Research 7, 1–30 (2006)
14. Friedman, M.: The use of ranks to avoid the assumption of normality implicit in the analysis of variance. Journal of American Statistical Association 32, 675–701 (1937)
15. Nemenyi, P.B.: Distribution-free multiple comparisons, PhD thesis, Princeton University (1963)

Analysis of Building Blocks with Numerical Simplification in Genetic Programming

David Kinzett[1], Mengjie Zhang[1], and Mark Johnston[2]

[1] School of Engineering and Computer Science
[2] School of Mathematics and Operations Research
Victoria University of Wellington, PO Box 600, Wellington, New Zealand
{kinzetalan,mengjie.zhang}@ecs.vuw.ac.nz, mark.johnston@msor.vuw.ac.nz

Abstract. This paper investigates the effect of numerical simplification on building blocks during evolution in genetic programming. The building blocks considered are three level subtrees. We develop a method for encoding building blocks for the analysis. Compared with the canonical genetic programming method, numerical simplification can generate much smaller programs, use much shorter evolutionary training time and achieve comparable effectiveness performance.

1 Introduction

In tree based Genetic Programming (GP) there is a tendency for the size of programs to increase, a process known as *bloat* [1,2,3]. Among other problems, this leads to increased memory usage and computation time. Overly large programs may over-fit the training data, reducing the performance on unseen data. In standard practice all nodes have some chance of being the crossover point. As the programs become deeper, the average depth of the crossover point also becomes deeper, crossover is then less likely to produce children with significantly improved fitness, and the overall efficiency of the GP search is reduced.

Since the 1990s, a substantial effort has been made to reduce or remove the redundant code in GP. The existing methods can be categorised into two approaches. The first approach is to add a program complexity measure into the performance based fitness function or into the performance based fitness selection mechanism to "control" code bloating to some extent. Typical examples include parsimony pressure [4,5,6,7], explicitly defined introns [8], tarpian method [9] and better genetic operators (crossover and mutation) [10]. This approach aims to indirectly control the redundant code in the evolved programs but does not explicitly remove the redundancy in the evolved programs, and sometimes results in a degradation of the effectiveness performance [4,11].

In the second approach, redundant code is directly removed from the evolved programs in certain ways. Typical examples include Koza's editing operation [3], Banzhaf's intron removal [12], Hooper and Flann's expression simplification [13], Ekart's Prolog clause simplification [14], and early work on prime number simplification [15].

Recently, two program simplification methods have been reported, which explicitly remove the redundant program code during the evolutionary process and have been successfully applied to regression and classification tasks. The first method [16] uses

A.I. Esparcia-Alcazar et al. (Eds.): EuroGP 2010, LNCS 6021, pp. 289–300, 2010.

algebraic simplification to remove the "redundant code" during evolution, and the second method simplifies the evolved programs during evolution using simple numerical significance [17]. The empirical results on a number of symbolic regression and classification tasks show that both methods are more efficient in evolving programs than the canonical GP approach without simplification and that the evolved programs are much shorter and easier to understand. The empirical research also shows that both methods achieved comparable or slightly better effectiveness[1] performance than the canonical GP approach. As the simplification process changes the program structure, it is natural to think that the good building blocks in the programs might be destroyed by the simplification process and accordingly this process might deteriorate the system effectiveness performance. However this clearly does not happen.

In an earlier paper [18] we used images to visualise two and three level deep subtrees encoded as bit strings. These images showed that a few building blocks remained in the population for a substantial part of the run, while a much larger number of building blocks were created, remained for a few generations and were then dropped from the population. We concluded that while the two online simplification methods destroyed some existing building blocks, they generated additional, and more diverse, building blocks during evolution, which sufficiently compensated for the negative effect from the disruption of building blocks. The restricted size of the images meant that the encoding scheme used was a very coarse representation of the building blocks and each image could only illustrate a single run.

1.1 Goals

This paper aims to extend the analysis of [18] by using a more descriptive encoding scheme for the building blocks[2] and to use statistical techniques across multiple runs to examine whether the observed behaviours in [18] are present across a much larger set of runs with the more descriptive encoding.

We examine the *numerical simplification* method, and compare its behaviour with canonical GP with *no simplification*. Specifically, we investigate the following questions:

1. How are the building blocks distributed as the evolution proceeds through the generations?
2. How does numerical simplification change this distribution?
3. Does the simplification process affect the overall diversity of building blocks within the population?

2 Brief Overview of Numerical Simplification

The idea of *numerical simplification* [17,18] is to consider the numerical contribution that a node or subtree makes to the output of its parent node, removing those nodes

---

[1] By effectiveness, we mean fitness for a symbolic regression problem and classification accuracy on the test set for a classification problem.

[2] When we use the term *building block* we mean a subtree of the specified depth. It may occur at any point in the program of which it is a part. We do not imply anything about the fitness of the building block.

and subtrees whose impact on the result is too small to make much difference to the program result. The motivation here came from the fact that most data includes a noise component. Instead of trying to fit to this noise, we treat two values whose difference is smaller than the noise as being equal. For efficiency reasons, this implementation addresses only the local effect of simplification at each node in the program tree. There will be cases where it does affect the system performance of the whole program, but the aim is to minimise this. It may be easiest to think of numerical simplification as a kind of lossy compression, where we aim to get useful reductions in program size without obvious loss in quality.

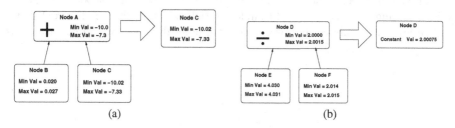

Fig. 1. Example trees used to explain numerical simplification

As the fitness is evaluated across the training set, each node keeps track of minimum and maximum values. The simplification process is performed from the bottom up, and each operator is responsible for making those simplifications that are meaningful for it. A significance tolerance (threshold) is chosen, which can be the result of preliminary trials, or if we have enough knowledge of our dataset then a good starting point will be the noise floor in the data. We used 0.001 in most of our experiments as a result of early trials. All our features have been normalised on the range [-1.0, +1.0] (see subsection 4.2) so this would represent a noise level of about 0.1% which seems reasonable without better information about the source data. For the addition and subtraction operators, a child node or subtree whose range of values is less than the threshold times the parent's minimum absolute value is discarded. Figure 1(a) gives an example of this. The range for Node B is $0.027 - 0.020 = 0.007$. The minimum absolute value for its parent Node A is 7.3. Since $0.007 < 0.001 \times 7.3$, the subtree headed by Node B will be discarded, and Node A will be replaced by Node C. Also, if the range of values a node takes is less than the threshold times its own minimum absolute value, the node is replaced by a constant terminal taking its average value. Figure 1(b) gives an example of this. The range for Node D is $2.0015 - 2.0000 = 0.0015$. The minimum absolute value for Node D is 2.0000. Since $0.0015 < 0.001 \times 2.0000$, the subtree headed by Node D will be discarded, and Node D will be replaced by a constant terminal with the value 2.00075. Note that the second type of simplification takes precedence over the first.

3   Encoding the Building Blocks: A New Scheme

As the number of possible building blocks in GP is usually very large, analysing the behaviour of the building blocks in GP is almost always a difficult task. This also applies to GP with program simplification during evolution. In this paper, we examine the behaviour of three level deep subtrees, which is large enough to be useful while keeping the encoding length within manageable bounds. In our earlier work [18] the encoding scheme used was a very coarse representation of the building blocks. There were many different building blocks that produce the same encoding. This was necessary because of the restrictions imposed by using images as the presentation medium. This paper aims to develop a new encoding scheme with a much more precise description of the building blocks. This is possible because we are using statistical measures rather than images to present the results.

Our approach is to encode each building block into a bit string in such a way that similar building blocks result in similar encodings. The nodes are encoded one level at a time, starting from the root, and from left to right within each level. Figure 2 shows a three level deep subtree. In this example the order the nodes would be encoded is × − + − F2 0.3 F3.

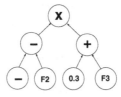

Fig. 2. An example tree to illustrate the encoding order

A three level deep tree with all operators having no more than two operands has a maximum size of seven nodes. This allows us to use eight bits to describe each node for a total of 56 bits. A 64 bit integer can then be used to hold the encoding.

- The operators are encoded as 111 followed by five bits identifying the operator. For these experiments this results in the following:

  1. 11100000 - *addition* operator.
  2. 11100001 - *subtraction* operator.
  3. 11100010 - *multiplication* operator.
  4. 11100011 - *division* operator.

- A feature is encoded as 10 followed by six bits identifying the feature, this allows us to use up to 64 features, and more could be handled by using part of the encoding space allocated to operators.
- An ephemeral constant is encoded as 0 followed by seven bits which are a signed integer that maps [-1.0,1.0] on to the range [-64,63] (*encoding = Const × 64*) provided by the seven available bits. Any encoding less than −64 is set to −64 or if greater than 63 then it is set to 63.

All of the operators and feature terminals are completely described. It is only the ephemeral constants that lose some precision. In the example of Fig. 2, the order of encoding is [×] [−] [+] [−] [F2] [0.3] [F3], which is encoded as [11100010] [11100001]

[11100000] [11100001] [10000010] [00010011] [10000011], the resulting encoding is then:
1110001011100001111000001110000110000010000100111100000011 or in hexadecimal *E2E1E0E1821383*.

4 Experimental Setup

4.1 Datasets

We use three classification tasks in the experiments.

- The first dataset (*coins*) consists of a series of 64×64 pixel images of New Zealand five cent pieces against a random noisy background [16]. There are 200 images of each of heads, tails and background only. Fourteen frequency features are extracted based on a discrete cosine transform of the image, as described in [19].
- The second dataset (*wine*) [20] gives the result of a chemical analysis of wines grown in the same region in Italy but derived from three different cultivars. The analysis determined the quantities of thirteen constituents found in each of the three types of wine. The thirteen constituents are the features, and the three classes are the cultivar from which the wine comes. This dataset was sourced from the Weka project described in [21].
- The third dataset (*faces*) comes from the ORL face data set [22]. We used four individuals thus the set was four classes with ten examples of each. This is a very small number of examples and makes evolving a good classifier difficult. The features used were simple pixel statistics from various portions of the image. More details about pixel statistics can be found in [23].

4.2 GP System Configuration

We consider GP with *no simplification* and *numerical simplification*. The terminal set for each dataset consists of the features used in that dataset and random "constant" numbers. The function set for all the datasets consists of the four standard arithmetic functions (addition, subtraction, multiplication and protected division). The fitness function uses the error rate on the training set. Experiments are all conducted with the same set of parameters. The population size is 200. Initial programs are five levels deep. Tournament selection is used with a tournament size of four. For the coin dataset we use 40 generations, for the wine dataset we use 200 generations, and for the faces dataset 100 generations.

These parameter values were determined using heuristic guidelines and preliminary trials via empirical experiments to obtain good results for these datasets.

For generating the next generation we use 5% reproduction, 85% crossover and 10% mutation. We use ten-fold cross validation and where simplification is used it is performed after the first generation, and every fourth generation thereafter. Note that we intend *not* to set any maximum program size. The runs are done in pairs, one for each of *no simplification* and *numerical simplification*. Because we are comparing building blocks between the two runs in each pair, both runs in the pair use the same starting population, the same folds, and the same starting seed. Each pair was run 50 times.

5   Results and Discussion

To investigate the distribution of building blocks as the run proceeds, we use three level deep building blocks encoded with the new scheme to examine (1) the lifespan of building blocks; (2) the rate at which new building blocks are added to the population; (3) the rate at which building blocks are removed from the population; (4) the number of distinct building blocks; and (5) the distribution of building block counts.

5.1   Lifespan of Building Blocks

If at a given generation, a building block (encoding) is present in the population, and at the previous generation it was not, then this is a *creation*. If at a given generation, a building block (encoding) is not present in the population, and at the previous generation it was, then this is a *destruction*.

Each time a *destruction* event occurs we record the number of generations that the building block has been in the population. This is a *lifespan*. At the end of the run we add the *lifespan* for each of the building blocks still in the population. We then plot the number of lifespans against each possible number of generations. The two different GP methods have different average program sizes and therefore different numbers of building blocks in their populations. Therefore we plot the lifespan counts as a percentage of the total number of lifespans for that run and method.

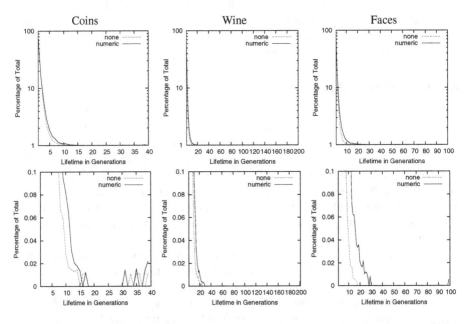

Fig. 3. Distribution of building block lifespans for the coin dataset (left), wine dataset (middle) and the faces dataset (right). The top row uses a logscale for the vertical axis, the bottom row is an enlargement of only the lowest frequencies to show the small number of building blocks with a long lifespan.

Figure 3 shows the *lifespan* distributions for the three datasets over 50 runs. The range of lifespan counts turned out to be very large and so the top row of graphs presented here use a logarithmic scale for the percentages. We added 1 to each count to avoid any problem with $log(0)$. We can see a small difference between the two methods for short lifespans but all the lifespan percentages for lifespans of greater than 10 are very small. The bottom row of plots in Fig. 3 is an expansion of just the lowest frequencies. In the coins dataset we can clearly see the small number of building blocks with long lifespans; they are harder to see for the other datasets but they are there. We tested the statistical significance of the differences between the two methods using the Wilcoxon Signed-Rank non-parametric test [24,25], and there was no significance to the differences we can see in Fig. 3.

5.2   Creation and Destruction Rates

We now examine the rate at which new building blocks are added to the population (creation) and the rate at which building blocks are removed from the population (destruction). Figure 4 shows the creation and destruction rates. Note the periodic oscillations in the simplification lines due to simplification being done every four generations. We can see that after the first one or two simplifications that the *numerical simplification* method has consistently lower rates, for both creation and destruction, than the *no-simplification* case. After the first few generations the creation and destruction rates show remarkably little long-term variation.

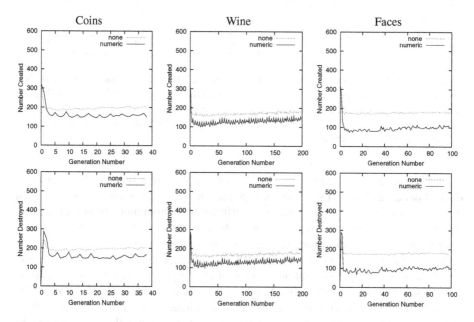

Fig. 4. Building block creation and destruction rates for the coin dataset (left), wine dataset (middle) and the faces dataset (right). The top row is the creation rate and the bottom row is the destruction rate.

5.3 Number of Distinct Building Blocks

Figure 5 shows the number of distinct building blocks, and the total number of building blocks in the population. The lines for the total number have been scaled by a factor of 5 to better fit the graph. We see that in all cases the total number of building blocks tends to rise through the run as the average program size increases. There are many small variations, but most of this growth (and occasional fall) is in a number of discrete steps. It is not easily seen on these graphs but these steps are two or three generations long. Note that there is no corresponding step in the number of distinct building blocks. One possible explanation for this effect is that when a genetic operation creates a program that is both larger than average and of high fitness, this program will often be the tournament winner and the building blocks in this program will propagate through the population causing both an increase in the average program size and an increase in total number of building blocks. The creation of such programs only occurs every few generations resulting in this stepped behaviour.

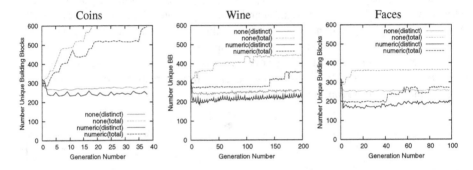

Fig. 5. The solid lines show the number of distinct building blocks in the population. The dashed lines show the total number of building blocks scaled to fit the graph (scale factor of 5). The left column is the coin dataset, the middle column is the wine dataset and the right hand column is the faces dataset. Note the periodic nature of the simplification lines, this is due to simplification only being run every fourth generation.

The first one, or sometimes two, rounds of simplification reduces the number of distinct building blocks. It starts to rise again and then the next round of simplification reduces it. The long term trend remains nearly constant throughout the rest of the run. As with the creation and destruction rates, the number of distinct building blocks is clearly lower for *numerical simplification* than for *no simplification*.

These results are not what we might have expected. The number of crossover and mutation operations per generation is constant at one per program in the population. For a given number of distinct building blocks already present in the population, the chance of a building block being created that is not already in the population is likely to also be constant. Therefore if the population size is large enough the creation rate will probably also be approximately constant.

What is not obvious is why the destruction rate and the number of distinct building blocks should remain constant or nearly so. We will examine this further in Sect. 5.4.

The consistancy of the patterns shown in Figs. 4 and 5 would suggest that they are statistically significant. We tested the significance of the differences between *numerical simplification* and *no simplification* using the Wilcoxon Signed-Rank non-parametric test. Because of the periodic nature of the numbers, the significance testing was done using averages over four successive generations, this being the number of generations per simplification. The significance was tested at the beginning and end of the run, and at three points in between.

The actual Z scores are not presented here because of space considerations but they show that for all three datasets, the *numerical simplification* method has significantly lower creation and destruction rates than the *no simplification* case. We see the same pattern with the number of distinct building blocks. All of the tests are at least the 95% level and most show a significance level of higher than 99%.

The number of unique building blocks is a measure of diversity in the population. This has a significantly lower value for the *numerical simplification* method. Other published results [16,17,18] have reported that there is no loss of classification accuracy with simplification methods. Table 1 shows the means and standard deviations of the test accuracy for the three datasets. We can see that the differences are very small and much smaller than the standard deviations. Tests showed that there is no statistical significance to these differences.

Table 1. Classification accuracy (as a percentage) on the test set of the two methods

	No Simplification		Numerical Simplification	
	Mean	StdDev	Mean	StdDev
Coins Dataset	93.9	3.0	93.0	3.1
Wine Dataset	97.9	4.2	97.9	5.1
Faces Dataset	66.1	6.3	65.8	6.2

5.4   Distribution of Building Block Counts

In section 5.2 we saw that the number of distinct building blocks remains constant or very nearly so. Intuitively we would expect that as the run proceeds and the building blocks in the high fitness individuals start to dominate the population, that the number of distinct building blocks in the population would drop. This is clearly not the case. It may be that it is only the distribution amongst the building blocks that changes. To test this we took the building blocks and sorted them in order of frequency in the final population. We have plotted the result in 3D in Fig. 6. These graphs are the average over the 50 runs. The *rank* axis is the frequency order at the end of the run: 1 at the back is the building block (encoding) with the highest number present in the final population; 2 is the second most numerous and so on. There are 100–200 different building blocks present in any generation but we show just the 20 most common in the final population as most of the building blocks are present in only small numbers. In general only about twenty have more than ten copies in the population at any generation. Each slice parallel to the generation axis is the same building block, showing the number present in the population at each generation.

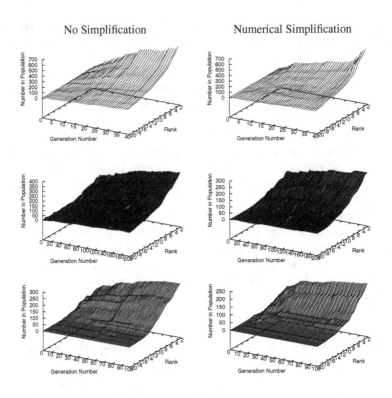

Fig. 6. The distribution of building blocks through the run. The top row is the coins dataset, the middle row is the wine dataset and the bottom row is the faces dataset.

The two graphs for the coins dataset show a clear tendency for the population to become more concentrated in the most numerous building blocks as the run proceeds. The other two datasets do not show this effect as clearly but there is still some indication. What is clear in all six graphs is that those building blocks that are common at the end of the run were in most cases among the most common at all generations in the run. We can see some small ridges in the surface, particularly in the early part of the run. These are caused by building blocks becoming slightly more or less common with respect to those near them in ranking, but very few building blocks change their ranking by more than a few places.

During the runs the genetic operators have moved building blocks between programs and they have slowly been arranged into the most advantageous arrangement. We can see from Fig. 6 that those building blocks that are common in the early generations remain common throughout the run and are therefore not among those building blocks whose destruction is shown in Fig. 4. These results suggest that the composition of the initial population is very important, if it is dominated by building blocks that are not useful in forming a good solution then it will be much more difficult to evolve a good solution.

6   Conclusions and Future Work

We have shown that there are many short lived building blocks that are created in small numbers and within one or two generations have been deleted from the population. There are also a much smaller number of building blocks that remain in the population for 60% or more of the run. This confirms the results from the image based encoding methods of [18]. We have also shown that *numerical simplification* does not appear to change that distribution.

We have shown that after the first few generations the rate at which new building blocks are added to, or building blocks removed from, the population is nearly constant. The number of distinct building blocks present in the population at any generation in the run is also nearly constant. The number of distinct building blocks in the population is reduced by *numerical simplification*. This means that in some sense at least, the *numerical simplification* process reduces the overall diversity of building blocks within the population. We were able to show that at least for these three datasets this loss of diversity has not adversely affected the classification accuracy.

In future work we will investigate further why the number of distinct building blocks remains constant and how *numerical simplification* reduces their number without adversely affecting the classification performance. We will also extend this work to regression problems in addition to the current classification problems.

References

1. Soule, T., Foster, J.A., Dickinson, J.: Code growth in genetic programming. In: Koza, J.R., et al. (eds.) Genetic Programming 1996: Proceedings of the First Annual Conference, Stanford University, CA, USA, pp. 215–223. MIT Press, Cambridge (1996)
2. Blickle, T., Thiele, L.: Genetic programming and redundancy. In: Hopf, J. (ed.) Genetic Algorithms within the Framework of Evolutionary Computation (Workshop at KI 1994), Saarbrücken, Germany, pp. 33–38 (1994)
3. Koza, J.R.: Genetic Programming: On the Programming of Computers by Means of Natural Selection. MIT Press, Cambridge (1992)
4. Nordin, P., Banzhaf, W.: Complexity compression and evolution. In: Eshelman, L. (ed.) Genetic Algorithms: Proceedings of the Sixth International Conference (ICGA 1995), USA, 15-19 July, pp. 310–317. Morgan Kaufmann, San Francisco (1995)
5. Zhang, B.-T., Mühlenbein, H.: Balancing accuracy and parsimony in genetic programming. Evolutionary Computation 3(1), 17–38 (1995)
6. Gustafson, S., Ekart, A., Burke, E., Kendall, G.: Problem difficulty and code growth in genetic programming. Genetic Programming and Evolvable Machines 5(3), 271–290 (2004)
7. Langdon, W.B.: Quadratic bloat in genetic programming. In: Whitley, D., et al. (eds.) Proceedings of the Genetic and Evolutionary Computation Conference (GECCO 2000), USA, 10-12 July, pp. 451–458 (2000)
8. Banzhaf, W., Nordin, P., Keller, R.E., Francone, F.D.: Genetic Programming: An Introduction on the Automatic Evolution of Computer Programs and its Applications. Morgan Kaufmann Publishers, San Francisco (1998)
9. Poli, R.: A simple but theoretically-motivated method to control bloat in genetic programming. In: Ryan, C., Soule, T., Keijzer, M., Tsang, E.P.K., Poli, R., Costa, E. (eds.) EuroGP 2003. LNCS, vol. 2610, pp. 204–217. Springer, Heidelberg (2003)

10. Langdon, W.B., Poli, R.: Fitness causes bloat. In: Chawdhry, P.K., Roy, R., Pant, R.K. (eds.) Soft Computing in Engineering Design and Manufacturing, pp. 13–22. Springer, Heidelberg (1997)
11. Parrott, D., Li, X., Ciesielski, V.: Multi-objective techniques in genetic programming for evolving classifiers. In: Corne, D., et al. (eds.) Proceedings of the 2005 IEEE Congress on Evolutionary Computation, Edinburgh, UK, September 2–5, vol. 2, pp. 1141–1148. IEEE Press, Los Alamitos (2005)
12. Brameier, M., Banzhaf, W.: A comparison of linear genetic programming and neural networks in medical data mining. IEEE Transactions on Evolutionary Computation 5(1), 17–26 (2001)
13. Hooper, D., Flann, N.S.: Improving the accuracy and robustness of genetic programming through expression simplification. In: Koza, J.R., et al. (eds.) Genetic Programming 1996: Proceedings of the First Annual Conference, Stanford University, CA, USA, July 28–31, p. 428. MIT Press, Cambridge (1996)
14. Ekart, A.: Shorter fitness preserving genetic programs. In: Fonlupt, C., Hao, J.-K., Lutton, E., Schoenauer, M., Ronald, E. (eds.) AE 1999. LNCS, vol. 1829, pp. 73–83. Springer, Heidelberg (2000)
15. Zhang, M., Zhang, Y., Smart, W.D.: Program simplification in genetic programming for object classification. In: Khosla, R., Howlett, R.J., Jain, L.C. (eds.) KES 2005. LNCS (LNAI), vol. 3683, pp. 988–996. Springer, Heidelberg (2005)
16. Wong, P., Zhang, M.: Algebraic simplification of GP programs during evolution. In: Keijzer, M., et al. (eds.) GECCO 2006: Proceedings of the 8th annual conference on Genetic and evolutionary computation, USA, vol. 1, pp. 927–934. ACM Press, New York (2006)
17. Kinzett, D., Zhang, M., Johnston, M.: Using numerical simplification to control bloat in genetic programming. In: Li, X., Kirley, M., Zhang, M., Green, D., Ciesielski, V., Abbass, H.A., Michalewicz, Z., Hendtlass, T., Deb, K., Tan, K.C., Branke, J., Shi, Y. (eds.) SEAL 2008. LNCS, vol. 5361, pp. 493–502. Springer, Heidelberg (2008)
18. Kinzett, D., Johnston, M., Zhang, M.: How Online Simplification Affects Building Blocks in Genetic Programming. In: Proceedings of the 11th Annual Conference on Genetic and Evolutionary Computation GECCO 2009, Montreal, Quebec, Canada, July 08–12, pp. 979–986. ACM, New York (2009)
19. Marshall, D.: The discrete cosine transform (2001),
    http://www.cs.cf.ac.uk/Dave/Multimedia/node231.htm
20. Forina, R., Leardi, M., Armanino, C., Lanteri, S.: Parvus: an extendable package of programs for data exploration, classification and correlation. Elsevier Scientific, Amsterdam (1988)
21. Witten, I., Frank, E.: Data Mining: Practical Machine Learning Tools and Techniques, 2nd edn. Morgan Kaufmann, San Francisco (2005)
22. Samaria, F., Harter, A.C.: Parameterisation of a stochastic model for human face identification. In: Proceedings of the Second IEEE Workshop on Applications of Computer Vision (1994)
23. Zhang, M., Andreae, P., Pritchard, M.: Pixel Statistics and False Alarm Area in Genetic Programming for Object Detection. In: Raidl, G.R., Cagnoni, S., Cardalda, J.J.R., Corne, D.W., Gottlieb, J., Guillot, A., Hart, E., Johnson, C.G., Marchiori, E., Meyer, J.-A., Middendorf, M. (eds.) EvoIASP 2003, EvoWorkshops 2003, EvoSTIM 2003, EvoROB/EvoRobot 2003, EvoCOP 2003, EvoBIO 2003, and EvoMUSART 2003. LNCS, vol. 2611, pp. 455–466. Springer, Heidelberg (2003)
24. Wilcoxon, F.: Individual comparisons by ranking methods. Biometrics 1, 80–83 (1945)
25. LaVange, L.M., Koch, G.G.: Rank score tests. Circulation 114(23), 2528–2533 (2006)

Fast Evaluation of GP Trees on GPGPU by Optimizing Hardware Scheduling

Ogier Maitre, Nicolas Lachiche, and Pierre Collet

LSIIT - UMR 7005 Pôle API Bd Sébastien Brant BP 10413 67412 Illkirch France
{ogier.maitre,nicolas.lachiche,pierre.collet}@unistra.fr

Abstract. This paper shows that it is possible to use General Purpose Graphic Processing Unit cards for a fast evaluation of different Genetic Programming trees on as few as 32 fitness cases by using the hardware scheduling of NVIDIA cards. Depending on the function set, observed speedup ranges between ×50 and ×250 on one half of an NVidia GTX295 GPGPU card, *vs* a single core of an Intel Quad core Q8200.

1 Introduction

General Purpose Graphic Processing Units (GPGPU) are about to revolutionize evolutionary computing because they have been designed for a workflow that is very similar to that of evolutionary algorithms. This means that our community can directly benefit from the R&D investments in very specialised chips made by the billion dollars gaming industry, provided that we understand how these cards work, and how we can make full use of their power and massive parallelism.

The current GTX295 card used in this paper contains 2×240 cores and has right now a computing power that is comparable to the cluster of 1000 350Mhz Pentiums that John Koza used to obtain the ground breaking results (leading to patentable inventions) published in [6], for less than $500.

A quick look at the design of these cards could get one to think that their seemingly SIMD[1] architecture would be a serious limiting factor, making them unsuited to execute many different genetic programming trees. However, this is not really the case, because the architecture of GPGPU cards is more complex, and allows to cut down SIMD execution to much smaller clusters of "virtual" cores, as will be shown below.

2 Description of the Problem

The workflow of image rendering algorithms is virtually the same as that of evolutionary algorithms (EAs), as the same pixel shader algorithm (read "fitness function") must be executed in parallel on millions of different pixels (read "genomes") of the image (read "population").

---

[1] Single Instruction Multiple Data means that all cores must excute the same instruction at the same time. Standard multi-core CPUs are MIMD, for Multiple Instruction Multiple Data (different instructions can be executed on different data).

A.I. Esparcia-Alcazar et al. (Eds.): EuroGP 2010, LNCS 6021, pp. 301–312, 2010.

In terms of hardware, this very special SIMD workflow allows in theory to mutualize all needs. For example only one Fetch&Dispatch unit (which provides code instructions to arithmetic and logic units ALUs) can be used for all ALUs (that execute the same instruction at the same time). Conversely on an MIMD processor, the fact that all ALUs must be able to execute *different* instructions in parallel means that independent Fetch&Dispatch units must be associated to all MIMD ALUs.

Then, since rendering algorithms work on millions of pixels, each core must execute the very same code for several hundreds of different pixels, meaning that heavy pipelining can be envisaged. This allows to do without a memory cache and use the silicon space for yet more cores: high latency memory is not a problem if enough threads can be stacked up on one core. If a single memory access takes as much time as the execution of 100 instructions, data will be ready when the 100th thread will have made its memory request (pipelining). If this workflow is totally compatible with GAs, and allows for an "easy" porting of an EA on a GPGPU [9], things are different for GP, where conceptually speaking, the algorithm must evaluate thousands of *different* programs (or functions) on what can be a *very small* learning set. On a standard SIMD architecture, two cores cannot execute different instructions simultaneously. They have to execute the 2 instructions sequentially.

As a consequence, two basic options can be used to evaluate GP trees:

1. Run one tree per core. But this guarantees to have many cores waiting for each other, since different trees will contain different operators and will be of different lengths (cores will often be idle, waiting for others to execute different instructions).
2. Run the same tree on all the cores, which necessitates enough different test cases to load the pipelines of the card. The problem is that on a 100 cores card, if one memory access takes the same time as executing 100 instructions, as many as 10,000 fitness cases will be needed to avoid the bottleneck on memory access time if all 100 cores evaluate the same GP tree.

3   Related Work

Several attempts have already been made at running interpreted or compiled Genetic Programming algorithms on GPGPU cards [8].

In the case of compiled GP on GPGPU, the first work by Chitty in 2007 [2] uses the relatively high-level *C for Graphics* (Cg) language with option 2 (one tree on all the cores, on different fitness cases). The author obtained speedups of ×10 for the whole algorithm on an NVidia 6400GO card with 4 pixel pipelines and 3 vertex pipelines (this is an old architecture) *vs* a 1.7GHz Intel processor on a symbolic regression problem with 400 fitness cases, and speedups of ×30 on the 11 way multiplexer with between 100 000 and 150 000 fitness cases.

In 2007, Harding *et al.* [3] applied approximatively the same technique using .Net and MS Accelerator framework. Option 2 was selected again, with impressive speedups of ×7000 for a compiled evaluation function on an NVidia 7300

GO card (4 pixel pipelines, 3 vertex pipelines) *vs* an Intel T2400 1.83GHz processor, but in the case of GP individuals with 10,000 nodes and 65,536 fitness cases for the sextic regression problem.

In 2008, Langdon *et al.* [7] used RapidMind to evaluate GP individuals with a sequential interpreter on GPU. They used option 1, where individuals are spread across all cores of the GPU. Each core executes all the functions in the function set on all nodes of the tree and keeps only the desired result. They obtain a speed up of ×12 on a 128 Shading Processors 8800GTX NVidia card compared to a 2.2GHz AMD Athlon 64 3500+ CPU for the whole algorithm, applied to a real world problem. They suggest that the SIMD nature of the implementation generates a loss of ×3, which is roughly proportional to the 5 functions of their functions set.

In 2008 and 2009, Robilliard *et al.* [13,12] use the NVidia CUDA environnement to perform GP interpretations on NVidia cards. This approach is the closest to the hardware among those discussed above. They used the SPMD (Single Program Multiple Data) architecture of NVidia GPUs to execute multiple individuals on multiple fitness cases at the same time. This work has been applied to sextic regression and 11-multiplexer on which a speed up of ×80 is obtained (for evaluation only) on the sextic regression problem with 2,500 fitness cases, on a 8800GTX NVidia card *vs* an Intel 2.6GHz processor.

4   CUDA

As seen above, different environments are used to execute GP individuals on GPU hardware. RapidMind and Accelerator are high level languages that allow to write portable code across multi-core architecture: RapidMind allows the execution of a C-like program through the OpenGL library while Accelerator uses DirectX to do so. Even if this high level approach is convenient, this results in a loss of performance, which is easy to understand in [7]. Programs are compiled as vertex or pixel shaders and data arrays are bound to textures. Those environments force the execution to be SIMD, even if the underlying hardware is SPMD.

The CUDA environment used in this paper allows direct access to the NVidia hardware without going through DirectX or OpenGL layers, and is therefore more efficient. Unfortunately, this means that the code is more complex to write, and portability is limited to NVidia cards.

4.1   Software Architecture

CUDA (released in 2004 by NVidia) is an abstract representation of a unified "computing accelerator." Its goal is to achieve a hardware abstraction of the underlying computing device by defining portable concepts across different architectures without any modification. The model handles threads of parallel tasks which can be executed on the accelerator. A thread is, as per the classical definition, an independent process, which executes instructions on data. Threads can be arranged in 2D arrays (called blocks), allowing them to map a 2D data array as a 2D texture. Every thread inside a block can communicate with any other thread in the same block, thanks to a small amount of high speed shared memory.

The CUDA software architecture defines a complex memory hierarchy, built separately from the main memory system of the computer. This hierarchy contains a large global memory (without a cache), a small very fast shared memory used for communication between threads inside a block, and read-only caches for textures, constants and instructions.

4.2 Hardware Architecture

Concepts in software abstraction are more or less mapped onto a hardware instantiation. The CUDA implementation uses NVidia GPUs as a "computing accelerator." Threads are executed by a Streaming Processor (SP). The card used for this paper holds 2 GPUs that contain 240 SP each while the future g300 chip of GTX395 cards will contain 2×512 streaming processors.

Things begin to get interesting when rather than having one Fetch and Dispatch (F&D) unit for all SPs as on a pure SIMD architecture, NVidia cards implements only one unit for 8 SPs . Unfortunately, all instructions must be executed 4 times by every SP, due to the difference in terms of speed, between the SP clock and the F&D unit clock. This means that 8 SPs act like a 32 core SIMD CPU, so at least 32 tasks must be present on the 8 linked SPs in order to fill every thread slots. This makes for virtual 32 SP *bundles* that are called Multi-Processors (MPs), knowing that a dual-chip 295GTX card holds 2×30 multi-processors.

A block of threads is executed on only one MP, but an MP can execute 4 blocks at a time, if enough resources are available (enough registers and shared memory for executing the 4 blocks).

The memory model is implemented on the GPU by using a global memory of several hundred MegaBytes (2×896MB on a 295GTX), read only caches, and memory banks for shared memory (16kB). Even if the global memory has a large bandwidth (2×111 GigaBytes per second), it suffers a very high latency, estimated to several hundred cycles for each memory access, partially due to the lack of cache.

4.3 Hardware Scheduling

The latency problem could be really embarrassing, but the GPU fortunately embeds a *hardware* scheduling mechanism on each MP which acts like the Hyper-Threading mechanism of *Pentium IV* and *Core i7* Intel processors, i.e. to be able to overcome memory stalls, as each MP can schedule between many threads. When a thread (actually, a bundle of 32 threads) makes a memory access, it is frozen for hundreds of cycles. The hardware swaps the bundle with another bundle that is ready to execute, by placing it onto the processor.

The CUDA documentation asserts that each MP can schedule between 24 bundles of 32 threads (*i.e.* 768 threads), coming from all the 4 thread blocks loaded onto an MP.

NVidia released a profiler for CUDA which allows to watch the scheduling ability and obtain an "occupancy" value. It is interesting to note that occupancy is not directly related to performance. Maximizing occupancy is only useful to overcome memory latencies. In some situations, increasing the occupancy can yield no improvement in performance, for example if a code has a high computation/memory_access ratio.

5   Implementation

The proposed implementation uses Reverse Polish Notation (RPN) to represent GP individuals, which is very parsimonious in memory. Copying the whole population onto the GPU with a real tree representation would drastically slow down the transfer from the CPU memory point of view. With RPN notation, the whole population occupies only one memory buffer, which can be transferred in one go, therefore exploiting the very high memory bandwidth of the graphic PCIEx interface on which the card is plugged. Trees are evaluated on the GPU card using a multi-thread RPN interpretor, which is able to evaluate multiple individuals on multiple fitness cases at the same time as explained in the next section. All interpretor stacks are allocated in the very fast shared memory as in [13].

There are several ways to deal with such an RPN representation. In [13], Robilliard *et al* flatten GP trees just before transferring them onto the card, which shows the feasibility of the approach. However the time spent in this operation will increase with population size and tree depth. Other ideas are for the GP algorithm to directly deal with flat individuals written in RPN. This has been done in [7,12] but it can introduce biases, such as using an equal (and maximal) sized buffer for each and every individual. Another approach would be to use linear GP, CGP, FIFTH or PUSH algorithms [1,10,4,14] that do not require a tree representation.

The current paper focuses only on parallel evaluation of different GP individuals on a GPGPU card, not on the GP algorithm that goes behind.

6   Evaluation Step

As discussed in section 4.3, GPUs are designed to execute many tasks in parallel. Evaluating a GP population of size n over k fitness cases is equivalent to evaluating $n \times k$ parallel tasks. We have seen that these tasks will be SIMD *within* bundles of 32 threads but can be MIMD *across* the bundles. The trick now consists in organising the tasks in order to keep all units busy while making sure they all fit in shared memory and registers so as to maximise the efficiency of the hardware scheduling process.

Threads within a bundle execute the same GP individual on different fitness cases, but different bundles can evaluate different individuals. This technique allows to make improved use of the underlying hardware for as few as 32 fitness cases, which is the main contribution of this work, although the presented implementation still allows for good speedups down to 8 test cases as will be shown below.

This is very important as many GP problems can only use a very limited number of test cases (very often less than 1,000 and often less than 100). This limits the potential of all previously published implementations of GP on GPUs (cf. section 3).

Because 32 fitness cases produce 32 threads, and because an MP can handle 4 blocks (the hardware scheduler can automatically map 4 individuals), evaluating 4 different individuals in the same block results in using 512 threads per MP, which improves performance. Therefore each MP will evaluate 16 individuals on 32 fitness cases. This is possible, because, as asserted by the CUDA documentation [11] a divergence in the execution path will result in loss of performance *only if this divergence occurs within one SIMD bundle.*

7   Experiments

7.1   Experimental Process

The experiments have been performed on a GTX295 NVidia card *vs* a recent Intel Quad core Q8200 (2.33GHz) processor and 4GB RAM, under linux 2.6.27 64 bits with NVidia driver 190.18 and CUDA 2.3. The GTX295 is a dual GPU card, but to simplify things, we use only one GPU to evaluate GP individuals, the second card being used for the standard display. A multi-GPU implementation has been tested by distributing the population on the two GPUs of the GTX295 card. No drawback has been observed other than the need for the population size to be large enough to fully load the two GPUs.

CPU code has been compiled with gcc 4.3.2 using the -O2 optimisation option and run on one core of the CPU only, so as to avoid poor multi-core implementation that would bias measurements towards an even better speedup for GPUs. By not implementing a multi-core CPU GP, one still has the possibility to imagine that in the best case, a perfect multi-core implementation would show a linear speed up, with respect to the number of cores of the CPU.

The evaluation algorithm is applied on a regression problem, using randomly generated trees, without any evolution (this paper is only about maximising GP tree evaluation speedup over GPUs). Trees are grown using the grow or full method from Koza's book [5]. They are evaluated on CPU and flattened before being evaluated on GPU so that the very same trees are used to compare CPU and GPU evaluation time. Timings are performed with the `gettimeofday()` POSIX function. For the CPU, timing is done on the evaluation function only, whereas on the GPGPU timing also includes transfer of the population from the CPU to the GPU memory and transfer of the results back to the CPU. Buffers for population, fitness cases, results and hits are allocated for the whole run only once. As for a real GP problem, fitness cases are constant and are sent to the GPU board during memory allocation (cf. fig. 1).

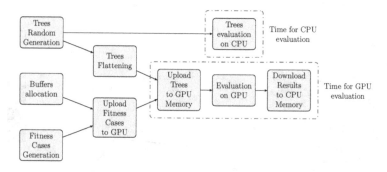

Fig. 1. Global scheme for GP simulation and timing process

7.2 Evaluation Time *vs.* Number of Fitness Cases

Four different implementations are compared in fig. 2, for depth 7 trees, with a population of 60 000 individuals. The three implementations which evaluate 32 fitness cases with 1, 2 and 4 different individuals per MP, are named MP1×32, MP2×32 and MP4×32. The last implementation (named MP1×128) evaluates 128 fitness cases with one individual per MP. MP1×32 is similar to the implementation presented in [13].

Curves are stair-shaped and the length of each step is equal to the number of fitness cases computed in parallel, which is reasonable. MP1×128 is the most efficient implementation on large fitness case sets, mainly because it greatly improves the scheduling capability of the GPU without incurring overhead for handling multiple individuals per MP. However, it is interesting to note that the curve for *MP4×32* is roughly identical to the curve for *MP1×128*, showing that it is possible to get a near-optimal use of GPGPUs with as few as 32 fitness cases.

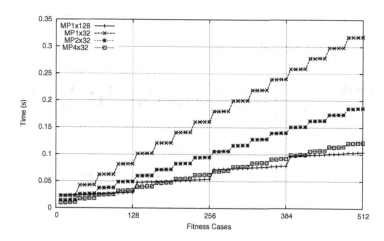

Fig. 2. Evaluation time for depth 7 trees for different implementations with a sampling size of 8 fitness cases

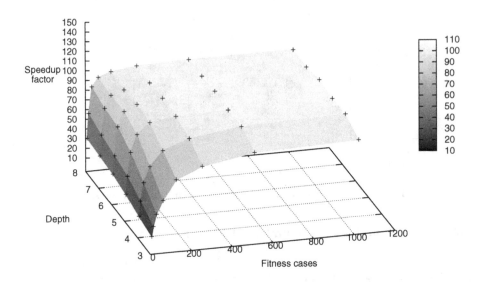

Fig. 3. Resulting speedup between GPGPU and CPU

7.3 Influence of Tree Depth on Speedup

Figure 3 shows the speedups for different numbers of fitness cases and different tree sizes with MP4×32 using a $\{+,-,\oplus,\times,\cos,\sin\}$ (where $\oplus$ is the protected division) function set, and a full method for tree construction. With this particular function set, trees are not full in the binary sense because of unary operators. One can see that the depth of trees has an influence on performance, but with less impact than the number of fitness cases. Indeed, an increase in tree depth not

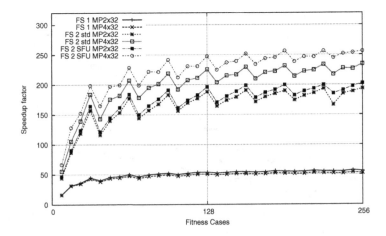

Fig. 4. Resulting speedup for depth 7 trees on GPGPU against CPU for different function sets

only increases the number of computations, but also the size of the population buffer *i.e.* the memory transfer time.

Above 32 fitness cases, the curve is not flat because of memory transfer time. Under 32 fitness cases, the GPGPU is not optimally loaded, but interesting speedups can nevertheless be obtained (×60 for tree depth 10 on 8 fitness cases only).

The surface reaches a plateau with a speedup of around ×250 when the card is fully loaded and memory transfer overhead is minimised.

7.4 Influence of Function Set

Fig. 4 shows that the computational complexity of the function set has an influence on speedup as well. Three different sets have been tested:

F1	F2	F2SFU
+, -, ⊘, ×	+, -, ⊘, ×, cos, sin, log, exp	+, -, ⊘, ×, cos, sin, log, exp

Function set 1 has a poor computational intensity. Execution time of the operators is so small that speedup stagnates at around ×50. Speedup is about the same for MP4×32 and for MP2×32 (that needs to handle twice as many threads), meaning that the bottleneck probably comes from memory access rather than thread management.

Function set 2 has a higher computational intensity. It keeps the hardware busy and speedup again depends on the number of fitness cases. The curve shows teeth because given that the execution time is flat between two multiples of 32 (cf. stairs in fig. 2), speedup decreases brutally at each new step *vs* CPU time that increases linearly with the number of test cases.

Function set 2 with Special Function Units uses interesting features that can be found on GPGPU cards, as explained in [11]: functions {sin, cos, log, exp} can be approximated by fast Special Function Units (SFU) which are inherited from the 3D rendering design of GPU cards. Function set 2 with SFU shows a gain in speedup obtained at a cost of less precise results. However using them in GP is not really problematic since GP will take the approximations into account. (One must only make sure that the obtained function is not used on another computer where the exact same SFU functions are not implemented.) Robilliard *et al.* used SFU functions to obtain their results in [12].

7.5 Influence of Tree Shapes on Speedup

Up to now, tests concerned "full" trees in the Koza sense (*i.e.* created with a full() function). Unfortunately, during a real GP run, trees are usually created using a ramped half and half initialisation method that tries to create as diverse a population as possible. Then as evolution goes on, the shape of the trees becomes more homogeneous, but they are certainly not full. In order to estimate the speedup that could be obtained during a real GP run, a population of trees created with Koza's grow() function [5] has been tested, that results in a performance loss if for instance a very large tree is part of the same bundle

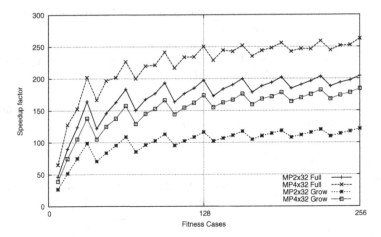

Fig. 5. Resulting speedup for depth 7 trees on GPGPU against CPU for different tree construction methods

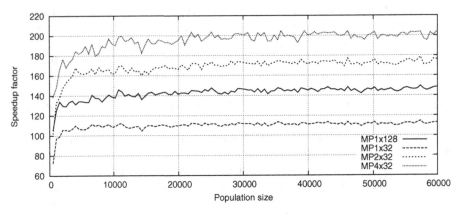

Fig. 6. Resulting speedup for depth 7 trees, function set FS2SFU and 32 fitness cases on GPGPU against CPU *wrt* the population size for different implementations of GP evaluations

as 3 other very small trees. Therefore, threads containing the small trees will have to wait for the execution of the thread containing the large tree before the bundle can be replaced.

Fig. 5 shows that speedup drops from around 250 with full trees down to around 170 with trees obtained with the *grow* method.

7.6   Influence of Population Size

Another important parameter is the size of the population. CUDA documentation says that many tasks must be loaded on the GPU to allow for scheduling between different tasks. If x individuals evaluating 32 fitness cases will fully load the card using an MP1×32 (or MP1×128) implementation, then, twice the number of individuals is necessary to load the card with an MP2×32 implementation, since 2 individuals will be put in the same bundle. An MP4×32 implementation will therefore need 4 times more individuals than an MP1×32 (or an MP1×128) implementation to load the card.

This is clearly shown in figure 6 where the curves for MP1×32 and MP1×128 attain their top speedup much faster than MP2×32 and MP4×32. However, this is not much of a problem since MP2×32 or MP4×32 curves show a much better speedup than MP1×32 or MP1×128 even for small population sizes.

8 Conclusion and Future Work

Few papers have been written on how Genetic Programming could benefit from being run on GPGPU hardware. However, this work is to our knowledge the first to focus on hardware scheduling of GPGPU cards in order to efficiently evaluate different individuals with as few as 32 fitness cases (interesting speedups are also obtained with learning sets as small as 8 fitness cases, but these do not allow to fully load the card).

Speedups ranging from ×50 up to ×250 (depending on the function set) have been obtained on a recent NVidia card *vs* a single core of a recent Intel processor. According to figures published by NVidia, the new generation of Fermi GPGPU cards could allow speedups of ≈ ×5,000 on a single PC with 4 GTX395 cards, *i.e.* much more than the power of the 1,000 350MHz Pentium cluster that Koza used to obtain patentable inventions in [6]. Such a speedup means that 1 day of computation on a GPGPU would be equivalent to 5,000 days on a modern PC, *i.e.* more than 13 years ! Even if this maximum speedup is not achieved on all kinds of problems, having years of calculation on a single PC done in one day may allow to start working on totally new kinds of problems that are simply out of reach without GPGPU cards.

The presented speedups only concern individuals evaluation time, not the full GP algorithm. Evaluation is usually considered to be the most time-consuming part of a GP, but GPGPU cards make this statement obsolete, as preliminary tests show that the standard GP evolutionary engine is now the bottleneck, since the trees need to be flattened before they are passed over to the GPGPU. Linear GP, CGP, FIFTH or PUSH [1,10,4,14] therefore look like good candidates to feed the cards with enough individuals, fast enough to satisfy their greed.

Concerning future work, a dynamic load balancing system could be implemented thanks to atomic functions available on GPGPUs that could yet improve speedup when trees have very different shapes, but the KISS principle says that it is now time to work on the GP engine until eventually, individuals evaluation becomes the bottleneck again. As soon as good results are obtained on a full GP program, our concern will be to make parallel GP programming over CUDA available in a language such as EASEA, making GPGPU-based GP (GPGPGPU ?) available to all researchers who would be interested in trying them out without needing to program the cards themselves.

References

1. Brameier, M., Banzhaf, W.: Linear Genetic Programming. Genetic and Evolutionary Computation, vol. XVI. Springer, Heidelberg (2007)
2. Chitty, D.M.: A data parallel approach to genetic programming using programmable graphics hardware. In: Procs of the 9th annual conference on Genetic and evolutionary computation, London, England, pp. 1566–1573. ACM, New York (2007)
3. Harding, S., Banzhaf, W.: Fast genetic programming on GPUs. In: Ebner, M., O'Neill, M., Ekárt, A., Vanneschi, L., Esparcia-Alcázar, A.I. (eds.) EuroGP 2007. LNCS, vol. 4445, pp. 90–101. Springer, Heidelberg (2007)
4. Holladay, K., Robbins, K., von Ronne, J.: FIFTH: A stack based GP language for vector processing. In: Ebner, M., O'Neill, M., Ekárt, A., Vanneschi, L., Esparcia-Alcázar, A.I. (eds.) EuroGP 2007. LNCS, vol. 4445, pp. 102–113. Springer, Heidelberg (2007)
5. Koza, J.R.: Genetic Programming: On the Programming of Computers by Means of Natural Selection (Complex Adaptive Systems). MIT Press, Cambridge (1992)
6. Koza, J.R., et al.: Genetic Programming IV: Routine Human-Competitive Machine Intelligence. Kluwer Academic Publishers, Dordrecht (2003)
7. Langdon, W., Banzhaf, W.: A SIMD interpreter for genetic programming on GPU graphics cards. In: O'Neill, M., Vanneschi, L., Gustafson, S., Esparcia Alcázar, A.I., De Falco, I., Della Cioppa, A., Tarantino, E. (eds.) EuroGP 2008. LNCS, vol. 4971, pp. 73–85. Springer, Heidelberg (2008)
8. Langdon, W.B.: A field guide to genetic programing. Wyvern, 8 (April 2008)
9. Maitre, O., Baumes, L.A., Lachiche, N., Corma, A., Collet, P.: Coarse grain parallelization of evolutionary algorithms on gpgpu cards with easea. In: GECCO, pp. 1403–1410 (2009)
10. Miller, J.F., Harding, S.L.: Cartesian genetic programming. In: GECCO 2008: Proceedings of the 2008 GECCO conference companion on Genetic and evolutionary computation, pp. 2701–2726. ACM, New York (2008)
11. NVIDIA. NVIDIA CUDA Programming Guide 2.0 (2008)
12. Robilliard, D., Marion, V., Fonlupt, C.: High performance genetic programming on GPU. In: Proceedings of the 2009 workshop on Bio-inspired algorithms for distributed systems, Barcelona, Spain, pp. 85–94. ACM, New York (2009)
13. Robilliard, D., Marion-Poty, V., Fonlupt, C.: Population parallel GP on the G80 GPU. In: O'Neill, M., Vanneschi, L., Gustafson, S., Esparcia Alcázar, A.I., De Falco, I., Della Cioppa, A., Tarantino, E. (eds.) EuroGP 2008. LNCS, vol. 4971, p. 98. Springer, Heidelberg (2008)
14. Spector, L., Robinson, A.: Genetic programming and autoconstructive evolution with the push programming language. Genetic Programming and Evolvable Machines 3(1), 7–40 (2002)

Ensemble Image Classification Method Based on Genetic Image Network

Shiro Nakayama, Shinichi Shirakawa, Noriko Yata, and Tomoharu Nagao

Graduate School of Environment and Information Sciences, Yokohama National University, 79-7, Tokiwadai, Hodogaya-ku, Yokohama, Kanagawa, 240-8501, Japan
{shiro,shirakawa,yata}@nlab.sogo1.ynu.ac.jp, nagao@ynu.ac.jp

Abstract. Automatic construction method for image classification algorithms have been required. Genetic Image Network for Image Classification (GIN-IC) is one of the methods that construct image classification algorithms automatically, and its effectiveness has already been proven. In our study, we try to improve the performance of GIN-IC with AdaBoost algorithm using GIN-IC as weak classifiers to complement with each other. We apply our proposed method to three types of image classification problems, and show the results in this paper. In our method, discrimination rates for training images and test images improved in the experiments compared with the previous method GIN-IC.

1 Introduction

Automatic construction method for image classification algorithms have been required. In general, image classification algorithms consist of image preprocessing, feature extraction, and classification process. It is very difficult to construct an algorithm suitable for all image classification problems. Therefore, a method is required to construct an image classification algorithm that would automatically adjust to the target problem is needed. Genetic Image Network for Image Classification (GIN-IC) [1] is one of the methods that construct image classification algorithms automatically, and its effectiveness has already been proven. GIN-IC automatically constructs the adequate classification algorithm (including image transformation, feature extraction and arithmetic operation components) using evolutionary computation. The process of GIN-IC is, first, to transform original images to easier-to-classify images using image transformation nodes, and next, to select adequate image features using feature extraction nodes. The greatest advantage of GIN-IC is its image transformation (preprocessing) component, which influences image feature selection. However, learning failure or over fitting of the training images sometimes occurs in the constructed algorithms because of GIN-IC's simple output to decide the classification.

In this paper, we extend GIN-IC by adding the AdaBoost algorithm [2]. AdaBoost is one of the greatest general ensemble learning methods to make a strong classifier, which has higher performance, by combining weak classifiers, which have lower performance. AdaBoost is applied to various image classification problems and has shown its effectiveness, such as the face detection

A.I. Esparcia-Alcazar et al. (Eds.): EuroGP 2010, LNCS 6021, pp. 313–324, 2010.

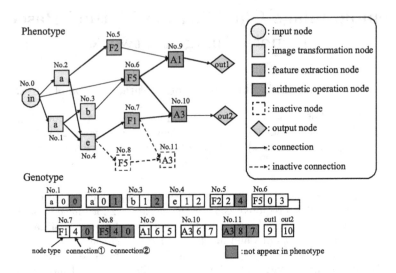

Fig. 1. Example of a structure in Genetic Image Network for Image Classification

method proposed by Viola and Jones [3]. Moreover, aggregating the classifiers constructed by genetic programming [4,5,6], particle swarm optimization [7] or neural networks [8] has been studied to improve their classification performance. In our method, a set of output nodes in GIN-IC is treated as a weak classifier. The performance is expected to be improved by using GIN-IC as weak classifiers that complement with each other.

The next section of this paper is an overview of GIN-IC. In section 3, we describe our proposed method. In section 4, we apply the proposed method to three kinds of image classification problems and show their results in section 5. Finally, in section 6, we describe conclusions and future work.

2 Genetic Image Network for Image Classification (GIN-IC)

2.1 Structure of GIN-IC

The image classifier GIN-IC consists of image transformation, feature extraction, and arithmetic operation components based on the Genetic Image Network [9]. GIN-IC constructs an acyclic network-structured image classifier automatically. Fig. 1 shows an example of the phenotype (feed-forward network structure) and genotype (string representing the phenotype) of GIN-IC.

One of the benefits of this type of representation is that it allows the implicit reuse of nodes in its network. The nodes of GIN-IC are categorized into five types: input nodes, image transformation nodes, feature extraction nodes, arithmetic operation nodes, and output nodes. Input nodes correspond to the original images. Image transformation nodes execute image transformation using the corresponding well-known image processing filters. Feature extraction nodes extract an image feature from the input images. Arithmetic operation nodes execute arithmetic operations. Image classification is performed using the values of the output nodes. In GIN-IC, these processes evolve simultaneously.

In GIN-IC, the feed-forward network structure of nodes is evolved, as shown in Fig. 1. Numbers are allocated to each node, beforehand. Increasingly large numbers are allocated, in order, to the input nodes, image transformation nodes, feature extraction nodes, arithmetic operation nodes, and output nodes. Connections, such as the feedback structure, that cannot be executed are restricted at the genotype level. The nodes take their input from the output of the previous nodes in a feed-forward manner. Because GIN-IC constructs a feed-forward network structured image classification procedure, it can represent multiple outputs. Therefore, GIN-IC enables easy construction of a multiclass image classification procedure using a single network structure.

To adopt an evolutionary method, GIN-IC uses genotype-phenotype mapping. This genotype-phenotype mapping method is similar to Cartesian Genetic Programming (CGP) [10]. The feed-forward network structure is encoded in the form of a linear string. The genotype in GIN-IC is a fixed length representation and consists of a string that encodes the node function ID and connections of each node in the network. However, the number of nodes in the phenotype can vary in a restricted manner, as not all the nodes encoded in the genotype have to be connected. This allows the existence of inactive nodes. In Fig. 1, node No. 8 and 11 are inactive nodes.

2.2   Genetic Operator and Generation Alternation Model

To obtain the optimum structure, an evolutionary method is adopted. The genotype of GIN-IC is a linear string. Therefore, it is able to use a standard genetic operator. In GIN-IC, mutation is used as the genetic operator. The mutation operator affects one individual, as follows:

- Select several genes randomly according to the mutation rate P_m for each gene.
- Randomly change the selected genes under the structural constraints.

$(1 + 4)$ Evolution Strategy $((1 + 4)$ ES) is used as the generation alternation model. The $(1 + 4)$ ES procedure in the experiments works as follows:

1. Set generation counter $j = 0$. Generate an individual randomly as a parent M.
2. Generate a set of four offspring C, by applying the mutation operation to M.
3. Select the elite individual from the set $M + C$ (the offspring is selected if it has the same best fitness as the parent). Then replace M with the elite individuals.
4. Stop if a certain specified condition is satisfied; otherwise, set $j = j + 1$ and go to step 2.

Since GIN-IC has inactive nodes, a neutral effect on fitness is caused by genetic operation (called neutrality [10]). In step 3, the offspring is selected if it has the same best fitness as the parent, then the searching point moves even if the fitness is not improved. Therefore, efficient search is achieved though a simple generation alternation model. This $(1 + 4)$ ES was adopted and showed its effectiveness in previous works [1,10].

2.3   Advantages and Limitations of GIN-IC

GIN-IC has many advantages to automatically construct image classification algorithms. The greatest advantage of GIN-IC is its image transformation (pre-processing) component, which is expected to influence image feature selection. In other words, GIN-IC generates and selects adequate image features by a combination of nodes. However, learning failure or over fitting of the training images sometimes occurs in the constructed algorithms because of GIN-IC's simple output to decide the classification. Moreover, more the size or the number of training images is increased, more time for learning it takes.

3   Proposed Method

3.1   Overview

To solve the problems noted in previous section, we apply the AdaBoost [2] algorithm to GIN-IC. A set of output nodes in GIN-IC is treated as a weak classifier. Thus, the total number of output nodes is $N \times T$, where N is the number of classes and T is the number of weak classifiers. Weak classifiers are evolved in sequence until each weak classifier achieves a specified error rate. In this process, the construction of the previous weak classifiers is fixed and can be reused in the subsequent weak classifiers. The effective process of other weak classifiers can be reused. Moreover, reuse is expected to reduce the time required for learning by avoiding recalculation at each operational node. In addition, all weak classifiers have a weight of their hypothesis. The final hypothesis is a weighted vote of the hypothesis of all weak classifiers. Fig. 2 shows an example of a structure in our proposed method for binary classification.

3.2   Process of the Proposed Method

The process of our proposed method is described as follows:

Step 1: Initialize the weights $D_1(i) = \frac{1}{m}$, $(i = 1, 2, \ldots, m)$, and weak classifier counter $t = 1$, where m is the number of training images.

Step 2: Focus the tth output set as the tth weak classifier. Here, add the new usable nodes to save enough nodes for constructing the new weak classifier. Add n_i of image transformation nodes, n_f of feature extraction nodes and n_a of arithmetic operation nodes.

Step 3: Evolve the weak classifier based on GIN-IC till the error rate ϵ_t is less than a threshold τ. ϵ_t is obtained by summing weights $D_t(i)$ corresponding to misclassified images as

$$\epsilon_t = \sum_{i:h_t(x_i) \neq y_i} D_t(i), \tag{1}$$

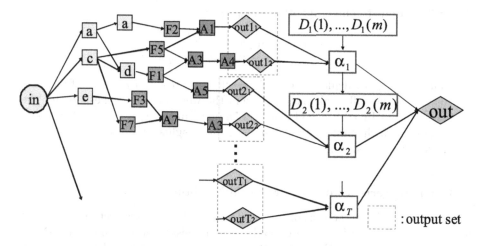

Fig. 2. Example of a structure in proposed method for binary classification

where $h_t(x_i)$ is the class label corresponding to the output node with the largest value of the weak classifier t when the input is image x_i, and y_i is the correct class label of image x_i. Here, we use $(1 + 4)$ ES as the generation alternation model. The $(1 + 4)$ ES procedure is the same as in section 2.2. Do not operate the fixed nodes in step 6 by genetic operation, and allow these nodes to be selected as the input of other nodes. When constructing the tth classifier, the structures of the classifiers from first to $(t - 1)$th can be reused.

Step 4: Calculate the weight of hypothesis α of the focused output set as

$$\alpha_t = \frac{1}{2} \log \left(\frac{1 - \epsilon_t}{\epsilon_t} \right). \tag{2}$$

Step 5: Update the weights as

$$D_{t+1}(i) = \frac{D_t(i)}{Z_t} \times \begin{cases} \exp(-\alpha_t) & \text{if } h_t(x_i) = y_i \\ \exp(\alpha_t) & \text{otherwise} \end{cases}, \tag{3}$$

where Z_t is the number for normalization. This operation adapts the weights corresponding to the training images based on the AdaBoost algorithm. By this operation, the weights corresponding to the training images classified correctly are decreased and the weights corresponding the training images misclassified by the previous weak classifiers are increased. Therefore, the misclassified images are classified correctly by the next weak classifier preferentially.

Step 6: Set $t = t + 1$. If $t \leq T$, fix the nodes connected with the focused output set and go back to step 2.

Step 7: Output the final hypothesis $h_{\text{fin}}(x_i)$ as

$$h_{\text{fin}}(x_i) = \arg\max_{y_i \in Y} \sum_{t:h_t(x_i)=y_i} \alpha_t. \tag{4}$$

This operation calculate the final classification results by a vote of all weak classifiers. For all weak classifiers, sum the weights of hypothesis α_t for the class output by tth weak classifier. The input image x_i is classified the class $h_{\text{fin}}(x_i)$, which maximizes the sum of the weights of weak classifiers that output the class.

3.3   Characteristics of the Proposed Method

We note some characteristics of our proposed method in this section. First, the classifier constructed by our proposed method consists of a number of GIN-IC as weak classifiers. We think that the performance is improved because weak classifiers complement with each other compared with GIN-IC. Second, the construction of the previous weak classifiers is fixed and can be reused in the subsequent weak classifiers. Therefore, the effective process of other weak classifiers can be reused since all nodes may be selected as the input of other nodes. Third, we stop evolving GIN-IC on the way to use it as weak classifiers. This operation is expected to reduce the time required for learning and to prevent over fitting.

4   Experiments

4.1   Settings of the Experiment

In this section, we evaluate our proposed method by applying it to three image classification problems. The problems are as follows:

1. Texture images
2. Pedestrian images
3. Generic object images

In these experiments, we transform all color images into grayscale. We also apply the previous method, GIN-IC, to the same problems to compare it with our proposed method. Table 1 shows the parameters used in the proposed method and the previous method, GIN-IC. We determined each parameter by the results of preliminary experiments.

We prepare simple and well-known image processing filters as the image transformation nodes in the experiments (26 one-input, one-output filters and 9 two-input, one-output filters), e.g., mean filter, maximum filter, minimum filter, Sobel filter, Laplacian filter, gamma correction filter, binarization, linear transformation, difference, logical sum, logical prod, etc. 17 simple statistical values are used as feature extraction nodes, e.g., mean value, standard deviation, maximum value, minimum value, mode, 3 sigma in rate, 3 sigma out rate, skewness,

Table 1. Parameters used in the experiments

Parameters	GIN-IC	Proposal
Generation alternation model	(1+4)ES	(1+4)ES
Mutation rate (P_m)	0.02	0.02
Image transformation nodes (n_i)	100	Add 50
Feature extraction nodes (n_f)	100	Add 50
Arithmetic operation nodes (n_a)	100	Add 50
Output nodes	6, 2, 5	6, 2, 5
The number of generations	112500	–
The number of weak classifiers (T)	–	100
Error rate threshold (τ)	–	0.4

kurtosis, etc. The arithmetic operation nodes are 20 well-known arithmetic operations, e.g., addition, subtraction, multiplication, division, threshold function, piecewise linear function, sigmoid function, absolute value, equalities, inequalities, constant value, etc. In both the proposed method and previous method (GIN-IC), we use the same kinds of nodes. The fitness function of GIN-IC as weak classifiers in proposed method is described as follows:

$$\text{fitness} = N_c \times m + \frac{1}{N_a}, \qquad (5)$$

where N_c is sum of the weights $D_t(i)$ of training images classified correctly, N_a is the number of active nodes, and m is the number of training images. If the classification performance is the same, the number of active nodes should be small in this fitness function. We describe the features of the training images used in each experiment as follows:

Experiment 1: Texture Images. We use texture images from the publicly available database VisTex.[1] We use six classes in this experiment. We make 128 images with 64×64 pixels each by dividing two texture images of 512×512 pixels for each class. The number of training images is 60 (10 images for each class). The main feature of these images is that the test images are comparatively similar to the training images. The training images used in this experiment are displayed in Fig. 3.

Experiment 2: Pedestrian Images. We use 924 pedestrian images from the publicly available database MIT Pedestrian Database[2] and 200 nonpedestrian images. We use two classes in this experiment. The size of all images is 64×128 pixels, and the number of the training images is 200 (100 images for each class). The pedestrian images have various resolutions while the pedestrians are roughly the same size. The nonpedestrian images are manually cut out from outdoor images. An example of the training images used in this experiment is displayed in Fig. 4.

---

[1] http://vismod.media.mit.edu/vismod/imagery/VisionTexture/vistex.html
[2] http://cbcl.mit.edu/software-datasets/PedestrianData.html

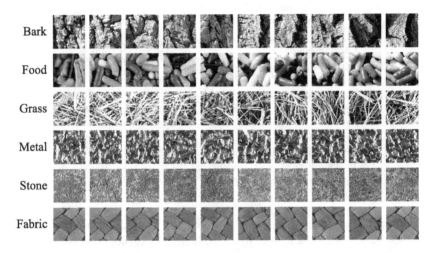

Fig. 3. Training images used in experiment 1 (texture)

Fig. 4. Example images used in experiment 2 (pedestrian)

Fig. 5. Training images used in experiment 3 (generic object)

Experiment 3: Generic Object Images. We use 500 generic object images from the publicly available WANG image database.[3] We use five classes in this experiment. The size of all images is 96×64 or 64×96 pixels, and the number of training images is 50 (10 images for each class). The main feature of these images is that target objects have various sizes, positions, types, and so on. Therefore, this problem is more difficult than the other two problems. The training images used in this experiment are displayed in Fig. 5.

5 Results and Discussion

5.1 Results

We compare our proposed method with GIN-IC in discrimination rate for training and test images and time required for learning in this section. The results are the average and the standard deviation (SD) over 10 different runs.

As the result of experiment 1, discrimination rates for the training and test images of textures are shown in Table 2. Our proposed method achieved 100% classification accuracy for all training runs against 98% on an average in GIN-IC. Moreover, the proposed method is about three times faster than GIN-IC, for the training images. For test images, the proposed method also obtained about 12% higher classification accuracy as compared to that in GIN-IC totally.

Table 2. Discrimination rate for the training and test images (texture)

Class	Training set		Test set	
	GIN-IC	Proposal	GIN-IC	Proposal
	Average	Average	Average $\pm$ SD	Average $\pm$ SD
Bark	99.0%	100.0%	70.7 $\pm$ 9.2%	91.7 $\pm$ 4.0%
Food	100.0%	100.0%	86.1 $\pm$ 5.8%	98.4 $\pm$ 1.8%
Grass	100.0%	100.0%	88.1 $\pm$ 3.2%	85.6 $\pm$ 6.5%
Metal	90.0%	100.0%	76.7 $\pm$ 16.2%	98.3 $\pm$ 1.9%
Stone	99.0%	100.0%	80.4 $\pm$ 10.5%	94.9 $\pm$ 5.7%
Fabric	100.0%	100.0%	94.7 $\pm$ 6.1%	99.4 $\pm$ 0.8%
Total	98.0%	100.0%	82.8 $\pm$ 8.2%	94.7 $\pm$ 1.5%

As the result of experiment 2, Table 3 shows discrimination rates for the training and test images of pedestrians. As for the results of experiment 1, the proposed method achieved 100% accuracy for all training runs against 90% on an average in GIN-IC. Moreover, the proposed method is about 50 times faster than GIN-IC, for the training images. Our proposed method also obtained higher classification accuracy for test images as compared to GIN-IC totally.

As the result of experiment 3, discrimination rates for the training and test images of generic objects are shown in Table 4. Similar to the results of experiments 1 and 2, the proposed method achieved 100% classification accuracy for

---

[3] http://wang.ist.psu.edu/docs/related

Table 3. Discrimination rate for the training and test images (pedestrian)

Class	Training set		Test set	
	GIN-IC	Proposal	GIN-IC	Proposal
	Average	Average	Average ± SD	Average ± SD
Pedestrian	89.5%	100.0%	81.4 ± 7.0%	88.6 ± 4.2%
Non-pedestrian	90.5%	100.0%	73.0 ± 10.5%	75.7 ± 4.0%
Total	90.1%	100.0%	80.5 ± 6.1%	87.2 ± 3.7%

Table 4. Discrimination rate for the training and test images (generic object)

Class	Training set		Test set	
	GIN-IC	Proposal	GIN-IC	Proposal
	Average	Average	Average ± SD	Average ± SD
Building	76.0%	100.0%	34.3 ± 19.5%	62.7 ± 6.9%
Bus	95.0%	100.0%	67.6 ± 12.4%	74.8 ± 7.8%
Elephant	95.0%	100.0%	66.3 ± 10.7%	84.0 ± 5.9%
Flower	100.0%	100.0%	70.9 ± 9.1%	86.4 ± 7.3%
Horse	96.0%	100.0%	56.6 ± 19.5%	73.4 ± 7.9%
Total	92.4%	100.0%	59.1 ± 6.3%	76.3 ± 3.5%

all training runs against about 92% on an average in GIN-IC. Moreover, the proposed method is about two times faster than GIN-IC, for the training images. The proposed method also obtained about 20% higher classification accuracy than GIN-IC totally, for test images.

5.2   Discussion

Our proposed method classified all training images completely in all runs and tends to prevent over fitting as compared to single GIN-IC in these experiments. We confirmed that GIN-IC and AdaBoost go well together. Since we use GIN-IC as weak classifiers, our proposed method can generate and select adequate image features by a combination of nodes. Although we only use simple image processing filters and image features as nodes in these experiments, we think that the performance is improved by adding more complex and effective processes such as SIFT descriptor [11]. We should investigate how GIN-IC contributes the performance of our proposed method compared with low level features.

Moreover, our proposed method took lesser time than single GIN-IC, for learning. We attribute this superiority to using GIN-IC as weak classifiers. An example of discrimination rate transition in experiment 2 (pedestrian) is shown in Fig. 6. About 60% classification accuracy is achieved in dozens of generations and higher accuracy costs hundreds and thousands generations. This graph indicates that error rate threshold τ should be small to reduce the number of generations to construct weak classifiers. However, too small τ brings a large number of weak classifiers. The relationship between the number of weak classifiers and τ

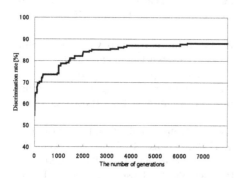

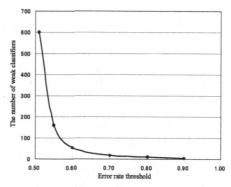

Fig. 6. Example of discrimination rate transition in GIN-IC

Fig. 7. Relationship between the number of weak classifiers and the error rate threshold τ

in pedestrian datasets is shown in Fig. 7. The vertical axis indicates the number of weak classifiers needed to completely classify the training images, and the horizontal axis indicates τ. This graph indicates that many weak classifiers are required if τ is small. From this preliminary experiment, we decide the parameters of τ and T.

6 Conclusions and Future Work

In this paper, we propose a method for automatic construction of an image classifier that aggregates GIN-IC as weak classifiers based on the AdaBoost algorithm. We applied the proposed method to three different problems of image classification, and confirmed that it obtained the optimum solution. In our proposed method, discrimination rates for the training and test images improved in the experiments as compared to that in the previous method GIN-IC. Also, our proposed method reduces the time required for learning.

However, the classifier obtained by the proposed method is constructed with 2500 nodes under 100 weak classifiers while single GIN-IC is constructed with 30 nodes. We will analyze the process of obtaining classifiers and what kind of preprocessing and features were evolved by our proposed method in future. Moreover, this method should be compared with other classifiers to evaluate its quality. Finally, we will apply it to other problems of image classification and object recognition with large scale variation and so on.

References

1. Shirakawa, S., Nakayama, S., Nagao, T.: Genetic Image Network for Image Classification. In: Giacobini, M., Brabazon, A., Cagnoni, S., Di Caro, G.A., Ekárt, A., Esparcia-Alcázar, A.I., Farooq, M., Fink, A., Machado, P. (eds.) EvoCOMNET. LNCS, vol. 5484, pp. 395–404. Springer, Heidelberg (2009)

2. Freund, Y., Schapire, R.E.: Experiments with a New Boosting Algorithm. In: Proceedings of the 13th International Conference on Machine Leaning (ICML 1996), pp. 148–156 (1996)
3. Viola, P., Jones, M.: Rapid Object Detection using a Boosted Cascade of Simple Features. In: Proceedings of the IEEE International Conference on Computer Vision and Pattern Recognition (CVPR 2001), vol. 1, pp. 511–518 (2001)
4. Iba, H.: Bagging, Boosting, and Bloating in Genetic Programming. In: Proceedings of the Genetic and Evolutionary Computation Conference 1999 (GECCO 1999), vol. 2, pp. 1053–1060 (1999)
5. Folino, G., Pizzuti, C., Spezzano, G.: Boosting Technique for Combining Cellular GP Classifiers. In: Keijzer, M., O'Reilly, U.-M., Lucas, S., Costa, E., Soule, T. (eds.) EuroGP 2004. LNCS, vol. 3003, pp. 47–56. Springer, Heidelberg (2004)
6. Folino, G., Pizzuti, C., Spezzano, G.: GP Ensembles for Large-scale Data Classification. IEEE Transaction on Evolutionary Computation 10(5), 604–616 (2006)
7. Mohemmed, A.W., Zhang, M., Johnston, M.: Particle Swarm Optimization Based Adaboost for Face Detection. In: Proceedings of the 2009 IEEE Congress on Evolutionary Computation, pp. 2494–2501. IEEE Press, Los Alamitos (2009)
8. Schwenk, H., Bengio, Y.: Boosting Neural Networks. Neural Computation 12(8), 1869–1887 (2000)
9. Shirakawa, S., Nagao, T.: Feed Forward Genetic Image Network: Toward Efficient Automatic Construction of Image Processing Algorithm. In: Bebis, G., Boyle, R., Parvin, B., Koracin, D., Paragios, N., Tanveer, S.-M., Ju, T., Liu, Z., Coquillart, S., Cruz-Neira, C., Müller, T., Malzbender, T. (eds.) ISVC 2007, Part II. LNCS, vol. 4842, pp. 287–297. Springer, Heidelberg (2007)
10. Miller, J.F., Thomson, P.: Cartesian Genetic Programming. In: Poli, R., Banzhaf, W., Langdon, W.B., Miller, J., Nordin, P., Fogarty, T.C. (eds.) EuroGP 2000. LNCS, vol. 1802, pp. 121–132. Springer, Heidelberg (2000)
11. Lowe, D.G.: Distinctive Image Features from Scale-Invariant Keypoints. International Journal of Computer Vision (IJCV) 60(2), 91–110 (2004)

Fine-Grained Timing Using Genetic Programming

David R. White[1], Juan M.E. Tapiador[1],
Julio Cesar Hernandez-Castro[2], and John A. Clark[1]

[1] Dept. of Computer Science, University of York, York YO10 5DD, UK
{drw,jet,jac}@cs.york.ac.uk
[2] School of Computing, University of Portsmouth, Buckingham Building,
Lion Terrace, Portsmouth PO1 3HE, UK
Julio.Hernandez-Castro@port.ac.uk

Abstract. In previous work, we have demonstrated that it is possible to use Genetic Programming to minimise the resource consumption of software, such as its power consumption or execution time. In this paper, we investigate the extent to which Genetic Programming can be used to gain fine-grained control over software timing. We introduce the ideas behind our work, and carry out experimentation to find that Genetic Programming is indeed able to produce software with unusual and desirable timing properties, where it is not obvious how a manual approach could replicate such results. In general, we discover that Genetic Programming is most effective in controlling statistical properties of software rather than precise control over its timing for individual inputs. This control may find useful application in cryptography and embedded systems.

1 Introduction

In previous work, we have combined Genetic Programming (GP), Multi-objective Optimisation (MOO) and simulation of hardware platforms to produce software with low power consumption [1] and reduced execution time [2]. We found that GP was indeed able to meet both functional and non-functional requirements, and also provide trade-offs between the two. Here we propose the notion of fine-grained resource control. For example, can we control the execution time of a program p on input x, $T(p, x)$, such that T can be an arbitrary function? Such control might allow us to solve some problems more efficiently than with functional computation alone, and to create software with useful security properties.

In this paper, we investigate the types of control that GP can achieve, and the effectiveness of the search algorithm in achieving these goals. We do not attempt to demonstrate that our solutions are the best, or that our parameter settings are optimal: only that GP has the potential to finely control timing behaviour in a way not previously considered. The results of single experimental runs are presented as proof of concept. We discuss example potential applications of these results to the domain of cryptography. Whilst we address timing properties, alternatives include power consumption and memory usage.

A.I. Esparcia-Alcazar et al. (Eds.): EuroGP 2010, LNCS 6021, pp. 325–336, 2010.
© Springer-Verlag Berlin Heidelberg 2010

2   Evolving Code with Specific Time Complexity

In this section, we demonstrate the difficulty of trying to manually control the low-level timing properties of software, as we attempt to create code that has a very specific time complexity relationship. This demonstrates the potential superiority of GP against manual design alone as a tool for such tasks.

We evolve individuals in the ECJ 19 Toolkit [3] and evaluate them by writing them out as C code, compiling them with a test harness using a cross-compiler, and executing them within the M5 Simulator [4]. The simulator is targeted for an Alpha architecture, using its default parameters. A trace file is produced, which is parsed by ECJ to measure the number of cycles used by the evolved code in each test case. Where handwritten solutions are examined in the following sections, the C source code has been manually written, and the rest of the evaluation method remains unchanged to ensure a fair comparison with evolved solutions.

2.1   Designing Linear Complexity

It is second nature to think about a program in terms of complexity: quadratic is good, linear is better, exponential is undesirable. For a moment, let us focus only on the complexity of a program rather than its purpose. Consider a program A that has linear complexity with respect to quantity n. Quantity n may be problem size, in which case we assume the conventional notion of the complexity of the program. If n an input, we have a program that has a linear relationship between its *input values* and its resource consumption. This is related to the theory of pseudo-polynomial time algorithms.

If we wish to construct code that may have this behaviour, we find that it is actually not as straightforward as one might assume, because the complex inter-action of hardware and software can easily lead to outliers in the relationship. For example, if we wish to construct a solution such that $T(p, k) = mk + c$, we can suggest such a program without regard to its functionality as thus:

```
float tmp = 0;
while (tmp < k)
    tmp++;
```

We have used `float` rather that `int` to maintain generality in the following sections, and because floating point operations have interesting timing properties. We now test this program with $k = 0 \ldots 99$. A test program provides these inputs, then parses a trace file to measure cycle usage for each call. Rather than implement this as a function, we have actually used a C `#define` macro to force the compiler to inline this code. This improves efficiency, and allows us to manipulate code embedded within a program rather than as an external function, interacting fully with the machine context of the surrounding code.

Figure 1(a) gives a graph of the results. Note that we do not experience a perfect relationship, due to the interaction between the test program and machine state. The primary cause of the outliers is data cache misses for the input values, such that the comparison operation causes a long delay prior to

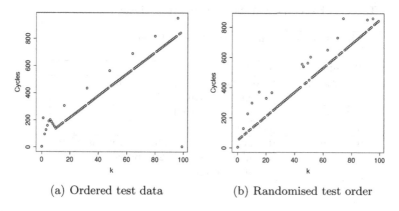

(a) Ordered test data   (b) Randomised test order

Fig. 1. Test results for handwritten linear solution

the next instruction. If we randomise the order of the inputs, we can measure the relationship in a more robust manner. The result is given in Figure 1(b).

Here we have even larger outliers, but they are spread throughout the input range rather than concentrated at the beginning. We can quantify the relationship by estimating Pearson's correlation coefficient for this sample:

$$r(k,T) = \frac{\sum_{i=1}^{n}(k_i - \bar{k})(T_i - \bar{T})}{\sqrt{\sum_{i=1}^{n}(k_i - \bar{k})^2}\sqrt{\sum_{i=1}^{n}(T_i - \bar{T})^2}} \tag{1}$$

Where k_i is the ith test case and T_i is the time taken to execute a code fragment p on this input. A perfect positive correlation would be 1, a negative correlation -1 and 0 for no correlation. The correlation coefficient for this manual attempt at linearity is 0.978, and by no means a perfect correlation due to the subtle interaction with the program's context. An interesting question, therefore, is: *can evolution find a better solution?*

2.2   Experiment A: Linear Behaviour

Experimental parameters are given in Table 1, chosen arbitrarily, and no tuning has been attempted. The intention is to demonstrate what is possible with GP, and not the most efficient way to achieve these results. The maximum number of instructions is limited to a similar value to that used by the handwritten solution, preventing GP from using larger solutions to mask the "noise" of program context. The randomised order of tests is varied at each generation, to avoid overfitting. "Increment tmp" increases the temporary variable by 1, whereas "update tmp" assigns a new value. `FixedLoop(n)` will loop for n iterations.

Genetic Programming is indeed able to locate a better solution, with a correlation coefficient of 0.993. A graph of this function's relationship and the code of the individual evolved is given in Figure 2. The key differences between the evolved and handwritten solutions are:

Table 1. Experiment A: Settings to evolve linear time behaviour

Objective	Find a program $p_*(k)$ such that $\Theta(f) = mk + c$
Terminal set	k, tmp
Function set	FixedLoop, $\leq$, increment tmp, +, *, −, /, if, sequence, skip, update tmp
Fitness cases	$k \in \{i \mid 0 \leq i < 100\}$
Fitness function	$r(k, T)$
Parameters	Initial tree depth = 3, generations = 10, population size = 20, prob(xo) = 0.9, prob(mutation) = 0.1

```
if (k) {
    for (c=0;c<k;c++) {
    };
} else {
    tmp++;
    tmp++;
    tmp++;
}
```

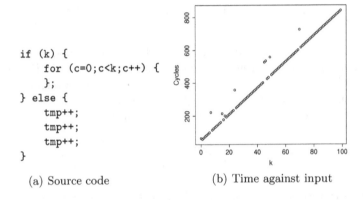

(a) Source code   (b) Time against input

Fig. 2. Evolved linear solution

– When $k = 0$, work will still be performed in the evolved version, namely testing for this case, and moving through further branches.
– When $k > 0$, an additional `if` statement evaluation will be performed.

If we examine the trace output for this evolved solution, we see that it includes exactly the same instructions executed in the manual solution, and adds some to either side of the loop. This effectively "smooths" the response (time taken) by suitably padding the instruction pipeline, as well as increasing the time taken for $k = 0$, i.e. setting a larger value for the intercept.

Note that we can now (approximately) calculate $f(k)$ by running the program and observing the time taken to execute, where in this case $f(k) = mk + c$.

2.3   Experiment B: Quadratic Behaviour

What if we wish instead to create a nonlinear relationship such as a quadratic curve with no linear term? We may try a handwritten solution as in Figure 3.

This solution takes the general approach of calculating $f(k)$ prior to repeating the strategy of looping to perform a multiple of a minimal unit of work

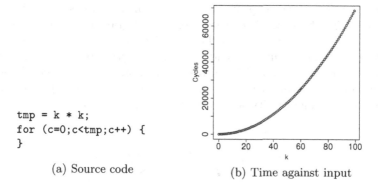

```
tmp = k * k;
for (c=0;c<tmp;c++) {
}
```

(a) Source code

(b) Time against input

Fig. 3. Test results for handwritten quadratic solution

(increasing c). This relationship appears to be a great improvement on the manual attempt at a linear solution, but we must quantify the relationship to be sure. We can estimate the derivative of the evolved function as:

$$f(k+1) - f(k) = m(2k+1) \tag{2}$$

Thus we can measure the correlation between the differences of successive timings and k in order to evaluate the fit of the quadratic relationship. For the handwritten solution above, we find a correlation of 0.962. Can we improve on this using evolution? We first used the correlation measure as a fitness function, and after some manual experimentation and analysis it became apparent that rewarding a certain amount of first-order correlation is also desirable in order to guide the search, and hence the fitness function was modified thus:

$$F(p) = w_0 \cdot r(k, T(p, k)) + w_1 \cdot r(k, T(p, k+1) - T(p, k)) \tag{3}$$

A simple selection of 0.2 and 0.8 for w_0 and w_1 respectively was sufficient to guide the search to a successful solution, found using the same parameter settings as given in in Table 1. The best individual evolved had a correlation of 0.967 between the input and derivative, a very modest improvement over the manually written version. The individual was:

```
for (c=0;c<(k * k );c++)
    tmp = tmp;
```

3   Time as a Functional Output

In the preceding section, we demonstrated that it is possible to search for programs that have simple relationships between their numerical input and total absolute execution time, and that exhibit those relationships more accurately than "obvious" handwritten alternatives.

Consider now a more complex relationship such as a Boolean function. Given two Boolean inputs a and b, can we evolve a program p with execution time $T(p, a, b) = f(a, b)$, where f could be a Boolean OR? For this to be literally true, the program's execution would have to take either 0 or 1 cycles, which is unrealistic as even a simple if will take more than a single cycle. Hence, we must find an *interpretation* of the timing output, denoted $I(T(p, a, b))$. This is an idea with much generality, and is illustrated in Figure 4.

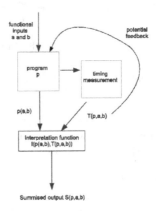

Fig. 4. Visualising the use of timing in calculation

A very simple interpretation that can be employed here is to measure the number of cycles the machine has executed and then take modulo 2 of this number. Thus the lowest "bit" of the execution time is used as output, and there are two output states: an even and odd number of cycles consumed. An interpretation such as this is arbitrary, and the idea can be generalised: perhaps interpretations can be cooperatively coevolved? The most interesting question here is: do such code fragments even exist, given the context of the test program within which they will be used?

It is not obvious how to go about manually constructing a solution, but we can imagine two ways in which it may be achieved: through something we could describe as either *implicit* or *explicit* time variation. In the former, we hope to rely purely on the low-level mechanics of the processor and memory subsystem to provide variation, such as floating point operations that consume a variable number of cycles. In the latter, we rely on some logical test to choose a path through the code. In practice, the latter cannot succeed without the former in order to "iron out" variation as in the handwritten solution from Section 2.2.

3.1   Experiment C: Timing OR Function

In this experiment, we give as input the four possible combinations of a pair of Boolean-valued floats and try to evolve a program that outputs their OR on the lowest bit of the cycle count. Initial experimentation revealed the following:

- the test cases could be passed by code that did not even evaluate the inputs.
- degenerate behaviours taking a single cycle ("always 1") were common.
- the ordering of test cases affected the performance of the search.

The code was therefore subsequently tested with the four possible inputs over four repetitions, and a randomised ordering of these 16 test cases used. In order to ensure that both inputs were evaluated at least once in any solution, the fitness function was specified as follows:

$$f(p) = w_1 \cdot c(p, a) + w_2 \cdot c(p, b) + w_3 \cdot (n - \sum_1^n |(T(p, a_n, b_n)\%2) - (a_n \vee b_n)|) \quad (4)$$

Where $c(p, a)$ is 1 if program p reads variable a, and 0 otherwise. The weightings w_1, w_2 and w_3 were 0.25, 0.25 and 0.5 respectively (an arbitrary choice). The parameters to the experiment are given in Table 2. Note that we added the constants 1 and Float_MAX (3.40282e38) to the terminal set. GP was indeed able to provide such a solution:

```
if (( 3.40282e+038f - b )) {
    for (c=0;c<(b + a );c++) {
        tmp++;
    };
} else {
    tmp =  3.40282e+038f;
}
```

This code passed all 16 test cases; it is quite straightforward to see how this might work. However, running the code again with a different test case order resulted in the code failing two test cases. This is because T is a function not only of p, a and b, but also of the machine context ϕ. We are trying to evolve code such that $T(p, a, b, \phi) \% 2$ is equivalent to $a \vee b$. The context is the machine state: stack

Table 2. Experiment C: Settings to evolve a Boolean OR function using time as an output channel

Objective	Find a program $p_*(a, b)$ such that $T(p, a, b)\%2 = OR(a, b)$
Terminal set	a, b, tmp, 1, Float_MAX
Function set	FixedLoop, $\leq$, increment tmp, +, *, -, /, if, sequence, skip, update tmp
Fitness cases	$a, b \in \{\{0, 0\}, \{0, 1\}, \{1, 0\}, \{1, 1\}\}$ (four reps, order randomised)
Fitness function	$f(p) = w_1 \cdot c(p, a) + w_2 \cdot c(p, b) + w_3 \cdot (n - \sum_{i=1}^n |T(p, a_i, b_i) - (a_i \vee b_i)|)$
Parameters	Initial tree depth = 3, generations = 20, population size = 100, prob(xo) = 0.9, prob(mutation) = 0.1

contents, the instruction pipeline, cache etc. This reliance on context is both a difficulty, where we wish to eliminate its effects, and also a useful resource, in the case where we want to exploit the machine state to achieve certain timing properties. This context caused problems for the manual solution in Section 2.1.

If we wish to implement this OR gate robustly, we must test on all $4! = 24$ input sequences. Even then, however, we cannot be sure that the context of the test program is not being exploited, such that if we wish to use the code in a new program we would have to again evolve and exhaustively test a new solution. Thus any such "absolute time manipulation" must be done in situ.

We did indeed attempt to evolve a program that is robust to input ordering, but failed to successfully do so even when testing each bit of timing output as a potential interpretation. Every run provided an individual with a few failed test cases out of 96. To achieve such control over absolute cycle usage it may be necessary to construct a function set exhibiting a variety of timing behaviours.

4   Timing Avalanche Criterion

In previous work [1], we have demonstrated that it is possible to evolve low-power pseudorandom number generators (PRNGs) using GP and simulation. As a measure of the randomness of the PRNG, we used the Strict Avalanche Criterion (SAC) [5], a cryptographic measure that estimates the nonlinearity of a function. SAC analyses the expected distance between outputs given a single bit flip in the input. SAC is an efficient measure of randomness that generalises well to other statistical qualities. Note that in this experiment we have used a single 32-bit input rather than 8 as in previous work, for the sake of simplicity.

Each output bit should have a probability of 0.5 of being flipped when a single input bit is changed, in order to maximise the nonlinearity of the PRNG. Hence, the Hamming distance between the two outputs should follow the binomial distribution $B(n, \frac{1}{2})$. By recording the Hamming distance between $p(a)$ and $p(a')$ for each test case, a χ^2 squared goodness-of-fit measure can be calculated against the ideal binomial distribution of bit flips. The performance measure of an individual program p is given by:

$$SAC(p) = \sum_{i=0}^{n} \frac{(C_i - E_i)^2}{E_i} \tag{5}$$

C_i is the counted frequency of i bit flip events, and E_i the expected number. In this experiment, *we take the radical step of applying the avalanche criterion to its timing behaviour*, $T(a, p, \sigma)$. We refer to this as the Timing Avalanche Criterion (TAC). This is a fascinating concept, which we suggest has never been considered due to the lack of any manual method capable of implementing it. It may enable us to evolve programs resistant to side-channel cryptanalysis, a major problem in designing secure algorithms. Kelsey [6] notes "It is probably not possible to protect against side-channel attacks in the design of algorithms."

Kocher et al. [7] were amongst the first to demonstrate that cryptographic primitives provably secure in the mathematical domain can become exposed to unseen vulnerabilities when implemented in a physical system. By monitoring the timing properties or power consumption [8] of a system, it is possible to deduce information about the state of executing software and compromise its security. A wide variety of attacks exist, from simple timing of operations to statistical analysis of power traces.

Counteracting such attacks is difficult: one method is to design code to consume the same number of cycles regardless of both the data input or output and the state of the system. For example, this can be achieved through the insertion of NOP instructions through the implementation. This defence is usually vulnerable to other forms of attack, such as detecting NOPs through other means, and a more robust method of defence is desirable.

4.1   Experiment D: Simple TAC

In this section, we attempt to evolve an expression that has a good TAC measure across the lowest 10 bits of its cycle count, which allows for up to 1023 cycles, sufficient for the evaluation of small expressions. Does such an expression even exist, given the context of a simple test loop that repeatedly uses the code with inputs separated by a single bit flip? It is not clear to us how we would proceed in designing such an expression, but can GP design one for us?

Table 3. Experiment E: Settings to evolve an expression with a good Timing Avalanche Criterion measurement

Objective	Find a program $p_*(a)$ such that $HD(T(p,a,\sigma),T(p,a',\sigma)) \approx B(n,\frac{1}{2})$ where $HD(a,a') = 1$.
Terminal set	a, Integer ERCs
Function set	If, <, LogicalShiftLeft (LSL), LSR, MULT, SUM, AND, NOT, OR, XOR
Fitness cases	a, a' where $HD(a,a') = 1$, sample size 4000
Fitness function	$\sum_{i=0}^{n} \frac{(C_i - E_i)^2}{E_i}$ over $n = 10$ bits of timing measurement, where C_i is the resulting frequency of i bits flipping and E_i is the expected frequency.
Parameters	Initial tree depth = 3, generations = 25, population size = 100, prob(xo) = 0.9, prob(mutation) = 0.1

We use a sample size of 4000, which is generous according to our previous work, and the same function set as we have previous employed. The experiment is summarised in Table 3. The best individual was subsequently tested over a sample size of 10000, which gave a good TAC measure of 0.0228. The p value of this result, effectively giving the probability that this sample is drawn from the ideal Binomial distribution, is 1.00 (to 3 s.f.). The distribution of bit flips is give in Figure 5. The individual is also reasonably small:

```
tmp = (((( a > (3594493887u)) ^ (( a * (1408948682u) ) > (( a > (3594493887u
)) ^ ( a * (609711807u) ) ))) ) ? ((( a * (1408948682u) ) >
((2302909662u) ^ a )) << ((( a > (a * (609711807u) )) ^ (a *
(609711807u) ) ) % 32u ) : (((( 2390510013u) * ((( a > (3594493887u))
^ (((( a * (1408948682u) ) > ((( a * (1408948682u) ) > ((2302909662u)
^ a )) << ((( a > (a * (609711807u) )) ^ (a * (609711807u) ) ) % 32u
) )) * (2540811676u) ) * ((( a * (1408948682u) ) & (( a > (3594493887u
)) ^ (a * (609711807u) ) ))) + a ) ) ) & (2490185230u)) ) ^ (a *
(609711807u) ) ) & (1135240832u)))
```

4.2 Experiment E: TAC and SAC

We now ask: is it possible to produce programs that perform two tasks at once, with both desirable functional and timing outputs? We attempt to produce code that has both good functional SAC (that is, it is a good random number generator) and also good TAC (it is resistant to side-channel analysis). Such a solution provides evidence that GP can evolve primitives resistant to side-channel analysis. It also suggests the feasibility of combining timing and functional properties of the software to improve the random number generator, or even to feedback the timing measure as input to improve the nonlinearity of the code over a series of evaluations, assuming we have the capability to measure time from the code.

The fitness function used was an even weighted combination of SAC and TAC, i.e. we assumed that the two objectives were not necessarily conflicting and that consequently Multi-objective Optimisation was not required. With a larger run of 25 generations, one of the best individuals produced was:

```
tmp = (((( a * (1408948682u) ) ^ (((((((( 1106785805u) * a ) >>
(((((1167812458u) + (2754164240u) ) & (~ a)) + ((2240102872u) > a) )
% 32u) ) * ((((((1106785805u) * a ) >> (( a ^ a ) % 32u) ) >> (( a ^
a ) % 32u) ) * ((((( 2390510013u) * a ) >> ((( 1106785805u) * a ) %
32u) ) * ((( 1106785805u) * a ) > (2390510013u)) ) ^ (~ a) ) * a ) )
^ (~ ((((1106785805u) * a ) > (3594493887u)) ^ a ))) ) ) ^
((1106785805u) * (~ (((( 1106785805u) * a ) > (3594493887u)) ^ a )) )
) >> ( a % 32u) ) * (1408948682u) ) ^ (((((( 2390510013u) * a ) >> ((
a ^ (((1876056559u) + (3922502476u) ) < (( 1106785805u) * a ) ) ) %
32u) ) * ((( 2390510013u) * a ) >> (( a ^ ((1106785805u) * a ) ) % 32u
) ) ) ^ (~ a) ) * a ) ) ) * (1408948682u) ) ^ (((((2390510013u) * a
) >> ((((((( a ^ ((2641736152u) ^ (1408948682u) ) ^ ((3594493887u)
* a ) )) >> (( a ^ a ) % 32u) ) * (((((( 2390510013u) * a ) >>
((( 1106785805u) * a ) % 32u) ) * ((( 1106785805u) * a ) > (2390510013
u)) ) * a ) >> (( a ^ ((1106785805u) * a ) ) % 32u) ) ) ^ (~ a) ) >>
(( a * (609711807u) ) % 32u) ) * (((((( 1670273051u) | a ) &
((3825661740u) + (3105575741u) )) ) ^ (((((( 2390510013u) * a ) >>
((( 1106785805u) * a ) % 32u) ) * ((( 1106785805u) * a ) > (2390510013
u)) ) ^ (~ a) ) * a ) ) ^ (~ (((( 1106785805u) * a ) > (3594493887u))
^ a )) ) ) ^ ((1106785805u) * a ) ) >> (a % 32u) ) % 32u) ) *
((( 2390510013u) * a ) >> (( a ^ ((1106785805u) * a ) ) % 32u) ) ) ^
(~ a) ) )
```

Comparing this to past results, there is a wider use of constants. Constants require memory access, introducing variation into the timing of the individual. The TAC and SAC distributions over a sample of 10000 are given in Figure 6. This individual had a SAC of 0.0189 and a TAC of 0.0399, equivalent to a p value of 1.00 (to 3 s.f.). These are excellent values, achieved surprisingly easily.

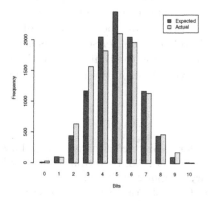

Fig. 5. Bit flip distributions for simple TAC

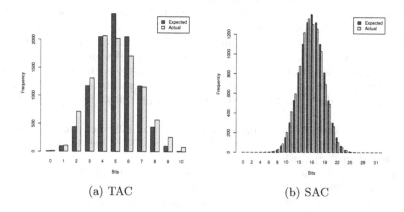

(a) TAC   (b) SAC

Fig. 6. Bit flip distributions for best individual

5   Conclusion

In this paper we have introduced several ideas regarding the application of Genetic Programming for fine-grained control over resource consumption. GP was shown to be most useful in controlling the behaviour of code over a series of evaluations, rather than the absolute value of a single evaluation. This opens up an avenue of further exploration in the concept of "doing two things at once", to liberate software from its role as an object of abstract calculation into a process that interacts with the host hardware platform and its execution context. At such a complex level of interaction, methods such as Genetic Programming may be essential to achieve desired behaviour.

Example applications can be found in cryptography, both in defending against side-channel attacks and exploiting side-channel properties. By exploiting covert timing channels [9], programs such as that evolved in Section 4.2 can be used to transfer information such that a *program is a key*, and the timing output of that program on a given input reveals the message. Only a party with the same code and platform can decode it. Another scenario is using such a program as a keystream generator, incorporating the timing properties of the software by (for example) XORing the functional output with the time taken.

References

1. White, D.R.: Searching for resource-efficient programs: Low-power pseudorandom number generators. In: GECCO 2008: Proceedings of the 10th annual conference on Genetic and evolutionary computation (2008)
2. Arcuri, A., White, D.R., Clark, J., Yao, X.: Multi-objective improvement of software using co-evolution and smart seeding. In: International Conference on Simulated Evolution And Learning (SEAL), pp. 61–70 (2008)
3. ECJ: Evolutionary computation in Java,
   http://www.cs.gmu.edu/~eclab/projects/ecj/
4. Binkert, N.L., Dreslinski, R.G., Hsu, L.R., Lim, K.T., Saidi, A.G., Reinhardt, S.K.: The M5 simulator: Modeling networked systems. IEEE Micro 26(4), 52–60 (2006)
5. Webster, A.F., Tavares, S.E.: On the design of s-boxes. In: Williams, H.C. (ed.) CRYPTO 1985. LNCS, vol. 218, pp. 523–534. Springer, Heidelberg (1986)
6. Kelsey, J., Schneier, B., Ferguson, N.: Yarrow-160: Notes on the design and analysis of the yarrow cryptographic pseudorandom number generator. In: Heys, H.M., Adams, C.M. (eds.) SAC 1999. LNCS, vol. 1758, pp. 13–33. Springer, Heidelberg (2000)
7. Kocher, P.C.: Timing attacks on implementations of diffie-hellman, rsa, dss, and other systems. In: Koblitz, N. (ed.) CRYPTO 1996. LNCS, vol. 1109, pp. 104–113. Springer, Heidelberg (1996)
8. Kocher, P., E, J.J., Jun, B.: Differential power analysis, pp. 388–397. Springer, Heidelberg (1999)
9. Kemmerer, R.A.: A practical approach to identifying storage and timing channels: Twenty years later. In: Computer Security Applications Conference, p. 109 (2002)

Author Index

Agapitos, Alexandros 122

Bader-El-Den, Mohamed 256
Banzhaf, Wolfgang 196
Bhowan, Urvesh 1
Brabazon, Anthony 14, 62
Brown, Gavin 232
Burland, Matt 244
Byrne, Jonathan 14

Castle, Tom 26
Caves, Leo S. 159
Clark, John A. 325
Collet, Pierre 301

Dignum, Stephen 38
Doucette, John 50

Fagan, David 62
Fatima, Shaheen 256
Fernández de Vega, Francisco 220
Folino, Gianluigi 74
Furuholmen, Marcus 86

Galván-López, Edgar 62, 134
Glette, Kyrre 86

Hernandez-Castro, Julio Cesar 325
Heywood, Malcolm I. 50
Hoock, Jean-Baptiste 268
Hovin, Mats 86

Jackson, David 98
Johansson, Ulf 278
Johnson, Colin G. 26
Johnston, Mark 1, 110, 289

Kattan, Ahmed 122, 134
Kinzett, David 289
König, Rikard 278

Lachiche, Nicolas 301
Langdon, W.B. 146
Liddle, Thomas 110
Löfström, Tuve 278
Lones, Michael A. 159

Maitre, Ogier 301
McDermott, James 14
McGarraghy, Sean 62
Miller, Julian F. 232
Moraglio, Alberto 171

Nagao, Tomoharu 313
Nakayama, Shiro 313
Nguyen, Quang Uy 184
Nguyen, Thi Hien 184
Nguyen, Xuan Hoai 184
Nicolau, Miguel 196
Niklasson, Lars 278

O'Neill, Michael 14, 62, 134, 184
O'Reilly, Una-May 244

Papuzzo, Giuseppe 74
Parcon, Jason 244
Poli, Riccardo 38, 122, 134, 208

Ribeiro, José Carlos Bregieiro 220

Schoenauer, Marc 196
Seaton, Tom 232
Shirakawa, Shinichi 313
Silva, Sara 171
Stepney, Susan 159

Tapiador, Juan M.E. 325
Teytaud, Olivier 268
Torresen, Jim 86
Tyrrell, Andy M. 159

Veeramachaneni, Kalyan 244
Vladislavleva, Katya 244

White, David R. 325

Yata, Noriko 313

Zenha-Rela, Mário Alberto 220
Zhang, Mengjie 1, 110, 289